STUDY GUIDE FOR
LIPSEY AND RAGAN

MACROECONOMICS

TENTH

William J. Furlong
University of Guelph

CANADIAN

E. Kenneth Grant
University of Guelph

EDITION

Addison
Wesley
Longman

Toronto

ISBN 0-201-66472-0

Acquisitions Editor: Dave Ward
Development Editor: Maurice Esses
Interior and Cover Design: Anthony Leung
Production Editor: Jennifer Therriault
Production Coordinator: Deborah Starks
Page Layout: Rena Potter

 2 3 4 5   05 04 03 02 01

Printed and bound in Canada

CONTENTS

TO THE STUDENT

The content of this book tests and reinforces your understanding of the concepts and analytical techniques stressed in each chapter of *Economics*, 10th Canadian edition, by Professors Lipsey and Ragan. Our own teaching experience has led us to believe that students have the most trouble understanding technical information and applying theoretical concepts to particular situations. Consequently, most multiple choice questions and exercises in this *Study Guide* are technical and numerical in nature. We feel that policy issues and specific applications of theory to real-world examples are primarily the responsibility of the textbook. You will find excellent discussions of issues and policy applications in the body of the text, especially in the boxes titled Applying Economic Theory and Extensions in Theory.

Each chapter in this *Study Guide* corresponds to a text chapter and is divided into seven basic sections. The **LEARNING OBJECTIVES** restate the learning objectives from the textbook. The **CHAPTER OVERVIEW** provides a brief summary of the important concepts and issues addressed in the chapter. It serves to enable you to anticipate topics covered in the chapter.

The **CHAPTER REVIEW** section is divided into subsections corresponding to the main sections and topics covered in the text chapter. The introduction to each topic reminds you of study goals and also provides some suggestions and tips for effective study. The multiple choice questions in this section are primarily nontechnical in nature. They are intended to give you quick feedback on your understanding of the material in the chapter, and to identify any areas that might need further study.

In some ways the greatest reinforcement to learning economics comes from doing the questions in the **EXERCISES** section. Some of our colleagues have indicated that some students rarely attempt the questions in this section, since the format of many introductory economics examinations consists primarily of multiple choice questions. We urge you *not* to make this mistake. These questions often require you to demonstrate numerically and/or graphically the sense of what has been expressed verbally. You may wish to review the mathematical exercises in Chapter 2 before attempting the questions in subsequent chapters. In addition, you are often asked to explain your method of analysis and your results. The ability to solve problems and to communicate and interpret results are important goals in an introductory economics course. We firmly believe that these exercises will enhance your ability to do well on multiple choice questions! Do not be discouraged if you have difficulty with certain exercises. The most effective learning sometimes comes from struggling with a problem. The solutions to the exercises (given at the end of the chapter) provide answers as well as explanations and/or derivations. A full appreciation of the points involved can be achieved only after you have participated in lectures, carefully read the text, and thought your way through the concepts and issues. We have also provided some more challenging problems in the subsection entitled **EXTENSION EXERCISES**.

The **PRACTICE MULTIPLE CHOICE TEST** reviews your comprehension of the entire chapter. Unlike the Chapter Review section, the Practice Test focuses more on analytical concepts and numerical techniques. When you answer these, avoid the temptation to leap at the first answer that seems plausible. There is one best answer for each question. You should be able to explain why any other answer is not as satisfactory as the one you have chosen.

At the end of each chapter, we provide **SOLUTIONS** for all the questions and exercises. However, we caution that our answers are brief. Your instructors often require much fuller explanations on midterm and final examinations.

Acknowledgments

We would like to thank those individuals who provided invaluable assistance in the preparation of this tenth edition of the *Study Guide*: Mara Grant for her computing and research assistance, and Evi Adomait for her critical review of the manuscript. In addition, we would like to thank Professors Larry Smith of the University of Waterloo and Cheryl Jenkins of John Abbott College for their valuable input as reviewers of the manuscript.

Finally, we dedicate this edition of the *Study Guide* to our respective families: Sally, Dylan and Liam; and Baiba, Mark and Mara.

William J. Furlong

E. Kenneth Grant

P A R T   O N E

WHAT IS ECONOMICS?

CHAPTER 1

ECONOMIC ISSUES AND CONCEPTS

 LEARNING OBJECTIVES

1 View the market economy as a self-organizing entity in which order emerges from a large number of decentralized decisions.

2 Understand the importance of scarcity, choice, and opportunity cost, and how all three concepts are illustrated by the production possibilities boundary.

3 Explain the circular flow of income and expenditure.

4 Recognize that there are several types of pure economic systems, but that all actual economies are mixed systems, having elements of free markets, tradition, and government intervention.

CHAPTER OVERVIEW

This introductory chapter discusses some of the major issues that confront all economies. An economy is endowed with scarce resources while human wants are unlimited. Choices must therefore be made regarding **production** and **consumption**. A central element of choice is the concept of **opportunity cost** which measures the benefit of the best foregone alternative when making a choice. An economy's opportunity cost in production is illustrated through its **production possibility boundary**. In addition to production and consumption choices, economies must also address how to avoid unemployment and how to ensure adequate growth over time. Different types of economic systems make these choices through different processes. This chapter reviews the main features of *command* and *market* economies.

Economists focus on three sets of decision makers in a market economy: individuals (consumers), firms (producers), and government. Consumers are assumed to have the objective of maximizing their well-being, while firms' decisions are made with the goal of maximizing their profits. (The objectives of government are discussed in later chapters). The interactions between households and firms through markets is best illustrated in a diagram depicting the circular flow of income and expenditure.

One of the great economic debates of the twentieth century concerns the relative merits of **centrally planned economies** (command economies) versus **free-market economies**. The pros and cons of each are reviewed. The central lesson from this chapter is that the market economy is a self-organizing entity that coordinates millions of decentralized, independent decisions made by self-interested consumers and producers.

CHAPTER REVIEW

The Complexity of the Modern Economy

Modern economies involve millions of economic decisions. The coordination of these decisions is the subject of this section. Coordination can occur through a centralized process—the command economy—or a decentralized process—the market economy. This section is intended to whet your appetite for study of "the economic problem."

1. One of the great insights of Adam Smith was that
   (a) modern economies require cental planning.
   (b) benevolence is the foundation of economic order.
   (c) the rich will get richer and the poor will get poorer in a market economy.
   (d) central coordination is required for any modern economy.
   (e) by acting in their own self-interest, people produce a spontaneous social order.

2. Which of the following is *not* one of the main characteristics of a market economy?
   (a) Individuals pursue their own self-interest.
   (b) Private property.
   (c) Sellers compete to sell their wares to potential buyers.
   (d) Firms seek to meet production quotas.
   (e) People respond to incentives.

3. The failure of central planning was caused by
   (a) production bottlenecks, shortages and gluts.
   (b) an incentive to produce goods of poor quality.
   (c) a failure to protect the environment.
   (d) poor incentives that didn't reward hard or efficient work.
   (e) all of the above.

Resources and Scarcity

After studying this section you should: understand the problem of scarcity, the need for choice and opportunity cost; be able to illustrate the relationship between scarcity, choice, and opportunity cost with a production possibility boundary (PPB); and, explain why growth in a country's productive capacity can be represented by an outward shift in its PPB and why unemployment of resources can be represented by points inside its PPB.

4. The fundamental problem of economics is, in short,
   (a) the existence of too many poor people.
   (b) the difficulty in finding jobs for all.
   (c) the scarcity of resources relative to wants.
   (d) constantly rising prices.
   (e) None of the above.

5. Scarcity is a problem that
   (a) more efficient production would eliminate.
   (b) is nonexistent in wealthy economies.
   (c) exists due to finite amounts of resources and unlimited human wants.
   (d) arises when productivity growth slows down.
   (e) exists in command economies but not market economies.

6. Which of the following is not an example of a factor of production?
   (a) a bulldozer.   (b) a mechanic.
   (c) a farm hand.   (d) a tractor.
   (e) a haircut.

7. Opportunity cost measures the
   (a) different opportunities for spending money.
   (b) the monetary cost of purchasing a commodity.
   (c) alternative means of producing output.
   (d) amount of one good forfeited to obtain a unit of another good.
   (e) market price of a good.

8. If a compact disc (CD) costs $10 and a cassette costs $5, then the opportunity cost of five CDs is
   (a) 50 cassettes.   (b) 10 cassettes.
   (c) 5 cassettes.   (d) 2 cassettes.
   (e) $25.

9. Assuming the alternative is employment, the opportunity cost of a university education is
   (a) tuition costs only.
   (b) tuition and book costs only.
   (c) the forgone salary only.
   (d) tuition costs plus book costs plus the forgone salary.
   (e) the direct costs of university such residence fees and books.

10. A downward-sloping production possibility boundary that is also a straight line implies
    (a) constant opportunity costs.   (b) zero opportunity costs.
    (c) only one good is produced.   (d) rising opportunity costs.
    (e) None of the above.

11. Which of the following causes an outward shift in the production possibility boundary?
    (a) A decrease in unemployment.
    (b) A loss in the productive capacity of agricultural acreage caused by a prolonged drought.
    (c) An increase in the productivity of all factors of production.
    (d) Shifting resources away from the production of one good towards another.
    (e) All of the above are correct.

12. Putting currently unemployed resources to work can be illustrated by
    (a) shifting the production possibility boundary outward.
    (b) a movement along a given production possibility boundary.
    (c) moving from a point on the boundary to a point outside it.
    (d) moving from a point inside the boundary to a point on it.
    (e) moving from a point on the boundary to a point inside it.

Who Makes the Choices and How?

This section will enable you to discuss the market interactions of consumers and producers through the circular flow of income and expenditure. You will also better understand how modern economies are based on the specialization and division of labour and appreciate the tendency towards economic globalization.

13. In economics, the term *market economy* refers to
    (a) institutions such as the Toronto Stock Exchange.
    (b) a place where buyers and sellers physically meet, such as at farmers' markets.
    (c) a society where individuals specialize in productive activities and enter voluntary trades.
    (d) a society where most economic decisions are made by marketing analysts.
    (e) an economy in which advertising is central to the marketing of goods and services.

14. In a barter economy, individuals
    (a) haggle over the price of each and every commodity.
    (b) trade goods directly for other goods.
    (c) use money to lubricate the flow of trades.
    (d) must each be a "jack of all trades."
    (e) All of the above.

15. The introduction of production lines where individuals specialize in performing specific tasks is known as
    (a) the division of labour.
    (b) the specialization of labour.
    (c) the market economy.
    (d) the advent of labour as a factor of production.
    (e) lean production.

16. Economic theory assumes that individuals
    (a) make choices to maximize their utility.
    (b) seek to maximize profits.
    (c) are the principal buyers of the factors of production.
    (d) specialize their labour.
    (e) are the sole buyers of goods and services in a market economy.

17. A central assumption in economic theory regarding firms is that they
    (a) are each owned by a single individual.
    (b) must be incorporated.
    (c) seek to maximize profits.
    (d) must all be making profits.
    (e) are the principal owners of the factors of production.

18. The two major types of markets in the circular flow of income are
    (a) public markets and private markets.
    (b) product markets and factor markets.
    (c) free markets and controlled markets.
    (d) markets for goods and markets for services.
    (e) regulated markets and open markets.

19. The circular flow of income and expenditure shows the flow of
    (a) goods and services from firms to consumers.
    (b) payments for goods and services from consumers to firms.
    (c) factor services from consumers to firms.
    (d) payments for factor services from firms to consumers.
    (e) All of the above.

20. The use of money when buying and selling makes
    (a) exchange easier.
    (b) barter more difficult.
    (c) specialization of labour more difficult.
    (d) opportunity cost lower.
    (e) the division of labour more difficult.

21. A barter economy
    (a) refers to the direct trading of goods.
    (b) does not require the use of money.
    (c) requires a double coincidence of wants.
    (d) involves costly searches for satisfactory exchanges.
    (e) All of the above.

22. Specialization of labour leads to a more efficient resource allocation because of
    (a) more self-sufficiency.
    (b) the use of barter.
    (c) the principle of comparative advantage.
    (d) a decrease in scarcity.
    (e) All of the above.

23. The market in which an individual sells his labour services is called a
    (a) product market.
    (b) factor market.
    (c) foreign-exchange market.
    (d) mixed market.
    (e) goods market.

Is There an Alternative to the Market Economy?

This section emphasizes the remarkable achievement of the market economy in providing order to millions of independent and decentralized decisions. After reading this section you will develop a better appreciation of the twentieth century's great economic debate on the relative merits of a market economy versus a command economy.

24. Which of the following would be a source of similarity among alternative types of economic systems?
    (a) Ownership of resources (private and public)
    (b) The process for making economic decisions.
    (c) The need to determine what is to be produced and how to produce it.
    (d) The role that tradition plays in determining production and employment.
    (e) Both (a) and (c).

25. In the Canadian economy, the majority of decisions on resource allocation are made by
    (a) consumers and firms through the price system.
    (b) the various levels of government.
    (c) negotiation between unions and firms.
    (d) business firms only.
    (e) legal contract.

26. Which countries are best characterized by public ownership of resources?
    (a) Canada and the United States.
    (b) Cuba and North Korea.
    (c) France and Germany.
    (d) Sweden and Norway.
    (e) (a), (c) and (d) are correct.

27. Complex economic plans for many sectors of the economy are most associated with
    (a) a market system.
    (b) the Canadian economy.
    (c) a command economy.
    (d) a feudal system.
    (e) a traditional economy.

EXERCISES

1. Four key economic problems are identified in Chapter 1:
   (1) What is produced and how? (resource allocation)
   (2) What is consumed and by whom? (distribution)
   (3) How much unemployment and inflation are there? (total employment and the price level)
   (4) How is productive capacity changing? (economic growth)

   After each of the following topics, identify which of the four types of economic problems applies. Use each classification only once.
   1 (a) Rises in oil prices during the 1970s encouraged a switch to alternative energy sources.
   4 (b) The standard of living in Canada, measured by real output per capita, has risen steadily over the past century.
   2 (c) Large harvests worldwide cause lower grain prices, thereby helping consumers but hurting farmers.
   3 (d) The unemployment rate has decreased in the late 1990s.

2. **The Production Possibility Boundary**

   The following exercise is designed to give you practice in constructing and interpreting a production possibility boundary.

   The economy of Islandia produces only two consumer goods, necklaces and fish. Only labour is required to produce both goods, and the economy's labour force is fixed at 100 workers. The table below indicates the daily outputs of *necklaces* and *fish* that can be produced with various quantities of labour.

Number of Workers	Daily Necklace Production	Number of Workers	Daily Fish Production (kilograms)
0	0	0	0
20	10.0	20	150
40	20.0	40	250
60	25.0	60	325
80	27.5	80	375
100	30.0	100	400

(a) Draw the production possibility curve for this economy, using the grid in Figure 1-1. (*Hint:* The labour force must always be fully employed along the production possibility boundary.)

Figure 1-1

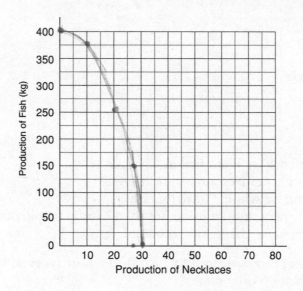

(b) What is the opportunity cost of producing the first 10 necklaces? What is the opportunity cost of producing the next 10 necklaces (i.e., from 10 to 20)? What happens to the opportunity cost of necklaces as their production is continuously increased?

(c) Suppose that actual production levels for a given period were 20 necklaces and 250 kilograms of fish. What can you infer from this information?

(d) Suppose a central planner in this economy were to call for an output combination of 35 necklaces and 150 kilograms of fish. Is this plan attainable? Explain.

(e) New technology is developed in necklace production, so that each worker can now produce double the daily amount indicated in the schedule. What happens to the production possibility curve? Draw the new curve on the grid. Can the planner's output combination in (d) now be met?

3. **Individual Choice and Opportunity Cost**

This exercise illustrates the concept of opportunity cost for an individual who faces fixed prices and has a fixed income.

Junior gets a weekly allowance of $10. He spends all of his allowance on only two commodities: video games at the arcade and chocolate bars. Assume that the price of a video game is 50 cents and the price of a chocolate bar is $1.

(a) Plot Junior's weekly attainable combinations of consumption.

Figure 1-2

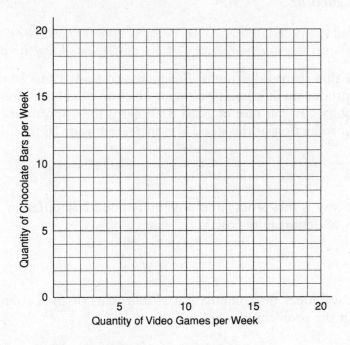

(b) Can Junior attain the following consumption combinations?
   (i)   15 video games and 2 chocolate bars
   (ii) 4 video games and 8 chocolate bars
   (iii) 7 video games and 7 chocolate bars

(c) What is the opportunity cost of Junior's first chocolate bar? his second? his third?

(d) By visual inspection of Junior's consumption possibility boundary, what could you say about his opportunity cost of consuming each of these commodities?

4. **The Opportunity Cost of University Education**

This question also explores opportunity cost but without diagrams.

Pamela, a first year student at Lakehead University, is considering whether or not to advance her studies by taking summer courses. Her monetary expenses would be: tuition, $1,000; books, $350; and living expenses, $1,500. Her alternative is to work as a lifeguard, which would earn her $3,500 for the summer. What is Pamela's opportunity cost of taking summer courses?

EXTENSION EXERCISES

E-1.   The following exercise addresses an economy's production possibilities algebraically. In the upcoming chapters you will be asked to make more use of algebra.

An economy's production possibility boundary is given by the mathematical expression $20 = 4A + B$, where A is the quantity of good A, and B is the quantity of good B.

(a)   If all resources in the economy were allocated to producing good A, what is the maximum level of production for this good? What is the maximum level of production for good B?

(b)   Suppose that the production of B is increased from 12 to 16 units and that the economy is producing at a point on the production possibility boundary. What is the opportunity cost per unit of good B? What is the opportunity cost per unit of good B if the production of this good was increased from 16 to 20?

(c)   In what way is this production possibility boundary different from that in Exercise 2 in terms of opportunity costs?

(d)   In what way does the combination of four units of good A and five units of good B represent the problem of scarcity?

E-2.   The following problem is conceptually challenging. The ability to solve it would reflect an excellent understanding of the production possibilities concept.

Consider the production possibilities for two totally dissimilar goods, such as apples and machine tools. Some resources are suitable for apple production and some for the production of machine tools. However, there is no possibility of shifting resources from one product to another. In this case, what does the production possibility boundary look like? Explain and show graphically.

PRACTICE MULTIPLE CHOICE TEST

1.   If the factors of production available to an economy were unlimited
   (a)   the opportunity cost of producing more goods would be zero.
   (b)   the price of cars would be infinitely high.
   (c)   there would be no unemployment.
   (d)   scarcity would become the most serious economic problem.
   (e)   All of the above.

2. If a 12-month membership in a fitness club costs as much as tickets for 24 Montreal Expos baseball games, the opportunity cost of a one-month membership in the fitness club is
   (a) 1/2 baseball game.   (b) 1 baseball game.
   (c) 2 baseball games.   (d) 12 baseball games.
   (e) 24 baseball games.

Questions 3 to 6 refer to Figure 1-3:

Figure 1-3

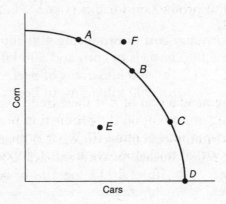

3. If a market economy is operating at point *A*,
   (a) resources are fully employed.
   (b) there is considerable unemployment.
   (c) the central planner values corn more than cars.
   (d) car producers are losing money due to low sales.
   (e) the opportunity cost of producing cars is zero.

4. Point *E* represents a situation that
   (a) is currently unattainable and can be expected to remain so.
   (b) will be attainable only if there is economic growth.
   (c) results from inefficient use of resources or failure to use all available resources.
   (d) has a higher opportunity cost than points on the boundary itself.
   (e) can never occur in a market economy.

5. With currently available resources, point *F* represents a situation that
   (a) results if resources are not fully employed.
   (b) can be achieved if consumers demand fewer cars than at point *C*.
   (c) is currently attainable.
   (d) can be achieved if all resources were allocated to the production of cars.
   (e) None of the above.

6. Assuming the initial situation is point *B*, which one of the following represents a reallocation of resources away from car production to corn production?
   (a) point *A*.   (b) point *C*.
   (c) point *E*.   (d) point *D*.
   (e) point *F*.

Questions 7 through 14 refer to the following schedule of production possibilities for combinations of corn and beef produced on a land tract of a given size and fertility.

Corn (bushels)	Beef (kilograms)
10,000	0
8,000	900
6,000	1,200
4,000	1,400
2,000	1,475
0	1,500

7. What would be the opportunity cost of producing 400 additional kilograms of beef if the current production were 8,000 bushels of corn and 500 kilograms of beef?
    (a) 500 bushels of corn.   (b) 400 kilograms of beef.
    (c) Zero.   (d) 900 kilograms of beef.
    (e) None of the above.

8. What would be the opportunity cost of producing 2,000 additional bushels of corn if the current production were 6,000 bushels of corn and 1,200 kilograms of beef?
    (a) 900 kilograms of beef.   (b) 1,200 kilograms of beef.
    (c) 300 kilograms of beef.   (d) Zero.
    (e) None of the above.

9. Which of the following combinations represent unattainable production levels with the current tract of land?
    (a) 8,000 bushels of corn and 500 kilograms of beef.
    (b) 8,000 bushels of corn and 1,200 kilograms of beef.
    (c) 2,000 bushels of corn and 1,475 kilograms of beef.
    (d) 6,000 bushels of corn and 1,300 kilograms of beef.
    (e) Both (b) and (d).

10. What is the opportunity cost of increasing beef production from 1,475 kilograms to 1,500 kilograms?
    (a) 2,000 bushels of corn.   (b) 50 bushels of corn.
    (c) 25 kilograms of beef.   (d) 800 bushels of corn.
    (e) None of the above.

11. The opportunity cost of increasing corn production from 4,000 to 6,000 bushels is
    (a) the same as the opportunity cost of increasing corn production from 8,000 to 10,000.
    (b) the same as the opportunity cost of increasing corn production from 2,000 to 4,000.
    (c) 0.1 kilograms of beef per bushel of corn.
    (d) 1,200 kilograms of beef.
    (e) None of the above.

12. Which of the following events is likely to lead to an outward shift of the production possibility boundary?
    (a) A reallocation of land use such that corn production increases from 6,000 bushels to 8,000 bushels while beef production decreases from 1,200 kilograms to 900 kilograms.
    (b) Some of the land is lost due to a flood.
    (c) Twenty of the existing acres are not used for either beef or corn production.
    (d) Corn prices fall relative to beef prices.
    (e) None of the above.

13. The opportunity cost per bushel of corn is 0.15 kilograms of beef when
    (a) corn production is increased from 8,000 to 10,000.
    (b) corn production is increased from 6,000 to 8,000.
    (c) corn production is increased from 4,000 to 6,000.
    (d) beef production is decreased from 1,500 to 1,475 kilograms.
    (e) None of the above.

14. Assuming that land is fully utilized and that corn production continually increases by 2,000 bushels, the opportunity cost in terms of beef production
    (a) increases.   (b) decreases.
    (c) is zero.   (d) remains constant.
    (e) is undefined.

15. In a command economy, where to produce on the production possibility boundary is determined by
    (a) the preferences of consumers, who spend their income accordingly.
    (b) a central plan established by the government.
    (c) traditional patterns of spending that change little from year to year.
    (d) the preferences of workers, who vote to indicate their preferences.
    (e) relative prices of goods.

16. Decisions on resource allocation are
    (a) necessary only in centrally planned economies.
    (b) made by central planners in traditional economies.
    (c) necessary only in economies that are not industrialized.
    (d) decentralized, but coordinated by the price system, in market economies.
    (e) primarily determined by traditional customs in market economies.

17. In a market economy, the allocation of resources is determined by
    (a) the government and its marketing boards.
    (b) the various stock exchanges in the country.
    (c) a central planning agency.
    (d) the millions of independent decisions made by individual consumers and firms.
    (e) the sobering discussions at the annual convention of the Canadian Economics Association.

18. The "invisible hand"
    (a) can only be seen by economists.
    (b) refers to excessive government taxation.
    (c) refers to a market economy's price system.
    (d) refers to the central planning agency of a command economy.
    (e) refers to hidden taxes.

SOLUTIONS

Chapter Review

1.(e) 2.(d) 3.(e) 4.(c) 5.(c) 6.(e) 7.(d) 8.(b) 9.(d) 10.(a) 11.(c) 12.(d) 13.(c) 14.(b) 15.(a) 16.(a) 17.(c) 18.(b) 19.(e) 20.(a) 21.(e) 22.(c) 23.(b) 24.(c) 25.(a) 26.(b) 27.(c)

Exercises

1. (a) 1 (b) 4 (c) 2 (d) 3

2. (a) **Figure 1-4**

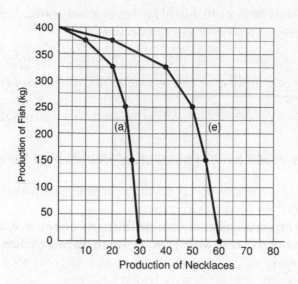

(b) 25 kilograms of fish (i.e., fish production decreases from 400 to 375). 50 kilograms of fish. The opportunity cost of producing necklaces is increasing — increasing necklace production by yet another 10 units from 20 to 30 would imply forgoing an additional 325 kilograms of fish.

(c) This production combination lies inside the production possibility boundary, so some workers are unemployed or inefficiently used.

(d) This combination is outside the production possibility boundary and is therefore unattainable with current resources and technology.

(e) The production possibility boundary shifts to the right as graphed in (a). The planner's output combination is now attainable but is inside the new boundary, implying that if it were indeed achieved, the economy would be inefficiently using its resources.

3. (a) **Figure 1-5**

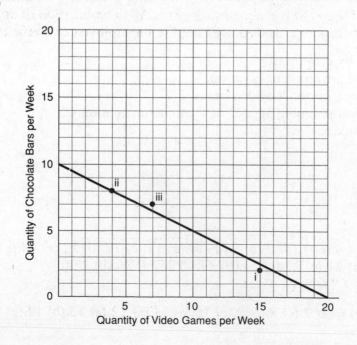

(b) (i) Yes, this combination lies inside his consumption possibility and is therefore afford-able with $10.

(ii) Yes, this combination is on his consumption possibility boundary and therefore costs exactly $10.

(iii) No, this combination lies outside his consumption possibility boundary and therefore costs more than a $10 allowance permits.

(c) To purchase the first chocolate bar, Junior must pay $1, which could have been used to purchase two video games. Thus the opportunity cost of the first chocolate bar is two video games. The opportunity cost of the second and third bars is also two video games each.

(d) Since the consumption possibility boundary is linear (i.e., a straight line), the opportunity cost is constant.

4. $4,850. Living expenses would have to be incurred regardless of her decision.

Extension Exercises

E-1. (a) If all resources were allocated to the production of good A, there would be no production of good B. Hence, according to the mathematical expression, the maximum production of good A is five units. If all resources were used to produce good B, then $B = 20$, and the production of good A is zero.

(b) The increase from 12 to 16 units of B requires a loss in production of good A of one (from two to one). An increase in B from 16 to 20 requires a loss in production of good A of one (from one to zero). Therefore, the opportunity cost *per unit* of good B is 0.25 units of A in each case.

(c) The opportunity cost is constant, whereas it was increasing for Exercise 2 above.

(d) According to the equation, four units of A and four units of B are possible. The combination of four units of A and five units of B is not feasible and indicates that more resources are required than are currently available.

E-2. When all resources suitable to apple production are employed, the resulting apple output is A' in Figure 1-6. When all resources suitable to machine tool production are employed, the resulting quantity of machine tools is M'. Since there is no possibility of shifting resources between these two outputs, the production possibility boundary is simply the point corresponding to the coordinates (A', M'). Any combination of apples and machine tools either inside or on the dashed lines implies unemployed or inefficiently used resources.

Figure 1-6

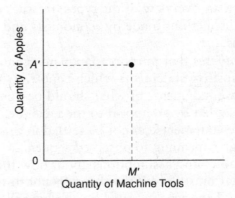

Practice Multiple Choice Test

1.(a) 2.(c) 3.(a) 4.(c) 5.(e) 6.(a) 7.(c) 8.(c) 9.(e) 10.(a) 11.(c) 12.(e) 13.(b) 14.(a) 15.(b) 16.(d) 17.(d) 18.(c)

CHAPTER 2

HOW ECONOMISTS WORK

LO LEARNING OBJECTIVES

1 Recognize the difference between positive and normative statements.

2 Understand how theorizing and model-building help economists think about the economy.

3 Explain the interaction between economic theories and empirical observations.

4 Understand why testing theories about human behaviour usually requires studying large numbers of individuals.

5 Recognize several types of economic data, including index numbers, time-series and cross-section data, and scatter diagrams.

6 Understand that economic theories involve relations between variables and that such relations can be expressed in words, equations, or graphs.

7 Recognize that the slope of a relation between *X* and *Y* is interpreted as the marginal response in *Y* to a unit change in *X*.

CHAPTER OVERVIEW

The previous chapter provided an overview of the types of issues economists consider. This chapter presents some important distinctions made by economists and discusses the approaches used to analyze economic questions.

Economists evaluate *hypotheses* that purport to explain economic behaviour. An important distinction is made between **positive statements** which concern what is, was or will be, and **normative statements** which are judgments of what should be done. Disagreements over positive statements are appropriately settled by an appeal to the facts (i.e., they are testable). Disagreements over normative statements cannot be settled in this way.

Theories are designed to give meaning to observed sequences of events. A theory typically consists of definitions of **variables** and assumptions about how things behave. Any theory has certain logical implications that must hold if the theory is not to be rejected. These are the theory's predictions or hypotheses. Theories are tested by checking their predictions against the evidence. In economics the evidence is most often comprised of data drawn from the real world.

The relationships among variables in economic theories are usually presented in tables, graphs or equations. These provide compact summaries of a large number of data observations, and play an important role in economic modelling.

CHAPTER REVIEW

Positive and Normative Advice

The objective of this section is to distinguish between positive and normative statements. Positive statements are assertions of fact that can, in principle, be tested. On the other hand, normative statements cannot be tested as they are value judgements.

1. Normative statements
   (a) concern an individual's beliefs in what ought to be.
   (b) are based on value judgments.
   (c) cannot be subjected to empirical scrutiny.
   (d) cannot be deduced from positive statements.
   (e) All of the above.

2. "Capital punishment deters crime" is an example of a
   (a) positive statement.   (b) value judgment.
   (c) normative statement.   (d) analytic statement.
   (e) untestable statement.

3. "Capital punishment should be reintroduced in Canada" is an example of a
   (a) positive statement.   (b) normative statement.
   (c) analytic statement.   (d) testable hypothesis.
   (e) None of the above.

Economic Theories and Models

This section contains a nontechnical discussion of the components of a theory and the role of models. After reading this section you should understand the basic structure of economic theories; the roles of variables, definitions, assumptions, and predictions in developing theories, and the purpose and usefulness of economic modelling.

4. Economic predictions are intended to
   (a) forecast the behaviour of each consumer.
   (b) forecast the behaviour of groups of individuals.
   (c) test normative statements.
   (d) anticipate the irrational behaviour of certain odd individuals.
   (e) Both (b) and (c) are correct.

5. If the assumptions imposed in an economic theory are unrealistic, then the theory
   (a) will always be refuted by the evidence.
   (b) is incorrect and should be rejected.
   (c) will not predict well and should be rejected.
   (d) will require more complex statistical techniques for testing.
   (e) may nonetheless predict better than any alternative theory.

6. The role of assumptions in theory is to
   (a) represent the world accurately.
   (b) abstract from reality.
   (c) avoid simplifications of the real world.
   (d) ensure that the theory considers all features of reality, no matter how minor.
   (e) None of the above.

7. A theory may contain all *but* which of the following?
   (a) Predictions about behaviour that are deduced from the assumptions.
   (b) A set of assumptions defining the conditions under which the theory is operative.
   (c) Hypotheses about how the world behaves.
   (d) A normative statement expressed as a functional relation.
   (e) Hypothesized relationships among variables.

Testing Theories

Economic theories are not intended to predict the behaviour of specific individuals. Rather, they attempt to predict "average" or "typical" behaviour in a group of individuals. The law of large numbers is essential to this objective; it suggests that random or erratic behaviours will tend to offset themselves. Although there tends to be broad agreement among economists on many issues, there are nonetheless some dissenting opinions and views. It is useful to recognize the causes of disagreement.

8. The "law" of large numbers basically says that
   (a) the greater the number of observations, the greater the sum of each variable.
   (b) measuring error increases with the number of observations.
   (c) a few observations are just as accurate as a large number of observations.
   (d) erratic behaviour by individuals tends to offset itself in a large group.
   (e) the greater the number of observations, the greater is the potential for prediction errors.

9. In measuring the area of a room, the "law" of large numbers implies that
   (a) more people will make small errors than large ones.
   (b) roughly the same number of people will understate the area as overstate it.
   (c) the average error of all individuals is approximately zero.
   (d) the more people taking the measurement, the smaller is the average error.
   (e) All of the above.

10. The statement that the quantity produced of a commodity and its price are positively related is
    (a) an assumption economists usually make.
    (b) a testable hypothesis.
    (c) a normative statement.
    (d) not testable as currently worded.
    (e) a value judgement.

11. The theory that extra-terrestrials exist and visit Earth in flying saucers
    (a) has been disproved by scientific evidence.
    (b) is inconsistent with scientific observation.
    (c) can never be disproved.
    (d) has been refuted.
    (e) Both (b) and (c).

12. Which of the following is not a possible source of disagreement among economists?
    (a) Use of different benchmarks.
    (b) Failure to distinguish between theories and models.
    (c) Failure to distinguish between short-term and long-term consequences.
    (d) Different values among economists.
    (e) Failure to acknowledge the extent of their ignorance.

Economic Data

Economists use data drawn from real world observations to test their theories. This section reviews two ways in which data can be examined: index numbers and graphs.

13. If a particular index number in 1999 is 159 and the base year is 1996, then the index shows an increase of
    (a) 5.9 percent between 1996 and 1999.
    (b) 59 percent between 1996 and 1999.
    (c) 159 percent between 1996 and 1999.
    (d) 0.59 percent between 1996 and 1999.
    (e) an indeterminable amount, since the value of the index in the base year is unknown.

14. Suppose the Consumer Price Index was 160 last month and rose by 2 percent over the base year during the current month. The price index for the current month is
    (a) 162.0.
    (b) 163.2
    (c) 160.02.
    (d) 160.2.
    (e) 80.0.

15. An unweighted index of prices for some group of goods
    (a) assigns all prices a weight of zero.
    (b) assigns all prices an equal weight.
    (c) merely calculates the sum of prices in the group.
    (d) assigns each price a weight according to its relative importance in the group.
    (e) adjusts each price based upon that good's weight in the group.

16. Which of the following is an example of cross-sectional data?
    (a) Annual unemployment rates for Canada.
    (b) Vancouver housing prices for the period 1950–1999.
    (c) Last year's crime rates for all Canadian cities.
    (d) A series of this year's daily interest rates.
    (e) None of the above.

17. Observations drawn repeatedly from successive months are
    (a) cross-sectional data.
    (b) time-series data.
    (c) unweighted data.
    (d) logarithmic data.
    (e) scattered data.

18. A scatter diagram can be used to plot
    (a) time-series data, but not cross-sectional data.
    (b) cross-sectional data, but not time-series data.
    (c) neither cross-sectional nor time-series data.
    (d) either cross-sectional or time-series data.
    (e) data in which time or location is a variable on one of the axis.

Graphing Economic Theories

Relationships between economic variables are often expressed algebraically and then displayed graphically. This is an important section that reviews the algebraic and graphical tools that are required for this course. After completing this section, you should be comfortable reading functional relationships, translating equations into graphs and interpreting graphs.

19. The slope of a straight line is
    (a) always positive.
    (b) calculated by dividing the variable measured on the horizontal axis by that measured on the vertical axis.
    (c) zero.
    (d) constant.
    (e) increasing or decreasing, depending upon whether the slope is positive or negative, respectively.

20. Suppose that economic analysis estimates the following relationship between imports (IM) and national income (Y): $IM = 100 + 0.15Y$. This means that
    (a) imports are negatively related to national income.
    (b) when national income is zero, imports are zero.
    (c) imports are 15 percent of national income.
    (d) imports are 15 times greater than national income.
    (e) other things remaining constant, for every increase of $1 in national income, imports will rise by 15 cents.

EXERCISES

1. **Positive and Normative Statements**

    After each phrase, write P or N to indicate whether a positive or a normative statement is being described.
    (a) A statement of fact that is actually wrong. _____
    (b) A value judgment. _____
    (c) A prediction that an event will happen. _____
    (d) A statement about what the author thinks ought to be. _____
    (e) A statement that can be tested by evidence. _____
    (f) A value judgment based on evidence known to be correct. _____
    (g) A hurricane forecast. _____
    (h) An opinion survey that indicates a majority of Canadians believe taxes ought to be reduced. _____

2. Endogenous and Exogenous Variables

In this exercise you are required to distinguish between cause and effect. In each of the following statements, classify the italicized variables as being endogenous (N) or exogenous (X).

(a) *Market price and equilibrium quantity* of a commodity are determined by demand and supply. _____
(b) The number of sailboats sold annually is a function of *national income*. _____
(c) The *condition of forest ecosystems* can be affected by regional air pollutants. _____
(d) The quantity of housing services purchased is determined by the *relative price of housing, income, and housing characteristics*. _____
(e) Other things being equal, *consumer expenditures* are negatively related to interest rates.
_____

3. A University Price Index

This exercise asks you to construct a price index for an item that is of concern to most students, the out-of-pocket cost of attending university. You may want to refer to Tables 2-2 and 2-3 of the text to review index numbers before attempting this exercise.

The following table presents data on three components of the out-of-pocket expenses for attending university: tuition, residence and meals. (Recall from the discussion in Applying Economic Concepts 1-1 of the text that these three do not represent the opportunity cost of a university education.) Tuition here refers to the annual fees for a B.A. degree; residence refers to the annual fee for a double occupancy room; and, food is the annual cost of a full meal plan in residence. The data are drawn from the University of Guelph for the years 1989–99, but are representative of all Ontario universities.

Year	Tuition	Residence	Food
1989–90	$1,374	$1,710	$1,660
1990–91	1,518	1,910	1,760
1991–92	1,638	2,050	2,000
1992–93	1,770	2,192	2,250
1993–94	1,894	2,352	2,400
1994–95	2,026	2,462	2,520
1995–96	2,228	2,462	2,600
1996–97	2,451	2,582	2,660
1997–98	2,930	2,672	2,670
1998–99	3,223	2,672	2,760

Source: University of Guelph Undergraduate Calendar (1989–1999).

(a) Using 1989–90 as the base year, construct a price index for each of the three expense items. (Note: Those students familiar with a spreadsheet software may wish to use it in answering this question).

(b) Which of these three items increased the most in percentage terms for the period 1989–90 to 1990–91? the period 1989–90 to 1998–99?

(c) Construct an unweighted (i.e., equal weight) index for all three fees.

(d) Use the proportion of each item's share of total cost in the base year, 1989–90, to construct a weighted index of all three fees.

(e) If you were president of the Student Council which index would you use when arguing against fee increases? If you were president of the university, which index would you use to support fee increases? Explain.

4. Linear Relationships

This exercise gives you practice in interpreting and graphing linear relationships.

Suppose that an economist hypothesizes that the annual quantity demanded of a specific manufacturer's personal computers (Q^D) is determined by the price of the computer (P) and the average income of consumers (Y). The specific functional relationship among these three variables is hypothesized to be the expression $Q^D = Y - 4P$.

(a) Which of these variables are endogenous and which are exogenous?

(b) What does the minus sign before the term $4P$ imply about the relationship between Q^D and P? What does the implicit positive sign before the term Y imply about the relationship between income and quantity demanded?

(c) Suppose for the moment that average income equals $8,000. Write a simplified expression for the demand relationship.

(d) Assuming that $Y = 8,000$, calculate the values of Q^D when $P = 0$, $P = \$500$, $P = \$1,000$, and $P = \$2,000$.

(e) Plot the relationship between P and Q^D (assuming $Y = \$8{,}000$) on the graph in Figure 2-1. Indicate the intercept value on each axis.

Figure 2-1

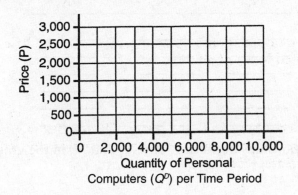

Quantity of Personal
Computers (Q^D) per Time Period

(f) Calculate the slope of this relationship.

(g) Assuming that $Y = \$8{,}000$, calculate the change in the quantity demanded when the price increases from \$1,000 to \$2,000. Do the same for a price increase from \$500 to \$2,000. Call the change in the quantity demanded ΔQ^D and the change in the price ΔP. Determine the ratio $\Delta Q^D / \Delta P$. Is this ratio constant?

(h) Now suppose that evidence indicates that in subsequent time periods, the average income of consumers changes to \$9,000 per month. Plot the new relationship between P and Q^D. What are the intercept values and the slope?

EXTENSION EXERCISES

The following exercises review two methods for solving a system of linear equations. The techniques reviewed here are used throughout the course. Although they are not required until Chapter 3 of the text when the demand and supply model is presented, it is useful to review them now while we are covering linear relationships. The first exercise works through the diagrammatic solution method while the next uses the algebraic approach. Students should be competent in using both solution techniques.

E-1.   Consider the following two linear equations:

$$(1)\ \ N_1 = 5 + 0.5X$$

$$(2)\ \ N_2 = 55 - 0.5X$$

(a) Complete the following table using the N_1 column for equation 1 and the N_2 column for equation 2.

X	N_1	N_2	N_3
10			
20			
30			
40			
50			
60			

(b) Plot the relationships between X and N_1 and N_2 in the graph provided below.

Figure 2-2

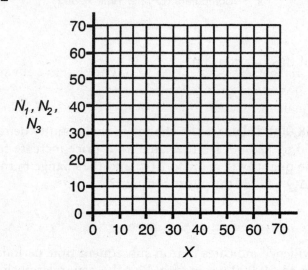

(i) The linear curve relating variables X and N_1 has a (positive/negative) _____ slope of _____.

(ii) The linear curve relating variables X and N_2 has a (positive/negative) _____ slope of _____.

(c) These equations are said to be solved when $N_1 = N_2$—call this the solution value N. At what value of X does $N_1 = N_2$? What are the corresponding values of N and X?

(d) Assume that the constant term in equation 1 increases from 5 to 25. Complete column N_3 in (a), and plot the new relationship on the graph in (b). The curve in equation (1) has shifted _____. The slope is _____.

(e) What is the new solution to this system of equations?

E-2. The following exercise reviews the procedure for solving a system of simultaneous equations by algebraic methods. This approach is extremely useful in both micro and macro chapters of this Study Guide. It is an alternative to diagrammatic solutions that were reviewed above in question E-1.

Consider two equations describing the relationships between two variables x and y

$$x_1 = a + by, \tag{1}$$

$$x_2 = c - dy. \tag{2}$$

where a, b, c and d are positive constants. The objective is to find values of x and y for which both equations are satisfied. First, note that there are two equations and three unknowns—the unknowns are the solution values to x_1, x_2 and y. Thus, if a unique solution exists, there is a missing equation. The missing equation to this system simply states that in the solution:

$$x_1 = x_2 \tag{3}$$

The solution procedure requires elimination of unknowns and equations by means of substitution. Each substitution must reduce the system by both an unknown and an equation, until all that remains is a single unknown in a single equation.

(a) Eliminate equation (1) and x_1 from the system. Count the remaining equations and unknowns.

(b) Now eliminate equation (2) and x_2 from the system. Count the remaining equations and unknowns.

(c) Solve for the solution value of y.

(d) Use the solution value of y to obtain solution values for x_1 and x_2.

(e) Often the constants in equations (1) and (2) are numerical. For example, suppose a = 200, b = 2, c = 400 and d = 3. Repeat questions (a) to (d) to solve for the numerical values of x and y.

PRACTICE MULTIPLE CHOICE TEST

1. Which of the following is the best example of a positive statement?
   (a) Equal distribution of national income is a desirable goal for society.
   (b) Foreign ownership is undesirable for Canada and should therefore be eliminated.
   (c) Although free trade may cause some Canadians to lose their jobs, it will significantly increase the income of the average Canadian.
   (d) Taxes should be lowered.
   (e) Deficit reduction should be the government's priority.

2. With respect to agriculture, weather is an example of
   (a) an exogenous factor of production.   (b) an endogenous input.
   (c) a dependent variable.   (d) an induced input variable.
   (e) a positive statement.

3. If annual per capita consumption expenditure decreases as average annual income decreases, these two variables are then said to be
   (a) negatively related.   (b) positively related.
   (c) randomly related.   (d) independent of each other.
   (e) None of the above.

4. Which of the following statements about economic theories is most appropriate?
   (a) The most reliable test of a theory is the realism of its assumptions.
   (b) The best kind of theory is worded so that it can pass any test to which it is applied.
   (c) The most important thing about the scientific approach is that it uses mathematics and diagrams.
   (d) We expect our theories to hold only with some margin of error.
   (e) Economic theories are based upon normative statements, and can therefore never be refuted.

5. A scientific prediction is a conditional statement because it
   (a) takes the form "if that occurs, then this will result."
   (b) is conditional on being correct.
   (c) is impossible to test.
   (d) is true in theory but not in practice.
   (e) is derived from normative statements.

6. The term "economic model" may refer to
   (a) an application of a general theory in a specific context.
   (b) a specific quantitative formulation of a theory.
   (c) a particular theory or subset of theories in economics.
   (d) an illustrative abstraction of some real world phenomenon.
   (e) All of the above.

7. Economic hypotheses are generally accepted only when
   (a) the evidence indicates that they are true with a high degree of probability.
   (b) they have been proved beyond a reasonable doubt.
   (c) they have been established with certainty.
   (d) the evidence supports the hypotheses in all cases.
   (e) Both (c) and (d) are correct.

8. Suppose that a scatter diagram indicates that imports are, on average, positively related to national income over time. If in one year imports fall when national income increases, the observation
   (a) disproves the positive relationship between the two variables.
   (b) suggests that other factors also influence the quantity of imports.
   (c) proves a negative relationship between the two variables.
   (d) suggests that a measurement error has necessarily been made.
   (e) suggests that the two variables are independent of each other.

9. Which of the following equations is consistent with the hypothesis that federal income tax payments (T) are positively related to family income (Y) and negatively related to family size (F)?
   (a) $T = -733 + 0.19Y + 344F$. (b) $T = -733 - 0.19Y - 344F$.
   (c) $T = -733 + 0.19Y - 344F$. (d) $T = +733 - 0.19Y + 344F$.
   (e) None of the above.

Use the following graph to answer questions 10 to 12:

Figure 2-3

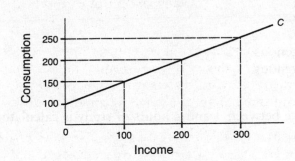

10. In the graph above, the slope of the line showing the relationship between consumption and income is
    (a) –2.   (b) 0.5.
    (c) 2.   (d) 2.5.
    (e) 150.

11. According to the graph above, when an individual has no income, consumption is
    (a) –200.   (b) –100.
    (c) 0.   (d) 100.
    (e) None of the above.

12. The line showing the relationship between consumption (C) and income (Y) can be represented mathematically as:
    (a) $C = 0.5Y$.   (b) $C = 2Y$.
    (c) $C = 100 + 0.5Y$. (d) $C = 100 + 2Y$.
    (e) $C = -100 + Y$.

Questions 13 to 17 refer to the following graph which depicts the relationship between performance on an economics examination and hours spent studying late the night before the early morning exam!

Figure 2-4

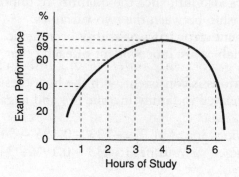

13. Exam performance is a(n) _____ variable and hours of study is a(n) _____ variable.
    (a) nonlinear; nonlinear.
    (b) marginal; contour.
    (c) exogenous; endogenous.
    (d) endogenous; exogenous.
    (e) slope; marginal.

14. The slope of this curve between 1 and 2 hours of study is calculated by
    (a) 60/2.
    (b) (60–30)/2.
    (c) (60–40)/2.
    (d) (60–40)/(2–1).
    (e) (60+40)/(2+1)

15. The marginal return to the third hour of study is
    (a) 69%.
    (b) 9%.
    (c) 23%.
    (d) 6%.
    (e) 3%.

16. As study time increases from 1 hour to 4 hours, the marginal return to study is _____ and the total return is _____.
    (a) diminishing; increasing.
    (b) increasing; increasing.
    (c) diminishing; diminishing.
    (d) increasing; diminishing.
    (e) diminishing; zero.

17. At four hours of study, the marginal return to a minute of study more or less (approxi-mately)
    (a) 75%.
    (b) increasing.
    (c) diminishing.
    (d) zero.
    (e) cannot be determined with information provided.

18. Due to a lack of sleep, exam performance suffers from a fifth and sixth hour of study. For this range of study hours, one can say
    (a) total returns are diminishing.
    (b) marginal returns are negative.
    (c) marginal returns are diminishing.
    (d) the slope of the performance curve is negative.
    (e) All of the above are correct.

SOLUTIONS

Multiple-Choice Questions

1.(e) 2.(a) 3.(b) 4.(b) 5.(e) 6.(b) 7.(d) 8.(d) 9.(e) 10.(b) 11.(e) 12.(b) 13.(b) 14.(a) 15.(b) 16.(c) 17.(b) 18.(d) 19.(d) 20.(e)

Exercises

1. (a) P (b) N (c) P (d) N (e) P (f) N (g) P (h) N.

2. (a) N (b) X (c) N (d) X (e) N

3.

Year	Tuition Index	Residence Index	Food Index
1989–90	100	100	100
1990–91	110	112	106
1991–92	119	120	120
1992–93	129	128	136
1993–94	138	138	145
1994–95	147	144	152
1995–96	162	144	157
1996–97	178	151	160
1997–98	213	156	161
1998–99	235	156	166

(b) The cost of residence increased by 12% for the period 1989–90, while that of tuition and food increased by 10% and 6%, respectively. During the decade 1989–1999, the fees for tuition, residence and food increased 135%, 56%, and 66%, respectively.

(c) The unweighted index is obtained by taking the average of the three indexes. For example, the unweighted index for 1998–99 is 186 = (235 + 156 + 166)/3.

Year	Unweighted Index	Weighted Index
1989–90	100	100
1990–91	109	109
1991–92	120	120
1992–93	131	131
1993–94	140	140
1994–95	148	148
1995–96	154	154
1996–97	163	162
1997–98	177	174
1998–99	186	182

(d) In 1989-90 the total fee was $4,744 = $1,374 + $1,710 + $1,660. Thus, the weights are: tuition, 0.29 = 1,374/4,744; residence, 0.36 = 1,710/4,744, and; food, 0.35 = 1,660/4,744. The weighted index is a weighted average of the indexes for each year. For example, in 1998–99, the weighted index is 182 = 0.29(235) + 0.36(156) + 0.35(166). See the table above for other years.

(e) The president of the Student Council would cite the tuition price index which shows a 135% increase over the decade to argue that fees have already increased enough. The university president would cite the weighted index to show that the cost of a university education has only increased 82% over the decade to justify higher fees. The difference is due to the small weight tuition has in the base year (0.29), relative to its weight in the most recent academic year (0.37). Note that tuition only became the most costly of the three items in 1997–98.

4. (a) Q^D and P are determined in the market for personal computers; they are endogenous variables. Average income, which is determined in many other markets, is not influenced to any significant extent by the computer market; it is exogenous to the market for computers.

(b) Q^D and P are negatively related; as P increases, Q^D falls. Q^D and Y are positively related; as Y increases, Q^D increases.

(c) The equation becomes $Q^D = 8,000 - 4P$.

(d) $Q^D = 8000; 6,000; 4,000; 0$.

(e) As shown in Figure 2-5, the intercept on the P axis is 2,000, and the intercept on the Q^D axis is 8,000.

Figure 2-5

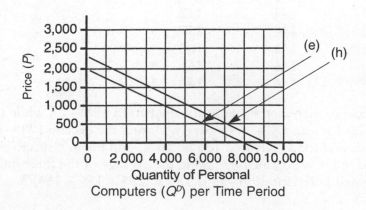

(f) The slope is calculated as $\Delta P / \Delta Q^D$; for example, $-2{,}000/8{,}000 = -1/4$.

(g) The change in quantity demanded is -4,000 when P increases from 1,000 to 2,000. When P increases from 500 to 2,000, quantity demanded falls by 6,000. In both cases the ratio $\Delta Q^D / \Delta P$ is equal to -4. It is the inverse of the slope.

(h) The intercept on the P axis is \$2,250, and the intercept on the Q^D axis is 9,000. The slope remains $-1/4$. See Figure 2-5 above.

Extension Exercises

E-1. (a)

X	N_1	N_2	N_3
10	10	50	30
20	15	45	35
30	20	40	40
40	25	35	45
50	30	30	50
60	35	25	55

(b)

Figure 2-6

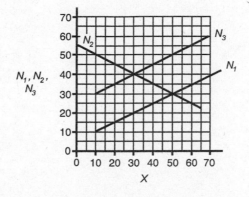

(i) positive; +1/2
(ii) negative; –1/2

(c) $N_1 = N_2$ when the two curves intersect. $N = 30$ and $X = 50$ solves this system of equations.

(d) leftward (or equivalently, upward); unchanged at +1/2.

(e) $N = 40$ and $X = 30$.

E-2. (a) Substitute equation (1) into equation (3) for x_1. This yields

$$a + by = x_2. \qquad\qquad (3')$$

There are two remaining equations, (2) and (3'), and two remaining unknowns, x_2 and y.

(b) Substitute equation (2) into (3') for x_2. This yields

$$a + by = c - dy. \qquad\qquad (3'')$$

There is only one equation remaining (3′) and only one unknown y.

(c) Rearranging terms in (3″) yields: $by + dy = c - a$, or equivalently, $(b + d)y = c - a$. Division by $(b + d)$ yields $y^* = (c - a)/(b + d)$ which is the solution value for y.

(d) Substitute y^* into equation (1), which yields

$$x_1{}^* = a + b(c - a)/(b + d)$$

which simplifies to $x_1 = (ad + bc)/(b + d)$. In view of equation (3), this is also the solution value to $x_2{}^*$.

(e) $x_1 = x_2 = x = 280$ and $y = 40$.

Practice Multiple Choice Test

1.(c) 2.(a) 3.(b) 4.(d) 5.(a) 6.(e) 7.(a) 8.(b) 9.(c) 10.(b) 11.(d) 12.(c) 13.(d) 14.(d) 15.(b) 16.(a) 17.(d) 18.(e)

PART TWO

AN INTRODUCTION TO DEMAND AND SUPPLY

CHAPTER 3

DEMAND, SUPPLY, AND PRICE

 ## LEARNING OBJECTIVES

1 Understand what determines "quantity demanded," the amount of some product that households want to purchase.

2 Distinguish between a shift in a demand curve and a movement along a demand curve.

3 Understand what determines "quantity supplied," the amount of some product that firms want to sell.

4 Distinguish between a shift in a supply curve and a movement along a supply curve.

5 Recognize the forces that drive market price to equilibrium.

6 Understand the four "laws" of demand and supply.

CHAPTER OVERVIEW

This chapter introduces you to the economic model of **demand** and **supply**, which describes how the interactions of buyers and sellers determine the **equilibrium price** and quantity exchanged in the markets for goods and services.

A downward-sloping **demand curve** shows the relationship between price and **quantity demanded**. From a buyer's perspective, the lower the (relative) price of a product, the more attractive it is to purchase. A **supply curve** shows the relationship between price and **quantity supplied**. From a seller's perspective, higher relative prices for a product make it more attractive to sell. If quantity supplied does not equal quantity demanded, the model predicts changes in price until the plans of buyers and sellers are satisfied at the equilibrium price.

Using the method of **comparative statics**, the effects of a shift in either demand or supply can be determined. The equilibrium price and quantity exchanged respond to changes in the determinants of demand (income, tastes, population, and prices of substitutes or complements) or supply (prices of inputs, technology, and the number of firms). These responses are called the "laws" of demand and supply.

CHAPTER REVIEW

Demand

The ability to distinguish between the concepts of quantity demanded and demand is an important objective in this section. Remember that quantity demanded refers to the amount of a product consumers desire to purchase at a specific price, whereas demand refers to the entire relationship between price and quantity demanded. It is of central importance that the student understand when there is a *movement along* a demand curve and when there is a *shift* in the demand curve. An understanding of the causes of shifts in demand curves is crucial to this distinction.

1. The term quantity demanded refers to the
   (a) amount of a good that consumers are willing to purchase at some price during some given time period.
   (b) amount of some good that consumers would purchase if they only had the income to afford it.
   (c) amount of a good that is actually purchased during a given time period.
   (d) minimum amount of a good that consumers require and demand for survival.
   (e) amount of a good that consumers are willing to purchase regardless of price.

2. An increase in quantity demanded refers to
   (a) rightward shifts in the demand curve only.
   (b) a movement up along a demand curve.
   (c) a greater willingness to purchase at each price.
   (d) an increase in actual purchases.
   (e) a movement down along a demand curve.

3. The demand curve and the demand schedule
   (a) each reflect the relationship between quantity demanded and price, *ceteris paribus*.
   (b) are both incomplete in that neither can incorporate the impact of changes in income or tastes.
   (c) are constructed on the assumption that price is held constant.
   (d) illustrate that in economic analysis, only two variables are taken into account at any one time.
   (e) characterize the relationship between price and actual purchases.

4. An increase in demand means that
   (a) consumers actually buy more of the good.
   (b) at each price, consumers desire a greater quantity.
   (c) consumers' tastes have necessarily changed.
   (d) price has decreased.
   (e) All of the above are correct.

5. If goods A and B are complements, an increase in the price of good A will lead to
   (a) an increase in the price of good B.
   (b) a decrease in the quantity demanded of good B.
   (c) a decrease in demand for good B.
   (d) no change in demand for good B because A and B are not substitutes.
   (e) a rightward shift in the demand for good B.

6. Increased public awareness of the adverse health effects of smoking
   (a) is a noneconomic event that cannot be incorporated into the demand and supply model.
   (b) is characterized as a change in tastes that leads to a leftward shift in the demand curve for cigarettes.
   (c) will lead to an eventual increase in the price of cigarettes due to shifts in the demand curve for cigarettes.
   (d) induces a decrease in the supply of cigarettes.
   (e) decreases the quantity demanded of cigarettes.

Supply

Similar to demand, it is important that the student understand the difference between quantity supplied and supply, as well as a movement along a supply curve as opposed to a shift in the curve. A movement along a supply (demand) curve is referred to a change in quantity supplied (demanded) while a shift in the entire curve is referred to as a change in supply (demand). Make sure you know what causes a shift in the supply curve.

7. A shift in the supply curve may be caused by any of the following except
   (a) an improvement in technology.
   (b) an increase in the wage paid to labour.
   (c) an increase in average consumer income.
   (d) an increase in the number of firms in the industry.
   (e) Both (b) and (c).

8. A rightward shift in the supply curve indicates
   (a) a decrease in price.
   (b) an increase in demand.
   (c) an increase in quantity supplied.
   (d) that at each price quantity supplied has increased.
   (e) an increase in consumers desire for a product.

9. An increase in the price of an input will
   (a) decrease quantity supplied.
   (b) decrease quantity supplied at each price.
   (c) decrease supply.
   (d) cause the supply curve to shift to the left.
   (e) (b), (c) and (d) are correct.

10. A movement along a supply curve could be caused by
    (a) an improvement in technology.
    (b) a change in the prices of inputs.
    (c) a shift in the demand curve.
    (d) a change in the number of producers.
    (e) an decrease in production costs.

The Determination of Price

If, at a particular market price, quantity demanded is not equal to quantity supplied, pressures are exerted on price to change until the market clears—i.e., until quantity demanded is equal to quantity supplied. You should understand these pressures. Furthermore, you should be able to show how equilibrium price and quantity exchanged are affected by changes in demand and supply—these are the laws of demand and supply.

11. Excess demand exists whenever
    (a) price exceeds the equilibrium price.
    (b) quantity supplied is greater than quantity demanded.
    (c) the equilibrium price is above the existing price.
    (d) there is downward pressure on price.
    (e) there is surplus production.

12. The "laws of demand and supply" are
    (a) federal statutes and are therefore enforced by the RCMP.
    (b) enshrined in the Canadian Constitution.
    (c) irrefutable propositions concerning economic behaviour.
    (d) basic assumptions in economic theory.
    (e) predictions of economic behaviour that have tended to withstand much, but not all, empirical testing.

13. An increase in both equilibrium price and quantity exchanged is consistent with
    (a) an increase in supply.   (b) a decrease in supply.
    (c) a decrease in quantity supplied.   (d) an increase in demand.
    (e) a decrease in demand.

14. Assuming a downward-sloping demand curve, an improvement in production technology for some good is predicted to lead to
    (a) a decrease in supply.
    (b) an increase in both equilibrium price and quantity exchanged.
    (c) a decrease in equilibrium price and an increase in equilibrium quantity exchanged.
    (d) a decrease in equilibrium price but no change in equilibrium quantity exchanged.
    (e) an increase in equilibrium price and a decrease in equilibrium quantity exchanged.

15. Comparative statics
    (a) is the analysis of market equilibria under different sets of conditions.
    (b) is the analysis of demand without reference to time.
    (c) refers to constant equilibrium prices and quantities.
    (d) describes the path by which equilibrium price changes.
    (e) refers to disequilibrium prices and quantities.

EXERCISES

1. This question asks you to solve for market equilibrium using demand and supply schedules.

   The demand and supply schedules for athletic shoes sold at Trendy Shoes Inc. at the local mall are hypothesized to be as follows (in pairs per week):

(1) Price	(2) Quantity Demanded		(3) Quantity Supplied	(4) Excess Demand (+) Excess Supply (−)
	D	D′		
$120	40	____	130	____
110	50	____	110	____
100	60	____	90	____
90	70	____	70	____
80	80	____	50	____
70	90	____	30	____
60	100	____	10	____

(a) Using the grid provided in Figure 3-1, plot the demand and supply curves (approximately). Indicate the equilibrium levels of price and quantity.

Figure 3-1

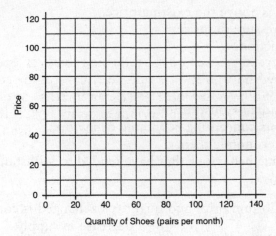

Quantity of Shoes (pairs per month)

(b) Fill in column 4 for values of excess demand and excess supply. What is the value of excess demand (supply) at equilibrium?_____

(c) Suppose there is a change in teenage fashion such that a substitute shoe, Doc Martens, becomes trendy. As a result, the quantity demanded of athletic shoes at Trendy Shoes Inc. decreases by 30 units per week at each and every price. Fill in the new quantity demanded in column (2) above, and draw the new demand curve D' on the grid.

(d) Supposing that price initially remains at the level you reported in answer (b). Explain the pressures that are exerted upon price by this change in tastes.

(e) After price has adjusted to the new equilibrium, what are the equilibrium price and quantity?

2. **Fair Pricing at Equality U?**

The executive of the Students' Association at the University of Equality has recently announced that "in the interests of fairness" all seats for on campus concerts will sell at the same price regardless of the popularity of the performer (clearly, there are no economics majors on the executive). The campus concert hall has a seating capacity of 5,000. Suppose that *average* demand for tickets for a *typical* concert or performer is as follows:

Price	Quantity Demanded
$6	8,000
8	5,000
10	2,500
12	1,500
14	1,000

(a) If the executive sets a price of $10 per seat, is there an excess demand or supply of concert tickets (on average)?

(b) What price would fill the concert hall without creating a shortage of seats at a typical concert?

(c) Suppose the quantity of tickets demanded at each price doubles when a particularly popular performer is booked. What would be the equilibrium ticket price for a popular performer?

(d) Do you think ticket scalping would be more profitable if the executive set price equal to, above or below equilibrium? Explain.

3. **The Laws of Demand and Supply**

Read the description of events in each of the following markets. Predict the economic impact of these events by drawing the appropriate shifts of curves in the accompanying diagram. Also, use + and – to indicate whether there will be an increase or decrease in demand (D), supply (S), equilibrium price (P), and equilibrium quantity (Q). If there is no change, use 0. If the change cannot be deduced with the information provided, use U for uncertain.

Figure 3-2

Market	Event		D	S	P	Q
(a) Canadian wine	Early frost destroys a large percentage of the grape crop in British Columbia	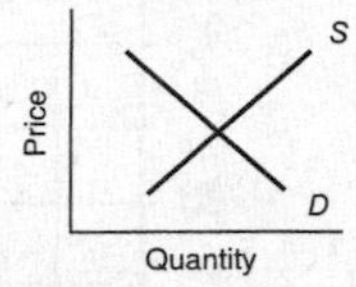	___	___	___	___
(b) Wood-burning stoves	The price of heating oil and natural gas triples	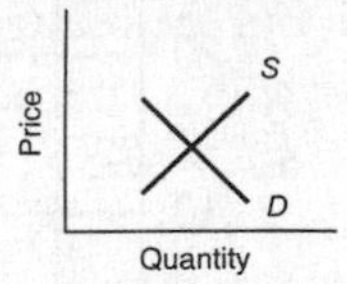	___	___	___	___
(c) Laser printers	Technological advances reduce the costs of producing laser printers	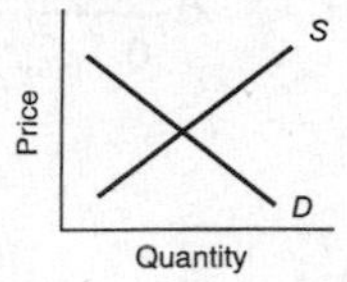	___	___	___	___
(d) Gold	Large gold deposits are discovered in northern Ontario	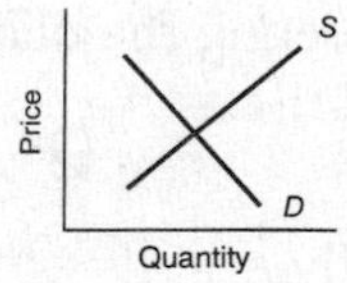	___	___	___	___
(e) Fast foods	The public show greater concern over high sodium and cholesterol; also, there is an increase in the minimum wage	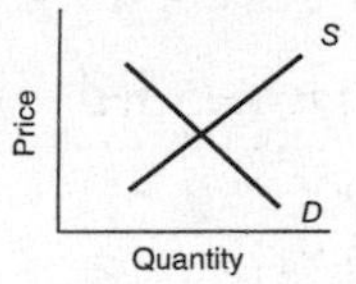	___	___	___	___
(f) Bicycles	There is increasing concern about physical fitness; also the price of gasoline rises	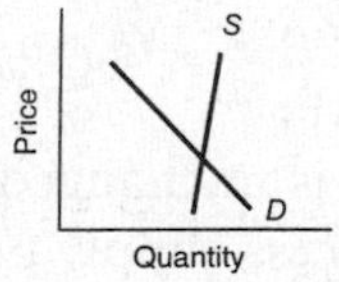	___	___	___	___
(g) Beer	Population of drinking age increases; also, brewery unions negotiate a large increase in remuneration	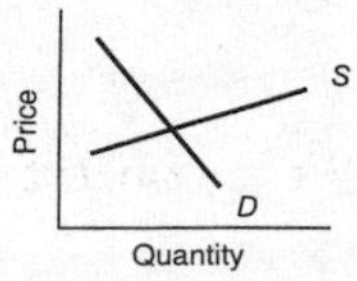	___	___	___	___
(h) Candles	Ice storm knocks out electrical power for an extended period of time	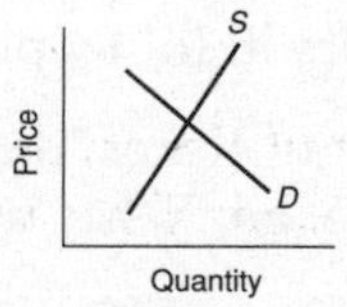	___	___	___	___

4. **Algebraic Solution of Equilibrium**

The purpose of this question is to encourage you to obtain the market equilibrium by algebraically solving a system of simultaneous equations. The required algebra is reviewed in Exercise E-2 of Chapter 2.

The demand and supply of widgets are given by

$$Q^D = 30 - 1.0P, \text{ and}$$

$$Q^S = 1.0P, \text{ respectively.}$$

(a) Plot the demand and supply curves on the graph below, and label them D and S, respectively.

Figure 3-3

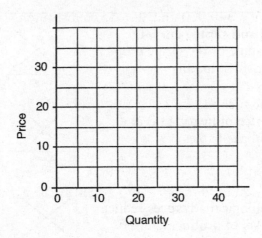

(b) Determine the equilibrium price and the equilibrium quantity by using two methods. First, solve by interpreting the diagram. Second, impose the equilibrium condition that

$$Q^D = Q^S$$

and solve algebraically.

(c) Now suppose that the demand curve changes to

$$Q^D = 30 - 1.5P$$

but the supply curve is unchanged. Before price adjusts from your answer in (b), is there excess demand or excess supply in the market? How much? Use algebra to solve for the new equilibrium.

(d) Confirm your answers in (c) by plotting the new demand curve and label it D'.

5. **Equilibrium Again!**

The following question demonstrates how changes in exogenous variables impact upon market equilibrium. This question walks you through both the algebraic and diagrammatic solution methods.

The quantity demanded of gadgets (Q^D) depends on the price of gadgets (P) and average household income (Y) according to the following relationship:

$$Q^D = 30 - 10P + 0.001Y$$

The quantity of gadgets supplied (Q^S) is positively related to the price of gadgets and negatively related to W, the price of some input (e.g., labour) according to

$$Q^S = 5 + 5P - 2W$$

(a) Assume initially that $Y = \$40,000$ and $W = \$5$. Substitute these values into the equations to obtain the demand and supply curves.

(b) Now use the equilibrium condition $Q^D = Q^S$ to solve the demand and supply curves simultaneously for the equilibrium price.

(c) Finally, substitute the equilibrium price into either the demand or supply curve to obtain the equilibrium quantity.

(d) Use the grid in Figure 3-4 to graph the demand and supply curves for gadgets in (a), and label them D_0 and S_0, respectively. Confirm that your answers in (b) and (c) are correct.

Figure 3-4

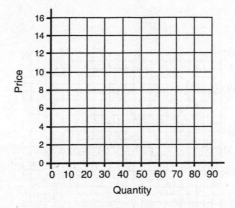

(e) Now, suppose that average household income increases to $55,000 but W remains constant. What are the new levels of equilibrium price and quantity? Plot the new demand curve, label it D_1, and confirm your answer.

(f) Now assume that the input price W increases to $12.50. Using the demand curve you derived in (e), determine the new levels of equilibrium price and quantity. Plot the new supply curve, label it S_1, and again confirm your answer.

6. **Movements versus Shifts**

For each of the following statements, determine if the sentence is referring to a change in demand, a change in quantity demanded, a change in supply or a change in quantity supplied. If applicable, indicate the resulting change in equilibrium.

(a) Oil prices rise as OPEC members agree to new restrictions on output.

(b) Prices of personal computers fall despite a substantial increase in the number sold.

(c) Apartment rental prices rise as student enrolment swells.

(d) Lower air fares spark the busiest-ever air travel over a holiday period.

(e) Increases in the prices of Christmas trees spur tree planting on land previously used by dairy farmers.

(f) The moratorium on fishing east coast cod is linked to an increase in the price of west coast salmon.

EXTENSION EXERCISE

E-1. This extension exercise introduces government intervention in the market. Specifically, government is introduced as an additional demander of a product.

The diagram in Figure 3-5 illustrates a hypothetical market for farm machinery in Canada.

Figure 3-5

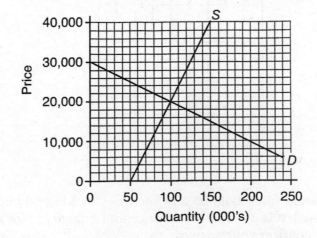

The federal government has decided that output in this industry should increase by 50 percent. Since current industry output is 100,000 units, it therefore plans to purchase 50,000 units of farm machinery *regardless of price*. The government intends to give away these units to less developed countries as part of Canada's foreign aid.

(a) Draw the new demand curve for farm machinery that takes into account government demand. What are the new levels of equilibrium price and quantity?

(b) By how much does industry output increase in percentage terms? Why does this increase fall short of the government's target of 50 percent?

(c) How many units would the government have to purchase in order to satisfy its objective of increasing industry output to 150,000 units? What is the associated quantity demanded by the private sector (i.e., by nongovernment consumers in Canada)?

(d) What erroneous assumption did the government make about the supply of farm machinery if they believed that buying 50,000 units would increase production by 50 percent?

PRACTICE MULTIPLE CHOICE TEST

1. When the Multiple Listing Service (MLS) reports that in the month of April at an average selling price of $250,000, total sales of homes in Toronto were 2,000 units, they are referring to
   (a) quantity demanded.
   (b) quantity supplied.
   (c) equilibrium quantity.
   (d) actual purchases, which may or may not equal quantity demanded or quantity supplied.
   (e) Both (a) and (c) are correct.

2. A decrease in the price of VCRs will result in
   (a) an increase in demand for VCRs.
   (b) a decrease in supply of VCRs.
   (c) an increase in the quantity demanded of VCRs.
   (d) a movement up along the demand curve for VCRs.
   (e) a rightward shift in the demand curve for VCRs.

3. A decrease in the price of compact disc (CD) players will induce
   (a) a leftward shift in the demand curve for cassette players (a substitute).
   (b) an increase in demand for cassette tapes.
   (c) a rightward shift in the demand curve for CDs (a complement).
   (d) a rise in demand for CD players.
   (e) Both (a) and (c) are correct.

4. A change in demand could be caused by *all but which* one of the following?
   (a) A decrease in average income.
   (b) An increase in the price of a substitute good.
   (c) A decrease in the cost of producing the good.
   (d) An increase in population.
   (e) A government program that redistributes income.

5. An increase in the supply of broccoli could be caused by *all but which* of the following?
   (a) A decrease in the price of broccoli.
   (b) A decrease in the price of labour employed in harvesting broccoli.
   (c) An improvement in pesticides, thereby decreasing the variability in broccoli output.
   (d) An increase in the number of producers.
   (e) An improvement in harvesting technology.

Questions 6 and 7 refer to the following diagram.

Figure 3-6

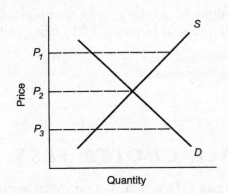

6. At a price of P_1,
   (a) there is upward pressure on price.
   (b) demand will rise to restore equilibrium.
   (c) quantity supplied is greater than quantity demanded.
   (d) the market has reached an equilibrium price.
   (e) a shortage exists.

7. When price equals P_3,
   (a) quantity exchanged equals quantity demanded.
   (b) there is excess supply.
   (c) there is a tendency for price to rise.
   (d) the market is in equilibrium.
   (e) a surplus exists.

8. Should polyester leisure suits become fashionable, economic theory predicts
   (a) a decrease in the price of these suits but an increase in the quantity exchanged.
   (b) an increase in both equilibrium price and quantity.
   (c) a shift in the supply curve to the right.
   (d) an increase in equilibrium price and a decrease in equilibrium quantity.
   (e) a leftward shift of the demand curve.

9. Simultaneous increases in both demand and supply are predicted to result in
   (a) increases in both equilibrium price and quantity.
   (b) a higher equilibrium price but a smaller equilibrium quantity.
   (c) a lower equilibrium price but a larger equilibrium quantity.
   (d) a larger equilibrium quantity but no predictable change in price.
   (e) a higher price, but no predicable change in equilibrium quantity.

10. A decrease in input prices as well as a simultaneous decrease in the price of a good that is substitutable in consumption will lead to
    (a) a lower equilibrium price and a larger equilibrium quantity.
    (b) a lower equilibrium price but no change in equilibrium quantity.
    (c) a lower equilibrium price and an uncertain change in quantity.
    (d) a lower equilibrium price and a smaller equilibrium quantity.
    (e) an unpredictable change in both price and quantity.

11. Which of the following is *not* a potential cause of an increase in the price of housing?
    (a) Construction workers' wages increase with no offsetting increase in productivity.
    (b) Cheaper methods of prefabricating homes are developed.
    (c) An increase in population.
    (d) An increase in consumer incomes.
    (e) The price of land (an input) increases.

12. Today the price of strawberries is 60 cents a quart, and raspberries are priced at 75 cents a quart. Yesterday strawberries were 80 cents and raspberries $1. Thus, for these two goods,
    (a) the relative price of raspberries has fallen.
    (b) the relative price of strawberries has fallen by 20 cents.
    (c) the relative prices of both goods have fallen.
    (d) relative prices have not changed.
    (e) the relative price of strawberries has risen.

13. In price theory, which of the following represents a relative price increase for strawberries, assuming that the average price level rises by 10 percent?
    (a) An increase in price from $1.00 to $1.05 per quart.
    (b) An increase in price from $1.00 to $1.10 per quart.
    (c) An increase in price from $1.00 to $1.15 per quart.
    (d) Both (a) and (c) are correct.
    (e) All of the above are correct.

Questions 14 to 20 refer to the following diagram which depicts the market for hamburgers in Collegeville, Ontario.

Figure 3-7

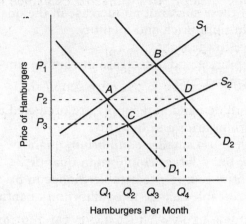

14. A change in Collegeville's market equilibrium from *A* to *B* may be caused by
    (a) a decrease in wages of part-time workers.
    (b) a decrease in the price of hot dogs.
    (c) an increase in the student population of Collegeville.
    (d) an increase in the price of hamburgers.
    (e) Both (c) and (d) are correct.

15. An increase in the price of hot dogs may be depicted in the hamburger market by a change in equilibrium from
    (a) *A* to *D*
    (b) *A* to *C*
    (c) *C* to *D*
    (d) *A* to *B*
    (e) Both (c) and (d) are correct.

16. A change in equilibrium from *A* to *D* may be explained by
    (a) an increase in Collegeville's student population.
    (b) a decrease in the price of beef patties.
    (c) an increase in the price of hot dogs coupled with an increase in the wages of restaurant employees.
    (d) a technological improvement in the production of hamburgers coupled with consumer concern about Mad Cow disease.
    (e) a decrease in the price of fries (a complement to hamburgers) coupled with a reduction in the wages of restaurant employees.

17. Which event would best explain a decrease in equilibrium quantity from Q_4 to Q_3?
    (a) An increase in the price of beef patties.
    (b) A decrease in Collegeville's student population.
    (c) A decrease in the price of fries (a complement to hamburgers).
    (d) An increase in the supply of hamburgers due to entry of new firms.
    (e) Consumer concern about Mad Cow disease.

18. If equilibrium changes from *A* to *B*, one could say
    (a) there has been an increase in demand.
    (b) quantity supplied has increased.
    (c) price has increased.
    (d) supply has not changed.
    (e) all of the above are correct.

19. A decrease in equilibrium price from P_1 to P_3, may be explained by
    (a) a decrease in supply.
    (b) a decrease in quantity supplied.
    (c) a decrease in demand and a decrease in supply.
    (d) a decrease in demand and an increase in supply.
    (e) an increase in supply and a decrease in quantity supplied.

20. An increase in average student incomes and an increase in the number of hamburger firms can be depicted by a change in equilibrium from
    (a) D to B.
    (b) C to D.
    (c) D to A.
    (d) C to B.
    (e) A to D or B to C, depending upon whether the demand for hamburgers is normal or inferior, respectively.

SOLUTIONS

Review Questions

1.(a) 2.(e) 3.(a) 4.(b) 5.(c) 6.(b) 7.(c) 8.(d) 9.(e) 10.(c) 11.(c) 12.(e) 13.(d) 14.(c) 15.(a)

Exercises

1. (a)

    Figure 3-8

    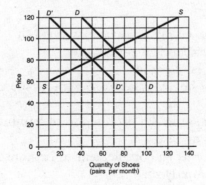

    Equilibrium price and quantity are $90 and 70 pairs per month, respectively.

(b)

Price	Excess demand (+) or excess supply (−)
$120	−90
110	−60
100	−30
90	0
80	+30
70	+60
60	+90

There is no excess demand or supply.

(c) See above diagram.

(d) With the change in tastes (i.e., along D') quantity demanded at the original price of $90 is now 40 units per week while quantity supplied remains at 70 units. Thus, 30 units remain unsold each week; this accumulating inventory exerts downward pressure on price.

(e) The new equilibrium is obtained at a price of $80 and quantity of 50 units per week.

2. (a) Excess supply of 2,500 seats.

(b) At $8, quantity demanded and quantity supplied each equal 5,000 seats.

(c) Since quantity demanded doubles at every price, 5,000 tickets would be demanded if price were $10.

(d) Scalpers would do better if price were set below equilibrium which creates excess demand. For example, at a price of $6, the quantity demanded for an "average" concert is 8,000 but only 5,000 are sold. Thus, scalpers who are fortunate to purchase at $6 have a better chance of finding a buyer who is willing to pay more than $6.

3.

	D	S	P	Q
(a)	0	−	+	−
(b)	+	0	+	+
(c)	0	+	−	+
(d)	0	+	−	+
(e)	−	−	U	−
(f)	+	0	+	+
(g)	+	−	+	U
(h)	+	0	+	+

4. (a)

Figure 3-9

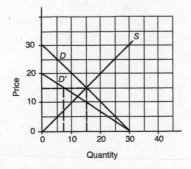

(b) $Q^D = Q^S$ is equivalent to: $30 - 1.0P = 1.0P$ which solves for $P = \$15$. Now substitute the equilibrium price into the equation for either Q^D or Q^S, and obtain the equilibrium quantity $Q = 15$. (e.g., $Q^S = 1.0(15) = 15$).

(c) When price is $15, $Q^S = 15$ and $Q^D = 7.5$; thus there is excess supply of 7.5 units. The new equilibrium now obtains where $30 - 1.5P = 1.0P$, which solves for $P = \$12$ and $Q = 12$.

(d) see Figure 3-9

5. (a) $Q^D = 30 - 10P + 0.001(40,000) = 70 - 10P$.
   $Q^S = 5 + 5P - 2(5) = -5 + 5P$.

   (b) For equilibrium, $Q^D = Q^S$, so that: $70 - 10P = -5 + 5P$, which solves for the equilibrium price of $5.

   (c) Substituting this value into either Q^D or Q^S, one obtains the equilibrium quantity of 20 units.

   (d)

Figure 3-10

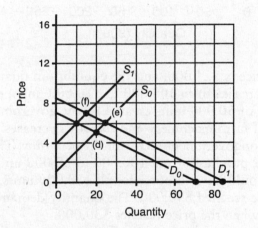

(e) Now $Q^D = 85 - 10P$. Setting $Q^D = Q^S$, or $85 - 10P = -5 + 5P$ yields $P = \$6$ and $Q = 25$.

(f) Now $Q^S = -20 + 5P$ and $Q^D = 85 - 10P$, so that $Q^D = Q^S$ solves for $P = \$7$ and $Q = 15$.

6. (a) The supply curve for oil shifts to the left, resulting in a higher equilibrium price.

   (b) The supply curve for computers shifts to the right, resulting in a lower equilibrium price and a greater quantity exchanged. (Although, demand may have also shifted to the right, the effect of the supply shift dominates, resulting in a lower price.)

   (c) The demand for apartments increased (i.e., demand curve shifts to the right), resulting in higher rents.

   (d) Increase in quantity demanded. Lower air fares induce a movement down along the demand curve for air travel.

   (e) Increase in quantity supplied. The higher price results in a movement up along the supply curve for Christmas trees.

   (f) The supply of east coast cod shifts to the left, resulting in a higher price for cod. To the extent that east coast cod and west coast salmon are substitutes, the higher price for cod will induce a rightward shift in the demand for salmon, leading to a price increase in salmon.

Extension Exercise

E-1.   (a)

Figure 3-11

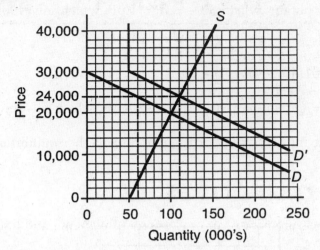

The equilibrium price is $24,000, and the equilibrium quantity is 110,000 units.

(b)   Industry output increases from 100,000 to 110,000 units, or by 10 percent. The additional demand of 50,000 units created by the government exerts upward pressure on the price of farm machinery and thereby decreases the quantity demanded by the private or nongovernment sector of the economy. These private-sector consumers reduce their purchases from 100,000 to 60,000 units.

(c)   The government would have to purchase all 150,000 units, which would be supplied only when the price reached $40,000. The quantity demanded by the private sector is reduced to zero when the price reaches $30,000.

(d)   They erroneously assumed the supply curve was horizontal.

Practice Multiple Choice Test

1.(d) 2.(c) 3.(e) 4.(c) 5.(a) 6.(c) 7.(c) 8.(b) 9.(d) 10.(c) 11.(b) 12.(d) 13.(c) 14.(c) 15.(e) 16. (e) 17.(a) 18.(e) 19.(d) 20.(e)

CHAPTER 4

ELASTICITY

🔵 LEARNING OBJECTIVES

1 Understand the measurement of price elasticity of demand, and know its determinants.

2 Understand the measurement of price elasticity of supply, and know its determinants.

3 Explain how an excise (or sales) tax affects the producer price and the consumer price.

4 Recognize that the incidence of a sales tax depends on relative demand and supply elasticities.

5 Understand the effect of income on quantity demanded, and how this elasticity defines normal and inferior goods.

6 Recognize the difference between substitute and complement goods, and how the degree of substitutability can be measured by the cross elasticity of demand.

CHAPTER OVERVIEW

The interaction of demand and supply was shown to determine equilibrium price and quantity in the previous chapter. The present chapter examines another important aspect of the interaction of demand and supply: the responsiveness of quantity demanded (or supplied) to changes in price (or other determinants of demand and supply).

Price elasticity of demand is measured as the percentage change in quantity demanded divided by the percentage change in price. When the percentage change in quantity demanded exceeds the percentage change in price (in absolute terms), demand is said to be **elastic** (as opposed to **inelastic** when the reverse holds, or unit elastic when the two percentage changes are of equal magnitude). If the price elasticity of demand for a product is known, one can predict the percentage change in quantity demanded that would result from a given percentage price change. The magnitude of a product's elasticity also allows us to predict whether an increase in its price will result in an increase or a decrease in total expenditure on the good. Whether demand (supply) is elastic or inelastic depends upon the availability of substitutes.

Tax incidence refers to the distribution of the *burden* of a tax between consumers and producers. This chapter shows that tax incidence is independent of who pays the tax. Rather, the distribution of the burden of a sales tax critically depends upon the relative magnitudes of the elasticities of demand and supply.

Additional elasticity measures are relevant when consumer income or the price of another good changes, which involves the **income elasticity** and **cross-price elasticity**, respectively. The sign of the income elasticity indicates whether the good is **normal** or **inferior,** while that of the cross-price elasticity indicates whether the goods are substitutes or complements.

CHAPTER REVIEW

Price Elasticity of Demand

In this section we focus on the responsiveness of quantity demanded to changes in price—the elasticity of demand. Pay particular attention to the formula for elasticity: there are several alternative ways of expressing the same thing. Sometimes elasticity is expressed in percentages, other times it is expressed in discrete changes. The nature of the information you are provided determines which form of the equation you should use. Depending upon its magnitude, elasticity is classified as elastic, inelastic or unit elastic. Make certain you understand the implications of this classification for the effect of a commodity's price change on its total expenditure.

1. The price elasticity of demand refers to a measure that shows the
    (a) responsiveness of quantity demanded of a good to changes in its price.
    (b) variation in prices due to a change in demand.
    (c) size of price changes caused by a shift in demand.
    (d) degree of substitutability across commodities.
    (e) magnitude of the shifts in a demand curve.

2. The price elasticity of demand is measured by the
    (a) change in quantity demanded divided by the change in price.
    (b) change in price divided by the change in quantity demanded.
    (c) slope of the demand curve.
    (d) percentage change in quantity demanded divided by the percentage change in price.
    (e) average quantity demanded divided by the average price.

3. If the percentage change in price is greater than the percentage change in quantity demanded, demand
    (a) is elastic.   (b) is inelastic.
    (c) is unit-elastic.   (d) shifts outward to the left.
    (e) shifts to the right.

4. An increase in the price of a good and a decrease in total expenditure on this good are associated with
    (a) inferior goods.   (b) substitute goods.
    (c) normal goods.   (d) elastic demand.
    (e) inelastic demand.

5. The price elasticity of demand for a good will be greater
    (a) the less available are suitable substitutes for this good.
    (b) the longer the time period considered.
    (c) for a group of related goods as opposed to an element of that group.
    (d) the greater is income.
    (e) All of the above are correct.

6. If a 10 percent increase in the price of ski lift tickets causes a 5 percent decrease in total expenditure on lift tickets, then demand is
   (a) elastic.   (b) inelastic.
   (c) perfectly inelastic.   (d) normal.
   (e) inferior.

7. Which of the following commodities is more likely to have an elastic demand?
   (a) Toothpicks.   (b) Cigarettes.
   (c) Heart pacemakers.   (d) Broccoli.
   (e) Vegetables.

Price Elasticity of Supply

The responsiveness of quantity supplied to a change in price can also be classified as elastic or inelastic. Make sure you understand the special case when the supply curve is linear and goes through the origin—if you are uncertain about it, review the discussion associated with Figure 4-6 of the text. Similar to demand, the magnitude of elasticity of supply depends upon the availability of substitutes.

8. A value of zero for the elasticity of supply of some product implies that
   (a) the supply curve is horizontal.
   (b) supply is highly responsive to price.
   (c) the supply curve is vertical.
   (d) the product will not be supplied at any price.
   (e) None of the above.

9. The elasticity of supply for a product will tend to be larger
   (a) the higher is the elasticity of demand for the product.
   (b) the lower is the elasticity of demand for the product.
   (c) the harder it is for firms to shift from the production of one product to another product.
   (d) the easier it is for firms to shift from the production of one product to another product.
   (e) the shorter the time period involved.

10. In the short run, a shift in demand will generally cause
    (a) the price to overshoot its long-run equilibrium value.
    (b) the price to undershoot its long-run equilibrium value.
    (c) the quantity exchanged to overshoot its long-run equilibrium values.
    (d) both price and quantity exchanged to overshoot their long-run equilibrium values.
    (e) None of the above.

11. Suppose that the short-run demand for a good is relatively more inelastic than its long-run demand. A given rightward shift in the supply curve will lead to a
    (a) smaller decrease in price in the long-run than in the short-run.
    (b) smaller increase in quantity in the long-run than in the short-run.
    (c) larger decrease in price in the long-run than in the short-run.
    (d) smaller decrease in both price and quantity in the long-run than in the short-run.
    (e) larger decreases in both price and quantity in the long-run than in the short-run.

An Important Example Where Elasticity Matters

Who bears the burden of a tax, consumers or producers? Surprisingly, the answer does not depend upon who pays the tax. Rather, it depends on the relative magnitudes of the elasticities of demand and supply. The more elastic is demand (supply), the smaller will be consumers' (producers') share of the burden of taxation. The distinction between consumer and seller prices is critical to understanding this section.

12. "Tax incidence" refers to
    (a) who is legally responsible for paying the tax revenue to the government.
    (b) the legislative process taxes must pass through.
    (c) the economic costs of avoiding taxes.
    (d) who ultimately bears the burden of the tax.
    (e) None of the above.

13. Suppose the market supply curve for some good is upward sloping. If the imposition of a sales tax causes no change in the equilibrium quantity sold in the market, the good's demand curve must be_____, meaning that the burden of the tax has fallen completely on the _____.
    (a) vertical, firms.
    (b) vertical, consumers.
    (c) horizontal, firms.
    (d) horizontal, consumers.
    (e) not enough information to answer this question.

14. Since the Goods and Services Tax (GST) is added to the price a consumer must pay for a commodity the
    (a) entire burden of the tax is borne by consumers.
    (b) consumer price increases by the amount of the tax.
    (c) seller price is unaffected.
    (d) burden is borne by producers who must collect the tax.
    (e) distribution of the burden depends upon the elasticities of demand and supply.

15. Consumers bear a greater share of the burden of the tax, the more
    (a) inelastic is supply.   (b) elastic is supply.
    (c) inelastic is demand.   (d) elastic is demand.
    (e) Both (b) and (c) are correct.

Other Demand Elasticities

Elasticity measures the responsiveness of one variable to another. It is an arithmetic measure and is not unique to economics (any more than the measurement "average" is). The income elasticity of demand and the cross-price elasticity of demand provide insights into the nature of the products being discussed. Are they luxuries or necessities, substitutes or complements, normal or inferior? Review the Terminology of Elasticity (see Extensions in Theory 4-1 in the text) to ensure a thorough understanding of the classification of the various elasticity measures.

16. Which of the following pairs of commodities is likely to have a cross-elasticity of demand that is positive?
    (a) Hockey sticks and pucks.   (b) Bread and cheese.
    (c) Cassettes and compact discs.   (d) Perfume and garden hoses.
    (e) Hamburgers and French fries.

17. Margarine and butter are predicted to have
    (a) the same income elasticities of demand.
    (b) very low price elasticities of demand.
    (c) negative cross-elasticities of demand with respect to each other.
    (d) positive cross-elasticities of demand with respect to each other.
    (e) elastic demands with respect to price.

18. Inferior commodities have
    (a) zero income elasticities of demand.
    (b) negative cross-elasticities of demand.
    (c) negative elasticities of supply.
    (d) highly elastic demands.
    (e) negative income elasticities of demand.

19. Which of the following goods is more likely to have an income elasticity of demand that is less than one?
    (a) Hot dogs.   (b) Microwave ovens.
    (c) Perfume.   (d) Winter vacations.
    (e) Sailboats.

Appendix to Chapter 4—More Details About Demand Elasticity

The material in this appendix examines the relationship between arc and point elasticity. It also discusses some diagrammatic features of linear demand curves that characterize the magnitude of elasticity.

Use the following figure to answer questions 20 to 23.

Figure 4-1

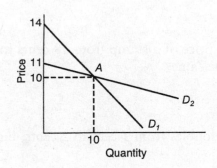

20. The point elasticity of D_1 at point A is [Hint: Multiply the ratio of price to quantity at point A by the reciprocal of the slope.]
    (a) 0.1   (b) 2.5
    (c) 1.0   (d) 10.0
    (e) 4.0

21. The point elasticity of demand for D_2 at point A is
    (a) 0.1   (b) 2.5
    (c) 1.0   (d) 10.0
    (e) 4.0

22. At a price of $10, demand curve D_1
    (a) has the same elasticity as any other point along D_1.
    (b) is more elastic than at any other price below $10.
    (c) is more elastic than D_2.
    (d) is inelastic.
    (e) None of the above.

23. Starting from point A, a 10 percent reduction in price along D_1 will result in an increase in quantity demanded of
    (a) 25 percent.   (b) 100 percent.
    (c) 10 percent   (d) 1 percent.
    (e) 2.5 percent.

EXERCISES

1. **Calculating and Classifying the Price Elasticity of Demand**

   This exercise reviews your ability to calculate and classify elasticity. Recall that there are alternative ways of expressing the elasticity formula; the data you are provided with determines which one you use.

   In each of the following scenarios, categorize the price elasticity of demand as *elastic, inelastic*, or *unit-elastic*. Where calculations are required, use average price and quantity. Note that categorization may not always be possible with the information provided.

   (a) The price of personal computers falls from $2,750 to $2,250, and the quantity demanded increases from 40,000 units to 60,000 units.

   (b) Canada Post increases the price of a stamp from 48 cents to 50 cents, but expenditure on postage stamps remains the same.

   (c) The price of matchbooks doubles from 1 cent to 2 cents, but the quantity purchased does not change.

   (d) An increase in the demand for blue jeans causes the price to increase from $45 to $55 and the amount purchased to increase from 1 million to 1.1 million.

   (e) A sudden decline in the supply of avocados leads to an increase in price by 10 percent and an accompanying reduction in quantity demanded by 20,000 units from the original level of 90,000 units.

(f) A 5 percent decrease in the price of gasoline results in a decrease in gasoline expenditure of 5 percent.

(g) A 10 percent increase in consumer income results in a 15 percent increase in the price of snowboards as well as a 15 percent increase in purchases.

2. Elasticity and Total Expenditure

This question reviews the relationship between the price elasticity of demand and total expenditure. Two alternative demand curves are depicted in the upper panels of Figure 4-2.

Figure 4-2

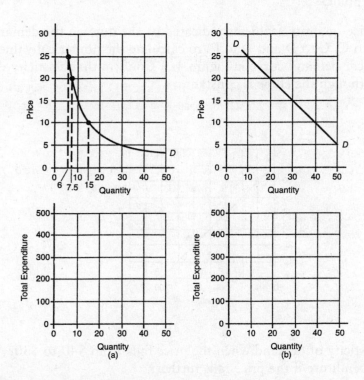

(a) Calculate the total expenditure associated with each demand curve at the following prices: $25, $20, $15, $10, and $5. Graph the respective total expenditure curves in the grids provided in the lower panels of Figure 4-2.

(b) By inspection of these expenditure curves, what can you say about the price elasticity of demand along each of the demand curves?

3. Elasticity and Total Expenditure Again

This exercise is designed to review your understanding of how the magnitude of elasticity determines the relationship between a price change and the resulting change in total expenditure. Fill in the following table:

	Price Elasticity	Change in Price	Change in Total Expenditure
(a)	2.0	up	___
(b)	1.0	down	___
(c)	___	up	none
(d)	0.0	down	___
(e)	0.6	___	up

4. Linear Demand and Elasticity

Even though the magnitude of elasticity is related to the slope of a demand curve, a constant slope does not imply a constant elasticity for a downward sloping demand curve. This exercise establishes the point.

(a) Use the four price-quantity segments indicated by the dots on the demand curve (i.e., the arcs A to B, B to C, C to D and D to E) to calculate the numerical values of price elasticity along the linear demand curve in Figure 4-3. Confirm that elasticity declines as price decreases even though the slope is constant.

Figure 4-3

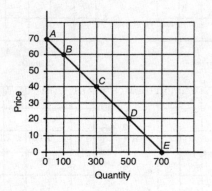

(b) What is the elasticity of demand when the price falls from $40 to $30? What would happen to total expenditure if the price falls further?

5. The Revenue-Maximizing Price

Policy makers sometimes erroneously presume that a price increase will always raise total expenditure. The following provides an vivid demonstration of this fallacy.

Suppose that you are hired as a consultant for the Guelph Transportation Commission. Its statisticians inform you that at the current fare of $1.30, the system carries 20,000 riders per day. They also indicate that for each $0.05 increase (decrease) in the fare, ridership decreases (increases) by 1,000 passengers.

(a) What is the arc price elasticity of demand at the current fare? (Hint: Consider a change in fare from 5 cents below the current fare to 5 cents above.)

(b) The commission has an objective of raising its total fare revenue (i.e., total expenditure by bus riders), and has asked you to determine by how much it should increase the fare. What do you advise? Why?

(c) What fare will maximize total revenue for the transit system? What is the associated ridership?

6. **The Honourable Member from Clearair**

The Honourable Mr. Camel, MP from the riding of Clearair, Ontario, has introduced a private member's bill in Parliament that will significantly increase taxes on cigarettes. He has argued this represents good social policy because it would reduce consumption of cigarettes, thereby increasing the amount of money families of low-income smokers would have leftover to spend on items such as food and shelter. Comment on Mr. Camel's reasoning using the concept of elasticity.

7. **Predicting Responses to Price Changes**

Elasticity measures are critical to the success of many policies. Consider the following example from the market for wheat:

(a) If the price of wheat falls 10 percent and farmers produce 15 percent less, what is the elasticity of supply for wheat?

(b) Suppose the government's goal is to raise wheat production by 30 percent to help fight famine. Based upon the elasticity calculated above, by what percentage must price increase to reach this goal?

(c) If the price of wheat falls by 5 percent, by what percentage will wheat production decline, given the elasticity you calculated above?

8. **The Elasticity of Supply**

This exercise reviews the calculation of the elasticity of supply.

(a) Given the supply curves in Figure 4-4, demonstrate that the elasticity of supply equals 1 along S_1 but falls as price increases along S. (Compute arc elasticities between the points indicated.)

Figure 4-4

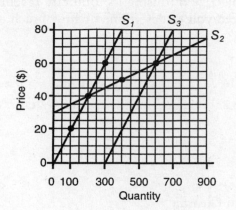

(b) How is the result for S_1 related to the fact that this supply curve passes through the origin?

(c) What does a supply curve such as S_3 imply when price equals zero?

9. **Tax Incidence**

Tax incidence depends upon the elasticities of demand and supply. This exercise emphasizes the relationship.

The following diagrams depict the demand and supply curves for the beer and orange juice markets in Ontario. Suppose a sale tax of t per litre is imposed in each of these markets.

Figure 4-5

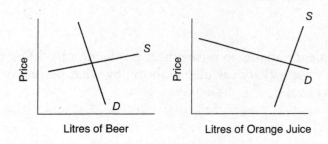

(a) Shift the appropriate curve to show the impact of the tax in each market. Label the new consumer price and seller price in the beer market P_{cb} and P_{sb}, respectively. In the market for orange juice, label them P_{cj} and P_{sj}, respectively.

(b) In which market is most of the burden of the tax borne by consumers? How would you characterize the elasticities of demand and supply in this market?

(c) In which market is most of the tax borne by producers? How would you characterize the elasticities of demand and supply in this market?

(d) In which market is the difference between the consumer price and the seller price greater?

EXTENSION EXERCISES

E-1.   Calculation of the elasticity of one variable in response to changes in another requires that all other variables are held constant. The following exercise establishes the point. WARNING: This exercise is *tough*! Successful completion of it would certainly indicate a thorough understanding of elasticity.

The following table provides data on income as well as prices and quantity demanded of goods x and y for five different periods (or observations):

Period	Income	P_x	Q_x^D	P_y	Q_y^D
(1)	$10,000	$25	10	$10	42
(2)	10,000	28	9	10	40
(3)	10,000	28	8	15	35
(4)	11,000	28	9	15	36
(5)	11,500	34	7	20	32

(a) Why should no elasticities be calculated between periods 4 and 5?

(b) Calculate the following elasticities, selecting appropriate periods and using arc formulas:

price elasticity for x _____, based upon periods _____ and ____;
price elasticity for y _____, based upon periods _____ and ____;
income elasticity for x _____, based upon periods _____ and ____;
income elasticity for y _____, based upon periods _____ and ____;
cross-elasticity of demand for y with respect to the price of x _____, based upon periods _____ and ____;
cross-elasticity of demand for x with respect to the price of y _____, based upon the periods _____ and ____.

E-2.   The classification of elasticity can often be determined by diagrammatic features of the relevant curves. This exercise explores the idea. The six diagrams in Figure 4-7 represent different combinations of elasticities of demand and supply at the equilibrium price P_E. Indicate which diagrams correspond to each of the following statements. (η_d refers to elasticity of demand, and η_s refers to elasticity of supply).

(a) η_d is greater than one and η_s is unity   _____
(b) η_d is unity and η_s is infinity   _____
(c) η_d is unity and η_s is unity   _____
(d) η_d is greater than one and η_s is zero   _____
(e) η_d is zero and η_s is unity   _____
(f) η_d is infinity and η_s is unity   _____

Figure 4-6

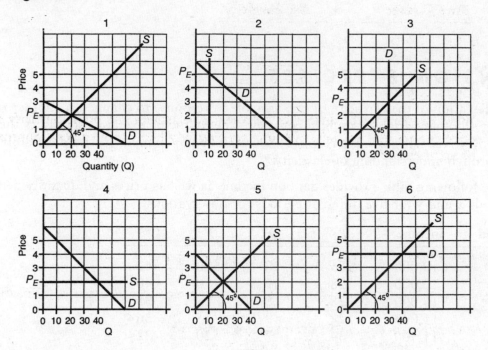

APPENDIX EXERCISE

The following exercise is based on the material in the appendix to this chapter. Read the appendix before attempting this exercise.

A-1. The appendix discusses the distinction between *point* and *arc* elasticity. Point elasticity measures elasticity at a particular point on the demand curve rather than over an interval (arc elasticity). This exercise requires you to calculate point and arc elasticities for the demand curve drawn in the following diagram. Note that the demand curve is linear with a constant slope of $\Delta P/\Delta Q = -1/2$ so that $\Delta Q/\Delta P = -2$ (the slope of the demand curve is $\Delta P/\Delta Q$ because price is measured on the vertical axis and quantity on the horizontal).

Figure 4-7

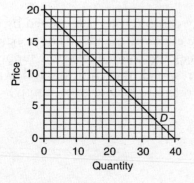

(a) Calculate the *point* elasticity of demand at a price of $10.

(b) Calculate the *arc* elasticity of demand for the following price changes (calculations should be to two decimal places).

Price Change	Arc Elasticity
$18 to $10	_____
$14 to $10	_____
$12 to $10	_____
$11 to $10	_____

(c) What happens to the difference between arc elasticity and point elasticity as the price change gets smaller? When is arc elasticity likely to be a good approximation of point elasticity?

PRACTICE MULTIPLE CHOICE TEST

1. If the price elasticity of demand for a good is 2 and price increases by 2 percent, the quantity demanded
    (a) decreases by 4 percent.   (b) decreases by 1 percent.
    (c) decreases by 2 percent.   (d) does not change.
    (e) is indeterminable with data provided.

Questions 2 through 5 refer to the four diagrams in Figure 4-8.

Figure 4-8

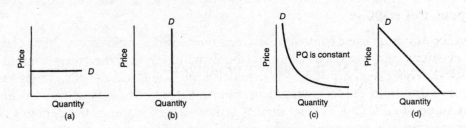

2. The demand curve with an elasticity of zero is
    (a) a.   (b) b.
    (c) c.   (d) d.
    (e) None of the above.

3. The demand curve with an elasticity of unity is
    (a) a.   (b) b.
    (c) c.   (d) d.
    (e) None of the above.

4. The demand curve with an elasticity of infinity is
   (a) a.   (b) b.
   (c) c.   (d) d.
   (e) None of the above.

5. The demand curve with an elasticity that is variable is
   (a) a.   (b) b.
   (c) c.   (d) d.
   (e) Both (c) and (d).

6. The price elasticity of demand for snowmobiles is estimated to be 1.2; thus an increase in price
   (a) always decreases quantity demanded by 12 percent.
   (b) always decreases quantity demanded by 1.2 percent.
   (c) increases total expenditure.
   (d) decreases total expenditure.
   (e) decreases total expenditure by 1.2 percent.

7. If the demand for some commodity has an elasticity of unity, a decrease in price
   (a) causes a 1 percent decrease in quantity demanded.
   (b) induces no change in quantity demanded.
   (c) results in no change in total expenditure.
   (d) is matched by a unit increase in quantity demanded.
   (e) Both (a) and (c) are correct.

Questions 8 to 10 refer to the following schedule. (Use average prices and quantities in your calculations.)

Price per Unit	Quantity Offered for Sale
$10	400
8	350
6	300
4	200
2	50

8. As price increases from $4 to $6, the elasticity of supply is
   (a) 1.0.   (b) 50.
   (c) 0.5.   (d) 5.0.
   (e) 2.0.

9. As price rises from $6 to $10 per unit, the supply response is
   (a) elastic.   (b) of unit elasticity.
   (c) of zero elasticity.   (d) inelastic.
   (e) infinitely elastic.

10. The supply curve implied by the schedule is
    (a) elastic for all price ranges.
    (b) inelastic for all price ranges.
    (c) of zero elasticity for all price ranges.

(d) of variable elasticity, depending on the initial price chosen.
(e) of constant elasticity.

11. A perfectly inelastic demand curve means that
    (a) a percentage decrease in price exactly increases quantity demanded by the same percentage.
    (b) an increase in price reduces quantity demanded.
    (c) the price elasticity of demand is infinity.
    (d) any change in price is perfectly matched by a change in quantity demanded.
    (e) quantity demanded does not change in response to any price change.

12. A decrease in income by 10 percent leads to a decrease in quantity demanded by 5 percent; the income elasticity of demand is therefore
    (a) -0.5.   (b) 2.0.
    (c) 0.5.   (d) 50.0.
    (e) 15.0.

13. A commodity is classified as a normal good if
    (a) a decrease in consumer income results in a decrease in demand.
    (b) it is consumed by a majority of the population.
    (c) its price and quantity demanded are negatively related, ceteris paribus.
    (d) an increase in its price leads to an increase in quantity supplied.
    (e) a decrease in consumer income results in an increase in demand.

14. If an individual allocates $200 as monthly expenditure on compact discs and decides to spend no more and no less regardless of price, this individual's demand for compact discs is
    (a) perfectly inelastic.   (b) perfectly elastic.
    (c) of unit elasticity.   (d) less than one but greater than zero.
    (e) of zero elasticity.

15. A shift in demand would not affect price when supply is
    (a) perfectly inelastic.
    (b) perfectly elastic.
    (c) of unit elasticity.
    (d) a straight line through the origin.
    (e) of zero elasticity.

16. The producers' share of the burden of a sales tax will be greatest
    (a) the more elastic is supply.
    (b) the more inelastic is supply.
    (c) the more elastic is demand.
    (d) the more inelastic is demand.
    (e) both (b) and (c) are correct.

17. Suppose the market supply curve is upward sloping. If the imposition of a sales tax causes no change in the price consumers pay, the good's demand curve must be _____, implying that the burden of the tax is _____.
    (a) vertical; entirely borne by producers.
    (b) horizontal; entirely borne by consumers.
    (c) perfectly inelastic; shared equally by consumers and producers.
    (d) perfectly elastic; entirely borne by producers.
    (e) downward sloping; shared by consumers and producers.

18. If two goods have a negative cross price elasticity of demand, we know that
    (a) they are both inferior goods.
    (b) they are substitutes.
    (c) they are both normal goods.
    (d) they are complementary goods.
    (e) one is inferior and the other is normal, but we can't determine which is which.

19. Pizza and hamburgers are likely to have
    (a) a positive cross elasticity of demand.
    (b) positive income elasticities of demand.
    (c) a negative cross elasticity of demand.
    (d) price elasticities of demand greater than one.
    (e) a cross elasticity of demand equal to zero.

20. A commodity with an income elasticity equal to –0.5
    (a) is said to have an inelastic demand.
    (b) is an inferior good.
    (c) is a complementary good.
    (d) has a downward sloping demand curve.
    (e) has a demand curve with a constant slope of 0.5 in absolute terms.

SOLUTIONS

Chapter Review

1.(a) 2.(d) 3.(b) 4.(d) 5.(b) 6.(a) 7.(d) 8.(c) 9.(d) 10.(a) 11.(a) 12.(d) 13.(b) 14.(e) 15.(e) 16.(c) 17.(d) 18.(e) 19.(a) 20.(b) 21.(d) 22.(b) 23.(a).

Exercises

1. (a) $\eta = 2.0 = (20{,}000/500 \times 2{,}500/50{,}000)$; elastic demand.
    (b) Elasticity of unity.
    (c) Perfectly inelastic demand.
    (d) η cannot be determined because the demand curve has shifted.
    (e) $\eta = 2.5 = ((20{,}000/80{,}000) \times 100)$ percent $\div$ 10 percent; elastic demand.
    (f) Perfectly inelastic demand.
    (g) η cannot be determined because the demand curve shifts.

2. (a)

    Figure 4-9

    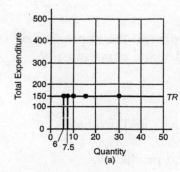 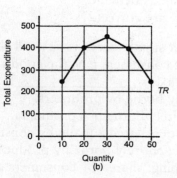

(b) Panel (a): Since total expenditure does not change along the demand curve, the price elasticity of demand is equal to unity at every point along this demand curve.

Panel (b): Since total expenditure increases as price falls from $25 to $20 to $15, demand is elastic over this range. Total expenditure is at its maximum value of $450 when price equals $15; this corresponds to unit elasticity. For further price decreases from $15 to $10 to $5, total revenue decreases, and hence demand is inelastic along this portion of the demand curve.

3. (a) down; (b) none; (c) 1; (d) down; (e) up.

4. (a) The following measures express elasticity as: $(\Delta Q/\Delta P)(P_A/Q_A)$, where Q_A and P_A are the average quantity and price, respectively.

   A – B, $\eta = (100/10)(65/50) = 13.0$;
   B – C, $\eta = (200/20)(50/200) = 2.5$;
   C – D, $\eta = (200/20)(30/400) = 0.75$;
   D – E, $\eta = (200/20)(10/600) = 0.167$.

   (b) $\eta = (\Delta Q/\Delta P)(P_A/Q_A) = (100/10)(35/350) = 1.0$. Over this interval, total expenditure is constant. With further declines in price, total expenditure will decline as we move into the inelastic portion of the demand curve.

5. (a) Calculate arc elasticity from $1.25 to $1.35 so that the average price corresponds to the current fare of $1.30.

$$\eta = \frac{2{,}000}{0.10} \times \frac{1.30}{20{,}000} = 1.3$$

   (b) Since demand is elastic, any increase in price only serves to decrease total revenue. Thus you should recommend that the price be decreased in order to increase total revenue.

   (c) Try successively lower fares until total revenue begins to decrease. The maximum total revenue is found to be $26,450, which obtains at a fare of $1.15 and a ridership of 23,000 passengers per day.

6. The Honourable Mr. Camel assumes a downward-sloping demand curve for cigarettes—as price increases, its consumption will fall. However, he also assumes that total expenditure on cigarettes will decrease. This would only be correct if demand were elastic; in the case of cigarettes, demand is more likely to be inelastic so that total expenditure on cigarettes would increase in response to higher taxes. The impact of this bill would be the exact opposite of what the MP intended.

7. (a) $\eta_s = 15/10 = 1.5$.
   (b) The necessary price change is 20 percent. It is obtained by dividing the output increase of 30 percent by the elasticity of 1.5. Since $\eta_s = \%\Delta Q/\%\Delta P$, it follows that $\%\Delta P = \%\Delta Q/\eta_s$.
   (c) The fall in output is 7.5%, which is calculated by multiplying the price decrease of 5 percent by the elasticity of 1.5.

8. (a) Starting from the origin for S_1, the elasticities of supply are: $(100/20)(10/50) = (100/20)(30/50) = (100/20)(50/250) = 1.0$.
   For S_2 when price rises from 40 to 50, the price elasticity of supply is: $(200/10)(45/300) = 3.0$, but when price rises from 50 to 60, the elasticity is $(200/10)(55/500) = 2.2$.

(b) Because S_1 passes through the origin, P and Q always change in the same proportion, which gives an elasticity value of 1.

(c) S_3 implies that firms are willing to supply the good (300 units) even when the price they receive is zero.

9. (a)

Figure 4-10

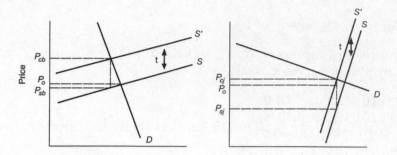

(b) The tax on beer is borne primarily by consumers. The relative slopes of the demand and supply curves in these markets suggest that the demand for beer is relatively inelastic, while its supply is relatively elastic.

(c) The tax on orange juice is borne primarily by producers. Demand in this market is relatively elastic, while supply is inelastic.

(d) The difference between consumer and seller prices are the same in each market. Specifically, the vertical distance by which each supply curve shifts is $\$t$ in each market.

Extension Exercises

E-1. (a) Elasticity measures are calculated under the *ceteris paribus* assumption that other factors affecting demand are unchanged. Between periods 4 and 5, not only has income changed, but so have the prices of x and y.

(b) periods (1) to (2), price elasticity for

$$x = \frac{9 - 10}{28 - 25} \times \frac{(28 + 25)/2}{(9 + 10)/2} = 0.93$$

periods (2) to (3), price elasticity for

$$y = \frac{35 - 40}{15 - 10} \times \frac{(15 + 10)/2}{(35 + 40)/2} = 0.33$$

periods (3) to (4), income elasticity for

$$x = -\frac{9 - 8}{11,000 - 10,000} \times \frac{(11,000 + 10,000)/2}{(9 + 8)/2} = 1.24$$

periods (3) to (4), income elasticity for

$$y = -\frac{36 - 35}{11,000 - 10,000} \times \frac{(11,000 + 10,000)/2}{(36 + 35)/2} = 0.30$$

periods (1) to (2), cross-elasticity of demand for y with respect to the price of

$$x = \frac{40 - 42}{28 - 25} \times \frac{(28 + 25)/2}{(40 + 42)/2} = -0.43$$

periods (2) to (3), cross-elasticity of demand for x with respect to the price of

$$x = \frac{8 - 9}{15 - 10} \times \frac{(15 + 10)/2}{(8 + 9)/2} = 0.29$$

E-2. (a) 1 and 6.   (b) 4.
      (c) 5.   (d) 2.
      (e) 3.   (f) 6.

Appendix Exercise

A-1. (a) Point elasticity = −1.00 = (−2)(10/20), or 1.00 neglecting the negative sign.

      (b)

Price Change	Arc Elasticity
$18 to $10	2.33
$14 to $10	1.50
$12 to $10	1.22
$11 to $10	1.11

      (c) As the change in price gets smaller, the values of arc elasticity and point elasticity converge. Thus arc elasticity serves as a good approximation of point elasticity for small changes in price.

Practice Multiple Choice Test

1.(a) 2.(b) 3.(c) 4.(a) 5.(d) 6.(d) 7.(c) 8.(a) 9.(d) 10.(d) 11.(e) 12.(c) 13.(a) 14.(c) 15.(b). 16.(e) 17.(d) 18.(d) 19.(a) 20.(b)

PART SEVEN

AN INTRODUCTION TO MACROECONOMICS

CHAPTER 19

WHAT MACROECONOMICS IS ALL ABOUT

LEARNING OBJECTIVES

1 View most macroeconomic issues as being about either long-run growth or short-run fluctuations, and see that government policy enters both categories.

2 Understand the meaning and importance of the key macroeconomic variables, including national income, unemployment, inflation, interest rates, exchange rates, and trade flows.

CHAPTER OVERVIEW

Macroeconomics examines the behaviour of such broad aggregates and averages as the **price level, nominal and real national output (income)**, output per person, the **output or GDP gap, employment, unemployment**, the **exchange rate**, and the **balance of payments**.

One central concept is the value of total output of the economy, which is often measured as gross domestic product (GDP). Comparing actual GDP to **potential GDP (potential output)** indicates the economy's position of the business cycle and the social loss from unemployment and underutilized resources. Long-term economic growth is reflected by an increasing real GDP, which allows the standard of living to increase.

The average price level is measured by a price index, which measures the cost of a set of goods in one year relative to their cost in a "base" year. Applying Economic Concept 19.3 in the textbook discusses how a consumer price index is constructed. The **inflation** rate measures the rate of change of the price level. Unanticipated changes in inflation redistribute purchasing power within an economy. The expected rate of inflation is an important determinant of the nominal interest rate. The **real interest rate** is the difference between the nominal rate and the expected rate of inflation.

The exchange rate is the number of Canadian dollars needed to purchase one unit of foreign currency. An **appreciation** of the exchange rate is a reduction in the **external value** of the Canadian dollar. The balance of payments is a record of all international transactions made by Canadian firms, households, and governments.

CHAPTER REVIEW

Growth Versus Fluctuations

Macroeconomic aggregates result from activities in many different markets and from the combined behaviour of households, governments, and firms. The most important macroeconomic issues can be divided into two broad categories—the causes of long-term economic growth, and the size and sources of short-term fluctuations. Broad government policies, such as monetary policy and fiscal policy, typically play a role in both discussions.

1. Which of the following is not a macroeconomic issue?
   (a) Changes in the unemployment rate.
   (b) A fall in the Consumer Price Index.
   (c) Historical trends in the growth of real per capita national income.
   (d) Short-term fluctuations in national income around its long-run trend.
   (e) The change in the price of VCR machines relative to the price of movie theatre tickets.

2. Which of the following macroeconomic issues are normally not associated with the causes of economic growth?
   (a) Increases in living standards over a decade.
   (b) A temporary tax cut.
   (c) Sustained increases in output per person.
   (d) An increased stock of resources for future production.
   (e) The role of increases in investment in generating a higher capital stock for a nation.

3. An upward trend in real national income is called
   (a) an inflationary boom.
   (b) a recessionary gap.
   (c) economic growth.
   (d) an inflationary gap.
   (e) a positive output gap.

Key Macroeconomic Variables

You should understand the issues that arise in measuring and interpreting various macroeconomic variables, especially the need to correct for inflation to express macroeconomic variables in real (constant-dollar) terms. The distinction between real and nominal values of macroeconomic variables will continue to be critical in the material that follows. Make sure that you understand how to calculate an inflation rate from price index information.

As you will see, the concept of an output (GDP) gap is an important macroeconomic variable. The output gap is defined as real actual national income minus real potential national income. If the gap is negative, then the economy is experiencing a recessionary gap situation.

Finally, a warning: students often do not understand the difference between a foreign exchange rate and the external value of a domestic currency. When one hears in the popular media that the Canadian dollar is appreciating or depreciating, it is external value of the Canadian dollar that is being referenced. Remember, the external value of the Canadian dollar is the reciprocal of the exchange rate.

4. Changes in real national income reflect only changes in output, whereas changes in current-dollar national income reflect
   (a) only price changes.
   (b) only changes in potential output.
   (c) changes in neither output nor price.
   (d) changes in both price and output.
   (e) only changes in real purchasing power.

5. According to Figure 19-1 in the textbook, what is an *injection* into the circular flow?
   (a) imports.
   (b) domestic production.
   (c) investment.
   (d) taxes.
   (e) consumption.

6. Real national income is also known as
   (a) nominal national income.
   (b) current-dollar national income.
   (c) constant-dollar national income.
   (d) potential national income
   (e) after-tax national income.

7. An inflationary gap
   (a) occurs when actual national income exceeds potential national income.
   (b) is when the value of the GDP gap is negative.
   (c) occurs when resource use is lower than its normal rate of utilization.
   (d) occurs when actual output is lower than potential output.
   (e) is mostly likely observed during periods of declining economic activity.

8. Actual GDP may exceed potential GDP for a short period of time when
   (a) the unemployment rate is high.
   (b) factors of production are employed at levels that are above normal utilization levels.
   (c) nominal GDP is less than real GDP.
   (d) there is a recessionary gap.
   (e) None of the above.

9. An economy that currently has a negative output gap
   (a) suffers a loss in output and economic well-being.
   (b) experiences less severe social problems because individuals are able to enjoy more leisure time.
   (c) has reached the peak stage of the business cycle.
   (d) will have rapidly rising prices.
   (e) Both (c) and (d).

10. In the long run, real national income per person grows when
   (a) there are persistent inflationary pressures on the economy.
   (b) the same amount of output can be produced by less units of inputs.
   (c) the resource base, including population, increases.
   (d) output per capita decreases.
   (e) Both (b) and (c).

11. The unemployment rate is defined as
    (a) the number of unemployed people expressed as a fraction of the total population
    (b) the number of unemployed people expressed as a fraction of the total number of employed persons.
    (c) the number of unemployed people expressed as a fraction of the labour force.
    (d) the number of unemployed people who receive unemployment insurance as a fraction of the total number of individuals who contribute to unemployment insurance.
    (e) the percent increase in the number of unemployed people over some time period.

12. Full employment in Canada
    (a) implies that the measured unemployment rate is zero.
    (b) occurs when the natural rate of unemployment is zero.
    (c) occurs when the output gap is positive.
    (d) has not been achieved in the past 50 years.
    (e) occurs when the only existing unemployment is structural and frictional.

13. An example of frictional unemployment is when
    (a) carpenters are laid off because of a decline in housing starts.
    (b) Montreal textile workers lose jobs due to a loss in Canadian export shares of textile products in world markets.
    (c) unemployed textile workers are refused jobs since they do not have knowledge of computer software packages required by firms in another industry.
    (d) a teenager quits a job at Canadian Tire in order to find a better-paying job at one of the three large hardware stores in the same city.
    (e) flight crews lose their jobs when the airline industry restructures.

14. An inflation rate is calculated by
    (a) subtracting the value of two price levels.
    (b) dividing the second price level by the first.
    (c) dividing the difference between two price levels by the initial price level and then multiplying by 100 percent.
    (d) taking the average value between two price levels.
    (e) None of the above.

15. Unforeseen inflation is likely to benefit
    (a) creditors.
    (b) pensioners whose monthly pension payments are fixed in nominal terms.
    (c) landlords who, because of rent controls, cannot raise nominal rents during the lease period.
    (d) those who have large balances in chequing accounts.
    (e) firms who have negotiated wage freezes in a new contract period.

16. Assume that prices over the year increase by 4 percent. Who of the following will experience a decrease in purchasing power?
    (a) A creditor who negotiated an annual contract at a nominal rate of interest of 6 percent and who wanted a 2 percent real rate of return.
    (b) A firm that is committed to increasing its wages by 5 percent over the year but whose prices are likely to increase only by the overall rate of inflation.
    (c) A person whose pension is totally indexed for price inflation.
    (d) A landlord who successfully negotiates a 7 percent increase in rent over the year.
    (e) An entrepreneur who makes a 5 percent annual rate of return on her wealth portfolio.

17. Inflation is likely to have no effects on purchasing power if
    (a) some decision-makers do not know the inflation rate over the life of any contract.
    (b) all private financial obligations are stated in real terms.
    (c) all individuals are not able to adjust quickly and easily to any inflation.
    (d) All of the above.
    (e) None of the above.

18. The exchange rate is defined as
    (a) the number of the domestic currency required to purchase one unit of foreign currency.
    (b) the difference between the real and the nominal interest rate.
    (c) the number of foreign currency units required to purchase one unit of domestic currency.
    (d) the ratio of a Canadian produced good to a foreign produced good.
    (e) the rate at which goods and services are exchanged between trading partners.

19. If 1.46 Canadian dollars trades for 1 U.S. dollar, then
    (a) 1.46 is the exchange rate between Canadian and U.S. dollars.
    (b) 1.46 is the external value of the Canadian dollar.
    (c) .46 is the external value of the Canadian dollar.
    (d) .46 is the exchange rate between Canadian and U.S. dollars.
    (e) both (a) and (c) are correct.

20. If 0.5 pound sterling trades for 1 Canadian dollar, then
    (a) the exchange rate is .5.
    (b) the external value of the Canadian dollar is .5 pounds.
    (c) the external value of the Canadian dollar is 2 pounds.
    (d) the exchange rate is $2 Canadian for every pound sterling.
    (e) both (b) and (d) are correct.

21. If the exchange rate between Japanese yen and Canadian dollars increases, then
    (a) it takes fewer Japanese yen to buy 1 Canadian dollar.
    (b) the external value of the Canadian dollar also increases.
    (c) the exchange rate is said to have depreciated.
    (d) it takes more Japanese yen to buy 1 Canadian dollar.
    (e) Both (b) and (d).

22. If the value of a country's merchandise imports exceeded the value of its merchandise exports by $50 million, it follows that
    (a) it has a $50 million deficit on its trade account.
    (b) the country must also have a positive output gap of $50 million.
    (c) its balance of payments must necessarily be in a deficit position of $50 million.
    (d) Both (a) and (c).
    (e) it has a $50 million surplus on its trade account.

EXERCISES

1. An economy produces four different goods and services within the current year. The level of production and the price per unit of each are listed here.

Item	Production Level	Price per Unit
Steel	500,000 tons	$100 per ton
Wheat	15,000 tons	$8 per ton
Haircuts	6,000	$9 each
Television sets	10,000 sets	$500 per set

(a) Calculate the value of the economy's nominal national income in the current year.

(b) In the next year nominal national income is measured at $55,725,740. Express this value as an index of last year's value.

(c) What is the percentage increase in nominal national income (compared with the base year)? Do this calculation two ways.

2. Here are some historical data for Canadian national income measured in terms of gross domestic product (GDP). The first column refers to current dollar (nominal) GDP, the second displays constant dollar (real) GDP, and the third refers to real potential GDP. All values are in billions. For this example, real GDP uses 1981 as the base year. *Note:* The real GDP data in the textbook use 1992 as the base year.

Year	Nominal GDP	Real GDP	Real Potential GDP
1980	309.9	343.4	348.7
1981	356.0	356.0	362.7
1982	374.4	344.5	372.6
1983	405.7	355.5	376.0
1984	444.7	377.9	385.9
1985	478.0	395.9	398.6
1986	504.6	408.1	411.8
1987	550.3	426.4	426.4
1988	601.5	447.8	446.1
1989	648.5	460.6	464.1

(a) Express the 1985 constant dollar value of GDP as an index (to one decimal place) of the 1981 constant dollar value of GDP. Do the same for the 1980 constant dollar value of GDP as an index in terms of 1981.

(b) What is the value of the output gap in 1984? In 1988? Were resources fully employed in these two years?

(c) What phase of the business cycle is represented by the 1981–1982 period?

(d) What was the percentage increase in current dollar GDP between 1981 and 1985?

What was the percentage increase in constant dollar (real) GDP in the same period?

What does the difference in the two percentages represent (approximately)?

(e) In what year did the economy have a GDP gap of 0? Referring to the unemployment rate data in Exercise 4, what was the natural rate of unemployment? What "kind" of unemployment exists when unemployment is equal to the natural rate?

3. You are given the following price indexes for various years. The base year (year 1) has an index of 100.

Year	Price Index	Annual Inflation Rate (percent)
7	118.1	n.a.
8	121.9	___
9	125.1	___
10	___	1.1

(a) Calculate the annual inflation rate (to one decimal place) for years 8 and 9, and fill in the blanks in the third column.

(b) What was the inflation rate over the period from the base year through year 9?

(c) Calculate (to one decimal place) the price index for year 10.

4. The following table provides information about the Canadian economy for a seven-year period.

Year	Real GDP 1992 Prices (billions)	Labour Force (thousands)	Unemployed (thousands)	Employed (thousands)	Unemployment Rate (percent)	Population (millions)
1985	614.8	13,123	____	11,742	10.5	25.2
1986	635.2	13,378	1,283	____	9.6	25.3
1987	661.7	13,361	____	____	8.9	25.6
1988	694.6	13,900	1,081	____	____	25.9
1989	711.6	14,151	1,065	13,086	7.5	26.2
1990	709.9	____	1,164	13,165	8.1	26.6
1991	697.3	14,408	1,492	12,916	____	27.0

(a) Fill in the missing values in the table.

(b) Calculate the percentage change in real GDP between 1987 and 1988. Compare this value with the percentage change in employment in this period. Do the same analysis for the two-year period 1990–91.

(c) Does there appear to be a positive or negative relationship between real GDP and employment for these two periods?

(d) Between 1989 and 1990 the unemployment rate increased while employment increased. How is this possible?

(e) Calculate the value of real per capita GDP for 1985 and 1991.

5. The exchange rate is another important macroeconomic variable discussed in Chapter 19. The information here is intended to provide practice interpreting exchange rate changes. The values are actual figures for the Canadian dollar relative to both the German mark and the Japanese yen.

| | Exchange Rate | | External Value of the Dollar | |
Year	Dollars per Mark	Dollars per Yen	Marks per Dollar	Yen per Dollar
1991	$0.924	$0.01418	_____	_____
1992	0.934	0.01427	_____	_____
1993	1.001	_____	_____	64.267
1994	*External value* _____	0.01625	1.003	_____

(a) Fill in the missing entries.

(b) Over the period 1991–92, the external value of dollar with respect to the German mark (increased, decreased) and the external value of the dollar with respect to the yen (increased, decreased). Over the period 1992–93, the external value of the dollar with respect to the mark and the yen (decreased, increased).

(c) Suppose that you paid 100 marks for a one-year asset at the end of 1991 (at an exchange rate of $0.924). How many dollars did you require to buy this asset?

100 × exchange rate

(d) If the German asset had an annual nominal interest rate of 6 percent, how many marks would you have received at the end of 1992? How many Canadian dollars would you have received when you converted the marks into dollars at the end of 1992? What would be your rate of return over the year as a percentage of the dollar amount you invested?

(e) Suppose that at the end of 1993 you purchased (at an exchange rate of 1.001) a one-year asset worth 10,000 marks which promised a nominal interest rate of 6 percent. What would be your rate of return at the end of 1994 as a percentage of the dollar amount you invested at the end of 1993?

6. This problem deals with the real interest rate on five-year conventional mortgages in Canada. Suppose that the lender, a financial institution, wishes to have a 4 percent real rate of return on an annual basis. Consider the following data. The nominal interest rates are stated for five-year conventional mortgages beginning in 1975, 1980, and 1985.

| | Nominal Annual Interest Rate on New | Annual Average Inflation Rate | | |
Year	Five-Year Mortgages	Expected	Actual	Period
1975	11.4		8.9	1975–1979
1980	14.3		8.7	1980–1984
1985	12.2		4.3	1985–1989

(a) Calculate the institution's expected annual rate of inflation when it set the five-year mortgage rate in 1975. Do the same for the two other five-year periods, and complete the entries in the table.

(b) By comparing the actual annual inflation rate with the nominal interest rate, in what five-year periods did the financial institution make more than its 4 percent real rate of interest on five-year mortgages?

(c) If borrowers shared the same expectations of inflation rates with the financial institution, in what five-year periods did borrowers unexpectedly pay less than a 4 percent real rate of interest?

7. Canadian international trade in goods and services is shown below (in millions of dollars).

Year	Exports	Imports	Net Exports
1993	218,443	218,963	_____
1994	260,917	252,286	_____
1995	300,914	276,379	_____

(a) Calculate net exports in each of the three years.

(b) Which year(s) did Canada have a trade surplus?

EXTENSION EXERCISE

E.1. This exercise features the construction of a Consumer Price Index which is explained in the textbook box "Applying Economic Concepts 19-3."

Suppose that the government's data collection agency has estimated the prices of six broad groups of consumer expenditure as well as the average proportions of consumers' income that is spent on these expenditure groups as follows:

	Prices (base year)	Prices (next year)	Proportion of Income Consumers Spend (on average)
Shelter	$3,000	$3,300	30%
Food	2,500	2,500	25
Transportation	5,000	5,000	15
Clothing	100	110	10
Entertainment	60	60	10
Other	300	330	10

(a) Compute the average price level in the base year and in the next year. (Assume that the proportions do not change.)

(b) The price index for the base year, by definition, is 100. Compute the price index for the next year.

(c) You may have noticed that the price of shelter, clothing, and other goods increased by 10 percent each. Does your answer to (b) indicate a 10 percent increase in the price index from the base year? Why or why not?

(d) Suppose that a group of households in this country consumes the products listed in the table in the following proportions: shelter, 40 percent; food, 30 percent; transportation, 5 percent; clothing, 15 percent; entertainment, 0 percent; other, 10 percent. Does the increase in the overall price index in (b) underestimate or overestimate the cost of living increase for this particular group of households?

PRACTICE MULTIPLE CHOICE TEST

1. If real potential GDP is 893 billion and current real GDP is 890 billion, then
   (a) there is an inflationary gap of 3 billion.
   (b) unemployment consists only of structural and frictional unemployment.
   (c) there is a recessionary gap of 3 billion.
   (d) the GDP gap is positive.
   (e) Both (a) and (d).

2. If a particular index number in 1999 is 149 and the base year is 1996, then the index shows an increase of
   (a) 4.9 percent between 1996 and 1999.
   (b) 149 percent between 1996 and 1999.
   (c) 49 percent between 1996 and 1999.
   (d) .49 percent between 1996 and 1999.
   (e) an indeterminable percent, since the value of the index in 1996 is unknown.

3. A price index changes from 120 to 114 over a particular time period. The percentage change in the price level was
   (a) 6 percent.
   (b) −5 percent.
   (c) 5 percent.
   (d) −6 percent.
   (e) −5.26 percent.

4. Suppose that a price index was 160 last month and rose by 2 percent during the current month. The price index for the current month is
   (a) 162.0.   (b) 163.2.
   (c) 160.02.   (d) 198.4.
   (e) 192.

5. *Statistics Canada* reported that the CPI increased from 104.2 to 105.9 from 1995 to 1996. The rate of inflation during that one-year period was
   (a) 1.7 percent.   (b) 5.9 percent.
   (c) 4.2 percent.   (d) 1.63 percent.
   (e) None of the above.

6. Suppose that a family's income grew from $38,000 to $38,100 over the period 1995 to 1996. Along with your answer to question 5, we can conclude that this family experienced
   (a) an increase in both nominal and real income.
   (b) a decrease in both nominal and real income.
   (c) a decrease in nominal income but an increase in real income.
   (d) a decrease in real income but an increase in nominal income.
   (e) an increase in nominal income but no change in real income.

7. If inflation is expected to be 5 percent in the coming year and the annual nominal interest is 8 percent, then the real rate of interest is
   (a) 13 percent.   (b) 3 percent.
   (c) −3 percent.   (d) 40 percent.
   (e) .4 percent.

8. If the CPI increased from 108.6 to 109.0 between September and October 1998, the monthly inflation rate was
   (a) 0.37 percent.   (b) 0.40 percent.
   (c) 9.0 percent.   (d) 3.7 percent.
   (e) None of the above.

9. According the information in question 8, the CPI between September and October 1998 was growing at an approximate *annual* rate of
   (a) 0.37 percent.   (b) 0.40 percent.
   (c) 4.4 percent.   (d) 4.8 percent.
   (e) None of the above.

adian nominal and real interest rates in 1998 were 4.7 percent and 3.5 percent, pectively. The expected percentage rate of inflation in 1998 was therefore
(a) 1.2. (b) −1.2.
(c) 24. (d) 2.4.
(e) 1.6.

11. Harry insists on an annual real rate of return of 4 percent. What nominal interest rate should he charge his brother, Bill, if he expects an annual inflation rate of 2.5 percent?
(a) 6.5 percent. (b) 2.5 percent.
(c) 1.5 percent. (d) 4 percent.
(e) less than 2.5 percent; after all, Bill is his brother.

12. The *Canadian Economic Observer* reported that between 1997 and 1998, one German mark increased from 79.9 Canadian cents to 84.5 Canadian cents. Hence, from a Canadian perspective,
(a) the external value of the dollar increased.
(b) the exchange rate (the dollar price of marks) increased.
(c) the external value of the dollar decreased.
(d) Canadians could buy more marks per dollar in 1998 than in 1997.
(e) Both (b) and (c).

13. Between 1996 and 1997, the Japanese yen fell from .0125 Canadian dollars to .0115 Canadian dollars. It follows that
(a) the external value of the Canadian dollar rose from 80 yen to 87 yen.
(b) the external value of the Canadian dollar fell from 125 yen to 115 yen.
(c) it was more expensive for Canadians to buy yen in 1996 than in 1997.
(d) it was more expensive for the Japanese to buy Canadian dollars in 1996 than in 1997.
(e) None of the above.

14. If employment in a country were 12 million and unemployment is 1 million, the unemployment rate is
(a) 13 million. (b) 7.7 percent.
(c) 8.3 percent. (d) 9.1 percent.
(e) None of the above.

SOLUTIONS

Chapter Review

1. (e) 2. (b) 3. (c) 4. (d) 5. (c) 6. (c) 7. (a) 8. (b) 9. (a) 10. (e) 11. (c) 12. (e) 13. (d) 14. (c) 15 (e) 16. (b) 17. (b) 18. (a) 19. (a) 20. (e) 21. (a) 22. (a)

Exercises

1. (a) $55,174,000 (Calculate price times quantity for each item and add the products of the four equations together)
   (b) 101 (55,725,740 divided by 55,174,000 × 100)
   (c) 1 percent. This can be obtained two ways. First, divide the change in income (551,740) by 55,174,000 and multiply by 100 percent. Alternatively, the index value for the next year indicates that the nominal value of output has increased by 1 percent.

2. (a) For 1985: 111.2 (395.9 divided by 356.0 × 100). For 1980: 96.5 (343.4 divided by 356.0 × 100).

(b) The output gap is defined as actual real GDP minus real potential GDP. Hence there was a negative (recessionary) output gap of –8 (377.9 – 385.9) in 1984 and a positive (inflationary) output gap of +1.7 in 1988. There was unused productive capacity (less than full employment) in 1984, whereas resources in 1988 were fully employed, although their utilization rate was greater than the normal level.

(c) Between the two years, real GDP fell and the output gap increased (compare –6.7 with –28.1). This period represented a recessionary phase or a slump. The trough occurred sometime in 1982.

(d) Current dollar GDP increased by 34.3 percent; constant (real) dollar GDP increased by 11.2 percent. The difference between these represents approximately the percentage increase in prices of all final goods and services over this period.

(e) The GDP gap is zero in 1987; real GDP and potential GDP are both 426.4. The unemployment rate in 1987 (refer to Exercise 4) was 8.9%. Structural and frictional unemployment are the only two components of the 8.9% unemployment rate.

3. (a) Year 8: 3.2 percent (3.8 divided by 118.1 × 100 percent).
Year 9: 2.6 percent (3.2 divided by 121.9 × 100 percent).

(b) 25.1 percent.

(c) 126.5 (125.1 × 1.011).

4. (a) Labour force: 1990: 14,329 (1,164 + 13,165).
Unemployed: 1985: 1,381 (13,123 – 11,742); 1987: 1,213 (13,361 × .089).
Employed: 1986: 12,095 (13,378 – 1,283); 1987: 12,418 (13,631 – 1,213); 1988: 12,819 (13,900 – 1,081).
Unemployment rate: 1988: 7.8% (1081/13,900 × 100%); 1991: 10.4% (1,492/14,408 × 100%).

(b) 1987–88; Real GDP increased by 4.97 percent while employment increased by 3.23 percent. 1990–91; Real GDP decreased by 1.77 percent while employment decreased by 1.89 percent.

(c) Positive relationship; they changed in the same direction.

(d) The labour force increased more in percentage terms than did employment. That is, more of those who entered the labour force became unemployed than employed.

(e) 1985: $24,397; 1991: $25,826.

5. (a) Marks per dollar: 1991: 1.082; 1992: 1.071; 1993: 0.999.
Yen per dollar: 1991: 70.522; 1992: 70.077; 1994: 61.539.
Dollars per yen: 1993: 00156.
Dollars per mark: 1994: 0.997.

(b) decreased, decreased; decreased.

(c) $92.40.

(d) 106 marks (100 × 1.06); $99.00 (106 × .934); 7.14 percent [($6.60/$92.40) × 100%].

(e) To obtain 10,000 marks in 1993, you paid $10,010. At the end of 1994 you receive 10,600 marks which converted into Canadian currency is $10,568. Your return is 5.6 percent [(10,568 – 10,010)/10,010] × 100.

6. (a) Expected inflation: 1975: 7.4 percent (11.4 – 4.0); 1980: 10.3 percent; 1985: 8.2 percent.

(b) Mortgages in 1980 yielded annually over five years 5.6 percent in real terms (14.3 – 8.7) and mortgages in 1985 garnered a 7.9 percent real rate of return per annum.

(c) Mortgages extended over the 1975–79 period; the actual, real rate of interest was 2.5 percent (11.4 – 8.9).

7. (a) Net exports are defined as exports minus imports. Net exports were –520 in 1993; +8,631 in 1994; +24,535 in 1995.
   (b) There was a trade deficit in 1993, trade surpluses in 1994 and 1995.

Extension Exercise

(a) Base year: $(3,000 \times 0.3) + (2,500 \times 0.25) + (5,000 \times 0.15) + (100 \times 0.1) + (60 \times 0.1) + (300 \times 0.1) = 2,321$. Next year: $(3,300 \times 0.3) + (2,500 \times 0.25) + (5,000 \times 0.15) + (110 \times 0.1) + (60 \times 0.1) + (330 \times 0.1) = 2,415$.

(b) Index = $(2,415/2,321) \times 100 = 104.0$.

(c) No; prices increased by approximately 4 percent. This is because shelter, clothing, and other goods are only 50 percent of total expenditures.

(d) The price increase from the base year for this group of households (using their fixed weights) is 5.5 percent. Hence the overall price increase reflected by the overall price index underestimates the cost of living increase of this group.

Practice Multiple Choice Test

1. (c) 2. (c) 3. (b) 4. (b) 5. (d) 6. (d) 7. (b) 8. (a) 9. (c) 10. (a) 11. (a) 12. (e) 13. (a) 14. (b)

CHAPTER 20

THE MEASUREMENT OF NATIONAL INCOME AND PRODUCT

LEARNING OBJECTIVES

1 Recognize the problem of "double counting" and how the concept of value added solves this problem when measuring national income.

2 Understand that the circular flow of income implies three ways of computing national income—total value added, total expenditure, and total income.

3 Explain the basic methods of measuring national income, using either the income approach or the expenditure approach.

4 Understand the difference between real and nominal GDP, and why GDP per worker is a better measure of living standards than just GDP itself.

5 Recognize that many things affecting our well-being are omitted from official measures of GDP.

CHAPTER OVERVIEW

Each firm's contribution to total output is equal to its **value added.** Value added equals revenue minus the costs of **intermediate goods.** The sum of all the values added produced in an economy is the economy's total output, which is called **gross domestic product (GDP).**

GDP can be calculated from the expenditure side, from the income side, or as the sum of values added in the economy. The expenditure side gives the total value of expenditures required to purchase the nation's output, and the income side gives the total value of income claims generated by the production of that output. By standard accounting conventions, these three aggregations define the same total.

Several concepts related to GDP are discussed, including **gross national product** and **disposable personal income.** Nominal GDP is distinguished from real GDP. Real measures of national income are calculated to reflect changes in real quantities. Nominal measures of GDP are calculated to reflect changes in both prices and quantities. Appropriate comparisons of nominal and real measures yield **implicit GDP deflators.**

GDP must be interpreted with its limitations in mind. GDP excludes illegal activities, the "underground economy," home production activities, and economic "bads." Hence, GDP does not measure everything that contributes to (or detracts from) human welfare.

CHAPTER REVIEW

National Output and Value Added

You should be aware that the concept of value added gets around the problem of "double" or "multiple" counting when measuring national income. Exercises 1 and 2 test your understanding of value added and the problem of double counting.

1. Value added in production is equal to
   (a) total value of output excluding the value of intermediate goods.
   (b) profits of all firms.
   (c) total value of output including intermediate goods.
   (d) the total costs in producing final outputs.
   (e) Both (a) and (d).

2. Estimating final output (GDP) by adding the sales of all firms
   (a) will overstate total output because it counts the output of intermediate goods more than once.
   (b) will understate the total value of national output.
   (c) is a measure of income accruing to Canadian residents.
   (d) provides the same value as net national income.
   (e) is the best measure of economic activity.

3. All goods and services used as inputs into a further stage of production are called
   (a) value added.
   (b) final goods.
   (c) intermediate goods.
   (d) consumption goods.
   (e) investment goods.

National Income Accounting: The Basics

The circular flow of income implies there are three ways of computing national income—total value added, total expenditure, and total income. This section outlines the two basic methods of measuring national income: from the expenditure side and from the income side.

It is important that you learn to distinguish the four broad categories of final expenditures (consumption, investment, government expenditure, and net exports) and understand the reasons for treating them separately. GDP accounting from the income side aggregates all factor payments: wages and salaries, profits, interest, and indirect taxes. The sum of wages and salaries, interest, and profits is called *net domestic income at factor cost*.

4. To calculate GDP from the expenditure side, one must add together
   (a) wages, profits, government purchases, and net exports.
   (b) consumption, government purchases, and interest.
   (c) wages, rent, interest, and profits.
   (d) consumption, investment, government purchases, and net exports.
   (e) consumption, investment, government purchases, and exports.

5. Which of the following would not be included in measures of the consumption component of aggregate expenditure?
   (a) Expenditures for new houses.
   (b) Expenditures for durable goods, such as new automobiles.
   (c) Expenditures for services.
   (d) Expenditures for nondurable goods.
   (e) Expenditures on rental accommodations by households.

6. The term "investment" in macroeconomics means
   (a) the total amount of capital goods in the country.
   (b) total amount of money invested in bonds and stocks.
   (c) the same things as profits.
   (d) the production of goods not for immediate consumption use such as factories, machines, residential housing, and changes in inventories.
   (e) the production of goods for immediate consumption.

7. Which of the following would *not* be included in the measures of the investment component of aggregate expenditure?
   (a) Sally Smith buys Air Canada shares.
   (b) An accounting firm buys three micro computers.
   (c) General Motors (Canada) increases its inventory holdings of parts produced in Brantford, Ontario.
   (d) A construction company builds 20 new homes in Kelowna, British Columbia.
   (e) An oil company expands its refinery facilities in Calgary, Alberta.

8. Government purchases are calculated at their
   (a) imputed market value.
   (b) factor cost.
   (c) labour cost.
   (d) opportunity cost.
   (e) actual market value.

9. Which of the following would not be included in measures of the government expenditure component of aggregate expenditure?
   (a) Salaries of civil servants whose responsibilities include the collection of the Goods and Service Tax (GST).
   (b) The city of Edmonton's purchase of forms from a Regina printing company.
   (c) Canada pension payments to residents of Sherbrooke, Quebec.
   (d) Expenditures for new naval minesweepers built in Nova Scotia.
   (e) The government of Newfoundland pays a New York engineering consulting company.

10. Gross domestic product
    (a) is equal to net national product minus depreciation.
    (b) excludes indirect taxes but includes capital consumption allowances.
    (c) must equal gross national product since both include capital consumption allowances.
    (d) includes replacement investment, which is measured by the level of capital consumption allowances.
    (e) is equal to GNP plus capital consumption allowances.

11. Which of the following would *not* be included in the measurement of GDP from the income side of the national accounts?
    (a) Consumption expenditures.
    (b) Depreciation or capital consumption allowances.
    (c) Indirect business taxes net of subsidies.
    (d) Wages and salaries.
    (e) Profits.

12. Net domestic income at factor cost
    (a) includes wages and salaries.
    (b) includes interest and profits.
    (c) excludes replacement investment.
    (d) excludes net indirect taxes.
    (e) All of the above are correct.

13. Suppose a Canadian firm imports $4,000 worth of sport uniforms and sells them for $5,000. The net effect on Canadian GDP would be
    (a) to decrease the value of GDP by $4,000.
    (b) to increase the value of GDP by $5,000.
    (c) to increase the value of GDP by 1,000.
    (d) to decrease the value of GDP by $5,000.
    (e) no effect on GDP since the sports uniforms were produced outside of Canada.

National Income Accounting: Some Extra Issues

There are several critical issues in this section. First, the distinction is made between Gross Domestic Product and Gross National Product. GDP measures the total output produced in Canada. GNP measures the total amount of income received by Canadian residents, no matter where that income was generated. Secondly, the section illustrates how real GDP measures are derived from nominal (or current-dollar) GDP values and from the "*Implicit GDP Deflator.*" Real measures of national income are calculated to reflect changes in real quantities. Thirdly, this section distinguishes between **per capita GDP** (overall living standards) and **labour productivity** (GDP divided by the number of employed persons). Lastly, this section emphasizes that GDP and related measures of national income must be interpreted with limitations in mind. Specifically, you should know the various activities that are **omitted from GDP** measurement.

14. Disposable personal income is
    (a) always the same as personal income.
    (b) income that is used only for consumption.
    (c) personal income remaining after net income taxes.
    (d) exclusive of transfer payments such as unemployment insurance payments.
    (e) personal income minus capital consumption allowances.

15. GNP
    (a) measures the value of production that is located in Canada.
    (b) measures the value of income that is earned from production in Canada.
    (c) measures the income accruing to Canadian residents.
    (d) excludes Canadian government purchases.
    (e) includes the value of illegal activities in Canada.

16. The implicit GDP deflator
    (a) can be used only on the Expenditure Side of the national accounts.
    (b) is GDP at base-period prices divided by GDP at current prices times 100.
    (c) is the index used to measure the prices of goods and services purchased by households.
    (d) is GDP at current prices divided by GDP at base-period prices times 100.
    (e) is both (b) and (c).

17. Real GDP is calculated by
    (a) dividing the nominal value of GDP by the implicit GDP deflator.
    (b) dividing the implicit GDP deflator by the nominal value of GDP.
    (c) dividing the constant dollar GDP by the implicit GDP deflator.
    (d) multiplying nominal GDP by the implicit GDP deflator.
    (e) dividing the nominal value of GDP by the implicit GDP deflator and then multiplying by 100.

18. Measures of labour productivity are
    (a) real GDP divided by the population.
    (b) real GDP divided by the number of employed workers.
    (c) total wage and salary income divided by the number of workers.
    (d) real GDP divided by the total number of hours worked.
    (e) Both (b) and (d).

19. If do-it-yourself homeowners stopped building their backyard decks and instead hired self-employed university students, then national income would
    (a) be reduced as now measured.
    (b) be unaffected if the students reported their earnings.
    (c) increase if the students reported their earnings.
    (d) be unaffected since the students are not wage earners.
    (e) include only the costs of materials, but not wages.

20. GDP understates the total production of goods and services for all but which one of the following reasons?
    (a) No allowances are included for rental income.
    (b) Illegal activities are not included in the GDP estimate.
    (c) Legal production in the "underground economy" is not reported for income tax purposes.
    (d) Nonmarketed household services such as gardening and cleaning performed by family members are not included.
    (e) Both (c) and (d).

21. As a measure of human well-being, GDP may be inadequate because it
    (a) overemphasizes the inequality of the distribution of income.
    (b) overstates the value of nonmarket work, such as home do-it-yourself activities.
    (c) focuses on production, not income.
    (d) ignores the influence of government transfer programs on household spending.
    (e) ignores the way current production methods may reduce the quality of life.

EXERCISES

1. The value of a product in its final form is the sum of the value added by each of the various firms throughout the production process. Using the information provided here, calculate the value of one loaf of bread that is ultimately sold to a household. In doing so, calculate the value added at each stage of production. (This example demonstrates that the value added approach avoids multiple counting.)

Stage of Production	Selling Price to the Next Stage	Value Added
1. Farmer (production of wheat)	$0.30	30
2. Milling company (flour)	0.55	25
3. Bakery (production of wholesale bread)	0.90	35
4. Retailer (sale to household)	1.00	10
Total	2.75	100

2. Suppose that the total output of the metal container industry were $11,522 million and $7,938 million in intermediate inputs were purchased to produce that amount in 1987.

   (a) Calculate the value added in the metal container industry in 1987.

   11,522 − 7,938 = 3,584.

   (b) Indicate which of the following items represent value added in the metal container industry.

   Intermediate   payment for an independent auditor to examine business accounts
   F ✓   wages of production workers who make cans
   F ✓   profits of metal container companies
   Intermediate   payments for aluminum used in producing cans
   F ✓   interest paid to banks by metal container companies

3. There are two other methods of measuring GDP—from the income side and from the expenditure side. This problem deals with the calculation of gross domestic product using these two approaches. Select only the appropriate items. (Figures are in billions of dollars.)

E	Government purchases of goods and services	$58.5
I	Indirect taxes less subsidies ✓	29.0
	Personal income taxes	41.5
✓	Wages and employee compensation (including personal income taxes)	165.5
	Interest on the public debt	15.5
E	Consumption expenditure	168.4
E	Exports	90.9
I	Capital consumption allowance ✓	33.5
E	Imports	93.3
E	Gross investment	67.2
I	Net interest income	19.0
E	Statistical discrepancy (expenditure side)	+0.2
I	Business profits before taxes	45.1
I	Statistical discrepancy (income side)	−0.2

Calculate the following values.
(a) GDP from the income side __29.0 +__. $165.5 + 15.5 + 33.5 + 19.0 + 45.1 + -0.2$
(b) GDP from the expenditure side __58.5 +__. $168.4 + 67.2 + 90.9 + 93.3 + 0.2 = 291.9$
(c) Assuming that net payments to foreigners had been $8 billion, calculate the value of GNP
_____. $291.9 - 8.0 = 283.9$
(d) Net domestic income at factor cost _____. $291.9 - 33.5 - 29.0 = 229.4$

4. You are given the following information about an economy over the five-year period, 1987–1991. All GDP values are in billions of dollars, the population (popln) figures are in millions, and all indices have a base year of 1986 (1986 = 100).

Year	Current Dollar GDP	Implicit GDP Deflator	Constant Dollar GDP	Popln	Index of Output per Person Employed
1987	551.6	104.7	_____	25.6	101.9
1988	605.9	_____	553.0	25.9	103.1
1989	649.9	114.8	566.1	26.2	102.4
1990	_____	118.6	563.1	26.6	101.7
1991	674.4	121.8	_____	27.0	102.3

(a) Fill in the missing entries in the table.
(b) Current dollar GDP increased by 9.84 percent between 1987 and 1988. Calculate the percentage increases in constant dollar (real) income and in the implicit GDP deflator. Why doesn't the sum of the two percentages equal the percentage increase in nominal GDP?

(c) Calculate the growth rate in real GDP per capita for 1987–1988 and 1990–1991. Which of the two periods is likely to represent a recessionary phase of the economy?

(d) Calculate the growth rate in "productivity" as measured by output per person employed for 1987–1988 and 1988–1989.

5. This exercise focuses on other measures of national income. You are given the following national income measures for an economy in a particular year. (Figures are in billions of dollars.)

Gross domestic product at market prices	$285	285.
Capital consumption allowances (depreciation)	32	+ 5
Retained earnings	12	− 32
Government transfers to households	30	− 30
Personal income taxes	42	− 12
Indirect taxes less subsidies	30	− 12
Consumer expenditure	168	+ 30.
Business taxes	12	
Net foreign investment income received	5	− 42
		192

(a) Calculate the value for disposable personal income.

192

(b) Define personal saving as disposable personal income minus consumption expenditure. What is its magnitude?

192 – 168 = 24

6. Which of the following transactions (or events) will be recorded in the GDP accounts in that year? Explain.

(a) Jim, who normally earns $20 per hour, volunteers 100 hours of his time to assist a local politician in the 1999 Ontario provincial election.

Non-market   not included

(b) The federal government increases the defence budget in order to send ten jet aircraft to Italy during the Yugoslavia-Kosovo crisis in spring 1999.

Included in expenditure

(c) Drug smugglers, using funds from the drug trade, purchase a new hotel in Vancouver.

Drug trade Illegal activity however this is Investment Expenditure

(d) A self-employed carpenter buys $1,000 worth of nails and lumber to build a fence for one of his customers. He charges the customer $1,800 but doesn't report the $800 of wages or profits to the tax authorities.

1000.00 included
800.00 not included

(e) Pollution of the Toronto beachfront forces the city of Toronto to lay off three lifeguards.

pollution not recorded, income lost will be

(f) All welfare recipients in St. John's are hired as municipal workers.

welfare not included however if hired as municipal workers their Salaries would be included

(g) Publicly supported abortion clinics are closed when the Supreme Court rules that abortions are illegal under the Criminal Code.

If financed by Gov't they would be included

7. Figures for the GDP and GNP (1990) values are reported below for five countries (in billions of units of their home currency).

Country	GDP	GNP	Currency
Canada	661.2	636.9	dollar
United States	5,392.2	5,441.0 ✓	dollar
Switzerland	314.0	327.6 ✓	franc
France	6,492.0	6,468.7	franc
Japan	425,735.0	428,667.0 ✓	yen

Source: *National Accounts, Main Aggregates*, OECD, Paris, 1992 and 1993.

(a) Explain what the difference between GDP and GNP implies about net payments of factor income in each country to the rest of the world.

GNP is greater than GDP in US, Switzerland & Japan / Canada + France must have made payments to the rest of the world

(b) Calculate the Canadian dollar value (in billions) of France's nominal GDP at an exchange rate of .215 Canadian dollars per franc.

6,492 × .215 = 1395.8

(c) Which countries are net creditors on a world-wide basis?

US, Switzerland & Japan.

EXTENSION EXERCISE

E1. This exercise focuses on nominal and real output and the implicit GDP deflator outlined in "Applying Economic Concepts 20-2." It also demonstrates that the value of the implicit GDP deflator depends on the selection of the base year. Assume that there are only two industries in an economy. Output and unit price for each industry are shown for three years.

Year	Quantity of Industry A (tons)	Quantity of Industry B (metres)	Price in Industry A (per ton)	Price in Industy B (per metre)	Nominal Value of Output
1	4,000	20,000	$20	$5	$ *80,000*
2	6,000	21,000	22	4	$ *132,000*
3	6,000	18,000	24	6	$ *144,000*

(a) Calculate the nominal value of output in Industry A in each of the three years. Do the same for Industry B. Find national output in nominal terms for each of the three years by adding the two output values for A and B.

(b) Using Year 1 prices, calculate the real value of output in Industry A for each of the three years. Do the same for Industry B. What is the value of real output in the economy for each of the three years?

(c) Calculate the value of the implicit GDP deflator (base year 1) for each of the three years.

(d) Repeat question (b) but now use Year 2 prices and calculate the real value in Industry A and B and then aggregate to determine the value of real output in the economy for each of the three years.

(e) Calculate the new value of the implicit GDP deflator (base year 2) for each of the three years.

(f) Comment on your answers to parts (c) and (e).

PRACTICE MULTIPLE CHOICE TEST

1. Suppose that a firm sells its output for $40,000, that it pays $22,000 in wages, $10,000 for materials purchased from other firms, and $3,000 to bankers, and that it declares profits of $5,000. The firm's value added is
   (a) $18,000.   (b) $40,000.
   (c) $30,000.   (d) $35,000.
   (e) $27,000.

2. Suppose that the steel industry has a total output of $63.8 billion and purchases $49.0 billion in intermediate inputs. Hence, the value added in billions of the steel industry in that period is
   (a) $112.8.   (b) -$14.8.
   (c) $63.8.   (d) $14.8.
   (e) $49.0.

3. Measured from the expenditure side, GDP equals
   (a) $C_a + I_a + G_a + (X_a - IM_a)$.
   (b) $C_a + I_a + G_a - T_a + (X_a - IM_a)$.
   (c) $C_a + I_a + G_a - X_a + IM_a$.
   (d) GNP minus depreciation.
   (e) None of the above.

4. Company *XYZ* receives $50 million from a new issue of stock. It uses $30 million of the proceeds to build a new factory and uses the other $20 million to retire debt with various banks. This transaction increases measured GDP in millions of dollars by
    (a) 50.   (b) 30.
    (c) 20.   (d) 100.
    (e) 80.

For questions 5 to 14, identify the items in the statements according to the following code: *C* = consumption; *I* = investment; *G* = government spending on goods and services; *NX* = net exports (*X − IM*); and *N* = not a component of aggregate spending.

5. The Bank of Nova Scotia expands its computer facilities in its Halifax offices.
    (a) *C*.   (b) *I*.
    (c) *G*.   (d) *NX*.
    (e) *N*.

6. As part of her duties, the sales manager of a Canadian-based company stays at the Savoy Hotel in London, England.
    (a) *C*.   (b) *I*.
    (c) *G*.   (d) *NX*.
    (e) *N*.

7. China buys beef cattle from Alberta beef cattle breeders.
    (a) *C*.   (b) *I*.
    (c) *G*.   (d) *NX*.
    (e) *N*.

8. Moncton residents purchase $200 million in newly constructed homes.
    (a) *C*.   (b) *I*.
    (c) *G*.   (d) *NX*.
    (e) *N*.

9. Montreal Stock Exchange sales in January are $2 billion.
    (a) *C*.   (b) *I*.
    (c) *G*.   (d) *NX*.
    (e) *N*.

10. Nova Scotians take holidays in Prince Edward Island.
    (a) *C*.   (b) *I*.
    (c) *G*.   (d) *NX*.
    (e) *N*.

11. The government of New Brunswick pays for the services of a Vancouver consulting company.
    (a) *C*.   (b) *I*.
    (c) *G*.   (d) *NX*.
    (e) *N*.

12. Sue buys a used motorcycle from her friend Chuck.
    (a) *C*.   (b) *I*.
    (c) *G*.   (d) *NX*.
    (e) *N*.

13. Ford (Canada) increases its inventory holdings of glass windshields produced in Ontario.
    (a) C.   (b) I.
    (c) G.   (d) NX.
    (e) N.

14. The city of Cornerbrook issues welfare cheques to some of its needy residents.
    (a) C.   (b) I.
    (c) G.   (d) NX.
    (e) N.

15. If the implicit GDP deflator increased from 120 in year 7 to 126 in year 8, then prices of final goods and services
    (a) increased 20 percent on average from the base year to year 7.
    (b) increased 5 percent on average between years 7 and 8.
    (c) increased by 6 percent since the index increased by 6 points.
    (d) Both (a) and (b).
    (e) None of the above.

16. If nominal GDP is $150 and real GDP is $125, the value of the implicit GDP deflator is
    (a) 120.   (b) 0.83.
    (c) 1.2.   (d) 83.
    (e) 125.

17. If an economy's annual nominal GDP increases by 11 percent and prices increase on an annual basis by 9 percent, then real GDP
    (a) increases by approximately 18.3 percent.
    (b) increases by 1.8 percent.
    (c) decreases by approximately 1.8 percent.
    (d) decreases by $2/9 \times 100$ percent.
    (e) remains constant.

18. If nominal GDP rises from $400 billion to $408 billion and the implicit GDP deflator rises from 125 to 127,
    (a) real GDP has risen from 3.2 billion to 3.21 billion.
    (b real GDP has risen from 500 billion to 518 billion.
    (c) real GDP is unchanged.
    (d) everyone is necessarily better off since nominal GDP has increased.
    (e) real GDP has risen from 320 billion to 321 billion.

19. In a particular year an economy's GDP is $401 billion, net payments to foreigners are $46 billion, and indirect taxes less subsidies are $5 billion. The value of the economy's GNP is
    (a) $447 billion.   (b) $355 billion.
    (c) $350 billion.   (d) $360 billion.
    (e) $452 billion.

For questions 20 to 22 use the information in the table below for a hypothetical economy that produces only two goods, A and B.

Year	Price	Quantity
1992		
Good A	$1.00	100 units
Good B	$2.00	200 units
1993		
Good A	$2.00	120 units
Good B	$3.00	160 units

20. The values of nominal GDP in 1992 and 1993 were, respectively
   (a) $500, $720.　　　　　(b) $500, $440.
   (c) $800, $720.　　　　　(d) $440, $800.
   (e) $720, $500.

21. The real GDP in 1993, expressed in 1992 dollars, was
   (a) $500.
   (b) $440.
   (c) $720.
   (d) $800.
   (e) 280 units.

22. The value of the implicit GDP deflator in 1993 was approximately
   (a) 164.
   (b) 114.
   (c) 64.
   (d) 144.
   (e) 88.0

SOLUTIONS

Chapter Review

1. (a) 2. (a) 3. (c) 4. (d) 5. (a) 6. (d) 7. (a) 8. (b) 9. (c) 10. (d) 11. (a) 12. (e) 13. (c) 14. (c) 15. (c) 16. (d) 17. (e) 18. (e) 19. (c) 20. (a) 21. (e)

Exercises

1. (a) The market value of one loaf of bread is $1.00. This is found by the sum of the value added (0.30 from the first stage plus 0.25 from the second stage plus 0.35 from the third stage plus 0.10 from the fourth stage). Thus, the sum of the valued added at each stage equals the value of the final product. Notice that the total $2.75 counts the contribution of the farmer four times.

2. (a) $3,584 = $11,522 − $7,938.
   (b) Items that represent value added are wages of production workers and profits of metal container companies, and interest paid by metal container companies. Payments for aluminum or an independent auditor are intermediate inputs.

3. (a) 29.0 + 165.5 + 33.5 + 19.0 + 45.1 − 0.2 = 291.9.
   (b) 58.5 + 168.4 + 67.2 + 90.9 − 93.3 + 0.2 = 291.9.
   (c) 291.9 − 8.0 = 283.9.
   (d) 291.9 − 33.5 − 29.0 = 229.4.

4. (a) GDP in current dollars: 1990: 667.8 (563.1 × 1.186).
   Implicit GDP deflator: 1988: 109.6 [(605.9 ÷ 553.0) × 100)].
   GDP in constant dollars: 1987: 526.8 [(551.6 ÷ 104.7) times 100]; 1991: 553.7.

   (b) Real GDP increased by 4.97 percent while the prices increased by 4.68 percent. The increase in nominal GDP is equal to the product of the two (1.0497)(1.0468) rather than the sum of the two percentages. See footnote #3 in the textbook chapter.

   (c) The growth rate in real GDP per capita for 1987–1988 is calculated by first determining real GDP per capita for each of the years. In 1987 per capita real GDP is $20,578 (526.8 billion ÷ 25.6 million) and in 1988 it is $21,351, and hence the percentage increase is 3.76 percent. The percentage change in real per capita GDP between 1990 and 1991 is −3.13 percent (−662 ÷ 21,169 × 100%). The period 1990–1991 was considered a recessionary period.

   (d) The percentage changes in productivity in 1987–1988 and 1988–1989 were 1.2 percent and −0.7 percent, respectively.

5. (a) Disposable personal income = GDP + net foreign investment income − capital consumption allowance − indirect taxes less subsidies − retained earnings − business taxes + government transfers − personal income taxes; 285 + 5 − 32 − 30 − 12 − 12 + 30 − 42 = 192.

   (b) Personal saving = disposable personal income minus consumption expenditure; in this case, S = 192 − 168 = 24.

6. (a) This is an example of a nonmarketed activity and therefore would not be included in GDP accounts. If the politician had paid Jim $2,000 for his 100 hours of work, then Jim's income would have been included in the GDP accounts.

   (b) This is a straightforward example of an increased government expenditure that would be recorded in the GDP accounts.

   (c) Even though the funds used to purchase the hotel are from illegal activities, the actual purchase would be recorded in the investment component of the GDP accounts.

   (d) The $1,000 purchase of nails and lumber would be recorded in the GDP accounts. The carpenter's value added ($800) is not included since the carpenter did not report his income. The $800 represents an "underground" economy transaction.

   (e) Although pollution costs are not recorded in the GDP accounts, the effects of pollution on market activity can appear in the GDP accounts. In this case, three lifeguards lost their jobs, and hence the income approach will indicate a decline in overall income (assuming that they were unemployed for a period of time after their dismissal).

   (f) The income paid to welfare recipients is not included in the measure of GDP. However, if all were hired as municipal workers, their salaries would be included in the government expenditure component of aggregate expenditures.

   (g) Abortion clinics, if financed by some level of government, would be included in the expenditure approach in measuring GDP. However, all other things being equal, their closure would decrease government expenditure. The purchases of abortion services from illegal, private clinics would presumably not be recorded in the GDP accounts.

7. (a) GNP is greater than GDP for the United States, Switzerland, and Japan while GNP is less than GDP for Canada and France. Clearly, Canada and France made net payments to the rest of the world. The other three countries received net payments from the rest of the world.

   (b) 1,395.8 billion Canadian dollars (6,492 × .215).

   (c) Japan, Switzerland, and the United States.

Extension Exercise

(a) Nominal value of output (in dollars)

Year	In A	In B	In economy
1	80,000	100,000	180,000
2	132,000	84,000	216,000
3	144,000	108,000	252,000

(b) Real value

Industry A:
in year 1 = 4,000 × 20 = $80,000
in year 2 = 6,000 × 20 = $120,000
in year 3 = 6,000 × 20 = $120,000

Industry B:
in year 1 = 20,000 × 5 = $100,000
in year 2 = 21,000 × 5 = $105,000
in year 3 = 18,000 × 5 = $90,000

Total Economy:
in year 1 = 80,000 + 100,000 = $180,000
in year 2 = 120,000 + 105,000 = $225,000
in year 3 = 120,000 + 90,000 = $210,000

(c) year 1: 180,000 ÷ 180,000 × 100 = 100.0
year 2: 216,000 ÷ 225,000 × 100 = 96.0
year 3: 252,000 ÷ 210,000 × 100 = 120.0

(d) Real value

Industry A:
in year 1 = 4,000 × 22 = $88,000
in year 2 = 6,000 × 22 = $132,000
in year 3 = 6,000 × 22 = $132,000

Industry B:
in year 1 = 20,000 × 4 = $80,000
in year 2 = 21,000 × 4 = $84,000
in year 3 = 18,000 × 4 = $72,000

Total Economy:
in year 1 = 88,000 + 80,000 = $168,000
in year 2 = 132,000 + 84,000 = $216,000
in year 3 = 132,000 + 72,000 = $204,000

(e) year 1: 180,000 ÷ 168,000 × 100 = 107
year 2: 216,000 ÷ 216,000 × 100 = 100
year 3: 252,000 ÷ 204,000 × 100 = 124

(f) Although the ranking is the same, the values differ because relative prices are different in the two years. The relative price of A to B is 4 in year 1 but is 5.5 in year 2. Hence, output is weighted by different relative prices in the two years.

Practice Multiple Choice Test

1. (c) 2. (d) 3. (a) 4. (b) 5. (b) 6. (d) 7. (d) 8. (b) 9. (e) 10. (a) 11. (c) 12. (e) 13. (b) 14. (e) 15. (d) 16. (a) 17. (b) 18. (e) 19. (b) 20. (a) 21. (b) 22. (a)

CHAPTER 21

SHORT-RUN VERSUS LONG-RUN MACROECONOMICS

LO *LEARNING OBJECTIVES*

1 Recognize why economists think differently about short-run and long-run changes in macroeconomic variables.

2 Explain why any change in GDP can be decomposed into changes in: the amount of factors, the employment of factors, and the productivity of factors.

3 Realize that short-run changes in GDP are mostly caused by changes in factor utilization, whereas long-run changes in GDP are mostly caused by changes in factor supplies and productivity.

4 Recognize that fiscal and monetary policy each have different effects in the short run than in the long run.

CHAPTER OVERVIEW

This chapter focuses on the difference between short-run and long-run macroeconomic change; short-run fluctuations and long-run trends. The equation, accounting for GDP change, explains how changes in three fundamental components (factor supplies, productivity, and utilization rates of factors) change GDP.

Since factor supply and productivity tend to be constant in the short run, short-term movements (fluctuations) in GDP are mostly accounted for by changes in factor utilization (measured by the ratio of employed factors to total available factor supplies) during periods of changing GDP gaps. Since factor utilization rates eventually return to their "normal" levels, long-run changes in potential GDP are mostly accounted for by changes in factor supplies and productivity (measured by the GDP to employed factors ratio).

The difference between the short run and long run forces economists to think differently about macroeconomic relationships that exist over a few months as compared to those that exist over several years. Moreover, the effects of monetary and fiscal policy are usually different in the short run as compared to the long run.

CHAPTER REVIEW

Two Examples

In response to a shock or a change in government policy, the economy behaves differently over several months (the short run) than its does over several years (the long run). The short run is a time period over which changes in economic conditions tend to cause changes in output and employment, with relatively small changes in prices or wages. The long run is a time period over which wage and price adjustment takes place.

1. Changes in national income in the short run
   (a) are primarily supply determined.
   (b) are primarily due to changes in factor productivity.
   (c) must equal changes in its potential level according to the GDP Accounting Equation.
   (d) are primarily caused by changes in aggregate demand.
   (e) will reflect price and wage adjustments.

2. A short-run increase in the interest rate is likely to lead to
   (a) adjustments in prices and wages.
   (b) increases in planned expenditures.
   (c) decreases in GDP and employment.
   (d) an increase in potential GDP.
   (e) an inflationary gap.

Accounting for Changes in GDP

To better understand the issues associated with the short run as compared to the long run, it is important for you to comprehend the GDP Accounting Equation (Identity). GDP is created by three components: available factors, factor utilization rates and productivity. Make sure you know the correct definition for each component, understand why each component can change, and identify within a short-run versus long-run taxonomy when the component is mostly likely to change.

3. Long-run increases in real GDP are usually associated with
   (a) increases in the sizes of output gaps.
   (b) increases in potential GDP, with no change in the output gap.
   (c) decreases in factor utilization.
   (d) increases in real interest rates.
   (e) None of the above are correct.

4. According to Equation 21-1 in the textbook, which of the following will cause decreases in real GDP?
   (a) decreases in factor supplies.
   (b) decreases in factor utilization rates.
   (c) decreases in productivity.
   (d) all of the above.
   (e) none of the above.

5. Which of the following will *not* increase an economy's supply of labour?
   (a) an increase in emigration.
   (b) an increase in the labour-force participation rate.
   (c) an increase in the birth rate.
   (d) a decrease in the mortality rate.
   (e) greater immigration.

6. Changes in factor supplies are
   (a) expressed by the term *GDP/employed factors* in the GDP Accounting Equation.
   (b) fixed in the long run since factor prices don't vary.
   (c) very important for explaining short-run fluctuations in national output.
   (d) the primary explanation of GDP gaps.
   (e) important determinants of long-term economic growth.

7. A low factor utilization rate
   (a) describes an inflationary gap situation.
   (b) describes *excess supply* in the factor market.
   (c) implies that unemployment is also low.
   (d) would tend to lead to increases in factor prices such as wage rates.
   (e) implies that the ratio of employed factors to total factor supply is high.

8. *Excess supply* in the factor market will be associated with
   (a) a reduction in employment in the short run.
   (b) a reduction in production in the short run.
   (c) a decrease in factor prices in the long run.
   (d) a restoration of normal utilization rates of factors in the long run.
   (e) All of the above are correct.

9. When short-run actual GDP is above potential GDP,
   (a) there is an excess supply of factors.
   (b) factor prices will tend to fall in the long run.
   (c) utilization rates of factors are above "normal" levels.
   (d) unemployment is high.
   (e) potential GDP will increase in the long run.

Policy Implications

Fiscal and monetary policies affect the short-run level of GDP because they alter the level of demand. But unless they are able to affect the level of potential output, they will have no long-run effect on GDP.

10. The consensus among economists is that monetary policy
    (a) effects real macroeconomic variables only in the long run.
    (b) involves taxation and government expenditure programs.
    (c) affects potential GDP in the short run.
    (d) affects nominal macroeconomic variables in the long run.
    (e) affects both real and nominal macroeconomic variables in the long run.

11. There is consensus among economists that changes in government spending (fiscal policy)
    (a) have no effects in either the short run or the long run.
    (b) must be neutral in terms of long-run effects.
    (c) have long-run impacts that must be quantitatively equal to short-run impacts.
    (d) must change potential GDP in the same direction as short-run changes in actual GDP.
    (e) do affect the level of potential output, but that it is opposite to its short-run effect on actual GDP.

EXERCISES

1. The information below reflect time series of real actual GDP and potential GDP for a hypothetical economy over a seven-year period.

Year	Actual GDP	Potential GDP
1989	1,000	1,100
1990	1,105	1,105
1991	1,120	1,110
1992	1,125	1,115
1993	1,000	1,117
1994	1,180	1,120
1995	1,205	1,205

   (a) What type of output gap existed in 1989 and what is its magnitude? What type of gap existed in 1995 and what is its magnitude?

   (b) In 1991 was there an excess supply of or an excess demand for factors? Are utilization rates of resources lower or higher than "normal levels"? Do you expect factor prices to eventually fall or rise?

   (c) In 1993 was there an excess supply of or an excess demand for factors? Are utilization rates of resources lower or higher than "normal levels"? Do you expect factor prices to eventually fall or rise?

   (d) According to the textbook, the time period between what two years is appropriate to measure long-run changes in output? Explain. Calculate the percentage change in long-run growth. Provide two possible explanations of why there was long-run growth in real national income.

2. Consider a debate between two economics professors about the effects of personal and business income tax cuts on an economy which currently has a zero GDP gap. Dr. Dove argues strongly that tax cuts do not effect potential GDP. Dr. Hawk argues that tax cuts can cause long-run growth in GDP. *Hint:* You might want to reread the textbook section entitled, "*Inflation and Interest Rates in Canada*" before you attempt this exercise.

(a) Analyse the short-run effects of tax cuts on real output, factor prices and the price level because of increased consumer buying and business investment. Identify the type of output gap that is likely to be created.

(b) Analyse Dr. Dove's long-run predictions for real output, factor prices, and the price level because of the tax cuts.

(c) What would have to happen in the economy for Dr. Hawk to be correct?

PRACTICE MULTIPLE CHOICE TEST

1. Referring to the data in Exercise 1, we observe in 1994
   (a) an inflationary gap of 60.
   (b) there was probably an excess demand for resources.
   (c) utilization rates were most likely above normal levels.
   (d) production is expected to increase in the short-run.
   (e) All of the above.

2. If actual real GDP were 240 and potential GDP were 250, then
   (a) an inflationary gap of 10 exists.
   (b) there is an excess demand for factors.
   (c) current utilization rates are below normal levels.
   (d) we would expect factor prices to rise in the long run.
   (e) long-run growth in output will fall.

3. Which of the following is likely to decrease potential GDP?
   (a) A decrease in taxes.
   (b) A decrease in productivity.
   (c) A decrease in the rate of factor utilization.
   (d) A decrease in emigration.
   (e) An increase in the participation rate of persons willing to work.

4. Which of the following is most likely to explain the creation of a short-run inflationary gap?
   (a) An increase in labour productivity.
   (b) An increase in factor supplies.
   (c) An decrease in import purchases.
   (d) An decrease in government purchases.
   (e) An increase in personal saving.

5. Which of the following is most likely to occur in the long run when there is a short-run excess supply of factors?
   (a) Factor prices will fall.
   (b) The rate of factor utilization will fall.
   (c) Productivity will fall.
   (d) Unemployment will increase permanently.
   (e) None of the above.

6. According to the data in Figure 21-2 in the textbook
   (a) Canadian labour productivity has steadily declined.
   (b) the most important cause of long-term economic growth in Canada has been sustained growth in employment rates.
   (c) the Canadian labour force has steadily increased.
   (d) Canada has experienced more short-term volatility in labour productivity than it has for employment rates.
   (e) percentage increases in Canadian labour productivity since the 1960s have surpassed percentage increases in the Canadian labour force.

SOLUTIONS

Chapter Review

1. (d) 2.(c) 3. (b) 4. (d) 5. (a) 6. (e) 7. (b) 8. (e) 9. (c) 10. (d) 11.(e)

Exercises

1. (a) In 1989, there was a recessionary gap of –100 (= 1,000 – 1,100). There was a zero gap in 1995.
   (b) There was an inflationary gap of 10 in 1991 which means there is excess demand in the factor market. Since actual real GDP exceeds real potential GDP, factor utilization is higher than normal levels. In the long run, we would expect factor prices to rise.
   (c) In 1993, actual real GDP was less than Potential GDP (a "recessionary gap" of –117). Factor utilization was lower than normal levels, and in the long run we would expect factor prices to fall.
   (d) The textbook views long run changes in GDP to be measured by changes in potential GDP, with no change in the output gap. The data in the table indicate that both 1990 and 1995 had zero output gaps. Hence, long-run growth in GDP is measured between 1990 and 1995, which in this case is 1,205 – 1,105 divided by 1,105 times 100 percent which equals 9.0 percent. Productivity and/or factor supply increased.

2. (a) Tax cuts increase disposable income for consumers and profits for firms. Both consumption and investment are likely to increase. An inflationary gap is created in the short run since potential GDP does not change. The demand for factors of production will increase and output will rise. Factor utilization will be higher than normal levels. In the short run factor prices and prices may be stable.
   (b) Dr. Dove would argue that the excess demand for factors in the short run will trigger increases in factor prices. This would result in the price level rising as firms pass factor price increases onto consumers. The rise in factor prices will eliminate excess demand, and the economy's real GDP level will be restored at its potential level (the zero output gap is restored).

(c) Dr. Hawk must believe that potential GDP is increased in the long run. Tax cuts must affect real variables such as the willingness of individuals to supply factor services. Moreover, increases in investment may increase the capital stock in the long run. Thus, long-run productivity may increase. Both factors may increase potential GDP in the long run. But, there is a catch; if tax cuts cause interest rates to rise, then private spending will be "crowded out." Dr. Hawk is on dangerous ground!

Practice Multiple Choice Test

1. (e) 2. (c) 3. (b) 4. (c) 5. (a) 6. (c)

PART EIGHT

NATIONAL INCOME AND FISCAL POLICY

CHAPTER 22

THE SIMPLEST SHORT-RUN MACRO MODEL

(LO) *LEARNING OBJECTIVES*

1 Understand the difference between desired expenditure and actual expenditure.

2 Explain the determinants of desired consumption and desired investment expenditures.

3 Understand the meaning of equilibrium national income.

4 Recognize the difference between movements along and shifts of the aggregate expenditure function.

5 Explain how a change in desired expenditure affects equilibrium income, and how this change is reflected by the multiplier.

CHAPTER OVERVIEW

The next four chapters discuss how equilibrium national income is determined. This chapter imposes three simplifying conditions:

• the price level is fixed;
• the economy has no government (no net taxes and no government purchases); and
• the economy is "closed" (no foreign trade).

Recall also that factor productivity and factor supplies are assumed constant in the short run. However, factor utilization rates can change. The chapter focuses on two sources of desired demand: consumption and investment.

The chapter introduces two important distinctions: desired versus actual expenditure and **autonomous** versus **induced expenditure**. Whereas national accounts measure actual expenditures, national income theory deals with *desired* expenditures. Desired expenditure refers to what people would like to spend out of the resources that are at their command as opposed to what they actually spend. An expenditure is said to be autonomous when its level *does not* depend on the level of actual national income. Components of aggregate expenditure that do change in response to changes in national income are called induced expenditures.

A key relationship in this chapter is the **consumption function**; the relationship between disposable income and desired consumption. The responsiveness of a change in consumption to a change in disposable income is measured by the **marginal propensity to consume (MPC)**. The ratio of consumption to the level of national income is called the **average propensity to consume (APC)**.

If consumption is known, then saving is known since disposable income must be consumed or saved. As result, we can derive a **saving** function, a relationship between desired saving and national income. The slope of the saving function is called the **marginal propensity to save (MPS)**; the ratio of saving to the level of national income is called the **average propensity to save (APS)**.

Desired consumption and investment (which is assumed to be autonomous) together determine aggregate desired expenditure (*AE*) in the economy which is depicted by an **aggregate expenditure function**. Equilibrium national income is defined as that level of national income where desired aggregate expenditure equals actual national income. If desired and actual income are not equal, production eventually will adjust to create an equilibrium situation. An alternative condition for national income equilibrium is where desired saving equals desired investment.

Changes in equilibrium occur from changes in autonomous expenditure which shift the aggregate expenditure function. The **simple multiplier** analysis indicates the quantitative change in equilibrium income from given changes in autonomous expenditure *with the price level held constant*. The size of the multiplier depends on the slope the *AE* curve.

CHAPTER REVIEW

Desired Expenditure

Households divide their disposable income (which is the equal to income since there are no taxes present in the simplest model) between consumption and saving. Two factors that influence desired consumption are (1) current disposable income and (2) wealth. Note that changes in current disposable income cause **movements along** the consumption and saving functions while changes in wealth cause the consumption and saving functions to **shift**. The distinction between the **marginal** and **average** propensities to consume and save is important. The slopes of the consumption and saving functions are the *marginal propensity to consume* and the *marginal propensity to save*, respectively.

Desired investment is assumed to be an autonomous expenditure. Make sure you understand how changes in the three important determinants of desired, aggregate investment expenditure—the real interest rate, changes in sales, and business confidence—shift the *investment function* up or down in a parallel fashion.

1. Autonomous expenditures
   (a) depend on desired national income.
   (b) do not depend on national income.
   (c) are induced expenditures.
   (d) are net of taxes.
   (e) include unintended increases in inventories.

2. The consumption function
   (a) describes the relation between desired consumption expenditure and the factors that determine it, like real disposable income.
   (b) refers to the relation between consumption expenditure and prices.
   (c) is relatively unimportant in macroeconomics, because consumption is such a small component of aggregate demand.
   (d) is a relationship between consumption expenditure and saving.
   (e) refers to the relation between an individual's consumption and import purchases.

3. The marginal propensity to consume is expressed as
   (a) the change in autonomous consumption.
   (b) the change in consumption divided by disposable income.
   (c) consumption divided by disposable income.
   (d) the change in consumption divided by the change in disposable income.
   (e) consumption divided by the change in disposable income.

4. Which of the following are the basic assumptions about the consumption function?
   (a) Below the break-even level, APC > 1 and MPC < 0.
   (b) The MPC and APC are always less than unity.
   (c) As income rises, the MPC falls and the APC rises.
   d) The APC is greater than zero and less than one and the MPC falls as income rises.
   (e) The MPC is greater than zero and less than one and the APC falls as income rises.

5. If aggregate real disposable income rose from $20,000 to $30,000 and desired consumption expenditure rose from $19,000 to $26,000, it can be concluded that the
   (a) the average propensity to consume fell as disposable income increased.
   (b) the marginal propensity to save is 0.30.
   (c) the marginal propensity to consume is 0.70.
   (d) desired saving increased from $1,000 to $4,000.
   (e) all of the above are correct.

6. Total saving divided by total income is called the
   (a) marginal propensity to save.
   (b) saving function.
   (c) average propensity to save.
   (d) marginal propensity not to consume.
   (e) total propensity to save.

7. An increase in households' real wealth is predicted to
   (a) shift the consumption function downward.
   (b) shift the saving function upward.
   (c) increase the marginal propensity to consume out of disposable income.
   (d) shift the consumption function upward.
   (e) Both (c) and (d).

8. Desired investment is most likely to rise when
   (a) real interest rates rise.
   (b) sales remain constant.
   (c) expectations of future profits become more optimistic.
   (d) All of the above.
   (e) None of the above.

9. A reduction in real interest rates
   (a) normally reduces the mortgage payments a home buyer must make.
   (b) reduces the incentive for businesses to hold inventories.
   (c) increases the financing costs to firms that must borrow funds.
   (d) will cause the investment function to shift down.
   (e) None of the above.

10. Which of the following events would shift the investment curve upward?
    (a) An increase in the real interest rate.
    (b) An increase in the level of sales.
    (c) An increasing expectation by firms that sales will decline.
    (d) An increasing expectation by firms that actual expenditures will exceed desired expenditures.
    (e) Speculation that business profits will be taxed more in the future.

11. An aggregate expenditure function shows that as national income rises
    (a) employment rises.
    (b) desired expenditures on currently produced goods fall.
    (c) prices rise.
    (d) interest rates must also rise.
    (e) desired expenditures on currently produced goods will rise by a proportion of the increase in national income.

12. The aggregate expenditure function is a relationship between
    (a) actual real expenditure and real national income.
    (b) desired real expenditure and nominal national income.
    (c) desired real expenditure and real actual national income.
    (d) real disposable income and saving.
    (e) actual nominal expenditure and nominal national income.

13. In a simple macroeconomic model, with a closed economy and no government, the aggregate expenditure function is the sum of
    (a) desired consumption and desired investment.
    (b) saving and desired investment.
    (c) consumption and disposable income.
    (d) desired consumption and desired saving.
    (e) actual consumption and actual investment.

14. The marginal propensity to spend
    (a) falls as actual national income increases.
    (b) is always equal to one.
    (c) is the slope of the aggregate expenditure function.
    (d) may be greater than one depending on the level of actual national income.
    (e) is the change in national income to the change in expenditure.

Equilibrium National Income

When something is in *equilibrium*, there is no tendency for it to change. In the context of national income theory, we need to determine the conditions for equilibrium national income. The chapter outlines two equilibrium conditions:
   (1) desired aggregate expenditure equals actual national income.
   (2) desired saving equals desired investment.

The first equilibrium condition is written as $Y = C + I$. When desired aggregate expenditure is greater than actual income, there will be pressure for national income to rise. For any level of income at which aggregate desired expenditure is less than actual output, there will be pressure for national income to fall.

The second equilibrium condition is written as $S = I$. When desired saving is greater than desired investment, there will be pressure for national income to fall. When desired saving is less than desired investment, there will be pressure for national income to rise.

15. In a macroeconomic model that includes consumption and investment, equilibrium real national income is attained when
   (a) actual real output is equal to desired real aggregate expenditure.
   (b) the aggregate expenditure function intersects the 45° line.
   (c) the average propensity of desired spending is unity.
   (d) there is no unintended inventory accumulation or reduction.
   (e) All of the above.

16. At a level of national income where aggregate desired expenditure falls short of actual national income, there will be a tendency for
   (a) national income to rise.
   (b) national income to fall.
   (c) inventories to unexpectedly decrease.
   (d) prices to rise.
   (e) None of the above.

17. If desired aggregate expenditures exceed actual national income,
   (a) inventories will build up, causing national income to rise.
   (b) national income will fall, because desired expenditures are less than actual expenditures.
   (c) shortages of goods and reductions in inventories will cause producers to increase output and national income to rise.
   (d) national income may increase or decrease, depending on the relative sizes of the average propensity to consume and the average propensity to save.
   (e) there will be no change in national income because only actual expenditure is relevant.

18. The requirement for equilibrium in the simple macro model (closed economy, no government) with a given price level is that
   (a) desired saving equals desired investment.
   (b) desired saving equals zero.
   (c) consumption equals desired investment.
   (d) desired investment equals zero.
   (e) desired investment equals actual saving.

19. On a graph depicting equilibrium national income (where desired aggregate expenditure equals actual national income) consider a level of actual national income where the vertical distance from the horizontal axis to the AE function is **less** than the vertical distance to the 45° line. At such an income level unintended inventories are _____, and so actual national income will tend to _____.
   (a) accumulating, rise.
   (b) equal to planned inventory accumulation, stay at that level.
   (c) being depleted, rise.
   (d) accumulating, fall.
   (e) being depleted, fall.

20. On a graph depicting equilibrium national income (where desired saving equals desired investment) consider a level of national income where the vertical distance from the horizontal axis to the saving function is less than the vertical distance to the investment function. At such an income level, inventories are ____, and so national income tends to ____.
    (a) accumulating, rise.
    (b) accumulating, fall.
    (c) being depleted, rise.
    (d) being depleted, fall.
    (e) constant, remain constant.

Changes in Equilibrium National Income

Shifts in the *AE* function are central to explaining why national income changes. An upward shift in the *AE* function will cause equilibrium national output to increase. A downward shift in the *AE* function will decrease equilibrium output. An upward shift in the *AE* function is caused by *increases* in autonomous expenditure. A downward shift in the saving function or an upward shift in the investment function will cause equilibrium national output to increase. An upward shift in the saving function or a downward shift in the investment function will cause equilibrium national output to decrease.

The ratio of the change in equilibrium national income to the change in autonomous expenditure *at a constant price level* is called the simple multiplier which is greater than one. The size of the simple multiplier depends on the slope of the *AE* function. Recall that the slope of the *AE* function is called the *marginal propensity to spend*. The multiplier is equal to $1/(1-z)$, where z is the marginal propensity to spend. For this chapter **only**, the marginal propensity to spend is equal to the marginal propensity to consume.

21. Which of the following will shift the *AE* function upward in a parallel fashion?
    (a) A decrease in autonomous consumption.
    (b) An increase in real national income.
    (c) The real rate of interest falls.
    (d) The marginal propensity to spend increases.
    (e) None of the above are correct.

22. An upward shift of the saving function causes equilibrium income to
    (a) fall.
    (b) rise.
    (c) remain constant but consist of more consumption and less investment.
    (d) remain constant but consist of less consumption and more investment.
    (e) remain constant but it does not affect desired aggregate expenditure.

23. The simple multiplier, which applies to short-run situations in which prices are given, describes changes in
    (a) investment induced by changes in equilibrium income.
    (b) saving caused by changes in investment.
    (c) the equilibrium level of income caused by changes in autonomous expenditure.
    (d) the rate of interest caused by increased demand for credit.
    (e) employment induced by changes in equilibrium income.

24. If the marginal propensity to spend is 0.75, then
    (a) the marginal propensity to not spend is 0.25.
    (b) the slope of the *AE* function is 0.75.
    (c) the value of the simple multiplier is 4.0.
    (d) in this simple model, the marginal propensity to consume is 0.75.
    (e) All of the above are correct.

25. If expenditure in the economy did not depend on the level of real national income, the value of the simple multiplier would be
    (a) zero.   (b) unity.
    (c) infinite or undefined.   (d) –1.
    (e) positive fraction.

26. The multiplier is larger
    (a) the higher the level of autonomous expenditures.
    (b) the steeper the slope of the *AE* function.
    (c) the flatter the slope of the *AE* function.
    (d) the steeper the slope of the saving function.
    (e) the lower the value of the marginal propensity to consume.

27. Assuming constant prices and a marginal propensity to spend of 0.75, an increase in autonomous investment of $1 million will increase equilibrium real national income by
    (a) $1 million.   (b) $4 million.
    (c) $250,000.   (d) $750,000.
    (e) $1.75 million.

EXERCISES

1. This question tests your knowledge of a Keynesian consumption function. For this example, the consumption function is given by the expression, $C = 80 + 0.5Y_d$. The first two columns of the following schedule depict this functional form for various levels of disposable income.

Y_d	C	S	ΔY_d	ΔC	MPC	APC
0	80	–80	n.a.	n.a.	n.a.	na
100	130	–30				1.30
			60	30	0.50	
160	160					1.00
				20	0.50	
200	180	20				____
					0.50	
400	280	120	____	____		0.70
			350	____	____	
750	455	____				____

(a) Fill in the missing values for the change in real disposable income (ΔY_d).

(b) Using the definition for the average propensity to consume (APC), fill in the missing values for APC. What did you notice happened to the value of APC as the level of Y_d increased?

(c) Fill in the missing values for ΔC.

(d) Using the definition for MPC, calculate it for the income change from 400 to 750.

(e) Using the definition for saving $S = Y_d - C$, fill in the missing values in the table. Using the formula $\Delta S / \Delta Y_d$, prove that the marginal propensity to save is constant and equal to 0.5.

(f) Prove that the algebraic expression for the saving function is $S = -80 + 0.5Y_d$.

(g) What is the break-even level of real disposable income? What is the amount of saving at this level of Y_d?

(h) Plot both the desired consumption (as line C) and desired saving functions (as line S) in Figure 22-1. In addition, draw the 45° line and prove that this line intersects the consumption function at a level of Y_d for which $S = 0$.

Figure 22-1

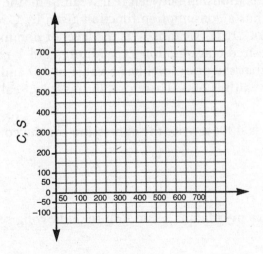

(i) Is desired consumption expenditure both autonomous and induced? Explain

2. The last question was based on a consumption function, $C = 80 + 0.5Y_d$ and a saving function, $S = -80 + 0.5Y_d$. Write the algebraic expression for the following cases:

   (a) The consumption function that has autonomous consumption of 100 and a marginal propensity to consume of 0.5.

   (b) The consumption function that has autonomous consumption of 80 and a marginal propensity to consume of 0.8.

   (c) The saving function for case (b).

   (d) The saving function that has autonomous saving of -50 and a marginal propensity to save of 0.6.

   (e) The consumption function for case (d).

   (f) Plot case (c) in Figure 22-1 and compare this curve with $S = -80 + 0.5Y_d$.

3. This exercise involves the relationship between real wealth and the consumption function. Suppose that an economy has a consumption function given by $C = 60 + 0.8Y + 0.1\,(W/P)$. The term W/P is the level of "real" wealth, W is the level of nominal wealth, and P is the price level. C represents desired consumption expenditure, and Y represents the level of real national income. Assume that the price level has a value of 1.0 and is constant and that the economy's total nominal wealth is 400. Therefore, in this case, real and nominal wealth are both equal to 400.

   (a) Given that real wealth is 400, rewrite the expression for the consumption function.

   (b) Fill in the missing values in columns 2 and 4 in the following schedule.

(1) Y	(2) C (W/P=400)	(3) C (W/P=2,400)	(4) S (W/P=400)	(5) S (W/P=2,400)
0	100	300	−100	−300
500	____	700	____	−200
1,000	900	1,100	100	−100
1,500	____	____	____	____
2,000	1,700	1,900	+300	+100

(c) Assume that the economy's real and nominal wealth increases from 400 to 2,400 (the price level remains at 1.0). Write the new consumption function, and fill in the missing values in columns 3 and 5.

(d) As a result of the wealth increase, what happens to the consumption function? The saving function? Check your answers against Figure 22-3 in the textbook.

4. Answer the following questions using Figure 22-2.

Figure 22-2

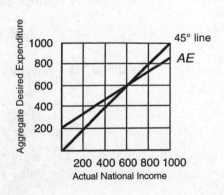

(a) When national income is 0, desired aggregate expenditure is _____.

(b) When national income is 600, desired aggregate expenditure is _____.

(c) If actual national income were 300, desired aggregate expenditure would be (less/greater) than income. Hence, inventories are likely to (fall/rise), and output and national income are likely to (expand/contract).

(d) If actual national income were 1,000, desired aggregate expenditure would be (less/greater) than national income, inventories would (fall/rise), and hence output and national income are likely to (expand/contract).

(e) In this case, the marginal propensity not to spend is _____, and the marginal propensity to spend is _____.

(f) The equilibrium level of national income is _____.

5. The following table summarizes desired levels of aggregate expenditure for an economy where the price level is assumed constant.

Y	C	S	I	AE
0	80	−80	120	200
100	140	−40	120	260
200	200	0	120	320
300	___	___	120	___
400	___	___	120	___
500	___	___	120	___
600	___	___	120	___
700	___	___	120	___

(a) Fill in the missing entries in the consumption, saving, and aggregate expenditure columns, assuming that the marginal propensity to consume out of disposable income remains constant.

(b) What is the equilibrium level of income in this economy?

(c) Explain why an output level (Y) of 400 is not an equilibrium situation.

(d) What is the marginal propensity not to spend on domestic goods? What is the simple multiplier for this economy?

(e) If investment were to increase by 60, what would the new equilibrium level of national income become? Show your answer in two ways, by using the table above and by applying the simple income multiplier.

(f) If investment is 120, what is the level of Y at which $S = I$?

6. Indicate whether or not the following separate event is expected to increase the equilibrium level of national income. Explain how the event would be depicted in an *AE* diagram for which the marginal propensity to spend is positive, but is less than one. Assume the economy is initially at equilibrium national income.

(a) An increase in actual national income.

(b) A decrease in autonomous consumption.

(c) A decrease in the real interest rate.

(d) A downward shift in the saving function by the same amount at every level of national income.

EXTENSION EXERCISES

E1.   This exercise involves an algebraic determination of equilibrium national income. You are given the following information about behaviour in an economy:

Equation 1, the consumption function:

$$C = 100 + 0.75Y_d$$

Equation 2, the relationship between national income and disposable income:

$$Y_d = Y$$

Equation 3, the investment function:

$$I = 50$$

(a)   What does equation (2) imply?

(b)   Aggregate expenditure is the algebraic sum of the various components. Derive the algebraic expression for *AE*.

(c)   What is the marginal propensity to spend? The marginal propensity not to spend?

(d) What is the algebraic equivalent to the statement, "equilibrium is achieved when the *AE* curve intersects the 450 line"?

(e) Using your answer for part (d), solve for the equilibrium level of Y.

(f) What is the value of the simple multiplier?

(g) If investment increased from 50 to 55, what is the new equilibrium level of Y?

(h) Now consider a different consumption function. All other equations remain the same. Suppose that the consumption function is $C = 100 + 0.8Y_d$ rather than equation (1). Answer the following questions.
  (i)   The slope of consumption function has (increased/decreased).
  (ii) The slope of the saving function has (increased/decreased).
  (iii) The value of the simple multiplier has (increased/decreased).
  (iv) The equilibrium level of Y has (increased/decreased).

E2. To confirm your answer to part (e) above, use the equilibrium condition that equilibrium occurs when $S = I$. (*Hint:* You must prove that the saving function is $S = -100 + .25Y$.)

PRACTICE MULTIPLE CHOICE TEST

Questions 1 through 6 refer to Figure 22-3:

Figure 22-3

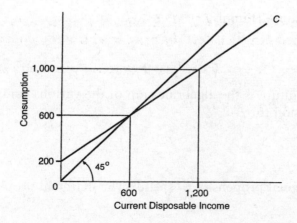

1. The Keynesian consumption function shown above assumes that an individual's desired consumption expenditures are
   (a) in part induced by increases in disposable income.
   (b) in part determined autonomously by factors other than income.
   (c) a function of disposable income in the current year rather than over a lifetime.
   (d) are a declining proportion of disposable income.
   (e) All of the above.

2. The marginal propensity to consume (MPC) out of disposable income according to Figure 23-3 is
   (a) 200.   (b) 100.
   (c) 2/3.   (d) 1/3.
   (e) 5/6.

3. As disposable income rises from 600 to 1,200, the average propensity to consume
   (a) rises from 1/3 to 1.   (b) falls from 1 to 5/6.
   (c) remains constant at 2/3.   (d) remains constant at 1.
   (e) falls from 1 to 1/3.

4. If the individual has no current disposable income,
   (a) consumption must be zero.
   (b) dissaving is 200.
   (c) the average propensity to consume is one.
   (d) consumption cannot be predicted.
   (e) saving is 200.

5. When disposable income is equal to 600,
   (a) aggregate saving is zero.
   (b) the average propensity to consume is unity.
   (c) the "break-even" level of disposable income is attained.
   (d) desired consumption is equal to actual consumption.
   (e) All of the above.

6. When disposable income is equal to 1,200,
   (a) the marginal propensity to consume is 5/6.
   (b) there is saving of 200.
   (c) there is dissaving of 200.
   (d) desired consumption expenditures exceed actual consumption by 200.
   (e) Both (c) and (d).

Questions 7 through 16 refer to the Figure 22-4. Assume that aggregate expenditure consists only of consumption and investment and that the price level remains constant.

7. According to the graph, the level of desired autonomous expenditure is
   (a) 120.   (b) 280.
   (c) 240.   (d) at point c.
   (e) can't be determined.

Figure 22-4

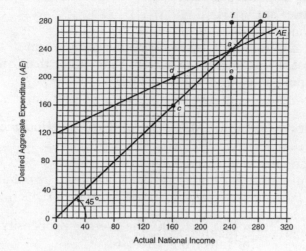

8. When actual national income is 160,
   (a) desired aggregate expenditure equals 160.
   (b) desired aggregate expenditure is less than 160.
   (c) equilibrium national income is attained.
   (d) saving is zero.
   (e) None of the above.

9. When actual national income is 280,
   (a) there will be a tendency for national income to fall.
   (b) inventories are unexpectedly decreasing.
   (c) the average propensity to spend is unity.
   (d) there is dissaving of about 20.
   (e) None of the above.

10. According to the aggregate expenditure curve labelled *AE*, the current equilibrium level of real national income is
    (a) 320.   (b) 240.
    (c) 120.   (d) 280.
    (e) 160.

11. The *AE* curve has a slope of
    (a) 0.5.   (b) 0.6.
    (c) 2.0.   (d) 1.0.
    (e) 0.4.

12. The value of the simple multiplier is therefore
    (a) 2.0.   (b) 0.5.
    (c) 2.5.   (d) 0.
    (e) 1.67.

13. The value of the marginal propensity not to spend is
    (a) 0.5.   (b) 0.4.
    (c) 1.0.   (d) 0.
    (e) 0.6.

14. Suppose that investment expenditure decreased by 40 at *all* levels of actual national income. The aggregate expenditure curve would
    (a) shift upward by 40 and intersect the 45° line at point *b*.
    (b) shift downward by 40, but its slope would also decrease.
    (c) shift downward by 40, have a slope of 0.5, and intersect the 45° line at point *c*.
    (d) not shift, but adjustment would involve a movement from point *a* to point *d*.
    (e) not shift, but adjustment would involve a movement from point *a* to point *b*.

15. According to the new *AE* curve associated with question 14, if output remains temporarily at 240, desired expenditure is
    (a) 240 (at point *a*), and hence inventories remain unchanged.
    (b) 200 (at point *e*), with the result that unplanned inventory accumulation is equal to 40.
    (c) 280 (at point *f*), with the result that unplanned inventory reduction is equal to 40.
    (d) 200, which is associated with point *d*.
    (e) 40, which is also the level of planned saving.

16. The decrease in desired investment of 40
    (a) will be illustrated by a movement from point *a* to point *c*.
    (b) will decrease real national income ultimately by 80.
    (c) will decrease consumption expenditures ultimately by 40.
    (d) will decrease saving ultimately by 40.
    (e) All of the above.

SOLUTIONS

Chapter Review

1. (b) 2. (a) 3. (d) 4. (e) 5. (e) 6. (c) 7. (d) 8. (c) 9. (a) 10. (b) 11. (e 12. (c) 13. (a) 14. (c) 15. (e) 16. (b) 17. (c) 18. (a) 19. (d) 20. (c) 21. (c) 22. (a) 23. (c) 24. (e) 25. (b) 26. (b) 27. (b)

Exercises

1. (a) 40, 200.
    (b) 0.90, 0.61; the value of *APC* fell.
    (c) 100, 175.
    (d) 0.50 = 175 ÷ 350.
    (e) 0, 295. The marginal propensity to save is 0.50 and is constant. For an increase in Y_d from 0 to 100, saving increases from −80 to −30. The ratio of the change is 0.50.
    (f) Saving is defined as $Y_d - C$, or $Y_d - (80 + 0.5Y_d)$. Hence, the saving function is, $S = -80 + 0.5Y_d$.
    (g) 160, at which $S = 0$.
    (h) **Figure 22-5**

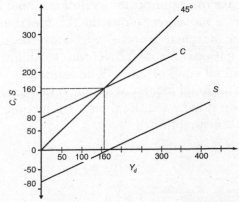

(i) Consumption expenditure is both autonomous and induced. It has an autonomous component because consumption is 80 when disposable income is zero. Since the marginal propensity to consume is 0.50, consumption is therefore induced as well.

2. (a) $C = 100 + 0.5Y_d$.
   (b) $C = 80 + 0.8Y_d$.
   (c) $S = -80 + 0.2Y_d$.
   (d) $S = -50 + 0.6Y_d$.
   (e) $C = 50 + 0.4Y_d$.
   (f) The new saving function has a smaller slope (0.2), the same intercept (–80), and intersects the income axis at $Y = 400$.

3. (a) When real wealth is 400, the consumption function becomes $C = 60 + 0.8Y + 0.1(400)$ or $C = 100 + 0.8Y$.
   (b) C is 500, 1,300. S is 0, +200.
   (c) The consumption function becomes $C = 60 + 0.8Y + 0.1(2,400)$ or $C = 300 + 0.8Y$. C is 1,500; S is zero.
   (d) The consumption function shifted up in a parallel fashion (an increase of 200 at every level of real national income). The saving function shifted down in a parallel fashion (a decrease of 200 at every level of real national income).

4. (a) 200.
   (b) 600.
   (c) greater; fall; expand.
   (d) less; rise; contract.
   (e) 1/3, 2/3.
   (f) 600.

5. (a) C: 260, 320, 380, 440, 500, AE: 380, 440, 500, 560, 620 –80, S: +40, +80, +120, +160, +200.
   (b) $Y = 500$ since $AE = Y$.
   (c) At $Y = 400$, aggregate expenditure is 440 (320 + 120). Since desired expenditure is greater than actual expenditure, there will be unplanned inventories reductions. Firms adjust to this situation by increasing output until the economy reaches an equilibrium of 500.
   (d) $0.4 = 1 - MPC$. The simple multiplier is $K = 1/1-z$, where z is the marginal propensity to spend. Hence, $K = 1 \div 0.4 = 2.5$.
   (e) Since, the multiplier is 2.5 and investment increases by 60, the total change in real national income is 150. Hence, the new equilibrium real income level is 650 (500 + 150). Using the schedule, the value $Y = 650$ is midpoint between 600 and 700. Hence, $C = 470$ and $I = 180$ for a total of $Y = 650$.
   (f) Saving (120) equals Investment at $Y = 500$.

6. (a) This event will not increase the equilibrium level of national income. An increase in actual national income causes a *movement along* the AE function. Desired expenditure increases, but because the marginal propensity to consume is less than one, the increase is less than the increase in national income. Inventories will accumulate, and firms will react by cutting output. The initial equilibrium will be restored.
   (b) The equilibrium level or national income will fall. A decrease in autonomous consumption shifts the AE function downward. Real national income will fall by a multiple of the decrease in autonomous consumption.

(c) This event will increase equilibrium national income. A decrease in the real interest rate will cause the investment function to shift up, and in turn, the AE function will shift upward. Real national income will increase by a multiple of the increase in investment (which is assumed to be autonomous expenditure).

(d) This event will increase equilibrium national income. A downward shift in the saving function is tantamount to an upward shift in the consumption function. As a result, the AE function will shift upward. Real national income will increase by a multiplier of the increase in autonomous consumption (or the decrease in autonomous saving).

Extension Exercises

E1. (a) Disposable income equals total income. Hence, there are no net taxes.

(b) $AE = C + I$, or $100 + 0.75Y + 50$. Hence, $AE = 150 + 0.75Y$.

(c) Inspecting the expression for the AE function, we see that the slope is 0.75 which is the marginal propensity to spend. In this case, the marginal propensity to spend is equal to the marginal propensity to consume. The marginal propensity not to spend (or in this case the marginal propensity to save) is equal to 0.25.

(d) $AE = Y$.

(e) $Y = 150 + 0.75Y$ implies $Y = 600$.

(f) $K = 1/1 - z$ where z is the marginal propensity to spend. In this case, the value of the simple multiplier is $1 \div 0.25 = 4.0$.

(g) An increase in real national income of 20 (5×4.0). Hence, the new equilibrium level is 620 ($600 + 20$).

(h) increased, decreased, increased, increased

E2. $S = Y - (100 + 0.75Y)$ or $S = -100 + 0.25Y$. Equating this equation to Investment (50) we obtain $Y = 600$.

Practice Multiple Choice Test

1.(e) 2.(c) 3.(b) 4.(b) 5.(e) 6.(b) 7.(a) 8.(e) 9.(a) 10.(b) 11.(a) 12.(a) 13.(a) 14.(c) 15.(b) 16.(e)

CHAPTER 23

ADDING GOVERNMENT AND TRADE TO THE SIMPLE MACRO MODEL

LO LEARNING OBJECTIVES

1 Understand how the government budget surplus is related to national income.

2 Understand how net exports are related to national income.

3 Recognize the difference between the marginal propensity to consume and the marginal propensity to spend.

4 Explain why net exports lead the economy to accumulate assets.

5 Understand why the presence of government and foreign trade reduces the value of the simple multiplier.

6 Explain how government can use its fiscal policy to influence the level of national income.

7 Recognize that the simple income-expenditure model of national income determination is based on the assumption of a given price level.

CHAPTER OVERVIEW

This chapter incorporates foreign trade and government into the national income model. The price level remains constant, and the exchange rate is assumed to be exogenous; it can change but not because national income changes.

Fiscal policy includes taxation, transfers, and government purchases. Government purchases of goods and services are part of autonomous expenditure. **Net taxes** (taxes minus transfers) affect national income indirectly through their influence on disposable income and hence consumption expenditure. A **public saving** function which incorporates net taxes and government expenditure is developed in this chapter. The slope of the public saving (or budget surplus) function is the *tax rate*. A higher tax rate decreases the size of the simple multiplier.

Net exports, another source of aggregate expenditure, are a negative function of real national income because imports rise with real income. A larger *marginal propensity to import* increases the slope of the net export function and reduces the size of the simple multiplier.

Equilibrium national income is determined using two approaches: the *aggregate expenditure* approach and the *saving-investment* approach. The latter involves calculating **national saving** $[S + (T - G)]$ and **national asset formation** $[I + (X - IM)]$. The simple multiplier now incorporates the tax rate and the marginal propensity to import.

CHAPTER REVIEW

Introducing Government

It is important for you to understand that government purchases of goods and services are a component of desired aggregate expenditure while taxes and government transfer payments are not. Net taxes *indirectly* affect desired aggregate expenditure (consumption) by altering disposable income. Government expenditures are autonomous components of aggregate expenditures while net taxes depend on the level of real national income. Now, disposable income is the difference between income and net taxes.

A **budget surplus** or **public saving** is the difference between net tax revenue and government purchases. The **public saving** or **budget surplus** function is upward sloping because net taxes increase as actual national income increases.

1. Which of the following items would *not* be considered a government purchase of goods and services?
   (a) The City of Quebec buys additional garbage trucks.
   (b) The Province of British Columbia pays a consulting firm to conduct an ecological impact study for a proposed new dam.
   (c) The federal government pays for new radar systems for the Canadian Navy.
   (d) The City of Moncton issues welfare payments to needy citizens. *→ Considered as transfer payments*
   (e) None of the above.

2. Transfer payments affect aggregate expenditure
   (a) directly.
   (b) through the consumption function. *→ Transfers are not part of GDP but are part of disposable income + therefore the consumption function*
   (c) through the investment function.
   (d) through net exports.
   (e) through the government purchases curve.

3. Public saving is equal to
   (a) net tax revenues minus government purchases.
   (b) disposable income minus consumption expenditure.
   (c) government purchases minus net tax revenues.
   (d) private saving plus government saving.
   (e) $I + NX$.

4. The slope of the budget surplus curve is *→ same as Public Saving*
   (a) equal to the marginal propensity to consume.
   (b) equal to the marginal propensity to save.
   (c) equal to income-tax rate.
   (d) equal to the value of the multiplier.
   (e) flat since all components are autonomous.

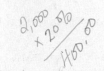

5. Suppose that G is 400 for all levels of income and the income-tax rate is 20%. When Y equals 1,000, national saving is ___-200___, denoting a budget ___deficit___.
   (a) 200, surplus.
   (b) 0, balance.
   (c) -200, deficit.
   (d) -200, surplus.
   (e) 200, deficit.

6. Suppose that G is 400 for all levels of national income and the income-tax rate is 20%. The government budget is balanced when Y equals
   (a) 1,000.
   (b) 8,000.
   (c) 80.
   (d) 2,000.
   (e) 500.

Introducing Foreign Trade

Net exports are defined as total exports minus total imports. The **Net Export** function relates net exports to actual national income. Exports are autonomous expenditures while imports are induced expenditures. The net export function is negatively related to actual national income since imports increase as national income increases. The slope of the net export function is the negative value of the *marginal propensity to import*.

The net export function will shift parallel to itself and upward if exports increase. Exports are determined by foreign income and relative international prices. In turn, relative international prices are determined by differential inflation rates and the exchange rate.

Imports are induced expenditures. Anything affecting the *proportion of income* that Canadian consumers wish to spend on imports will change the *slope* of the net export function. The proportion that Canadians spend on imports will change if relative international prices change.

7. In a simple macro model with an open economy, it is assumed that
   (a) exports and imports are autonomous.
   (b) exports and imports are induced.
   (c) exports are exogenous and imports are induced.
   (d) exports are induced and imports are autonomous.
   (e) none of the above.

8. Which of the following events is likely to increase export sales?
   (a) An increase in domestic real GDP.
   (b) A decline in the exchange rate.
   (c) An increase in the domestic price level.
   (d) A decrease in the foreign price level.
   (e) An increase in foreign income.

9. Which of the following events is likely to decrease import purchases into a particular country?
   (a) A decrease in the exchange rate.
   (b) A decrease in the external value of the country's currency.
   (c) A decrease in foreign income.
   (d) An increase in domestic GDP.
   (e) An increase in the foreign price level.

10. The marginal propensity to import
    (a) is the ratio of imports to real national income.
    (b) is equal to one minus the marginal propensity to consume.
    (c) is the change in real GDP divided by the change in imports.
    (d) determines the slope of the net-export function.
    (e) is usually believed to be greater than one for most developed countries.

11. Anything that increases the proportion of income that domestic consumers wish to spend on imports will
    (a) rotate the net-export function downward and thus increase the slope of the net-export function.
    (b) decrease the slope of the net-export function.
    (c) will cause net exports to increase at every level of real GDP.
    (d) decrease the propensity to import.
    (e) shift the net-export function upward in a parallel fashion.

Equilibrium National Income

Since net taxes have been introduced, disposable income nets out net taxes from income ($Y_d = Y - T$). Desired consumption expenditures depend on the level of disposable income. Hence, it is possible to define two different marginal propensity to consume values. The marginal propensity to consume out of *disposable income* relates desired consumption to disposable income while the marginal propensity to consume out of *national income* relates desired consumption to national income.

The marginal propensity to spend is no longer simply equal to the marginal propensity to consume. It now incorporates the tax rate and the marginal propensity to import, but not in a straightforward way. Some exercises help you to calculate the marginal propensity to spend.

There are two equilibrium conditions:
(i) Desired aggregate expenditure equals actual income, or $Y = C + I + G + NX$; and
(ii) National Saving equals National Asset Formation, or $S + (T - G) = I + NX$.

12. Equilibrium real national income occurs when
    (a) the AE function intersects the 45° line.
    (b) the average propensity to spend is one.
    (c) desired aggregate expenditure equals output.
    (d) $Y = C + I + G + (X - IM)$.
    (e) All of the above.

13. Which of the following is *not* a component of aggregate expenditure?
    (a) Investment.
    (b) Government purchases on goods and services.
    (c) Net exports.
    (d) Consumption expenditure.
    (e) Personal income taxes paid.

14. In our analytical model, all but which of the following are functions of current income?
    (a) Consumption.   (b) Net exports.
    (c) Investment.   (d) Personal incomes taxes.
    (e) Saving.

15. If $Y_d = 0.8Y$ and consumption were always 80 percent of disposable income, then the marginal propensity to consume out of total income would be
    (a) 0.8.   (b) 0.75.
    (c) 0.64.   (d) 0.2.
    (e) 1.6.

$Y = 0.8 \times .80 = 0.64$

16. National saving is
    (a) net tax revenue minus government purchases.
    (b) disposable income minus consumption expenditure.
    (c) private saving plus net asset formation.
    (d) private saving plus public saving.
    (e) private saving plus government net-taxation revenue.

17. Which of the following is a correct statement about national asset formation?
    (a) It is equal to investment plus net exports.
    (b) Net exports are central to determining the rate at which a country accumulates foreign assets or incurs foreign liabilities.
    (c) When plotted against actual national income, the national asset formation function is downward sloping since net exports fall as income increases.
    (d) An economy reaches equilibrium when national asset formation is equal to desired national saving.
    (e) All of the above are correct.

18. When national asset formation is greater than national saving, we would expect
    (a) real GDP to decrease.
    (b) the price level to fall.
    (c) firms to increase output, employment to expand, and GDP to rise.
    (d) actual national income to be greater than desired aggregate expenditure.
    (e) None of the above are correct.

Changes in Equilibrium National Income

The value of the simple multiplier is reduced by the presence of taxes and imports since they reduce the marginal propensity to spend out of national income. The higher is the marginal propensity to import, the lower the simple multiplier. The higher the income-tax rate, the lower the simple multiplier.

Stabilization policy deals with changes in government purchases and/or net taxes in order to deal with GDP gap problems. A reduction in tax rates or an increase in government purchases shifts the AE function upward, causing an increase in equilibrium national income. Such policy stances would be appropriate to eliminate a recessionary gap. For changes in government purchases, the ratio of the change in national income to the change in purchases is the multiplier value.

If tax rates change, the relationship between disposable income changes. For any given level of national income, there will be a different level of disposable income and hence a different level of consumption. This change in consumption results in a nonparallel shift of the AE function. The value of the multiplier will also change. You should also know what is meant by a balanced budget multiplier.

19. An increase in the tax rate would
    (a) increase disposable income.
    (b) decrease the slope of the *AE* function.
    (c) shift the *AE* function downward in a parallel fashion.
    (d) shift the *AE* function upward in a parallel fashion.
    (e) None of the above.

20. National income is likely to increase as the result of increases in all but which of the following, assuming other autonomous or exogenous variables remain constant?
    (a) The tax rate.   (b) Net exports.
    (c) Government purchases.   (d) Investment.
    (e) Autonomous consumption.

21. The simple multiplier becomes larger when which of the following variables increases?
    (a) The marginal propensity to save.
    (b) The marginal propensity to import.
    (c) The income tax rate.
    (d) The marginal propensity not to spend.
    (e) The marginal propensity to consume.

22. The balanced budget multiplier (where an increase in government spending is paid for with an equal increase in taxes) is likely to be
    (a) equal to the multiplier for an increase in *G* without tax increases.
    (b) zero under all circumstances.
    (c) greater than the multiplier for an increase in *G* without tax increases.
    (d) less than the multiplier for an increase in *G* without tax increases.
    (e) infinitely large.

Limitations of the Income-Expenditure Approach

Equilibrium in the simple model is demand determined. Whatever level of output is demanded by purchases will be "passively" provided by producers. This aspect of the model may be appropriate if firms have excess capacity or if they are price setters. Chapters 24 and 25 will consider the supply side of the economy. When the demand side and the supply side of the economy are considered simultaneously, changes in desired aggregate expenditures usually cause both prices and real national income to change. This is why the simple multiplier, derived under the assumption that prices do not change, is too simple.

23. The simple multiplier analysis assumes that
    (a) the price level changes when real GDP changes.
    (b) the exchange rate changes when autonomous expenditure changes.
    (c) changes in real GDP depend on the extent to which firms change prices and output.
    (d) the price level and exchange rate are exogenous and do not change when real GDP changes.
    (e) the supply side of the economy determines the multiplier effect of an increase in autonomous expenditure.

EXERCISES

1. This question deals with the *Keynesian* consumption function: the relationship between consumption and two variants of current income, real disposable income and total real income. You are given the following information:

Y	Y_d	Desired C	$S = Y_d - C$
0	0	44	−44
100	70	100	−30
200	140	156	−16
300	210	212	−2

(a) What relationship exists between Y and Y_d? Why is Y_d less than Y?

(b) Prove that the marginal propensity to consume out of real disposable income is constant and equal to 0.8.

$$-\frac{100}{44}\Big/56$$

(c) Derive the algebraic expression for the relationship between C and Y_d.

(d) Calculate the marginal propensity to consume out of real income (Y).

for every $100 Consumption increase, 56

(e) Derive the algebraic expression for the relationship between C and Y.

(f) Suppose that the marginal propensity to consume out of disposable income remains at 0.8 but that the relationship between income and disposable income becomes $Y_d = 0.6Y$. What economic event might have caused the change? Recalculate the values of C and Y_d for Y values equal to 100, 200, and 300. Recalculate the marginal propensity to consume out of total income.

2. As an economy expands in terms of real income, net exports fall. If $X - IM$ is negative, a deficit in the balance of trade is said to exist. To explain this we present the following hypothetical schedule, where Y represents real national income, X represents desired exports, and IM represents desired imports.

Y	X	IM	(X – IM)
0	40	0	_____
100	40	10	_____
200	40	20	_____
400	40	40	_____
800	40	80	_____

(a) Exports are assumed to be autonomous (independent of the level of Y). However, what specific relationship exists between IM (imports) and Y? Explain why there is a positive relationship between desired imports and real national income.

(b) Calculate the values for X – IM. Does the balance of trade fall (become smaller) as Y increases?

(c) Plot the net export curve in Figure 23-1.

Figure 23-1

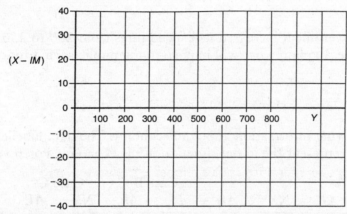

(d) Suppose that exports at each level of Y fell from 40 to 30. Recalculate the value of X – IM at each level of Y, and plot the new net export curve.

(e) Identify three factors that might have caused exports to decline as in (d).

– X change rate
+ Inflation –
– Foreign income

3. This exercise tests your knowledge of the concept of the public saving (budget surplus) function. You are given information about an economy in the following schedule:

Y	G	T
0	200	0
400	200	100
800	200	200
1,000	200	250
1,200	200	300

$6 - 200 = -200$

$100 - 200 = -100$

$200 - 200 = 0$

$250 - 200 = 50$

$300 - 200 = 100$

(a) Using the expression $[B = T - G]$, calculate the values of public saving (budget surplus) for each of the five national income levels.

(b) What is the value of the tax rate according to the schedule?

(c) If the economy experiences a recession and real national income falls from 1,000 to 800, what is the change in public saving, assuming government purchases and tax rates remain unchanged? Explain.

(d) Suppose that the government increased its expenditures from 200 to 250 at each level of real national income. Explain what will happen to the public saving function.

4. You are given the following information about an economy. The data labelled "Case A" in the following schedule represent the initial situation in the economy. Potential GDP is 450.

Y	C	I	G	NX	AE	I	AE	NX	AE	C	AE
		Case A				Case B		Case C		Case D	
0	10	50	10	10	80	60	90	−10	60	10	80
200	190	50	10	−10	240	60	___	−30	___	150	___
300	280	50	10	−20	320	60	___	−40	___	220	___
400	370	50	10	−30	400	60	___	−50	___	290	___
450	415	50	10	−35	440	60	___	−55	___	325	___

(a) For case A, determine the equilibrium level of real national income and the marginal propensity to spend.

(b) Graph the aggregate expenditure curve in Figure 23-2, and indicate the equilibrium level of real national income (case A). What is the value of the output gap?

Figure 23-2

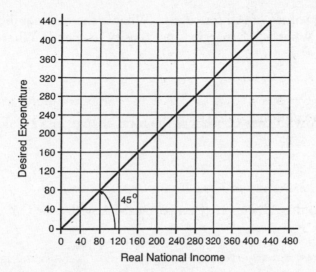

(c) Now assume that a change occurs in the economy so that case B holds. Case B is identical to case A except that investment *at every level of Y* increases from 50 to 60. Fill in the missing values in the table for *AE*, and plot the new aggregate expenditure curve. What has happened to the aggregate expenditure curve? (Compare case A with case B.)

(d) Using the *AE* curve for case B, what is the value of desired *AE* at a level of real national income of 400? What do you predict will happen to the equilibrium level of real national income in this situation? Explain.

(e) What is the equilibrium level of real national income for case B? What has been the total change in real national income (ΔY) between case A and B? Calculate the ratio $\Delta Y/\Delta I$ from A to B. What is the value of the simple multiplier? What has happened to the value of the output gap?

(f) Calculate the value of the marginal propensity to spend (denoted as z in the text) for case B. Using the formula $K = 1/(1 - z)$, confirm your answer for the value of the simple multiplier in (e).

(g) The total change in income is composed of two parts: the change in the autonomous component of $AE(\Delta A)$, which in this case is ΔI, and the *induced* change in aggregate expenditure (ΔN). What is the value for ΔN?

5. Assume that case A is the initial situation but now net exports at every level of income fall such that $X - IM$ (or NX) has fallen by 20 at every level of Y. This is case C in the schedule above.

   (a) Fill in the missing values of AE for case C. What is the new equilibrium level of real national income? What is the marginal propensity to spend? What is the value of the output gap.

   (b) Comparing case A with case C, what is the total change in Y? Calculate the value of the multiplier.

   (c) What happened to the AE curve? (Compare case A with case C.)

6. Assume that case A is the initial situation but that factors in the economy change so that case D in the above schedule applies. Case D is identical to case A except that the consumption function is now quite different.

   (a) Calculate the marginal propensities to consume out of national income for both cases, and indicate the nature of the behavioural change between the two cases.

   (b) Fill in the missing values of AE for case D. Graph the new aggregate expenditure curve on the grid in exercise 4(b) and compare it with the one for case A.

   (c) Calculate the marginal propensity to spend for case D, and compare it with that for case A. Calculate the multiplier value, and compare it with the multiplier for case A.

   (d) What is the equilibrium level of real national income for case D?

7. This exercise enforces your understanding of the saving-investment approach for the determination of equilibrium national income. Refer to the data in the schedule associated with questions 11 to 20 in the **Practice Multiple-Choice Test** section. Equilibrium national income was 400 according to the aggregate expenditure approach. We want to confirm this answer.

   (a) Calculate the level of private saving at $Y = 400$ using the expression $S = Y_d - C$.

(b) Calculate the level of public saving at $Y = 400$ using the expression $T - G$.

(c) Add your answers from (a) and (b) to find the level of national saving at $Y = 400$.

(d) Calculate the level of national asset formation at $Y = 400$ using the expression $I + NX$. Confirm that this value is equal to the level of national saving.

8. A newly elected government inherits an inflationary gap. Record high export sales of one of the country's manufactured goods have created an inflationary gap of 12 billion. The recently appointed minister of finance seeks advice from her advisers. After careful study, they advise her to increase taxes permanently by 3 billion, keeping government spending at its current level. Their recommendation is based on the following assumptions:

(a) The high level of export sales will continue, and potential GDP will remain at 1 trillion.
(b) The taxation multiplier is 4.
(c) Within the foreseeable future, changes in both prices and input prices are likely to be negligible.
(d) Since the government has a large majority, policy changes can be made quickly with few execution lags. Moreover, the advisers are confident that the private sector will respond quickly to this policy change.

The advisers have also been told by the chief economist in the ministry that both the export and government spending multipliers are 6.0.

(a) Assuming that all information is correct, do you agree that the recommended policy will eliminate the inflationary gap? Explain.

(b) The minister accepts the advice, the tax change becomes law, and the size of the output gap begins to decrease. However, shortly after the policy change, exports of one of the country's food products falls unexpectedly by 2.5 billion due to the introduction of a cheaper and higher-quality product by a foreign competitor. Assuming that input prices remain constant and that the chief economist's numbers are accurate, what will happen to the equilibrium level of GDP if no additional fiscal measures are introduced? What is the value of the output gap now?

(c) The finance minister is severely criticized in Parliament. The prime minister insists that she reverse the government's fiscal stance and restore taxes to their original levels (that is, reduce them by 3 billion). Will this reversal in fiscal policy resolve the output gap problem described in (b)? Explain.

(d) The finance minister threatens to resign. She argues that her credibility as minister is at stake. A reversal of policy would be political suicide for her. Moreover, her taxation increase was correct; unforeseen external factors caused the problem. She convinces the prime minister that the government's appropriate stance should be to retain the 3 billion increase in taxation, and also to increase government spending by 2.5 billion. Comment on this new policy stance.

EXTENSION EXERCISES

E1. This exercise involves an algebraic macroeconomic model. You should read the appendix to this chapter before attempting these questions. You are given the following information about behaviour in an economy that has a potential real national income of 300.

The consumption function is

$$C = 30 + 0.9Y_d. \tag{1}$$

The parameter 0.9 is the marginal propensity to consume out of disposable income and we will denote it as the parameter, b.

The relationship between Y_d and Y is

$$Y_d = 0.8Y. \tag{2}$$

Since equation (2) implies that the tax rate (t) is 0.2, the tax function can be written as

$$T = 0.2Y. \tag{3}$$

Investment expenditure is

$$I = 40. \tag{4}$$

Government expenditure is

$$G = 20. \tag{5}$$

The net export function is

$$X - IM = 20 - 0.12Y. \tag{6}$$

The term 0.12 is the marginal propensity to import and is denoted as m.

The AE expenditure identity is

$$AE = C + I + G + (X - IM). \tag{7}$$

The public saving (B) identity is

$$B = T - G. \tag{8}$$

Using the AE approach, the equilibrium condition is

$$AE = Y. \tag{9}$$

Solving for equilibrium real national income using the AE approach

The key to determining the equilibrium level of real national income is to derive the algebraic expression for the *AE* function. We do this step by step.

(a) Since *AE* is a relationship between desired expenditures and *Y*, it is necessary to express consumption as a function of *Y*. Hence, substitute equation (2) into (1), and form the new consumption function. Call this function equation (10). What is the marginal propensity to consume out of total income?

(b) The *AE* function is the algebraic sum of the components of desired aggregate expenditure. Substitute equations (10), (4), (5), and (6) into equation (7) and derive the algebraic expression for the *AE* function. Make sure you collect all of the autonomous terms as well as all the coefficients for the *Y* variable.

(c) The slope of the *AE* function (*z*) is given by, $z = b - bt - m$. Prove that this value is equal to the value of the coefficient of the *Y* term in part (b).

(d) Using equation (9), solve for the equilibrium level of *Y*. What is the value of the simple multiplier? What is the value of the output gap?

(e) What is the value of public saving (budget surplus) at the equilibrium level of GDP?

(f) What is the value of net exports at the equilibrium level of GDP?

Solving for equilibrium real national income using the saving-investment approach

(g) Prove that the private saving function is the expression $S = -30 + .08Y$.

(h) Prove that the public saving function is the expression $B = 0.2Y - 20$.

(i)   Prove that the national saving function is the expression $-50 + 0.28Y$.

(j)   Prove that national asset formation function is the expression $60 - 0.12Y$.

(k)   By equating the national saving function to the national asset formation function, prove that equilibrium national income is 275.

Fiscal Policy Issues

(l)   Assume that the government wishes to eliminate the output gap. What change in government expenditures would you recommend?

(m)   Eliminating the output gap by changing the tax rate is a much more difficult exercise. We use the *AE* approach to deal with this interesting policy issue. Suppose that equation (2) changed to $Y_d = 0.8367Y$. What has happened to the tax rate? Prove that the new equation for the *AE* function is given by, $AE = 110 + .633Y$. Using equation (9) and the new aggregate expenditure function, prove that the new equilibrium level of real national income is approximately equal to 300. Has the tax cut policy eliminated the output gap?

(n)   Could the government eliminate the output gap by changing its spending and its taxation by the same amount? This is called a balanced budget policy. This model has a balanced budget multiplier of 0.46 approximately. What is the needed equal change in government spending and taxation revenue that is required to eliminate the current output gap?

E2.   This exercise reinforces your understanding of equilibrium national income using the saving-investment approach. You are given the following information about an economy:
- the income-tax rate is 0.20.
- the marginal propensity to consume out of disposable income is 0.70.
- investment is 56 at all levels of income.
- government purchases on goods and services are always equal to 50.
- exports are always equal to 10.
- the marginal propensity to import is 0.10.
- autonomous consumption is 100.
- the algebraic expression for private saving is given by $S = -100 + .24Y$.

(a) Derive the algebraic expression for public saving.

(b) Derive the algebraic equation for national saving.

(c) What is the level of national saving at $Y = 400$?

(d) Derive the equation for national asset formation.

(e) What is the equilibrium level of national income?

E3. Test your knowledge of factors that shift the AE curve and/or change its slope. For each of the following events indicate if the AE curve shifts upward, downward, or not at all, and indicate if the slope of the AE curve increases (becomes steeper), decreases (becomes flatter), or is not affected.

(a) A provincial government reduces its income-tax rate.

(b) Sales of Toronto-produced computer software packages increase to Australia.

(c) Actual national income increases.

(d) The foreign exchange rate changes from 1.40 Canadian dollars for every U.S. dollar to $1.50 (Canadian).

(e) The real rate of interest increases.

PRACTICE MULTIPLE CHOICE TEST

Questions 1 to 4 refer to Figure 23-3

Figure 23-3

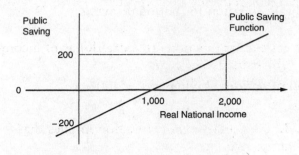

1. The marginal tax rate implied in the diagram is
   (a) zero.   (b) 0.1.
   (c) 0.2.   (d) 0.5.
   (e) 0.4.

2. When national income is 2,000,
   (a) the government has a surplus budget position of 200.
   (b) government purchases exceed taxes net of transfers by 200.
   (c) the government budget is balanced.
   (d) public saving is zero.
   (e) the government has necessarily accumulated more public debt.

3. If the government were to raise the income tax rate, the public saving function would be
   (a) shifted upward parallel to the current function.
   (b) rotated upward (steeper slope) from the current intercept.
   (c) shifted downward parallel to the current function.
   (d) unaffected.
   (e) rotated downward (flatter slope) from $Y = 1,000$.

4. If the government were to increase its purchases on goods and services, the public saving function would be
   (a) shifted upward parallel to the current function.
   (b) rotated upward from the current intercept.
   (c) unaffected.
   (d) rotated downward from the current intercept.
   (e) None of the above.

Questions 5 to 10 refer to Figure 23-4.

Figure 23-4

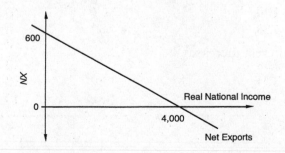

5. The net export function slopes downward because as income increases
   (a) imports increase, thereby reducing net exports.
   (b) exports fall, thereby reducing net exports.
   (c) prices of domestic goods rise, thereby raising the value of exports.
   (d) foreign income falls, thereby reducing net exports.
   (e) the exchange rate appreciates.

6. In a movement along the net export function, an extra dollar of income results in imports
   (a) rising by 60 cents.   (b) rising by 15 cents.
   (c) falling by 15 cents.   (d) falling by 40 cents.
   (e) falling by 60 cents.

7. When national income is 3,000, the net export function implies that
   (a) imports are greater than exports.
   (b) net exports are negative.
   (c) net exports are zero.
   (d) exports are greater than imports.
   (e) the marginal propensity to import is zero.

8. A net export function that is represented by a horizontal line would signify that
   (a) imports are not a function of income.
   (b) exports are induced.
   (c) imports are very close substitutes for domestic goods.
   (d) exports are very close substitutes for domestic goods.
   (e) imports are induced.

9. If foreign income rises, the net export function
   (a) becomes steeper.   (b) becomes flatter.
   (c) shifts upward.   (d) shifts downward.
   (e) is unaffected.

10. The net export function is most likely to shift downward when, other things being equal,
    (a) prices for the country's exports decrease.
    (b) the exchange rate depreciates.
    (c) domestic prices fall relative to foreign prices.
    (d) foreign income rises.
    (e) tariffs are imposed on imports.

Questions 11 to 20 refer the following information about an economy. Before attempting these questions, you should calculate the values of aggregate expenditure, the government's budget surplus, and national asset formation for each of the six levels of national income (Y) shown in the schedule.

Y	T	C	I	G	NX
0	0	100	56	50	10
100	20	156	56	50	0
200	40	212	56	50	−10
300	60	268	56	50	−20
400	80	324	56	50	−30
500	100	380	56	50	−40

11. Which of the following statements is correct?
    (a) Autonomous consumption is 100.
    (b) Autonomous exports are 10.
    (c) The marginal propensity to import is 0.1.
    (d) The marginal tax rate is 0.2.
    (e) All of the above.

12. The marginal propensity to consume
    (a) out of disposable income is 0.56.
    (b) out of total income is 0.56.
    (c) out of disposable income is 0.70.
    (d) out of total income is 0.70.
    (e) Both (b) and (c).

13. Which of the following statements is *not* correct?
    (a) Desired aggregate expenditure at $Y = 200$ is 308.
    (b) The marginal propensity to spend out of total income is 0.46.
    (c) At $Y = 500$, there is a budget deficit of 50.
    (d) At an income level of 400, imports are greater than exports.
    (e) At an income level of 300, there is a government budget surplus of 10.

14. The value of the simple multiplier is
    (a) 1.85 approximately.
    (b) equal to the marginal propensity not to spend which is 0.54.
    (c) equal to the slope of the *AE* function which is 0.46.
    (d) 2.17 approximately.
    (e) the reciprocal of the marginal propensity to import.

15. At an income level of 400, the value of national asset formation is
    (a) 26.   (b) 50.
    (c) 70.   (d) –30.
    (e) 30.

Equilibrium and Comparative Statics: Questions 16 to 18.

16. Which of the following statements is true?
    (a) According to the *AE* approach, equilibrium national income is 400.
    (b) The average propensity to spend is unity at $Y = 400$.
    (c) Total imports are 40 at $Y = 400$.
    (d) Public saving (budget surplus) is 30 at equilibrium national income.
    (e) All of the above.

17. Which of the following statements is *not* true?
    (a) The value of the simple multiplier is 1.85, approximately.
    (b) An increase in investment from 56 to 83 will increase equilibrium national income from 400 to 450, approximately.
    (c) An increase in the equilibrium value of real national income will have no effect on total taxes collected.
    (d) If exports fall from 10 to 0, real national income will fall by approximately 18.5.
    (e) An increase of 50 in the equilibrium value of real national income will decrease net exports by 5.

18. An increase in the tax rate from 20 to 30 percent will
    (a) decrease the slope of the AE curve.
    (b) change the value of the simple multiplier to 1.64, approximately.
    (c) decrease the marginal propensity to consume out of total income to a value of 0.49.
    (d) generate an equilibrium level of real national income that is less than 400.
    (e) All of the above.

Fiscal Policy: Questions 19 and 20.

19. Suppose that current equilibrium GDP was 400 and that the target or desired level of GDP was 418.5. Which of the following policies would achieve the target value of GDP?
    (a) Government expenditures should increase by 18.5.
    (b) The tax rate should be increased from 0.20 to 0.30.
    (c) Government spending should increase by 10.
    (d) The government should reduce the money supply and its expenditures by 10.
    (e) None of the above.

20. If the government wanted to reduce real GDP by 15 and the balanced budget multiplier was 0.75, then
    (a) government spending and taxation revenue should increase by 20.
    (b) government spending and taxation revenue should decrease by 15.
    (c) government spending and taxation revenue should increase by 15.
    (d) government spending and taxation revenue should decrease by 20.
    (e) government spending should decrease by 15.

SOLUTIONS

Review Questions

1. (d) 2. (b) 3. (a) 4. (c) 5. (c) 6. (d) 7. (c) 8. (e) 9. (b) 10. (d) 11. (a) 12. (e) 13. (e) 14. (c) 15. (c) 16. (d) 17. (e) 18. (c) 19. (b) 20. (a) 21. (e) 22. (d) 23. (d)

Exercises

1. (a) There is a positive relationship given by the expression, $Y_d = 0.7Y$. It is less because taxes outweigh transfer payments; net taxes are positive and are deducted from total income.
   (b) $\Delta C / \Delta Y_d = 0.8$ and is constant. When Y_d increases from 0 to 70, consumption increases by 56.
   (c) Since autonomous consumption (when $Y = 0$) is 44 and the marginal propensity to consume out of disposable income is 0.8, the consumption function is written as $C = 44 + 0.8Y_d$.
   (d) The marginal propensity to consume out of total real income is calculated from the first and the third columns. We observe that every 1 dollar increase in real income generates a 56 cent increase in consumption. Hence, the marginal propensity to consume out of total income is 0.56.
   (e) The consumption function is written as $C = 44 + 0.56Y$.
   (f) Since disposable income is less at every level of income, the tax rate must have increased. In this case, the tax rate has increased from 30 to 40 percent. As real income increases from 100 to 300, disposable income levels become 60, 120, and 180. Consumption levels become 92, 140, 188. The marginal propensity to consume out of total real income becomes 0.48 which is equal to 0.8×0.6.

2. (a) Imports are positively related to national income by the expression $IM = 0.1Y$. As real national income rises, households buy more imported goods; firms, in order to produce more goods, require more imported inputs; and it is possible for governments and firms to import various machines, goods, and services as part of their investment and expenditure programs.
   (b) 40, 30, 20, 0, –40. Yes, because imports rise as income rises.
   (c) See Figure 23-5.

Figure 23-5

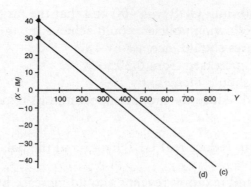

   (d) $Y = 0$, $NX = 30$; $Y = 100$, $NX = 20$; $Y = 200$, $NX = 10$; $Y = 400$, $NX = -10$; $Y = 800$, $NX = -50$.
   (e) The external value of the domestic currency appreciated (or the exchange rate fell); foreign income fell; domestic inflation was higher than foreign inflation.

3. (a) –200, –100, 0, 50, 100.
   (b) The tax rate is 0.25.
   (c) The budget surplus (public saving) falls from 50 to 0. As Y falls, tax revenue falls. Since G is constant, the government's budget surplus (public saving) falls.
   (d) The public saving function shifts down and to the right.

4. (a) $AE = Y$ at 400. The marginal propensity to spend is 0.80 and is constant ($\Delta AE = 160$, $\Delta Y = 200$, $\Delta AE/\Delta Y = 0.80$).
   (b) The AE curve has an intercept value of 80 on the vertical axis, has a slope of 0.80, and intersects the 45° line at an income level of 400. There is an output gap of –50 (a recessionary gap).
   (c) AE: 90, 250, 330, 410, 450. The AE curve shifts vertically upward by 10 in a parallel fashion.
   (d) $AE = 410$ when $Y = 400$. Since AE is greater than national income, real income and employment will rise.
   (e) $AE = Y$ at 450. The change in income is 50, and $\Delta Y/\Delta I = 5$. The value of the simple multiplier is 5. The output gap has been eliminated.
   (f) The marginal propensity to spend is 0.80. The marginal propensity not to spend is 0.20. $K = 1/0.2 = 5$.
   (g) Since the total change in income is 50 and $\Delta I = 10$, the value of ΔN is 40.

5. (a) AE: 60, 220, 300, 380, 420. Equilibrium is $Y = 300$. The marginal propensity to spend remains at 0.80. The output gap is now –150.
   (b) Y fell by 100. The multiplier is $\Delta Y/\Delta(X - IM) = -100/-20 = 5$.
   (c) The AE curve shifts downward by 20 in a parallel fashion.

6. (a) Case A: $MPC = 0.90$; case D: $MPC = 0.70$. Consumers have become more frugal; they are saving a higher proportion of national income.
   (b) AE: 80, 200, 260, 320, 350. The new AE has an intercept of 80 on the vertical axis, has a slope of 0.60, and intersects the 45° line at $Y = 200$. The AE curve for case D is flatter than that for case A.
   (c) The marginal propensity to spend for case D is 0.60, which is lower than 0.80 for case A. The multiplier for case D is therefore $1/(1 - 0.60) = 2.5$.
   (d) $AE = Y$ when $Y = 200$.

7. (a) Private saving equals –4 (=400 – 80 – 324).
   (b) Public saving equals +30 (=80 – 50).
   (c) National saving equals +26 (=30 – 4).
   (d) National asset formation equals +26 (= 56 – 30).

8. (a) The inflationary gap of 12 will be completely eliminated if taxes are increased by 3 billion since the tax multiplier is 4.
   (b) GDP declines for two reasons. The increase in taxation will decrease GDP by 12 billion, and the decrease in exports will decrease GDP by 15 billion (2.5×6). The total decrease is therefore 27 billion. The economy's initial GDP level must have been 1,012 billion. After the taxation and export changes, the new equilibrium level must be 27 billion less, or 985 billion. Hence the output (recessionary) gap is –15 billion.
   (c) No, a taxation cut of 3 billion will increase GDP by 12 billion, leaving a recessionary gap of –3 billion (997 – 1,000).
   (d) If nothing else happens, the minister's amended policy will restore potential GDP. As was discussed before, the taxation increase will eliminate the inflationary gap. The 2.5 billion increase in government spending will counteract the 2.5 billion reduction in food exports.

Extension Exercises

E1. (a) Equation (10) is $C = 30 + 0.72Y$. The marginal propensity to consume out of total real income is 0.72.
     (b) $AE = 30 + 0.72Y + 40 + 20 + 20 - 0.12Y = 110 + 0.60Y$.
     (c) $z = b(= 0.9) - bt(= 0.9 \times 0.2) - m(= 0.12) = 0.6$.
     (d) $110 + 0.6Y = Y$ or $Y = 275$. The value of the simple multiplier is $K = 1/(1 - z)$ or 2.5. The output gap is $275 - 300$ or –25. This is a recessionary gap.
     (e) $B = 0.2 \times 275 - 20 = 35$.
     (f) $(X - IM) = 20 - 0.12(275) = -13$.
     (g) Private saving is equal to $Y_d - C$ or $Y - 0.2Y - [30 + 0.9(Y - 0.2Y)]$.
     (h) Public saving is equal to $T - G$ or $0.2Y - 20$.
     (i) National saving is equal to $S + T - G$ or $0.28Y - 50$.
     (j) National asset formation is equal to $I + NX$ or $60 - 0.12Y$.
     (k) Equating the national saving function to the national asset formation function, we obtain $Y = 275$.
     (l) The output gap is –25 (275 – 300). The government spending multiplier in this model is 2.5. Hence, government expenditure should rise by 10.
     (m) The new consumption function (expressed as a function of total income) is $C = 30 + (0.836 \times 0.9)Y$ or $C = 30 + .753Y$. Hence aggregate expenditure is $30 + .753Y + 40 + 20 + 20 - 0.12Y$ or $110 + 0.633Y$. Using the condition that $AE = Y$, we obtain a new equilibrium level of real national income of 299.8 (approximately 300). The output gap has been eliminated.

(n) Both G and total taxation revenue must increase by 54.3. With a balanced budget multiplier of 0.46, GDP will increase by 25.

E2.   (a) Public saving is $T - G$. Since taxes are 20% of income, then the equation for public saving is $.2Y - 50$.

(b) National saving is the sum of public and private saving. Hence, the equation for national saving is $.2Y - 50 + [-100 + .24Y]$ or $.44Y - 150$.

(c) 26.

(d) National asset formation is investment plus exports minus imports. The equation for national asset formation is $66 - .1Y$.

(e) Equilibrium occurs when national asset formation is equal to national saving. Equating the two equations, we obtain an equilibrium of 400.

E3.   (a) Disposable income will increase. Hence, the marginal propensity to consume out of national income will increase. The AE curve will pivot up and its slope will increase.

(b) Since export sales have risen, the AE curve will shift up. Since exports are assumed to be autonomous, the slope of the AE curve is unaffected.

(c) Were you fooled by this question? An increase in actual national income causes a *movement* along a given AE curve not a shift.

(d) The U.S. dollar has appreciated; the Canadian dollar has depreciated. This change has two effects on the AE curve. First, exports to the U.S. are likely to increase. An increase in exports will shift the AE curve upward in a parallel fashion. Secondly, Canadians are likely to reduce the proportion of their income expended on imports. This will cause the AE curve to rotate upward and the slope of the AE curve will become steeper. Taking both effects into account, the AE curve will shift upward and its slope will increase. As a result the multiplier value will increase.

(e) A rise in the real interest rate will decrease investment. Since investment is an autonomous expenditure component, the AE curve will shift downward in a parallel fashion.

Practice Multiple Choice Text

1. (c) 2. (a) 3. (b) 4. (e) 5. (a) 6. (b) 7. (d) 8. (a) 9. (c) 10. (b) 11. (e) 12. (e) 13. (c) 14. (a) 15. (a) 16. (e) 17. (c) 18. (e) 19. (c) 20. (d)

CHAPTER 24

OUTPUT AND PRICES
IN THE SHORT RUN

LO *LEARNING OBJECTIVES*

1 Understand why an exogenous change in the price level shifts the *AE* curve and changes the equilibrium level of real GDP.

2 Explain the meaning of the *AD* curve, and which factors lead it to shift.

3 Explain the meaning of the *SRAS* curve and why changes in technology or factor prices cause it to shift.

4 Understand the concept of macroeconomic equilibrium.

5 Explain the effects of aggregate demand and aggregate supply shocks on real GDP and the price level.

CHAPTER OVERVIEW

The previous two chapters analysed national income determination under the assumption that the price level was fixed. In the next two chapters we consider the simultaneous determination of real national income and the price level. This chapter focuses on the short run, when technology and factor prices remain constant. Macroeconomic equilibrium of national income and the price level occurs at the intersection of the *AD* and *SRAS* curves.

A downward sloping **aggregate demand curve** is developed. A rise in the price level lowers private-sector wealth; this leads to a downward shift in the aggregate expenditure curve and a decrease in the equilibrium level of income. Moreover, a rise in the domestic price level shifts the net export function downward, which means a downward shift in the aggregate expenditure curve. Hence, national income equilibrium decreases.

The slope of the **short-run aggregate supply (*SRAS*) curve** is positive, but its value changes as output changes. Although factor prices are constant for any *SRAS* curve, unit costs usually increase as output increases. Hence, firms usually want higher prices for increased output.

The effects of **aggregate demand shocks** on real income and the price level depend on the range of the *SRAS* curve in which the demand shock occurs. The steeper the slope of the *SRAS*, the less the increase in real income and the greater the increase in the price level from any increase in aggregate demand. Hence, the value of the multiplier depends on the slope of the *SRAS* curve.

Aggregate supply shocks shift the *SRAS* curve. An upward shift in the *SRAS* curve, with a downward sloping *AD* curve, will cause the price level to rise and real income to fall. This combination of events is called *stagflation*. A downward shift in the *SRAS* curve will lead to a fall in the price level, but an increase in real output.

CHAPTER REVIEW

The Demand Side of the Economy

Now, you must understand the **relationship between *AE* and *AD* curves. An exogenous change in the price level** *shifts* the *AE* curve and changes the equilibrium level of real GDP for two reasons. First, a fall in the price level increases real wealth, and so the consumption function shifts up. Secondly, a decrease in the domestic price level (foreign prices held constant) will increase exports and decrease imports. Hence, the net export function shifts up. Both factors will increase the equilibrium level of real income. These two factors explain why the *AD* curve **is negatively sloped.** Do not be confused; a price change causes the *AE* curve to **shift**, but causes a movement along the *AD* curve. The *AD* curve shifts only because some autonomous expenditure changes (such as investment or government expenditures). A shift in the *AD* curve is called an **aggregate demand shock.**

1. All other things being equal, an increase in the domestic price level will
   (a) increase the value of real money balances and hence cause an upward shift in the consumption function.
   (b) decrease the value of real money balances and hence cause an upward shift in the consumption function.
   (c) cause exports to increase, thereby causing the net export function to shift downward.
   (d) decrease the value of real wealth and cause the consumption and aggregate expenditure functions to shift downward.
   (e) cause input prices to fall.

2. All other things being equal, a decrease in the domestic price level will shift the net export function
   (a) downward, thus causing the aggregate expenditure function to shift downward.
   (b) upward, thus causing the aggregate expenditure function to shift upward.
   (c) upward, thus causing the aggregate expenditure function to shift downward.
   (d) downward, thus causing the aggregate expenditure function to shift upward.
   (e) downward, thus causing the SRAS curve to shift upward.

3. The aggregate demand (*AD*) curve relates
   (a) real national income to desired expenditure for a given price level.
   (b) nominal national income to the price level.
   (c) equilibrium real national income to the price level.
   (d) consumption expenditure to the price level.
   (e) real national income to inflation rates.

4. All other things being equal, a fall in the domestic price level causes
   (a) the aggregate expenditure curve to shift upward and hence leads to a movement downward and to the right along the *AD* curve.
   (b) the aggregate expenditure curve to shift upward and hence leads to a movement upward and to the left along the *AD* curve.
   (c) the *AD* curve to shift to the right and a movement upward and to the right along the *AE* curve.
   (d) the *AD* and the *AE* curves to shift upward.
   (e) the *SRAS* curve to shift downward.

5. All other things being equal, the *AD* curve shifts to the right as a result of all but which of the following changes?
   (a) Increased government expenditure.
   (b) Increased imports.
   (c) Increased autonomous exports.
   (d) Increased investment expenditure.
   (e) Decreased tax rates.

6. All other things being equal, an increase in desired <u>investment</u> expenditures will
   (a) shift the *AE* curve upward.
   (b) shift the *AD* curve to the right.
   (c) cause the equilibrium levels of real national income and price to increase if the economy operates with a positively sloped *SRAS* curve.
   (d) All of the above.
   (e) None of the above.

7. Within an *AD-SRAS* model, the simple multiplier can be measured by
   (a) the extent of the horizontal shift of the *AD* curve in response to a change in autonomous expenditure.
   (b) the extent of the vertical shift of the *AD* curve in response to a change in autonomous expenditure.
   (c) the distance moved along the *AD* curve in response to a change in autonomous expenditure.
   (d) the distance between initial equilibrium and the new intersection of *AD* and *SRAS* in response to a change in autonomous expenditure.
   (e) the ratio of the change in price to the change in autonomous expenditure.

The Supply Side of the Economy

The **short-run aggregate supply (*SRAS*) curve** relates the price level to the quantity of output that firms would like to produce and sell on the assumption that the technology and the prices of all factors of production remain constant. For a given *SRAS* curve, unit costs tend to rise with output because less efficient factories may have to be used, or less efficient workers may have to be hired, or existing workers may have to be paid overtime rates. Unit cost increases trigger price increases. It is assumed that the *SRAS* curve not only slopes up but also gets steeper as real GDP increases. Hence, at low levels of GDP the *SRAS* curve is relatively flat, but as GDP rises the *SRAS* curve gets progressively steeper.

Each *SRAS* is associated with a specific set of factor prices. Hence, the *SRAS* curve will shift if factor prices change.

8. An upward-sloping *SRAS* curve indicates
   (a) firms' willingness to supply more output if the output can be sold at higher prices.
   (b) that expanding output means incurring higher unit costs and higher prices of output.
   (c) that expanding output means higher factor prices and therefore higher output prices.
   (d) Both (a) and (b).
   (e) None of the above.

9. If the *SRAS* curve is horizontal,
   (a) output can be increased at a constant price level.
   (b) any increase in *AD* will cause real national income and the price level to increase.
   (c) output is constant but the price level is variable.
   (d) the economy is most likely operating beyond its potential level of real national income.
   (e) potential output varies in the short run.

10. A rightward shift in the *SRAS* curve is brought about by
    (a) an increase in factor prices.
    (b) decreases in productivity.
    (c) increases in productivity and/or decreases in factor prices.
    (d) decreases in factor supplies.
    (e) increases in real wealth.

11. As real GDP increases, the change in the price level will be greatest
    (a) if the *SRAS* curve is relatively steep.
    (b) when the unemployment rate is high.
    (c) when unit costs do not change.
    (d) if the *SRAS* curve is flat.
    (e) Both (a) and (c) are correct.

Macroeconomic Equilibrium

The short-run equilibrium values of real GDP and the price level occur at the intersection of the *AD* and *SRAS* curves. The combination of real GDP and the price level that is on both the *AD* and *SRAS* curves is called a **macroeconomic equilibrium**.

Changes in the macroeconomic equilibrium are caused by shifts in the *AD* curve and/or the *SRAS* curve. Your task is to understand the economic factors that cause either the *AD* curve or the *SRAS* curve to shift and the direction of the shift. For example, an expansionary demand shock associated with export increases causes the *AD* curve to shift to the right. With an upward sloping *SRAS* curve, the equilibrium values of the price level and real GDP increase.

The shape of the *SRAS* has important implications on how the effects of an aggregate demand shock are divided between changes in real GDP and changes in the price level. Hence, the multiplier value associated with a demand shock must be less than the simple multiplier because the price level has increased. Do you understand why?

Aggregate supply shocks cause the *SRAS* curve to shift. Aggregate supply shocks cause the price level and real GDP to change in opposite directions.

12. With a given aggregate demand curve, a shift in the *SRAS* curve to the left will cause
    (a) increases in real national income and the price level in the short run.
    (b) an increase in the price level but a decrease in real national income in the short run.
    (c) decrease in the price level but an increase in real national income.
    (d) decrease in potential real national income.
    (e) a movement down an *AD* curve.

13. Assume that the *SRAS* curve slopes upward. After an economic shock, we observe that the equilibrium price level is lower than before but real equilibrium output has increased. Which one of the following events, by itself, could explain this observation?
    (a) An increase in input prices.
    (b) An increase in factor productivity.
    (c) An increase in exports.
    (d) A reduction in investment expenditure.
    (e) A decrease in the tax rate.

14. If the current price level is below the short-run macroeconomic equilibrium level,
    (a) the desired output of firms is greater than the level of output consistent with expenditure decisions.
    (b) desired aggregate expenditure is less than the amount of goods supplied in the short run.
    (c) the desired output of firms is less than the level of output consistent with expenditure decisions.
    (d) price will tend to adjust such that there will be movement downward and to the right along the *AD* curve.
    (e) price will adjust downward along the *SRAS* curve.

15. The multiplier value that allows for price changes will be equal to the value of the simple multiplier if the demand shock occurs in the
    (a) flat range of the *SRAS* curve.
    (b) intermediate range of the *SRAS* curve.
    (c) steep portion of the *SRAS* curve.
    (d) range characterized by increasing unit costs.
    (e) the inelastic portion of the *AD* curve.

16. Under what circumstances would an expansionary demand shock result in virtually no increase in real income but a large increase in the price level?
    (a) If the demand shock occurred in the flat range of the *SRAS* curve.
    (b) If the demand shock occurred in the intermediate range of the *SRAS* curve.
    (c) If the demand shock occurred in the steep portion of the *SRAS* curve.
    (d) If unit costs were constant before and after the demand shock.
    (e) If input prices decreased.

17. If autonomous investment increased, the multiplier would be zero if
    (a) price increases reduced consumption and net exports by the same amount as the increase in autonomous investment.
    (b) the demand shock occurred in the vertical range of the *SRAS* curve.
    (c) if the upward shift in the *AE* curve associated with the increase in investment was completely counteracted by the reduction in net exports and real wealth.
    (d) All of the above.
    (e) None of the above.

18. Assuming the *SRAS* curve is positively sloped, which of the following events would lead to a fall in both the equilibrium levels of real GDP and the price level?
    (a) An increase in productivity.
    (b) A decrease in government purchases.
    (c) An increase in exports.
    (d) A depreciation of the external value of the domestic currency.
    (e) A decrease in the marginal propensity to save.

EXERCISES

1. *The Derivation of an AD Curve from Consumption Theory*

   This exercise should enhance your understanding of why an *AD* curve is downward sloping. The exercise demonstrates the links among changes in price, the level of real wealth, consumption expenditure, and equilibrium real GDP.

   Desired consumption (*C*) is shown at two different price levels, $P = 1$ and $P = 2$. The consumption function is given by the expression $C = 100 + 0.8Y + 0.1(W/P)$, where W represents the total nominal wealth in the economy. We assume that nominal wealth is 3,000. All other components of aggregate expenditure are lumped together in one column, labelled $I + G + NX$. For the purposes of this exercise only, entries in that column are assumed to be unaffected by the price level, but because imports are included in this combination, the component is a negative function of real national income.

Y	C_1 (P=1)	C_2(P=2)	I+G+NX	AE_1(P=1)	AE_2(P=2)
0	400	250	1,200	1,600	1,450
2,500	2,400	2,250	700	3,100	2,950
2,875	____	____	625	____	____
3,250	____	____	550	____	____
3,625	____	____	475	____	____
4,000	____	____	400	____	____
4,375	____	____	325	____	____

   (a) Use the consumption equation above or assume that the marginal propensity to consume that you can derive from the initial data entries remains constant at all levels of national income. Fill in the missing values for C_1, C_2, AE_1, and AE_2.

   (b) Plot the aggregate expenditure functions in the left-hand panel in Figure 24-1 and determine the equilibrium level of national income at each price level.

   (c) What vertical shift in the *AE* function occurs as a result of a rise in a price level of $P = 1$ to $P = 2$? What is the change in the equilibrium level of national income after the change?

   (d) Use the two values in (b) to plot the aggregate demand curve in the right-hand panel of Figure 24-1. Assume that a linear approximation is satisfactory. Why does the aggregate demand curve slope downward?

   (e) If government spending rises at all levels of income by 150, by how much does the equilibrium level of national income rise? Plot the new aggregate expenditure function (AE_E) in the upper graph, assuming $P = 1$, and show the new equilibrium level of income.

Check your answer by determining the marginal propensity to spend, deriving the simple multiplier, and multiplying by the autonomous expenditure change.

(f) If government spending rises by 150, explain how this affects the position of the *AD* curve. How does your answer to (e) provide useful information regarding the size of any shift in the curve? Plot the new *AD* curve in Figure 24-1.

Figure 24-1

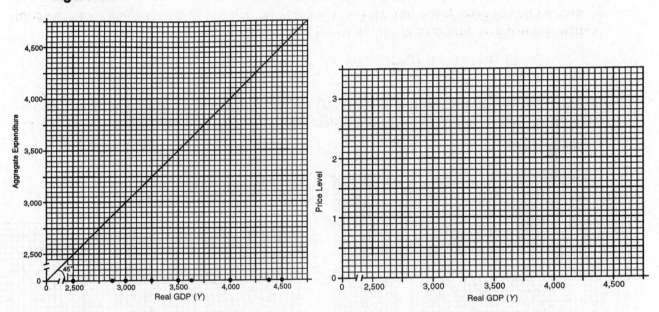

(g) In the examples above, if the price level falls from 2 to 1, the *AE* curve shifts up by 150, and if the government increases spending by 150, the *AE* curve shifts up by 150. Yet in one case the economy moves along the *AD* curve, and in the other case the *AD* curve shifts. Explain why these different results occur.

2. *The Derivation of an* AD *Curve from Net-Export Theory*

Another reason why the *AD* curve slopes downward is that a reduction in the domestic price level (assuming that the foreign price level remains constant) increases the domestic economy's competitiveness internationally, *ceteris paribus*. Thus net exports (*NX*) will increase if the domestic price level falls. This exercise has the same consumption function as exercise 1. However, now the component $X - IM$ depends on relative prices (the ratio of the domestic price level to the foreign price level). For our present purposes, the foreign price is assumed to be equal to 1.0 and constant. Thus the relative price can be represented by the domestic price level, P. The non-consumption items in aggregate expenditure are now determined by the equation

$$I + G + NX = 1,500 - 0.2Y - 300P.$$

There are two domestic price levels, $P = 1$ and $P = 2$.

(a) Using the equation just given, fill in the entries for $I + G + NX$ for both price levels. Then calculate AE_1 and AE_2 for all levels of income in the table.

Y	C_1	$(I+G+NX)_1$	AE_1	C_2	$(I+G+NX)_2$	AE_2
0	400	1,200	1,600	250	900	1,150
2,500	2,400	700	3,100	2,250	400	2,650
2,875	2,700	___	___	2,550	___	___
3,250	3,000	___	___	2,850	___	___
3,625	3,300	___	___	3,150	___	___
4,000	3,600	___	___	3,450	___	___
4,375	3,900	___	___	3,750	___	___

(b) Plot the two aggregate expenditure functions in the left-hand panel of Figure 24-2, and determine the equilibrium level of national income at each price level (P).

(c) Based on your answer to (b), plot the AD curve for this economy in Figure 24-2, assuming that a linear approximation is satisfactory.

Figure 24-2

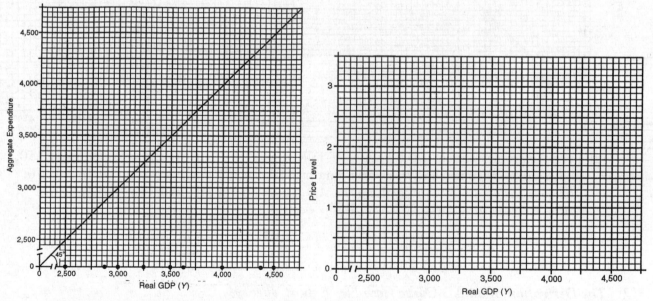

(d) How can you characterize the slope of this AD curve compared to the one you derived in exercise 1?

(e) Suppose that the expression for nonconsumption demand expenditures was $I + G + NX = 1,500 - 0.2Y - 600P$. Without solving the model formally, how would you expect this change to affect the slope of the aggregate demand curve?

(f) To summarize your findings, based on a common initial equilibrium price level and national income, the more price responsive foreign demand is for domestically produced goods and the more price responsive domestic demand is for foreign goods, the (flatter, steeper) is the slope of the *AD* curve, all other things being equal. Also, the more responsive consumption is to changes in real wealth, the (flatter, steeper) is the slope of the *AD* curve.

3. *Macroeconomic Equilibrium*

The aggregate demand function is given by $P = 40 - 2Y$, and the short-run aggregate supply function is given by $P = 10 + Y$, where Y refers to real national income and P is the price level.

(a) Graph the *AD* curve and indicate both intercept values in Figure 24-3.

(b) Plot the *SRAS* curve and indicate its intercept value on the price axis.

Figure 24-3

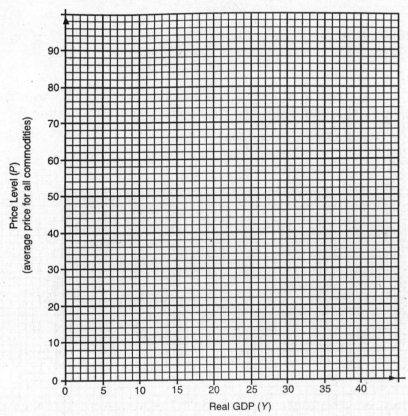

(c) Referring to the graph, what is the macroeconomic equilibrium (equilibrium levels of P and Y)? Prove algebraically that the intersection of the two equations yields these equilibrium values.

(d) Suppose that the expression for the *AD* curve became $P = 70 - 2Y$. Plot this expression in the graph, and discuss the changes that occurred to the levels of *P* and *Y*. Comment on the size of the horizontal shift in the *AD* curve in relation to the value of the change in output.

4. This exercise focuses on the value of the multiplier allowing for price changes. You are given the following information about an economy.

The aggregate demand function is

$$P = \frac{60}{0.2Y - 25}.$$

The short-run aggregate supply function is

$$P = 0.02Y.$$

The *AE* function is

$$AE = 0.8Y + 25 + 0.1(W/P).$$

P represents the price level, *Y* represents real national income, and *W* is nominal wealth. The marginal propensity to spend is 0.8, and the nominal value of wealth is 600.

(a) Graph the *AD* and *SRAS* curves in Figure 24-4.

Figure 24-4

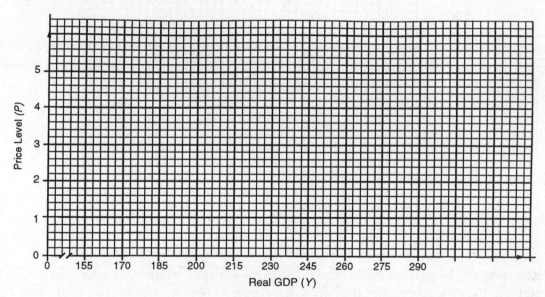

(b) According to the graph, what are the equilibrium values of *P* and *Y*?

(c) Using the equilibrium condition $Y = AE$, prove that your answer for the equilibrium value of Y (when $P = 4$) in (b) is confirmed.

(d) What is the value of the simple multiplier?

(e) Suppose that the AE function becomes $AE = 0.8Y + 10 + 0.1(W/P)$ because a component of autonomous expenditure decreases by 15. As a consequence, the AD function becomes $P = 60/(0.2Y - 10)$. When graphed, this expression lies to the left of the initial AD curve. If the price level remains at 4 for the time being, what is the new equilibrium level of Y according to the new AE function? (*Note:* This is not a permanent equilibrium value, as the next question in this exercise points out.)

(f) What is the quantity of output supplied at a price level of 4 according to the $SRAS$ function? What is the quantity demanded at a price level of 4 according to the new AD function?

(g) In the situation depicted in (f), the price level will fall. Prove that the new AD curve intersects the $SRAS$ curve at a price level of 3 and a real income level of 150.

(h) A fall in autonomous expenditure of 15 triggered a decline in the equilibrium level of Y of 50. What is the value of the multiplier that allows for price level changes? How does this value compare with the value of the simple multiplier? Explain.

5. *Aggregate Demand Shocks*

P	SRAS (Y)	AD_a	AD_b	AD_c	AD_e	AD_f
1.0	0–50	____	____	____	____	____
1.2	70	____	____	____	____	____
1.4	80	____	____	____	____	____
1.6	85	____	____	____	____	____
1.8	85	____	____	____	____	____
2.0	85	____	____	____	____	____

(a) Assume that the aggregate expenditure function is $AE = 30 + 0.5Y - 5P$. Determine the appropriate entries for column AD_a and plot them in Figure 24-5, labelling the curve AD_a. (As a shortcut in deriving the AD curve without plotting the separate AE curves for each price level, note that equilibrium values of national income occur when $Y = 30 -$

$0.5Y - 5P$, and then simplify by combining the Y terms.) Therefore, the AD curve is a linear function. Also plot the $SRAS$ curve. What is the equilibrium level of national income?

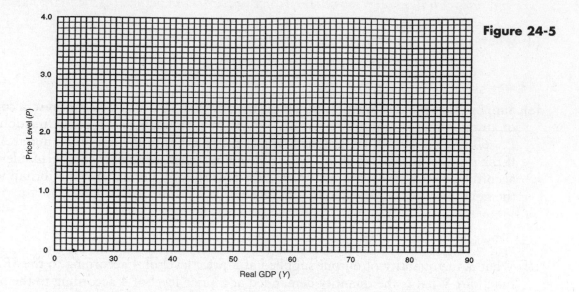

Figure 24-5

(b) Suppose that business confidence in the economy falls, so that investment declines by 10, and the AE function becomes $20 + 0.5Y - 5P$. Fill in the entries for the new AD curve under AD_b, and plot it on the graph. What is the new equilibrium level of national income?

(c) Suppose instead that business confidence rose, so that the AE function became $40 + 0.5Y - 5P$. Fill in the entries for the new AD curve (AD_c), and plot it on the graph. What is the new equilibrium level of national income?

(d) In (b) and (c), shifts in the AD curve by the same amount but in the opposite direction did not result in the same change in the absolute value of output. Explain why they did not.

(e) If the economy, instead, starts from a position where $AE = 47 + 0.5Y - 5P$, determine the appropriate AD curve entries (AD_e), plot them, and solve for the equilibrium level of income.

(f) Starting from a position where $AE = 47 + 0.5Y - 5P$, suppose that business confidence improves and investment rises by 10. What are the appropriate entries for the AD curve now (AD_f)? How does the resulting shift in the AD curve from (e) compare to the shift you determined from (a) to (c)? How does the change in equilibrium national income compare to what you found from (a) to (c)?

(g) From the various *AD* shifts you have examined, what can you conclude about the potential error from relying on the simple multiplier to predict changes in national income?

6. *"I don't give a . . . [expletive deleted] . . . about the slope of the* SRAS *curve."*

The Finance Minister is under extreme pressure from his caucus, the public, and the opposition parties to reduce unemployment and to eliminate a prolonged recessionary gap. He summons his key economic advisers in the central bank and the Department of Finance to (1) brief him on the current situation and to (2) advise him on various policy options.

After an hour's briefing, the Minister is assured that the officials from the central bank and his ministry have reached consensus on the following:

(1) The output (recessionary) gap is $8 billion.
(2) Private-sector autonomous expenditures are not likely to change in the foreseeable future.
(3) Over the period of the policy change, input (factor) prices will not change.
(4) The preferred policy change is an expansion in government expenditure.

The second hour of the briefing is acrimonious. The central bank officials argue that the slope of the *SRAS* curve is very steep with the result that the multiplier value is 1.2. Therefore, they recommend a government expenditure increase of $6.67 billion. The Finance officials argue vehemently that the slope of the *SRAS* curve is quite flat and recommend a government expenditure increase of $3.2 billion. Shouting occurs and accusations of incompetence are made by both parties. The Minister has heard enough! He slams his fist on the conference table and, paraphrasing the words of a former U.S. President, he replies, "I don't give a . . . [expletive deleted] . . . about the slope of the *SRAS* curve. Resolve the issue and give me a specific policy recommendation within 24 hours. And, you better be right, or many of you will find yourselves unemployed."

(a) What is the value of the government expenditure multiplier according to the Finance Department officials?

(b) Is the discrepancy between the two estimated multiplier values consistent with the differing views about the slope of the *SRAS* curve? Why might the two separate groups have differing views regarding the slope of the *SRAS* curve?

(c) Suppose that the views of the Department of Finance officials prevail. The Minister of Finance announces an increase in government expenditure of $3.2 billion. After all effects of the expenditure programs have been realized in the economy, it is reported to the Minister that real national income has increased by $3.8 billion and that the price level increase was larger than expected. The Minister is demoted to the backbenches without cabinet responsibility. What went wrong?

EXTENSION EXERCISE

E1. This exercise involves the construction of an upward-sloping *SRAS* curve. Students who have not studied microeconomics may find it difficult. All students may wish to refer to Chapters 10 and 12 in the text. The text explains that the *SRAS* curve represents the relationship between the price level and the supply of aggregate output when factor prices remain constant. The *SRAS* curve will have a positive slope when increases in output cause increases in unit costs and product prices even though factor prices do not change. The *SRAS* curve tends to be relatively flat when the economy operates below its potential output level. However, production increases beyond normal capacity levels will be associated with large increases in unit costs, which in turn generate large price level increases.

The complete explanation of a positively sloped *SRAS* curve is complex; the aggregate relationship between output and the price level reflects the overall behaviour of diverse firms that differ in market structure for products and inputs as well as in their objectives. This exercise deals with the concept of unit costs that increase in response to output increases by profit-maximizing firms that operate in competitive markets for inputs and products.

Short-run theory of competitive firms outlined in Chapter 12 yields the following principles: (1) a competitive firm's short-run supply curve is that part of its marginal cost curve which lies above the average variable cost curve; (2) a competitive firm maximizes profits (or minimizes short-term losses) by equating marginal cost to product price; and (3) short-run capacity is the level of output that corresponds to the minimum short-run average total cost. A firm that is producing at an output less than the point of minimum average total cost has excess capacity.

Consider a representative firm in the competitive sector. Assume that its total fixed costs (associated with a fixed capital stock) are $100 and that the firm pays $10 for each worker it hires. The following table provides detailed information about its production, employment of labour, and costs.

		Total Cost (dollars)			Marginal Cost (dollars/unit)		Average Cost (dollars/unit)	
(1) Labour	(2) Output	(3) Fixed	(4) Variable	(5) Total	(6) MC*	(7) Fixed	(8) Variable	(9) Total
0	0.0	100	0	100		—	—	—
					0.67			
1	15.0	100	10	110		6.67	0.67	7.33
					0.53			
2	34.0	100	20	120		2.94	0.59	3.53
					0.71			
3	48.0	100	30	130		2.08	0.62	2.71
					0.83			
4	60.0	100	40	140		1.67	0.67	2.33
					5.00			
5	62.0	100	50	150		1.61	0.81	2.42
					10.00			
6	63.0	100	60	160		1.59	0.95	2.54
					20.00			
7	63.5	100	70	170		1.57	1.10	2.68

*Marginal cost (in column 6) is shown between the lines of total cost because it refers to the change in total cost divided by the change in output that brought it about. An MC value of $0.71 is the $10 increase in TC (from $120 to $130) divided by the 14-unit increase in output from (34 to 48).

(a) What output level represents the firm's short-run capacity?

(b) Suppose that the firm considers increasing its production from 41 (the midpoint of the output range 34 to 48) to 54 (the midpoint of the output range 48 to 60). Will its marginal cost increase, decrease, or remain constant? What happens to the firm's average variable costs (unit variable costs)? Recalling that a firm equates product price with marginal cost, what change in price is required to induce the firm to increase its output from 41 to 54? Both output levels (41 and 54) are less than its capacity. Hence, when a firm has excess capacity, increases in output cause (large, small) increases in unit costs; therefore, its short-run supply curve is relatively (flat, steep).

(c) Why did marginal costs increase as output increased from 41 to 54? (*Hint:* What was the incremental contribution to output of hiring the third worker as output increased from 34 to 48 compared with the incremental contribution to output of hiring the fourth worker as output increased from 48 to 60?)

(d) Suppose that the firm considers increasing its output from 54 to 61 (the midpoint of the output range 60 to 62). Will its marginal costs increase, decrease, or remain constant? What happens to its average (unit) variable costs? What price will the firm require to maximize profits for the higher output? An output level of 61 is greater than the firm's short-run capacity. Hence, for output levels that are higher than capacity, the firm's short-run supply curve is relatively (flat, steep).

(e) The text also explains that the *SRAS* curve will shift to the left if input prices increase. Prove that the representative firm's marginal and average variable costs increase at every output level if the wage rate increases from $10 per worker to $20 per worker. Continue to assume that fixed costs are $100.

PRACTICE MULTIPLE CHOICE TEST

Questions 1 through 8 refer to Figure 24-6.

1. According to the curves AE_0 and AD_0, the equilibrium levels of price and real national income are, respectively,
   (a) 2.0 and 500. (b) 2.6 and 800.
   (c) 2.0 and 1,000. (d) 2.6 and 1,000.
   (e) None of the above.

2. Assuming that the AE_0 curve shifts upward from AE_0 to AE_1 but the price level remains constant at its initial level, we can say that
   (a) autonomous expenditures must have increased by 250.
   (b) real national income increases by 500.
   (c) the aggregate demand curve shifts to the right so that $Y = 1,000$ at the price level 2.0.
   (d) input prices must have remained constant.
   (e) All of the above.

Figure 24-6

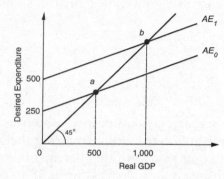

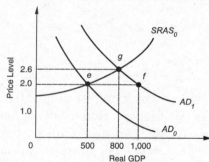

3. According to the diagram, the value of the simple multiplier is
   (a) 5.0. (b) 0.5.
   (c) 4.0. (d) 1.2.
   (e) 2.0.

4. Given the aggregate demand curve AD_1 and a price level of 2.0 (point f),
   (a) aggregate demand is less than aggregate supply.
   (b) aggregate demand is equal to aggregate supply.
   (c) firms are unwilling to produce enough to satisfy the existing demand at the existing price level, and hence the price level will rise.
   (d) the price level is likely to fall.
   (e) input prices must rise.

5. Given the increase in autonomous expenditure, moving from point *f* to point *g* represents the effect of an increase in the price level that
   (a) reduces both exports and real wealth.
   (b) reduces exports but increases consumption.
   (c) increases both exports and real wealth.
   (d) increases exports and saving.
   (e) increase input prices.

6. The movement from point *f* to point *g* implies that
   (a) the AE_1 curve shifts downward to intersect the 45° line at an output level of 800.
   (b) the AE_1 curve shifts downward to intersect the 45° line at an output level 500.
   (c) the economy moves along the AE_1 curve until it reaches an output of 800.
   (d) the economy moves along the AE_1 curve until it reaches an output of 500.
   (e) the economy moves along the AE_0 curve until it reaches an output of 800.

7. Assuming that input prices do not change, the new short-run macroeconomic equilibrium as a result of the increase in autonomous expenditure will be
   (a) at point *g*.
   (b) at an output level of 800.
   (c) at a price level of 2.6.
   (d) a 300 higher income than the initial situation.
   (e) All of the above.

8. The value of the multiplier after allowing for a price change is
   (a) 1.2.   (b) 2.0.
   (c) 1.0.   (d) 4.0.
   (e) 0.8.

Refer to Figure 24-7 when answering questions 9 through 13. Point *a* is the initial situation.

Figure 24-7

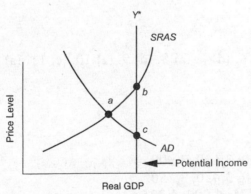

9.   When consumers become worried about the future and decide to save more out of additional income,
   (a) the *AD* curve shifts leftward, causing national income and the price level to fall.
   (b) the *AD* curve shifts rightward, causing national income and the price level to rise.
   (c) the *SRAS* curve shifts rightward, causing national income to rise and the price level to fall.
   (d) the *SRAS* curve shifts leftward, causing national income to fall and the price level to rise.
   (e) the positive output gap will decrease.

10. The dominant short-run effect of an increase in desired investment is to
    (a) shift the *SRAS* curve to the left.
    (b) shift the *SRAS* curve to the right.
    (c) shift the *AD* curve to the left.
    (d) shift the *AD* curve to the right.
    (e) increase the potential output level.

11. If the *AD* curve shifts to the right, we expect
    (a) the price level to increase and output to fall.
    (b) the price level to increase and output to rise.
    (c) unemployment to rise.
    (d) productivity to fall.
    (e) input prices to increase in the short run.

12. Rising oil prices would result in stagflation in this economy if the *SRAS* curve
    (a) shifted leftward, causing output and the price level to rise.
    (b) shifted rightward, causing output and the price level to fall.
    (c) shifted leftward, causing output to fall and the price level to rise.
    (d) shifted rightward, causing output to rise and the price level to fall.
    (e) intersected the *AD* curve at a higher output and price level.

13. In order to eliminate the current output gap (shown at point *a*),
    (a) government taxes should be increased such that the *AD* curve shifts from point *a* to point *b*.
    (b) net exports must increase in such a way that the *SRAS* curve shifts from point *a* to point *c*.
    (c) input prices must increase so that the *SRAS* curve shifts from point *a* to point *c*.
    (d) government expenditures must increase so that the new *AD* curve intersects the *SRAS* curve at point *b*.
    (e) input prices must fall so that the new *AD* curve intersects the *SRAS* curve at point *b*.

SOLUTIONS

Chapter Review

1. (d) 2. (b) 3. (c) 4. (a) 5. (b) 6. (d) 7. (a) 8. (d) 9. (a) 10. (c) 11. (a) 12. (b) 13. (b) 14. (c)
15. (a)   16. (c) 17. (d) 18. (b)

Exercises

1. (a) The missing entries are:
        C_1: 2,700; 3,000; 3,300; 3,600; 3,900.
        C_2: 2,550; 2,850; 3,150; 3,450; 3,750.
        AE_1: 3,325; 3,550; 3,775; 4,000; 4,225.
        AE_2: 3,175; 3,400; 3,625; 3,850; 4,075.
    (b) For $P = 1$, national income is 4,000. For $P = 2$, national income is 3,625. See Figure 24-8 for the completed graph.
    (c) *AE* shifts down by 150; national income falls by 375.
    (d) The *AD* curve slopes downward because consumption is an increasing function of real wealth. The *AD* curves drawn on the basis of two observations only are approximations, because the actual relationship based on the algebraic model is non-linear, as determined by W/P.
    (e) National income rises by 375. The marginal propensity to spend is 0.6 and the simple multiplier is 2.5. Note that $2.5 \times 150 = 375$.

(f) Greater government spending shifts the *AE* curve upward by 150 and the *AD* curve rightward by 375.

(g) The *AD* curve relates equilibrium national income to the price level, and therefore the change in the price level leads to a movement along the *AD* curve. The increase in government spending increases desired expenditures at all price levels, and therefore the *AD* curve shifts rightward.

Figure 24-8

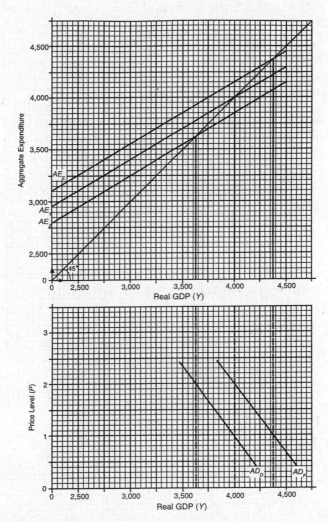

2. (a) Missing entries are as follows:

$(I+G+X-IM)_1$	$(I+G+X-IM)_2$	AE_1	AE_2
625	325	3,325	2,875
550	250	3,550	3,100
475	175	3,775	3,325
400	100	4,000	3,550
325	25	4,225	3,775

(b) Equilibrium levels are 4,000 at $P = 1$ and 2,875 at $P = 2$.

(c) See Figure 24-9.

(d) The slope of this *AD* curve is flatter than the *AD* curve in exercise 1.

(e) The larger the coefficient for the price term in the net export function (i.e., the more price-responsive net exports are), the flatter the *AD* curve.

(f) flatter, flatter.

Figure 24-9

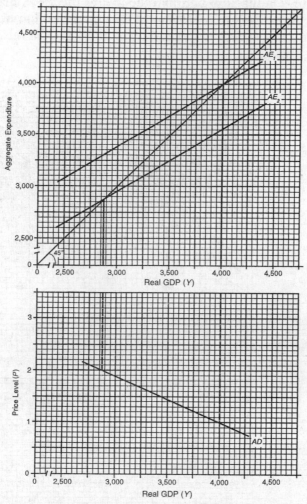

3. (a) and (b) **Figure 24-10**

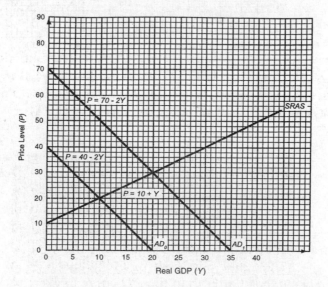

(c) Equilibrium is $P = 20$ and $Y = 10$. They can be solved algebraically by $40 - 2Y = 10 + Y$, which gives $Y = 10$. Substituting $Y = 10$ into either equation gives $P = 20$.

(d) See the graph. The new equilibrium is $P = 30$ and $Y = 20$. A demand shock has caused real income to increase by 10, but the horizontal shift in the AD curve is 15. Some of the stimulus from greater desired aggregate expenditures results in higher prices (a 50 percent increase) rather than greater output, because the expansion in output causes unit costs to increase.

4. (a) **Figure 24-11**

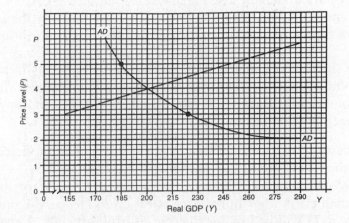

(b) The equilibrium levels are $P = 4$ and $Y = 200$.
(c) When $P = 4$, the value of real wealth is 150. Hence, consumption expenditure plus the autonomous components of AE are $40 + 0.8Y$. $AE = Y$ at $Y = 200$.
(d) Since the marginal propensity to spend is 0.8, the value of the simple multiplier is 5.0.
(e) Equilibrium is given by $Y = 0.8Y + 10 + 15$ or $Y = 125$.
(f) At $P = 4$, the quantity of aggregate supply is 200. At $P = 4$, the quantity of aggregate demand is 125.
(g) For equilibrium, aggregate supply equals aggregate demand or $0.02Y = 60/(0.2Y - 10)$. Substituting $P = 3$ into the SRAS equation, we obtain $Y = 150$. Moreover, when $P = 3$, $Y = 150$ according to the AD function.
(h) The value of the multiplier is $50/15 = 3.33$. This is smaller than the value of the simple multiplier, which in this case is 5.0. This is because the fall in the price level (from 4 to 3) increases the real value of wealth, thereby stimulating more consumption, and the domestic price level falls relative to foreign prices, thereby stimulating more exports and fewer imports.

5. (a) The AD_a entries are 50, 48, 46, 44, 42, 40. Equilibrium national income is 50.
   (b) The AD_b entries are 30, 28, 26, 24, 22, 20. Equilibrium national income is 30.
   (c) The AD_c entries are 70, 68, 66, 64, 62, 60. Equilibrium national income is a little more than 68 (68.2), and the price level is a little less than 1.2 (1.18).

Figure 24-12

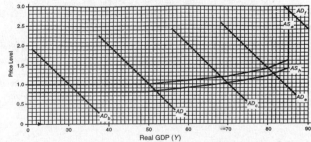

(d) When AD shifted leftward, the $SRAS$ curve was horizontal and the price remained unchanged. When AD shifted rightward, the price level rose because the $SRAS$ sloped upward, indicating that marginal costs of production were higher at higher levels of output. The higher price reduces quantity demanded, and the increase in national income is smaller in absolute value than reported in (b).

   (e) The *AD* entries are 84, 82, 80, 78, 76, 74. [(By extrapolation, *AD* is 70 at *P* = 2.4, a useful point in orienting the *AD* curve for (f)]. Equilibrium national income is 80, and the price level is 1.4.

   (f) The *AD* entries are 90 at *P* = 2.4, 88 at *P* = 2.6, 86 at *P* = 2.8, 84 at *P* = 3.0. Equilibrium national income is 85, and the price level is 2.9. *AD* shifts by the same amount in each case (10 times the simple multiplier, or 20), but here real output increases only from 80 to 85.

   (g) Applying the simple multiplier is least likely to result in errors in predicting changes in national income when the economy is operating in the relatively flat portion of the *SRAS* curve. It becomes progressively less appropriate when the economy operates in the (relatively) steep portion of the *SRAS* curve.

6. (a) To fill the recessionary gap of $8 billion, they believe that an increase in G of $3.2 billion is sufficient; their estimate of the multiplier value must be 2.5.

   (b) Yes. A steep slope of the *SRAS* curve implies that any rightward shift in the *AD* curve will have a small effect on *Y* but a large effect on *P*. Hence, the multiplier value of a given increase in G will be low for the central bank officials. A steep slope of the *SRAS* curve means that central bank officials believe that unit costs will increase rapidly as output increases are stimulated by expenditure increases.
In contrast, the Finance Department officials must believe that firms have a great deal of excess capacity and hence output increases will invoke only small changes in unit costs and the price level.

   (c) Your guess is as good as ours. Several possibilities exist. First, the assumption that private-sector spending was not likely to change might have been wrong. During the period of government expenditure expansion, private-sector spending may have fallen. Secondly, the central bank officials might have been right. The slope of the *SRAS* curve might have been quite steep. Notice, that the increase in real national income of $3.8 billion is quite close to their predicted value of $3.28 billion (1.2 × 3.2).

Extension Exercise

E1. (a) According to the schedule, the minimum *ATC* occurs at about 60 units.

   (b) Marginal cost increases from 0.71 to 0.83. Average variable cost increases. Price must also rise to (at least) 0.83. Small; flat.

   (c) The marginal productivity of labour falls for successive increments of workers; that is, the incremental contribution is falling. This can be shown by computing the ratio of the change in output associated with the change in labour. The third worker contributes 14 additional units of output; the fourth worker contributes only 12 additional units of output; the fifth worker contributes 2 additional units; and the sixth contributes only half a unit of output. Thus marginal and unit costs increase because of diminishing marginal productivity of labour.

   (d) Its marginal cost increases from 0.83 to 5.00. Unit variable costs increase as well. Price must rise to (at least) 5.00. Steep.

   (e) Total costs are now 100, 120, 140, 160, 180, 200, 220, and 240. The marginal costs are now 1.33, 1.05, 1.42, 1.66, 10.00, 20.00, and 40.00. Unit variable costs are now 1.33, 1.18, 1.25, 1.33, 1.61, 1.90, and 2.20.

Practice Multiple Choice Test

1. (a) 2. (e) 3. (e) 4. (c) 5. (a) 6. (a) 7. (e) 8. (a) 9. (a) 10. (d) 11. (b) 12. (c) 13. (d)

CHAPTER 25

OUTPUT AND PRICES
IN THE LONG RUN

LO LEARNING OBJECTIVES

1 Understand how wages and other factor prices respond to recessionary and inflation-ary gaps, and how this shifts the *SRAS* curve.

2 Explain how the economy adjusts following an aggregate demand or aggregate supply shock.

3 Define the economy's long-run aggregate supply (*LRAS*) curve.

4 Explain the different causes of short-run and long-run changes in real GDP.

5 Explain why the paradox of thrift applies in the short run but not in the long run.

6 Recognize how lags and uncertainty place limitations on the use of fiscal policy.

CHAPTER OVERVIEW

In the previous chapter, we considered the importance of supply conditions in determining national income and the price level, assuming factor prices could not change. In this chapter we allow for factor prices to change in the long run, but continue to assume that productivity is constant. Hence, a long-run aggregate supply (*LRAS*) is added to the aggregate demand and supply analysis. The flexibility of wages and other factor prices is one of the fundamental differences between the short run and long run in macroeconomics.

A short-run output gap (either inflationary or recessionary) is a convenient measure of the pressure on factor prices to change. An inflationary gap leads to higher factor prices (wages) and a leftward shift in the *SRAS* curve. The *SRAS* curve will continue to shift leftward until the price level rises enough to eliminate excess demand, and potential income is restored. Thus, the *LRAS* curve is vertical at the economy's potential output level. A decrease in aggregate demand causes a recessionary gap, leading to slower wage growth or possibly lower wages. If wages fall, the *SRAS* curve will shift rightward, thereby generating lower prices and greater output. However, some economists believe that this adjustment process takes a very long time because wages and other factor prices tend to be "sticky" downward. This is known as the **adjustment asymmetry** (flexible wages upward, but sticky wages downward).

Fiscal policies to stabilize the economy may encounter several difficulties. There are **lags (decision and execution)** in recognizing output gaps, making decisions to deal with them, implementing those decisions, and then reversing them when demand conditions change. However, some changes in taxation and transfer payments occur automatically as the economy changes; **automatic stabilizers**.

CHAPTER REVIEW

Induced Changes in Factor Prices

Short-run **output gaps can cause factor prices to change** in the long run. An inflationary gap generates a set of conditions—high profits for firms and unusually large demand for labour—that cause wages and thus unit labour costs to rise. As wages rise, the *SRAS* curve shifts upward and to the left. In the long run, the *AD* curve and a higher *SRAS* curve intersect at potential GDP; the nominal values of macroeconomic variables increase, but real values stay the same.

A recessionary gap generates low profits for firms and low demand for labour (factors), and hence wages and unit labour costs tend to fall. If wages do fall, the *SRAS* curves shifts downward and to the right. However, the experience of many developed economies suggests that the downward pressure on wages during slumps (recessionary gaps) often do not operate as quickly as the upward pressures on wages. Hence, recessionary gaps can be sustained for long periods of time.

The **Phillips Curve** indicates the relationship between the unemployment rate and the rate of change of wages. Inflationary gaps (when actual income exceeds potential GDP or the unemployment rate is less than the *NAIRU*) are associated with *increases* in wages while recessionary gaps are normally associated with *decreases* in wages. Be careful! The Phillips curve is not the same as the SRAS curve, although they are related. The economy's location on the Phillips curve indicates how the SRAS curve is shifting as a result of an existing output gap. Refresh your memory by rereading *Extensions in Theory* 25-1 in the textbook.

1. In an *AD-SRAS* diagram, a recessionary gap is shown by
   (a) the *AD* and *SRAS* curves intersecting at an output level that is to the right of potential GDP.
   (b) the *SRAS*, *AD*, and *LRAS* curves intersecting at the same output level.
   (c) the *AD* and *SRAS* curves intersecting at an output level that is to the left of potential GDP.
   (d) the horizontal distance between the *AD* and *SRAS* curves for any price level.
   (e) the vertical distance between the *AD* and *SRAS* curves for any output level.

2. A recessionary gap
   (a) will result in factor use that is lower than the normal rate of utilization.
   (b) will tend to trigger factor price increases since factor markets will have excess supply conditions.
   (c) will be depicted by a point on the Phillips curve associated with high percentage increases in prices.
   (d) will cause the *SRAS* curve to shift upward and to the left in the longer term as factor prices adjust to the recessionary gap.
   (e) causes potential GDP to fall.

3. Starting from a position in which potential national income is constant and equal to actual income, an expansionary demand shock will result in
   (a) short-run increases in both the price level and real GDP.
   (b) a recessionary gap, which creates pressure for factor price increases.
   (c) pressure for an upward shift of the *SRAS* curve in the long run.
   (d) All of the above.
   (e) Both (a) and (c).

4. If wage rates rise
   (a) the *AD* curve shifts to the left.
   (b) the *SRAS* curve shifts down and to the right.
   (c) the *SRAS* curve shifts up and to the left.
   (d) the *AD* curve shifts to the right.
   (e) Both (b) and (d) are correct.

5. A movement up and along a Phillips curve starting from the *NAIRU* (or from potential GDP) means that
   (a) wages are decreasing.
   (b) unemployment is above the *NAIRU*.
   (c) there is a short-run inflationary gap.
   (d) there will pressure for the *SRAS* curve to shift up and to the left.
   (e) Both (c) and (d) are correct.

6. When there is a short-run recessionary gap, we would expect
   (a) an excess supply of labour to cause wage rates to fall.
   (b) firms are operating beyond normal capacity levels.
   (c) current unemployment to be lower than the *NAIRU*.
   (d) the *SRAS* to shift up and to the left in subsequent time periods.
   (e) the rate of change of wage rates to be positive.

Demand and Supply Shocks

We now examine the **long-run consequences of demand and supply shocks.** The key point to remember when examining these issues is the extent to which factor prices (wages) are flexible upwards and downwards.

The short-run effects of a contractionary *AD* shock is a short-run recessionary gap. But, if wages (factor prices) are flexible downward, potential GDP is restored in the long run, albeit at a lower equilibrium price level. The story is different if wages are sticky downward. This does not mean that wages never fall, but they may do so slowly. The recesssionary gap may be prolonged and unemployment can persist because of the weakness of the adjustment mechanism.

Now, consider aggregate supply shocks. A negative supply shock will shift the *SRAS* curve upward and to the left. A short-run recessionary gap is created. Assuming wages are flexible, the economy's adjustment mechanism then reverses the *SRAS* shift and returns the economy to potential GDP. The long-run equilibrium occurs at the intersection of the *AD* curve and the *LRAS* curve. Long-run macroeconomic equilibrium will change only if the *LRAS* curve shifts.

7. Assuming wage rates are flexible, the long-run effect of a contractionary demand shock is
   (a) a restoration of potential GDP as the *SRAS* curve shifts up and to the left.
   (b) the creation of a permanent recessionary gap.
   (c) a permanent decrease in potential GDP.
   (d) permanently higher unemployment levels.
   (e) a restoration of potential GDP as the *SRAS* curve shifts down and to the right.

8. The short-run effect of a positive supply shock (associated with a decline in imported resource prices) is
   (a) to shift the *SRAS* curve initially up and to the left.
   (b) the creation of a recessionary gap.
   (c) factor utilization that is beyond normal levels.
   (d) would be shown by a movement up the Phillips curve.
   (e) an increase in the unemployment rate.

9. The long-run effect of a short-run positive supply shock is
   (a) an elimination of the short-run inflationary gap as wage increases cause the *SRAS* to shift up through time.
   (b) an increase in potential GDP, even though productivity does not increase.
   (c) a leftward shift in the *LRAS* curve.
   (d) an expansionary aggregate demand shock.
   (e) None of the above are correct.

National Income in the Short and Long Run

In the long run, the economy is at equilibrium at potential output represented by the vertical *LRAS* curve. The price level is determined where the *AD* curve intersects the *LRAS* curve.

10. With a vertical *LRAS* curve in the long run,
    (a) shifts in aggregate demand affect the price level but not the level of real GDP.
    (b) expansionary demand shocks are the primary source of long-run economic growth.
    (c) the price level depends upon the slope of the *AD* curve alone.
    (d) output is determined by demand factors alone.
    (e) economic growth occurs as the *LRAS* curve shifts to the left.

11. Which of the following depicts economic growth in the long run?
    (a) The SRAS curve shifts to the right.
    (b) The *LRAS* curve shifts to the right.
    (c) The *AD* curve shifts to the right.
    (d) Potential GDP increases over time.
    (e) Both (b) and (d).

12. The *LRAS* curve is likely to shift rightward if
    (a) tax changes reduce incentives for investment.
    (b) the nation's supplies of all factors of production increase.
    (c) tax decreases cause higher levels of aggregate demand.
    (d) factor prices increase.
    (e) national saving decreases.

13. The vertical long-run aggregate supply curve shows that, given full adjustment of input prices,
    (a) potential real income is compatible with any price level.
    (b) output is determined solely by the level of aggregate demand.
    (c) equilibrium real national income is indeterminate.
    (d) the price level is determined solely by aggregate supply.
    (e) output is at its utmost limit.

Fiscal Policy and the Business Cycle

Discretionary fiscal policy changes (tax rates, transfers, and government purchases of goods and services) may be used to solve short-run output gap situations by shifting the *AD* and the budget surplus functions. Aspects of the taxation and transfer system act as automatic stabilizers: as real national income changes, so do tax liabilities and claims on transfers. Make sure you understand the various limitations of discretionary fiscal policy because of **decision and execution lags**.

14. If there is currently an inflationary gap, an appropriate fiscal policy would be to
    (a) increase taxes.
    (b) increase government purchases of goods and services.
    (c) decrease taxes.
    (d) increase transfer payments.
    (e) reduce the budget surplus.

15. The appropriate fiscal policy to eliminate a recessionary gap would be to
    (a) increase taxes.
    (b) increase government purchases of goods and services.
    (c) decrease transfer payments.
    (d) increase the budget surplus.
    (e) decrease government purchases of goods and services.

16. Which of the following are potential limitations of discretionary fiscal policy?
    (a) There may be long decision lags.
    (b) The change in fiscal policy may overshoot its target because factor prices may be working simultaneously to eliminate the gap problem.
    (c) Private-sector decision makers may view the policy to be short-lived and hence they do not change their expenditure plans.
    (d) All of the above.
    (e) None of the above.

17. Assuming private expenditure functions do not shift, a decrease in the government's budget surplus due to a discretionary fiscal policy change
    (a) represents contractionary fiscal policy.
    (b) would be an appropriate policy for closing an inflationary gap.
    (c) will shift the aggregate demand curve to the right.
    (d) will have no effect on aggregate demand.
    (e) would not shift the budget surplus function.

18. The paradox of thrift suggests that
    (a) increased saving directly generates economic growth in the short run.
    (b) increased saving reduces aggregate demand and increases unemployment in the short run.
    (c) by providing larger funding sources for investment expenditure, increased domestic saving fosters economic growth in the long run.
    (d) Both (b) and (c).
    (e) increased thrift has no effect on the economy either in the short or long run.

EXERCISES

1. Show graphically, in Figure 25-1, and explain the short-run and long-run adjustments that you expect from the following economic changes, given that the economy starts from a

position where actual GDP equals potential income. Indicate what type of short-run output gap is created by the event. Assume that the *LRAS* curve is not affected by these events.

(a) An increase in desired investment due to greater optimism over future economic prospects.

(b) An increase in the savings rate due to a maturing of the baby-boom generation.

(c) An increase in the price of imported oil due to political instability in major producing regions.

(d) A decrease in export sales of raw materials.

Figure 25-1

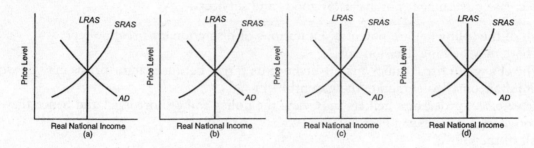

2. *The Short-run and Long-run Effects of a Demand Shock*

An economy's *SRAS* function is $P = 1 + 0.01Y$, which is presented below in schedule form, where P is the price level and Y is the level of real national income. The long-run aggregate supply curve is vertical at a real national income level of 1,000. Two schedules for the AD curve are presented, with Case I being the initial situation.

SRAS		LRAS		AD Case I		AD Case II	
Y	P	Y	P	Y	P	Y	P
0	1.0	1,000	1.0	0	111.0	0	116.5
500	6.0	1,000	6.0	500	61.0	500	66.5
1,000	11.0	1,000	11.0	1,000	11.0	1,000	16.5
1,050	11.5	1,000	11.5	1,050	6.0	1,050	11.5

(a) Taking Case I for the *AD* curve, what are the equilibrium levels of P and Y? What is the value of the output gap?

(b) Assume that the *AD* curve shifts right, represented by Case II. If the *SRAS* curve does not change immediately, what are the new short-run equilibrium values for *P* and *Y*? What type of gap exists, and what is its magnitude?

(c) Given the shift of the *AD* curve, what do you predict will happen in the long run to the equilibrium levels of *P* and Y? What will happen to the inflationary gap?

(d) Explain what is likely to happen to the *SRAS* curve in the long run.

3. The combination of $Y = 480$ and $P = 1.0$ in Figure 25-2 depicts the initial equilibrium situation in an economy.

Figure 25-2

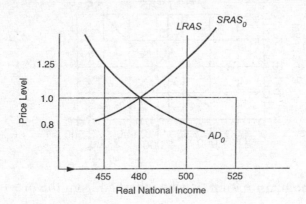

(a) The initial equilibrium reflects what sort of output gap?

(b) If the government chose to wait for factor price changes to eliminate the current gap, what predictions for future values of *Y* and *P*, assuming the appropriate factor price changes do occur, would you make?

(c) The government is concerned that the policy stance associated with part (b) will take too long. Thus, the government considers eliminating the gap by increasing its expenditures by 8. It has arrived at this number by knowing that the value of the simple multiplier is 2.5. Show this policy stance in the diagram above. (*Hint:* Draw the new *AD* curve parallel to AD_0.) Will this policy change eliminate the output gap? Explain.

(d) Demonstrate the consequences of a fiscal policy that expands government expenditures by 18. Draw the corresponding *AD* curve on the diagram (again, parallel to AD_0) and explain whether you would expect this equilibrium to change in the long run.

(e) What was the value of the multiplier for the policy stance in part (c)? Explain why this multiplier value is less than the simple multiplier.

4. *The Problems Associated with the Formulation of Fiscal Policy*

A newly elected prime minister inherits the economic situation depicted in Figure 25-3. Current potential real income is 1,800.

Figure 25-3

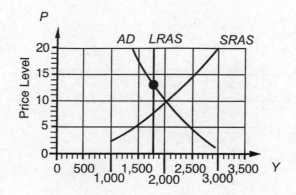

(a) Describe the economic situation that he inherited from the previous government.

(b) If the government does nothing, what is likely to happen to real national income and the price level in future time periods? Assume that aggregate demand (from the private sector) does not change.

(c) The new prime minister believes strongly that appropriate tax policies can increase investment and capital stock in the long run. His government initiates tax changes to affect the *LRAS* curve. Describe the general nature of the tax changes, and explain what this policy action is attempting to do.

(d) The opposition in the House of Commons vehemently objects to the government's policy. What arguments might they muster?

EXTENSION EXERCISE

E1.   You are given information about an economy in terms of the initial short-run aggregate supply and aggregate demand curves. Potential GDP (the *LRAS* curve) is constant at 1,000.

The initial *SRAS* equation: $P = .05Y$.

The initial *AD* equation: $P = 80 - .03Y$.

(a) Solve for the initial equilibrium values of Y and P. What type of gap exists?

(b) Suppose that the *AD* equation changed to $P = 100 - .03Y$. Solve for the new short-run equilibrium values of P and Y. What type of short-run gap exists, and what is its magnitude?

(c) What long-run adjustments in the economy would you expect?

(d) Predict the long-run values of the price level and real GDP. (*Hint:* By assuming that the slopes of the *AD* and *SRAS* curves do not change, and that potential GDP is not influenced by the aggregate demand shock, derive the algebraic expression for the new *SRAS* curve.)

PRACTICE MULTIPLE CHOICE TEST

Questions 1 through 6 refer to Figure 25-4. The curves with the subscript 0 refer to the initial situation.

Figure 25-4

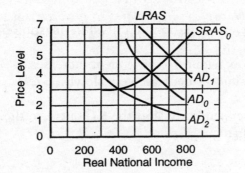

1. Given the *LRAS* curve, at the initial situation
   (a) we know that the economy has reached its potential real income level, and the price level is 4.
   (b) potential income is greater than actual real income, although the equilibrium price level is 4.
   (c) the economy is at a short-run equilibrium in terms of income and the price level, but not in terms of input prices.
   (d) the economy is in equilibrium, but factor use is above normal levels.
   (e) the economy is at its utmost limit of productive capacity.

2. Suppose that the *AD* curve shifts to AD_1 as government purchases rise. In the short run,
   (a) potential national income increases to 700 and the price level rises to 5.
   (b) real national income increases by 100 and the price level increases to 5 due to wage increases.
   (c) an inflationary gap of 100 occurs, unit costs increase even though factor prices are constant, and the price level increases to 5.
   (d) real national income increases by 200, factor prices remain constant, and the price level remains at 4.
   (e) real national income remains constant, but the price level increases to 6.

3. As a result of the short-run inflationary gap caused by the *AD* shock,
   (a) wage rates begin to fall.
   (b) wage rates begin to rise.
   (c) the *SRAS* curve shifts to the right.
   (d) the *LRAS* curve shifts to the right.
   (e) the *AD* curve shifts to the left as real wealth falls.

4. The economy's long-run equilibrium after this demand shift will be
   (a) a real income level of 600, higher nominal factor prices, and a price level of 6.
   (b) a real income level of 400 and a price level of 3.
   (c) a price level of 6 and real income of 800, due to an induced rightward shift of the *AD* curve.
   (d) potential and real income equal to 700 and a price level of 6.
   (e) a real income level of 800, and a price level of 4.

5. Suppose that the *AD* curve shifted from AD_0 to AD_2 because of a decline in investment expenditure. The short-run impact of this contractionary demand shock is
   (a) a recessionary gap of 200.
   (b) lower unit costs because of a reduction in output.
   (c) an equilibrium price level of 3.
   (d) an increase in unemployment.
   (e) All of the above.

6. Given the investment decline, the situation described in question 5 will persist, possibly for a long period of time, if
   (a) some other autonomous expenditure component increases.
   (b) factor prices remain constant or decrease very slowly.
   (c) factor prices fall rapidly.
   (d) increases in government expenditure shift the *AD* curve to the right.
   (e) None of the above are correct.

SOLUTIONS

Chapter Review

1. (c) 2. (a) 3. (e) 4. (c) 5. (e) 6. (a) 7. (e) 8. (c) 9. (a) 10. (a) 11. (e) 12. (b) 13. (a) 14. (a) 15. (b) 16. (d) 17. (c) 18. (d)

Exercises

1. (a) The *AD* curve shifts rightward in the short run, resulting in greater output and higher prices. A short-run inflationary gap is created and exerts pressure on wages to rise. Over time the *SRAS* curve shifts upward and to the left, thus restoring the initial level of potential income but at a higher price level.

    (b) The *AD* curve shifts leftward and rotates to become steeper as a result of an increase in the marginal propensity to save. A recessionary gap puts downward pressure on wages and prices. If wages decline, the *SRAS* curve shifts downard and to the right, restoring the initial level of potential income at a lower price level. Due to asymmetric adjustments in the labour market, the recessionary gap may remain for a considerable time. The question assumes that the *LRAS* curve is not affected by the short-run increase in saving.

    (c) The *SRAS* curve shifts leftward, resulting in higher prices and lower national income. The recessionary gap exerts downward pressure on wages and prices. If wages decline, the *SRAS* curve shifts rightward, and the economy may eventually reach its potential income again. If wages are slow to fall, then the recessionary gap may last for a long period of time.

    (d) The *AD* curve shifts leftward and down, resulting in lower prices and lower national income. A short-run recessionary gap situation is created. Downward pressure is put on all factor prices, including wages. If wages fall, the *SRAS* curve shifts downward and to the right through time. The economy returns to its long-run potential income but has a lower price level than before.

2. (a) The equilibrium levels are $P = 11$ and $Y = 1,000$. The output gap is 0.

    (b) The new equilibrium levels are $P = 11.5$ and $Y = 1,050$. The output gap is a positive value (+50). This is known as an inflationary gap.

    (c) Since the economy now tries to operate beyond its potential level, unusually high demand for factors will trigger increases in factor prices. As a consequence, the *SRAS* curve will shift upward and to the left. In the long run, potential national income will be restored at $Y = 1,000$. According to the new *AD* curve (Case II), $Y = 1,000$ is associated with a price level of 16.5. The short-run inflationary gap will be eliminated in the long run, but the long-run price level will be higher than that which resulted in the short run.

    (d) As explained above, the SRAS curve shifts upward and intersects the *AD* curve and the *LRAS* curve at $P = 16.5$ and $Y = 1,000$.

3. (a) The initial situation reflects a recessionary gap, since output of 480 is less than potential output of 500, shown by the *LRAS* curve.

    (b) The *SRAS* curve would shift down along the aggregate demand curve until potential income is reached ($Y^* = 500$) at a price level of 0.8.

    (c) An increase in government expenditure of 8 will shift the *AD* curve to the right by 20. The new *AD* curve intersects the *LRAS* curve at $P = 1$ and $Y = 500$, but it intersects the *SRAS* curve at a level of output less than potential output. Although the size of the recessionary gap has been reduced, a recessionary gap still remains. It is possible that the remaining gap will be eliminated if factor prices decrease thereby shifting the *SRAS* curve to the right.

(d) If the government expands its purchases by 18, the new *AD* curve will shift to the right and pass through the point $P = 1$ and $Y = 525$. If the new *AD* curve has the same slope as the initial one, it will also pass through the point $P = 1.25$ and $Y = 500$. There will be no need for factor prices to adjust in the long run since the recessionary gap has been eliminated.

(e) The multiplier is calculated by dividing 20 by 18 which is equal to 1.11 and is considerably lower than the simple multiplier value, 2.5. When unit costs and prices rise some aggregate expenditures are reduced. Specifically, real wealth decreases and hence some consumption expenditure is reduced. Moreover, as the domestic price increases, net exports are likely to fall.

4. (a) The prime minister has inherited an inflationary gap of 200. Current equilibrium levels of real national income and price are 2,000 and 10, respectively.

(b) If the government does nothing, the economy will adjust by itself. Factor prices will most likely increase, thereby shifting the *SRAS* curve upward and to the left until it intersects the *LRAS* curve at $Y = 1,800$ and $P = 13$. As a result, the economy will have an even higher price level, but the inflationary gap will have been eliminated.

(c) The prime minister's policies should involve lower tax rates, which stimulate more investment expenditure, which increases the capital stock. Thus potential real income is affected in the long run. If these policies are totally successful, the *LRAS* curve will shift to the right, perhaps to $Y = 2,000$ or beyond. Since equilibrium real national income equals the new potential level (2,000), the inflationary gap has been eliminated, and there will be no pressures for the *SRAS* curve to shift to the left.

(d) The opposition should base their arguments on the fact that tax reductions will stimulate increases in *AD*. In the short run, there will be even higher pressures for prices and factor prices to increase. Moreover, the added pressures caused by *AD* increases may prevail for some time, since it is possible that the tax changes may take a long time to increase the capital stock, thereby shifting the *LRAS* curve to the right.

Extension Exercise

E1. (a) Equilibrium is found by equating aggregate demand with the short-run aggregate supply curve, or $.05Y = 80 - .03Y$. Hence, $Y = 1,000$ and $P = 50$. Since actual real GDP is equal to potential real income, no output gap exists.

(b) The change in the equation for aggregate demand reflects an expansionary demand shock. If it were plotted, the new AD curve would be to the right of the initial curve. The new short-run equilibrium is found by equating the new AD curve with the initial *SRAS* curve. The new equilibrium is $Y = 1,250$ and $P = 62.5$. A short-run inflationary gap of 250 has been created. See Figure 25-5.

(c) The short-run inflationary gap creates pressure for wages to increase. As wages rise, the *SRAS* curve shifts upward and to the left until potential GDP is restored. The long-run price level is higher than the initial value.

(d) There are several ways to solve this problem. One way is to solve for the long-run price level using the new AD curve for $Y = 1000$. We obtain a new price level of 70 using the equation $P = 100 - .03Y$ and noting that $Y = 1,000$. Now, define the higher *SRAS* curve as $P = x + .05Y$, where x is a new intercept term. Since $Y = 1,000$ and $P = 70$, x is equal to 20. Hence, the equation for the new *SRAS* curve is $P = 20 + .05Y$.

Figure 25-5

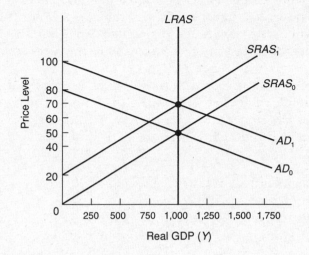

Practice Multiple Choice Test

1. (a) 2. (c) 3. (b) 4. (a) 5. (e) 6. (b)

PART NINE

MONEY, BANKING, AND MONETARY POLICY

CHAPTER 26

THE NATURE OF MONEY

LO *LEARNING OBJECTIVES*

1 Understand the Classical dichotomy and how this relates to the neutrality of money.

2 Explain the various functions of money.

3 Understand the historical origins of money.

4 Recognize that modern banking systems comprise both privately-owned commercial banks and government-owned central banks.

5 Explain how commercial banks create money through the process of taking deposits and making loans.

6 Know what items are included in various measures of the money supply.

CHAPTER OVERVIEW

This is the first of three chapters that discusses the role of money in the economy. This chapter discusses the functions of money, the evolution of money as a medium of exchange from gold to paper to demand deposits (chequing), and elements of the money supply in the current Canadian economy.

The largest component of the money supply is deposits created by commercial banks. The banking system in Canada consists of two main elements: the Bank of Canada (which is the central bank) and the commercial banks. The Bank of Canada is a publicly owned corporation that is responsible for the day-to-day conduct of monetary policy and provides banking services to commercial banks and the federal government. Commercial banks are profit-seeking institutions that allow their customers to transfer deposits from one bank to another by means of cheques.

When the banking system receives a new cash deposit, it can create new deposits to some multiple of this amount. The amount of new deposits created depends on the banks' **target reserve ratio**, the amount of cash drain to the public, and whether the banks choose to hold **excess reserves**.

The chapter concludes by distinguishing among various kinds of deposits. By doing so, different measures of the money supply can be identified. The distinctions between money, **near money,** and **money substitutes** are also discussed.

CHAPTER REVIEW

Two Perspectives on Money

This section discusses the effect of the monetary sector on real macroeconomic variables such as real GDP. Both the *Classical* and *Modern* views of the role of money hold that the **real sector** of the economy is not influenced by money in the long run since relative prices are not impacted. This is the doctrine of the *neutrality of money*. However, the modern view does not necessarily accept the neutrality of money in the short run.

1. The classical view of the neutrality of money states that
   (a) the allocation of resources is independent of the distribution of income.
   (b) the real part of the economy cannot affect relative prices.
   (c) the supply of money has no effect on the real part of the economy.
   (d) money is neutral in its effect on absolute prices in the economy.
   (e) money consists only of paper notes issued by a neutral central bank.

2. According to the classical view, a 50% reduction in the money supply will, in the long run,
   (a) reduce real GDP by 50 percent.
   (b) lower all money prices by 50%.
   (c) lower all money prices by 100%.
   (d) lower all relative prices by 50%.
   (e) have no effect on either relative or money prices.

3. Most modern economists believe that
   (a) money is neutral in the long run.
   (b) changes in money and changes in prices are closely linked over long periods of time.
   (c) changes in money supply may have impacts on the real GDP in the short run.
   (d) All of the above are correct.
   (e) None of the above are correct.

The Nature of Money

Three functions of money are identified: a **medium of exchange, a store of value,** and a **unit of account.** Different kinds of money vary in the degree of efficiency with which they fulfill these functions. By far, the largest component of modern money is **deposit** money; money held by the public in the form of chequing accounts in commercial banks that can be withdrawn on demand.

4. For money to serve as an efficient medium of exchange, it must have all but which of the following characteristics?
   (a) General acceptability.
   (b) Convertibility into gold or silver.
   (c) High value relative to its weight.
   (d) Divisibility.
   (e) Very difficult to counterfeit.

5. The value of money depends primarily on
   (a) the gold backing of the currency alone.
   (b) the gold backing of both currency and deposits.
   (c) its purchasing power.
   (d) who issues it.
   (e) a government decree.

6. To be a satisfactory store of value, money must have
   (a) a relatively stable value.
   (b) a direct relationship to national income.
   (c) a highly volatile value over time.
   (d) no interest payments for holding it.
   (e) the backing of a precious metal, typically gold.

7. "Debasing" metal coinage had the effect of
   (a) causing prices to fall in the economy.
   (b) changing relative prices.
   (c) increasing the purchasing power of each coin.
   (d) creating a loss for the person issuing the coins.
   (e) causing inflation.

8. A fractionally backed paper money system exists when claims against banks' reserves
   (a) have 100 percent backing in precious metals such as gold.
   (b) exceed the value of actual reserves.
   (c) have a direct relationship to national income.
   (d) have a fixed relationship to the quantity of coinage.
   (e) are less than the value of actual gold reserves.

9. Today, paper money in Canada is issued by
   (a) all chartered banks.
   (b) the federal Department of Finance.
   (c) all commercial banks.
   (d) the central bank of Canada (the Bank of Canada).
   (e) the Privy Council.

10. All Canadian currency (coins and paper notes) is
    (a) fractionally backed by gold reserves.
    (b) totally backed by gold.
    (c) interest-bearing.
    (d) fiat money.
    (e) backed by deposits in the commercial banks.

The Canadian Banking System

To understand banking practices and functions of banks, you should understand certain balance sheet (or "T-account") entries and transactions. A balance sheet has a left-hand and a right-hand side; by convention assets are listed on the left-hand side and liabilities on the right-hand side. For the very simple balance sheets used in the textbook, the sum of all assets must be equal to the sum of all liabilities. If one side changes, the other must also change by exactly the same magnitude.

As a banker to the banks, the Bank of Canada accepts commercial bank deposits (these are called *reserves*). Reserves are assets to the banks, but liabilities to the Bank of Canada. As a banker to the federal government, the Bank of Canada accepts government deposits and occasionally buys government bonds. The bonds held by the Bank of Canada are its assets while deposits of commercial banks and the federal government at the Bank are its liabilities. The Bank of Canada also regulates the money supply by changing two of its liabilities; reserves and currency (notes in circulation).

The principal assets of banks are the securities they own and the loans they make to individuals and businesses. The principal liabilities of banks are the deposits they accept from individuals, businesses, and governments. The banks hold reserves as assets to assure that depositors can withdraw their deposits on demand. Learn the differences between the terms *actual* versus *excess* (or *deficient*) reserve positions.

11. Which of the following is not an asset of a commercial bank?
    (a) Foreign currency holdings.
    (b) Reserves.
    (c) Loans.
    (d) Government of Canada securities.
    (e) Deposits of households.

12. The reserve ratio is the fraction of a bank's
    (a) deposits that it must hold in the form of currency.
    (b) deposits that it holds as reserves either in currency or as deposits with the Bank of Canada.
    (c) assets that it holds in the form of reserves.
    (d) reserves that it is required to hold in the form of deposits with the Bank of Canada.
    (e) None of the above.

13. Which one of the following is not a function of the Bank of Canada?
    (a) Providing banking services for the federal government.
    (b) Acting as a lender of last resort to the banks.
    (c) Controlling the supply of money and credit.
    (d) Lending to business firms.
    (e) Supporting money markets.

14. The deposits of banks at the Bank of Canada, which constitute a part of bank reserves, appear as
    (a) a liability on the Bank of Canada's balance sheet.
    (b) an asset on the Bank of Canada's balance sheet.
    (c) a liability on the balance sheet of the banks.
    (d) an asset on the balance sheet of the banks.
    (e) Both (a) and (d).

15. If Marie Swayne transfers $400 (Canadian) from a Michigan bank to a Toronto Dominion branch in Winnipeg, then the branch's balance sheet will show
    (a) only an increase in reserves of $400.
    (b) only an increase in deposits of $400.
    (c) no change, since the increase in reserves of $400 is cancelled by the increase in deposits of $400.
    (d) an increase in reserves and deposits of $400 each.
    (e) only an increase in assets of $400.

16. Which of the following is not an asset of the Bank of Canada?
    (a) Government of Canada deposits.
    (b) Government of Canada securities.
    (c) Advances to banks.
    (d) Foreign currency holdings.
    (e) All of the above.

17. If a bank currently holds $600 million in deposits and $40 million in reserves and has a target reserve ratio of 6 percent, this bank has
    (a) excess reserves of $36 million.
    (b) required reserves of $4 million.
    (c) target reserves of $2.4 million.
    (d) target reserves of $40 million.
    (e) excess reserves of $4 million.

Money Creation by the Banking System

Remember, deposit money is the major component of Canada's money supply. This section shows that when one bank receives more reserves because it attracts *new deposits*, the banking system can increase Canada's money supply by a multiple. If v is the target reserve ratio, the ultimate effect on the deposits of the banking system of a new deposit will be $1/v$ times the new deposit, assuming there is no **cash drain**. If there is a cash drain of c (the ratio of cash to deposits that people want to maintain), then the ultimate effect on the deposits of the banking system will be $1/(c + v)$ times the new deposits. When banks lose reserves because of a loss in deposits, the money supply is likely to contract by a multiple provided that there were no excess reserves to begin with.

18. The process of creating deposit money by banks
    (a) is possible because of a fractional reserve system.
    (b) is consciously undertaken by each bank.
    (c) must occur if there are excess reserves.
    (d) permits only small, gradual changes in the money supply.
    (e) None of the above.

19. A reduction in bank reserves by payments of currency to foreigners will
    (a) always cause a multiple contraction in deposits.
    (b) cause a multiple contraction in deposits only if there are no excess reserves.
    (c) never affect domestic deposits.
    (d) never affect the availability of domestic credit.
    (e) never affect GDP in the short run.

20. Suppose a bank has a target reserve ratio of 4 percent. It loses $10 million of its initial deposits of $100 million. Which of the following statements is true?
    (a) To maximize profits, the bank must have been holding initially $40 million in reserves.
    (b) After the loss in deposits, target reserves are $4 million.
    (c) After the loss in deposits, the bank has deficient reserves.
    (d) After the loss in deposits, the bank has excess reserves.
    (e) To maximize profits, the bank initially had more than $4 million in reserves.

21. Assuming a fixed target reserve ratio (v) of 10 percent in a banking system and no cash drain out of the banking system, a banking system that receives $1.00 in new deposits can ultimately create an expansion in deposits of
    (a) $10.00, which is $1/v$ times $1.00.
    (b) 10 cents, which is 10 percent of $1.00.
    (c) approximately $1.11 which is determined by the formula $1/(1 - v)$.
    (d) $1.10, which is $(1 + v)$ times $1.00.
    (e) $1.00 times $1/1 - z$.

22. The existence of a currency drain from the banking system will, other things being equal,
    (a) reduce the ability of the banking system to expand or contract the money supply.
    (b) have no effect on the ability of the banking system to contract the money supply.
    (c) have no effect on the ability of the banking system to expand the money supply.
    (d) increase the ability of the banking system to expand or contract the money supply.
    (e) increase the marginal propensity to save.

23. The multiple expansion of deposits triggered by a $1 new deposit into the banking system will be reduced if
    (a) the cash drain falls at every stage of the process.
    (b) every bank increases its target reserve ratio.
    (c) every bank lowers its target reserve ratio.
    (d) the Bank of Canada lowers a required reserve ratio.
    (e) None of the above.

The Money Supply

The measurement of the money supply varies with the type of deposits that is included. Of the three money supply measurements, the most narrowly defined is called **M1**. Assets that fulfill adequately the store-of-value function and are readily converted into a medium of exchange but are not themselves a medium of exchange are called near money, and they are included in **M2 and M2+**. Instruments that serve as a temporary media of exchange but are not a store of value are usually called money substitutes.

24. Different definitions of the money supply include different types of deposits. The narrowly defined money supply, called M1, includes currency and
    (a) term deposits.
    (b) demand deposits.
    (c) all deposits of chartered banks.
    (d) personal savings and terms deposits at all credit unions and trust companies.
    (e) foreign currency deposits.

25. A money substitute is something that serves as a
    (a) store of value.
    (b) unit of account.
    (c) temporary medium of exchange but not as a store of value.
    (d) temporary medium of exchange and also as a store of value.
    (e) medium of exchange and a unit of account.

26. Which of the following would qualify as a near money?
    (a) A demand deposit.
    (b) A Bank of Canada note.
    (c) A deposit at a trust company.
    (d) A credit card.
    (e) A gold bar.

EXERCISES

1. Indicate which of the three functions of money is demonstrated in each of the following transactions. Use the appropriate number: (1) medium of exchange, (2) store of value, (3) unit of account.
    (a) Farmer Brown puts cash in a mattress. _____
    (b) Storekeeper Jones adds up the total sales for the day. _____
    (c) Plumber Smith makes $500 per week. _____
    (d) Travelling salesperson Lee pays $100 by cash per week for gasoline. _____
    (e) The Blacks purchase by cheque a good oriental rug with the thought that it will keep its value for a long time. _____

2. Which of the following might be regarded in Canada as money, as near money, or as neither? Explain your answers briefly.

    (a) A share of stock in Bell Canada. _____

    (b) A $10 Bank of Canada note. _____

    (c) A Canada Savings Bond maturing in 2004. _____

    (d) A bank note issued by a Saskatchewan bank in 1897. _____

    (e) An ounce of gold in a Krugerrand (South African coinage provided for hoarders and speculators). _____

    (f) A fixed-term deposit account at a trust company. _____

    (g) A personal chequing deposit at the Bank of Montreal. _____

3. Do you understand the components of a bank's balance sheet? Confirm your understanding by arranging the following items on the proper side of a bank's balance sheet.

(a)	Demand deposits	2,000,000
(b)	Savings and time deposits	4,080,000
(c)	Currency in vaults	60,000
(d)	Deposits in the Bank of Canada	1,000,000
(e)	Loans to the public	4,000,000
(f)	Security holdings (Canadian government, provincial, municipal, and other)	1,500,000
(g)	Bank building and fixtures	360,000
(h)	Capital and surplus	920,000
(i)	Foreign currency assets	80,000

Assets	Liabilities

4. This exercise deals with a multiple contraction of deposits triggered by an international capital outflow (a loss in domestic deposits). Suppose that Bank A, a Canadian bank, begins with the T-account shown here. The target reserve ratio is assumed to be 10 percent, and there is no cash drain. Joe Doe, a holder of a deposit in Bank A, withdraws $1,000 and deposits this amount in a commercial bank in a foreign country (an example of an international capital outflow). Thus, $1,000 has been taken out of the Canadian banking system.

Bank A (initial situation)		Bank A (after the withdrawal)	
Reserves: $10,000	Deposits: $100,000	Reserves: $	Deposits: $
Loans: $90,000		Loans:	

   (a) What were Bank A's target reserves? Did it have excess reserves initially?

(b) Show the immediate effect of the withdrawal from Bank A.

(c) What is the status of Bank A's reserves now?

(d) Bank A reacts by calling in a loan that it had made to Mary Smith equal to the amount of its reserve deficiency. Mary repays the loan by writing a cheque on her account in Bank B, another Canadian bank that also has a fixed target reserve ratio of 10 percent. Bank B's initial T-account is shown next. Fill in the T-accounts for the effects of Bank A's receiving the payment from Mary and of Bank B's losing Mary's deposit.

Bank B (initial situation)				Bank B (after losing Mary's deposit)		
Reserves:	$ 5,000	Deposits:	$50,000	Reserves: $		Deposits: $
Loans:	$45,000			Loans:		

Bank A (after receiving the loan repayment)	
Reserves: $	Deposits: $
Loans:	

(e) After this transaction, does Bank A have deficient reserves? Does Bank B?

(f) In fact, Bank B has a deficiency of reserves. It reacts by calling in a loan made to Peter Piper equal to the amount of the deficiency. Peter cashes in a deposit that he held in Bank C; that is, Bank C loses a deposit and Peter repays Bank B. Bank C's initial situation is shown next; its target reserve ratio is also 10 percent. Fill in the T-accounts for the effects of Bank B's receiving the loan repayment and Bank C's losing Peter's deposit.

Bank C (initial situation)				Bank C (after losing Peter's deposit)		
Reserves:	$ 7,000	Deposits:	$70,000	Reserves: $		Deposits: $
Loans:	$63,000			Loans:		

Bank B
(after receiving loan repayment)

| Reserves: $ | Deposits: $ |
| Loans: | |

(g) After this transaction, does Bank B have deficient reserves? Does bank C?

(h) After this transaction, the reduction in the money supply has been Joe's original withdrawal plus $_____ in other deposits. Loans have been reduced by $_____.

(i) Assuming a 10 percent target ratio for all banks, the process will continue until the total reduction in the money supply will be $_____. The total reduction in loans will be $_____.

5. *The Multiple Expansion of the Money Supply*

Suppose that a foreign company withdraws money from its account in a foreign country, buys $1 million of Canadian currency, and deposits this sum into the Canadian banking system. This is an example of an international capital inflow. The target reserve ratio for each bank is assumed to be 8 percent, and there is no currency drain from the banking system. The initial situation in the Canadian banking system is depicted as follows:

All Banks

Reserves: $ 72 million	Deposits: $900 million
Loans: $728 million	
Securities: $100 million	

(a) According to the initial scenario, target reserves are $_____ and excess reserves are $_____.

(b) After the $1 million deposit, target reserves are $_____ and excess reserves are $_____.

(c) Assuming that all excess reserves are used to expand loans, the final (increase, decrease) in the money supply will be _____ times the new $1 million deposit, which is equal to _____.

(d) The final (increase, decrease) in loans will be $_____.

6. *Deposit Creation with Some Complicating Factors*

Star Bank, a Canadian commercial bank that currently has $300 million dollars in deposits, has been operating with a target reserve ratio of 8 percent. Judy Kupferschmidt has just inherited the equivalent of $1 million Canadian from a relative living in Florida and deposits this sum in this bank.

(a) If the bank continued to operate on an 8 percent target reserve basis, what is the magnitude of its excess reserves after Judy's deposit? (Assume Star Bank had no initial excess reserves.)

(b) If other Canadian banks also had 8 percent target reserve ratios and there was no cash drain from the banking system, what might be the final change in the Canadian money supply?

(c Suppose that Star Bank considers the risk of extending new loans from the excess reserves created by Judy's deposit to be too high. It decides to hold all of Judy's deposits in reserves. What is its new target reserve ratio, approximately? Will a multiple expansion in bank deposits occur?

(d) Assume that the scenario in (a) holds; Judy deposits $1 million in Star Bank. All Canadian banks, including Star, have a constant target reserve ratio of 8 percent. However, the Canadian public normally holds 2 percent of its money holdings in the form of currency (Bank of Canada notes and coins). If all banks used all of their excess reserves to extend loans, what would be the maximum possible change in the Canadian money supply?

PRACTICE MULTIPLE CHOICE TEST

Questions 1 through 4 refer to the following information about a banking system. Make the following assumptions:
  (a) There is a banking system in which each bank has a fixed target reserve ratio of 5 percent.
  (b) There is no currency drain from the banking system, and all banks are assumed to hold no excess reserves for a prolonged period of time.
  (c) Banks experiencing excess (deficient) reserves respond by increasing (decreasing) loans.
  (d) The current status of the balance sheet of all banks is as follows:

All Banks	
Reserves: $_____	Deposits: $300 million
Loans: $270 million	
Securities: $_____	

1. If all banks initially had no excess reserves,
   (a) the reserves of the banks must have been $30 million.
   (b) the holdings of securities by the banks must have been $15 million.
   (c) the reserves of the banks must have been 5 percent of loans, or $13.5 million.
   (d) the reserves of the banks must have been $300 million.
   (e) the reserves of the banks must have been 5 percent of securities.

2. If all banks initially had $16 million of actual reserves, then
   (a) excess reserves are $15 million.
   (b) the banks have $1 million in deficient reserves (negative excess reserves).
   (c) excess reserves are $1 million.
   (d) target reserves are equal to actual reserves.
   (e) the banks must borrow from the Bank of Canada.

3. Assuming that the banking system begins with no excess reserves, a loss of $1 million of deposits from the system will ultimately lead to
   (a) a reduction in the money supply of $19 million.
   (b) a reduction in the money supply of $500,000.
   (c) an increase in the money supply of $20 million.
   (d) deposit liabilities in the banking system of $280 million.
   (e) an increase in the money supply of $19 million.

4. Assuming that the banking system begins with no excess reserves, a gain of $1 million of deposits will ultimately lead to
   (a) increased deposits of $19 million.
   (b) increased loans of $20 million.
   (c) increased loans of $1 million.
   (d) a $5 million increase in the money supply.
   (e) increased deposits of $20 million.

Questions 5 to 7 are based on the following monetary aggregates (billions of dollars) for October 1995.

Demand deposits (at chartered banks)	33.8
Nonpersonal notice deposits and personal saving deposits	322.1
Currency outside banks	26.0
Deposits at non-bank financial institutions (trust mortgage and loan, credit unions, caisses populaires)	133.9
Money market mutual funds and deposits at other institutions	77.6

Source: *Bank of Canada Review*, Fall 1995.

5. The value of M1 at this date was (in billions),
   (a) 33.8.   (b) 26.0.
   (c) 381.9.   (d) 613.4.
   (e) 59.8.

6. The value of M2 at this date was (in billions),
   (a) 59.8.   (b) 381.9.
   (c) 355.9.   (d) 348.1.
   (e) 613.4.

7. The component(s) of M2+ at this date (in billions) not included in either M1 or M2 was (were)
   (a) 33.8.   (b) 77.6
   (c) 322.1.   (d) 133.9.
   (e) Both (b) and (d).

Questions 8 to 14 differ in their assumptions about the values of v and c in a banking system. Assume initially that the banking system in a particular country has no excess reserves before it receives $50 million in new deposits. For each question, determine the final change in deposits.

8. If $v = .10$ and $c = .10$, then the final change in deposits in the banking system will be
   (a) +$500 million.
   (b) +$5 million.
   (c) +$55.6 million.
   (d) +$250 million.
   (e) +$62.5 million.

9. If $v = .10$ and $c = .05$, then the final change in deposits in the banking system will be
   (a) +$500 million.
   (b) +$333.3 million.
   (c) +$1 billion.
   (d) +$58.8 million.
   (e) +10 billion.

10. If $v = .10$ and $c = .15$, then the final change in deposits in the banking system will be
    (a) +$200 million.
    (b) +$66.7 million.
    (c) +500 million.
    (d) −$1 billion.
    (e) +$333.3 million.

11. By comparing your answers to questions 8, 9, and 10, you have observed that when the cash drain increases, the final change in deposits in a banking system from an increase in new deposits
    (a) decreases.
    (b) is not affected.
    (c) reverts from an overall expansion to an overall contraction.
    (d) increases.
    (e) depends on the difference between v and c.

12. If $v = .05$ and $c = .10$, then the final change in deposits in the banking system will be
    (a) −$1 billion.
    (b) +$333.3 million.
    (c) +$58.8 million.
    (d) +$10 billion.
    (e) +500 million.

13. If $v = .20$ and $c = .10$, then the final change in deposits in the banking system will be
    (a) +$250 million.
    (b) +$500 million.
    (c) +$71.4 million.
    (d) +$166.7 million.
    (e) +$2.5 billion.

14. By comparing your answers to questions 8, 12, and 13, you have learned that when the target reserve ratio increases, the final change in deposits in a banking system from an increase in new deposits
   (a) decreases.
   (b) is not affected.
   (c) reverts from an overall expansion to an overall contraction.
   (d) increases.
   (e) depends on the difference between the cash drain ratio and the target reserve ratio.

Questions 15 to 19 test your knowledge of balance sheet entries for various bank transactions. Assume for simplicity that a bank's balance sheet has only three items: reserves, the combination of loans and securities, and deposits to customers. A positive sign (+) refers to an increase and a negative sign (–) refers to a decrease. Remember, a balance sheet must always balance.

15. If you deposited the total amount of your paycheque of $2,000 at your bank, the bank's balance sheet would change by
   (a) +$2,000 in deposits only.
   (b) +$2,000 in loans only, since your are lending the bank $2,000.
   (c) +$2,000 in deposits and +$2,000 in loans and securities.
   (d) +$2,000 in deposits and +$2,000 in reserves.
   (e) +$2,000 in reserves only.

16. If a bank sells $2,000 in securities to replenish its reserves, the bank's balance sheet would change by
   (a) –$2,000 in loans and securities and –$2,000 in deposits.
   (b) –$2,000 in loans and securities and –$2,000 in reserves.
   (c) +$2,000 in reserves only.
   (d) +$2,000 in loans and securities and +$2,000 in reserves.
   (e) –$2,000 in loans and securities and +$2,000 in reserves.

17. If a bank makes a loan of $2,000 to a Harry Smit, a local donut shop owner, and credits $2,000 to his chequing account, the bank's balance sheet would change by
   (a) –$2,000 in reserves and +2,000 in deposits.
   (b) +$2,000 in loans and securities and +2,000 in deposits.
   (c) –$2,000 in reserves and +2,000 in loans in securities.
   (d) +$2,000 in loans and securities only.
   (e) +$2,000 in deposits only.

18. If a commercial bank sells $2,000 of its securities to the Bank of Canada and receives $2,000 reserves in the Bank of Canada, the commercial bank's balance sheet would change by
   (a) +$2,000 in loans and securities and +$2,000 in deposits.
   (b) –$2,000 in loans and securities and +$2,000 in deposits.
   (c) –$2,000 in loans and securities and +$2,000 in reserves.
   (d) –$2,000 in loans and securities only.
   (e) None of the above are correct.

19. If a business uses $2,000 of its chequing account to pay off a $2,000 loan from the same bank, the bank's balance sheet would
   (a) change by –$2,000 in loans and securities and –$2,000 in deposits.
   (b) change by –$2,000 in deposits only.
   (c) change by +$2,000 in reserves and –$2,000 in loans and securities.
   (d) change by –$2,000 in loans and securities only.
   (e) not change because all entries are internal transactions.

SOLUTIONS

Chapter Review

1. (c) 2. (b) 3. (d) 4. (b) 5. (c) 6. (a) 7. (e) 8. (b) 9. (d) 10. (d) 11. (e) 12. (b) 13. (d) 14. (e) 15. (d) 16. (a) 17. (e) 18. (a) 19. (b) 20. (c) 21. (a) 22. (a) 23. (b) 24. (b) 25. (c) 26. (c)

Exercises

1. (a) 2; (b) 1 and 3; (c) 3; (d) 1; (e) 1, and the rug serves as function 2.

2. (a) neither; it is neither a medium of exchange nor a unit of account.
   (b) money; fiat money issued by the Bank of Canada.
   (c) near money; it is easily convertible to money.
   (d) neither; once money but now a collector's item.
   (e) neither, but readily convertible into money and considered by some to be a good store of value.
   (f) near money.
   (g) money.

3.

Currency in vaults	$60,000	Demand deposits	$2,000,000
Deposits in Bank of Canada	$1,000,000	Savings deposits	$4,080,000
Loans to public	$4,000,000		
Security holdings	$1,500,000		
Bank Buildings and fixtures	$360,000		
Foreign currency assets	$80,000	Capital and surplus	$920,000
	$7,000,000		$7,000,000

4. (a) Target reserves = $10,000; no.
   (b) Deposits −$1,000 to $99,000; reserves −$1,000 to $9,000.
   (c) Target reserves = $9,900; actual reserves = $9,000; hence its reserves are deficient by $900.
   (d) Bank A: reserves +$900, loans −$900; Bank B: reserves −$900 to $4,100; deposits −$900 to $49,100.
   (e) Bank A does not, but Bank B has a deficiency of $810.
   (f) Bank B: reserves +$810, loans −$810; Bank C: reserves −$810 to $6,190, deposits −$810 to $69,190.
   (g) No, but Bank C has a deficiency of $729.
   (h) −$900 + (−$810) + (−$729) = −$2,439; loans down by $1,710.
   (i) $10,000; $9,000.

5. (a) $72 million (0.08 × $900 million); 0.
   (b) $72.08 million (0.08 × $901 million); $920,000.
   (c) increase; 12.5 (1/0.08); $12.5 million.
   (d) increase; $11.5 million (12.5 − 1.0).

6. (a) $920,000.
   (b) $12.5 million (= 1/0.08 × $1 million).
   (c) Its initial reserve holdings were $24 million. After Judy's deposit, reserves are $25 million and total deposits are $301 million. Therefore, the new target reserve ratio is 8.3 percent. No; Star has no excess reserves to lend out. Thus no other bank receives additional reserves.
   (d) $10 million increase. This is obtained by multiplying $1 million by 1/(0.08 + 0.02). The value 0.08 is the target reserve ratio and 0.02 is the cash drain.

Practice Multiple Choice Test

1. (b) 2. (c) 3. (d) 4. (e) 5. (e) 6.(b) 7. (e) 8. (d) 9. (b) 10. (a) 11. (a) 12. (b) 13. (d) 14. (a) 15. (d) 16. (e) 17. (b) 18. (c) 19. (a)

CHAPTER 27

MONEY, OUTPUT, AND PRICES

LO LEARNING OBJECTIVES

1 Explain how the present value of an asset is related to the market interest rate.

2 Know the three motives for holding money.

3 Understand how changes in the demand for money or the supply of money influence the interest rate.

4 Explain the transmission mechanisms of monetary policy.

5 Distinguish between the short-run and long-run effects of changes in the money supply.

CHAPTER OVERVIEW

This chapter considers the **transmission mechanism** by which changes in the money supply influence macroeconomic variables such as the interest rate, real national income, and the price level in the short run. An important chain of causation is as follows: an increase in the money supply causes an initial disequilibrium in the money and bond markets, which leads to a decline in the equilibrium level of the real interest rate. The lower real interest rate causes an increase in desired investment expenditure (a movement down the **desired investment demand curve**, I^D). Hence, the aggregate demand curve shifts up and to the right.

In an open economy, there is another channel by which monetary shocks influence P and Y in the short run. A decrease in the money supply will increase interest rates. Higher interest rates attract more international capital (and generate lower international capital outflows). The exchange rate will depreciate (the external value of the domestic currency will appreciate) and hence net exports will fall. The decline in net exports will shift the AD curve down and to the left. Hence, in the short run, real GDP and the price level will fall.

The chapter discusses three motives for holding money. The negative relationship between the quantity demanded for money and the nominal interest rate is called the **liquidity preference function**. Bonds represent another asset that can be held in one's wealth portfolio. The relationship between the **yield (interest rate)** of a bond and its **price** is outlined at the beginning of the chapter.

The chapter concludes by demonstrating the short-run effects of a change of the money supply on real income and the price level in an *AD-SRAS* framework. The **strength of monetary forces** with respect to the quantitative impact on *Y* and *P* depend on the response of the quantity demanded for money and the quantity change of desired investment to changes in the interest rate. Moreover, the slope of the *SRAS* curve determines the extent to which a shift in the *AD* curve (caused by a change in the money supply) changes *Y* and *P* in the short run. In the long-run, money is neutral; that is, money shocks influence only the price level.

CHAPTER REVIEW

Understanding Financial Assets

For simplicity, all wealth holdings are classified as either money or bonds. Money, as a medium of exchange, has a low or zero rate of return. Bonds are not media of exchange, but they are interest-bearing assets. It is important for you to understand that the present value (or market price) of a bond is negatively rated to its interest rate. If necessary, reread Extensions in Theory 27-1. A special type of bond is a perpetuity.

1. In equilibrium, the market price of a bond will be
    (a) the present value of the income stream it produces.
    (b) unaffected by changes in the interest rate.
    (c) the sum of the annual returns, compounded to their value at the end of the asset's useful life.
    (d) positively related to its yield.
    (e) must be the same as its face value, or its principal value.

2. A rise in the market price of a bond with a given income stream
    (a) will have no effect on the bond's interest rate.
    (b) is equivalent to a reduction in the present value of the bond.
    (c) is equivalent to an increase in the bond's rate of return.
    (d) will not affect the present value of the bond.
    (e) is equivalent to a decrease in the bond's rate of return.

3. A bond promises to pay $1,000 one year from now. At an interest rate of 8 percent, the bond's present value is $_____. If the interest rate were 10 percent, the market value of the bond would be $_____.
    (a) $926; $909.   (b) $1,000; $1,000.
    (c) $920; $900.   (d) $1,080; $1,100.
    (e) $556; $500.

4. A bond that promises to pay $100 two years from now has a market price given by the formula
    (a) $PV = \dfrac{\$100}{(1 + i)}$.   (b) $PV = \dfrac{\$100}{(1 + i)^2}$.

    (c) $PV = \$100(1 + i)$.   (d) $PV = \$100(1 + i)^2$.
    (e) $PV = \$100/i^2$.

5. An asset that pays the same dollar annual value forever is called a
    (a) perpetuity.   (b) preferred share.
    (c) fixed-term bond.   (d) treasury bill.
    (e) a junk bond.

The Demand for Money

The amount of money balances everyone in the economy wishes to hold is called the **demand for money**. The opportunity cost of holding money balances is the nominal interest that could have been earned if the money had been used instead to purchase bonds. The total demand for money balance holding is comprised of three motives: the **transactions motive**, the **precautionary motive**, and the **speculative motives**. Both the transactions and precautionary demands for money depend positively on the level of national income. The total nominal demand for money is negatively related to the nominal interest rate and is positively related to the price level and real GDP. The total real demand for money is negatively related to the nominal interest rate and positively related to real GDP. The function relating money demanded to the nominal rate of interest is called the liquidity preference (*LP*) function.

Nominal and real interest rates may differ. However, since the chapter assumes that there is no ongoing inflation, nominal and real interest rates are the same.

6. The opportunity cost to firms and households of holding money balances is
   (a) zero, since all economic transactions require the use of money.
   (b) the foregone nominal interest that could have been earned on other assets.
   (c) low when nominal interest rates are high.
   (d) the nominal interest rate received on chequing accounts.
   (e) zero, since the Bank of Canada pays no interest for holding commercial bank reserves.

7. Suppose that the real and nominal supply of and demand for M1 was $16.7 billion in 1975 and that prices doubled between 1975 and 1983. What would be the nominal value of M1 in 1983 that maintains a constant real supply of money over this period?
   (a) $8.35 billion.   (b) $33.4 billion.
   (c) $16.7 billion.   (d) $41.75 billion.
   (e) None of the above.

8. The nominal amount of money held for transaction balances will
   (a) vary positively with national income measured in current prices.
   (b) vary positively with interest rates.
   (c) vary negatively with the value of national income.
   (d) be larger with shorter intervals between paydays.
   (e) be zero if there are interest-bearing assets.

9. Precautionary balances would be expected to increase if
   (a) business transactions were to become much less certain.
   (b) interest rates increased.
   (c) people were expecting securities prices to rise.
   (d) national income fell.
   (e) the market prices of bonds fall.

10. The speculative motive for holding money balances
    (a) applies to bonds but not other interest-earning assets.
    (b) varies positively with national income.
    (c) assumes that the opportunity cost of holding cash balances is zero.
    (d) suggests that individuals will hold money in order to avoid or reduce the risk associated with fluctuations in the market prices of other assets.
    (e) deals with the uncertainty of future transactions.

11. An increase in the price level
    (a) decreases the real demand for money.
    (b) increases the real demand for money.
    (c) decreases the nominal demand for money.
    (d) increases the nominal demand for money.
    (e) both (b) and (d).

Monetary Forces and National Income

This section outlines the transmission mechanism of monetary shocks on Y and P. You need to understand the condition for **monetary equilibrium**. Simply stated, monetary equilibrium occurs when the total quantity demanded for money is equal to the quantity of money supplied; the intersection of the LP function and the supply of money curve. The equilibrium rate of interest is determined at monetary equilibrium. In a disequilibrium situation, if the demand for money exceeds supply, then wealth holders will sell bonds in order to obtain more money. By doing so, the price of bonds will fall thereby increasing the interest rate on bonds. The equilibrium level of the interest rate will change if either the LP function or the money supply function shift.

A monetary expansion causes the equilibrium rate of interest to fall. There are two possible channels by which the monetary expansion affects real GDP and the price level in the short run. First, the quantity of desired investment may increase. Secondly, the lower domestic interest rate triggers capital outflows which cause the exchange rate to appreciate (the external value of the domestic currency depreciates) and thereby increases net exports (more exports and less imports).

12. If there is an excess supply of money, households and firms will
    (a) sell bonds and add to their holdings of money, thereby causing the interest rate to fall.
    (b) purchase bonds and reduce their holdings of money, thereby causing the interest rate to rise.
    (c) purchase bonds and reduce their holdings of money, thereby causing the interest rate to fall and bond prices to rise.
    (d) purchase bonds and reduce their holdings of money, thereby causing the price of bonds to fall.
    (e) sell bonds and add to their holdings of money, thereby causing the price of bonds to fall.

13. Changes in interest rates caused by money supply contractions or expansions
    (a) are usually of little consequence in influencing economic activity in the short run.
    (b) will not affect the market prices of bonds.
    (c) cause the liquidity preference function to shift if the price level remains constant.
    (d) cause the investment demand function to shift.
    (e) provide the link between changes in the money supply and changes in aggregate demand in the short run.

14. Other things being equal, a fall in the interest rate will cause
    (a) a shift in the I^D function to the left.
    (b) a shift in the I^D function to the right.
    (c) a movement down the I^D function.
    (d) a movement up the I^D function.
    (e) the market price of bonds to fall.

15. The investment demand curve illustrates the
    (a) positive relation between investment and the real rate of interest.
    (b) negative relation between investment and the real rate of interest.
    (c) negative relation between bonds and the nominal rate of interest.
    (d) positive relation between bonds and the nominal rate of interest.
    (e) relationship between asset demand and the real rate of interest.

16. A transition from a excess demand for money balances situation to a monetary equilibrium
    (a) tends to increase aggregate demand.
    (b) has an unpredictable effect on aggregate demand.
    (c) tends to decrease aggregate demand.
    (d) will affect aggregate demand but not the interest rate.
    (e) will increase the demand for bonds.

17. If the Bank of Canada increases the money supply, we would expect the
    (a) interest rate to fall, the *AE* curve to shift upward, and the *AD* curve to shift to the left.
    (b) interest rate to fall, the *AE* curve to shift downward, and the *AD* curve to shift to the right.
    (c) interest rate to rise, the *AE* curve to shift upward, and the *AD* curve to shift to the left.
    (d) interest rate to fall, the *AE* curve to be unaffected, and the *AD* curve to become flatter.
    (e) interest rate to fall, the *AE* curve to shift upward, and the *AD* curve to shift rightward.

18. A reduction in the Canadian supply of money which causes increases in Canadian interest rates relative to those in the rest of the world
    (a) will increase Canadians' demand for foreign assets.
    (b) will decrease foreigners' demand for Canadian assets.
    (c) will decrease Canadians' and foreigners' demand for Canadian assets.
    (d) will increase Canadians' and foreigners' demand for Canadian assets.
    (e) Both (a) and (b).

19. If Canadian interest rates rise relative to those in other countries,
    (a) the demand for Canadian dollars in international exchange markets will increase.
    (b) the demand for Canadian dollars in international exchange markets will fall.
    (c) the exchange rate will rise.
    (d) the external value of the Canadian dollar will rise.
    (e) Both (a) and (d).

20. With reference to your answer to question 19, you would therefore expect
    (a) net exports to increase and the *AD* curve to shift to the left.
    (b) the *AD* curve to shift to the right.
    (c) net exports to decrease and the *AD* curve to shift to the left.
    (d) net exports to decrease and equilibrium levels of *Y* and *P* to increase.
    (e) None of the above are correct.

The Strength of Monetary Forces

In the long run, monetary shocks are neutral; that is they influence nominal values but not the real sectors of the economy such as real GDP. This is because monetary shocks create only short-run output gap situations. Over time factor prices adjust, thus restoring potential real GDP, albeit at a different nominal price level.

In the short run, the strength of monetary shocks will depend on the sensitivity of money demand and desired investment to a change in the interest rate. The steeper the *LP* function, the greater the change in the equilibrium interest rate. Moreover, the steeper the investment demand curve (I^D), the lower the change in desired investment expenditures to a change in interest rates. You may wish to refresh your knowledge of the materials in Chapters 24 and 25 which explain the importance of the slope of the *SRAS* curve in determining the quantitative impacts of *AD* shocks on short-run equilibrium values of real GDP and the price level.

21. The short-run impacts of a monetary contraction are
    (a) a creation of a short-term recessionary gap.
    (b) an increase in the rate of interest.
    (c) a reduction in the level of desired investment expenditure.
    (d) an appreciation of the external value of the domestic currency.
    (e) All of the above.

22. The long-run impacts of a monetary contraction are
    (a) an elimination of the short-run recessionary gap.
    (b) of no effect on potential real GDP.
    (c) lower factor prices.
    (d) a lower equilibrium price level.
    (e) All of the above.

23. Monetary policy can eliminate a short-run inflationary gap by
    (a) raising interest rates, reducing investment, and increasing aggregate expenditure.
    (b) lowering interest rates, increasing investment, and increasing aggregate expenditure.
    (c) raising interest rates, reducing investment, and moving upward along the *AD* curve.
    (d) raising interest rates, reducing investment, and shifting the *AD* curve.
    (e) increasing the exchange rate.

24. A given change in the money supply will exert a larger effect on real national income in the short run
    (a) the flatter the *LP* curve and the steeper the I^D curve.
    (b) the flatter both the *LP* and I^D curves are.
    (c) the steeper both the *LP* and I^D curves are.
    (d) the steeper the *LP* curve and the flatter the I^D curve.
    (e) if the economy operates in the steep portion of the *SRAS* curve.

25. The short-run impact of a decrease in the money supply on real national income will be high if
    (a) the economy operates in the steep portion of its *SRAS* curve.
    (b) the liquidity preference curve is horizontal.
    (c) the I^D curve is perfectly inelastic.
    (d) if international capital flows are totally insensitive to interest rate changes.
    (e) None of the above.

EXERCISES

1. If you are not convinced that interest rates and present value are negatively related, perhaps this exercise will eliminate your doubt. The present value of a bond is the market equilibrium price of the bond. Consider two bonds, A and B. Bond A promises to pay $120 one year hence, and bond B promises to pay $120 two years from now.

(a) Calculate the present value for bond A when the interest rate is 8 percent. Calculate the present value for interest rates of 10 percent, 20 percent, and 25 percent. What happened to the market price when interest rates rose?

(b) If you were told that the market price (present value) of bond A increased, what would you conclude is happening to the interest rate on bond A?

(c) Calculate the present value for bond B for interest rates of 10 percent, 20 percent, and 25 percent.

(d) Which of the two bonds had the larger percentage change in its price when the interest rate rose from 10 to 20 percent?

(e) If the current rate of interest on both bonds were 20 percent, which bond would currently be selling for the higher market price? Why?

(f) An individual who insists on receiving a 14 percent return on all assets would be prepared to pay what market price for bond A? For bond B?

2. Suppose that a household is paid $1,000 at the beginning of each month. The household spends all of its income on the purchase of goods and services each month. Furthermore, assume that these purchases are made at a constant rate throughout the month. Consequently, payments and receipts are not perfectly synchronized.

(a) What is the value of currency holdings at the beginning of the month? At the end of the first week? At the end of the third week? At the end of the month?

(b) What is the magnitude of the *average* currency holdings over the month?

(c) Suppose that the household's income increases to $1,200 and purchases of goods and services during a month are equal to this amount. What is the *average* currency holding?

(d) Suppose that the household is paid $1,000 over the month but in instalments of $500 at the beginning of the month and $500 at the beginning of the third week. What is the magnitude of the *average* currency holdings per month?

3. Two liquidity preference curves are illustrated in Figure 27-1.

Figure 27-1

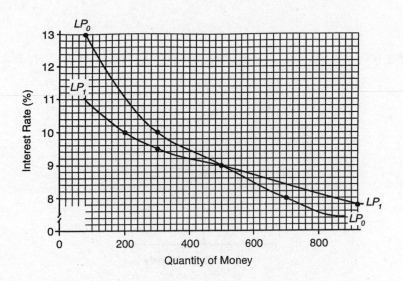

(a) Using your knowledge of the transactions and speculative motives for money, explain why the quantity of money demanded falls when interest rates rise.

(b) If the money supply is 500 and constant at all levels of interest rates, what interest rate is associated with monetary equilibrium? Plot the supply of money function in the graph, and indicate the monetary equilibrium interest rate.

(c) Suppose that the monetary authority decreased the money supply from 500 to 300. At an interest rate of 9 percent, what kind of situation exists in the money market? Would households and firms tend to buy or sell bonds? Explain. Predict what is likely to happen to bond prices and interest rates.

(d) As interest rates rise, what happens to the quantity of money demanded? Predict the new equilibrium level of interest rates first using LP_0 and then using LP_1.

(e) What increase in the money supply (from 500) would be necessary to achieve an equilibrium interest rate of 8 percent if LP_0 applies? If LP_1 applies?

4. (a) Explain and illustrate graphically an excess demand for money, and predict the effect on interest rates.

Figure 27-2

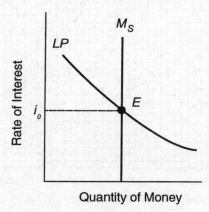

Quantity of Money

(b) Explain and illustrate graphically an excess supply of money, and predict the effect on interest rates.

Figure 27-3

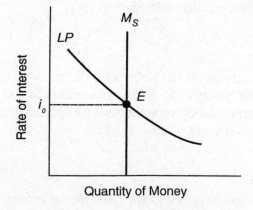

Quantity of Money

(c) Predict the effect of an increase in the money supply by the Bank of Canada on the rate of interest and desired investment expenditure. Initial equilibrium is MS_0, i_0, P_0, and I_0.

Figure 27-4

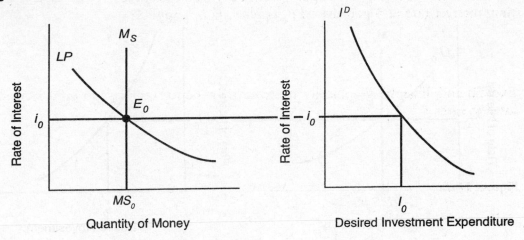

(d) Assuming a constant price of P_0, show the effect of an increase in desired expenditure on the equilibrium level of real national income. Initial equilibrium is E_0 in both graphs.

Figure 27-5

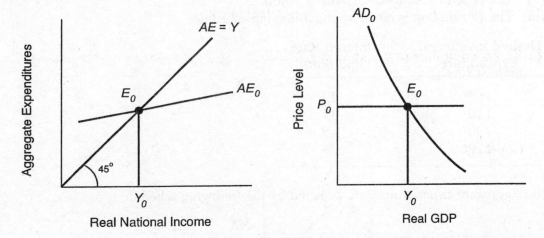

(e) Show the effect of an increase in the price level, other things being equal, on the rate of interest and investment expenditure in Figure 27-6. Start from equilibrium at E_0, i_0, and I_0, and assume that the supply of money remains constant.

Figure 27-6

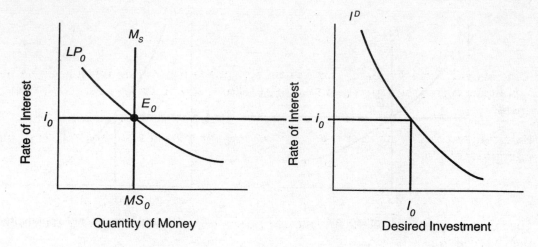

5. Suppose that the economy is currently experiencing unemployment. The central bank considers potential (full-employment) national income to be the policy objective. The economy's liquidity preference curve is that labelled LP_0 in exercise 3, and the current money supply is 500. Other information about the economy is described in points (i) through (vii).

(i)   The marginal propensity to spend is 0.50.
(ii) The potential national income is 1,600.
(iii) The I^D function is given by the following schedule:

Desired Investment Expenditure	Interest Rate (percent)
160	13
180	11
200	9
210	8

(iv) Aggregate expenditures are depicted by the following schedule:

Y	C	I	G	NX	AE
1,520	912	200	300	138	1,550
1,540	924	200	300	136	1,560
1,560	936	200	300	134	1,570
1,580	948	200	300	132	1,580
1,600	960	200	300	130	1,590

(v)   The LP curve is not influenced by changes in the level of national income.
(vi) The SRAS curve is horizontal at a price level of 2.0 for all levels of national income less than potential national income (1,600), at which level it becomes vertical.
(vii) International capital flows are totally insensitive to interest rate changes.

(a) Explain the relevance of assumptions (v) to (vii).

The central bank sets its research department to work in order to establish accurate information about the current situation and to suggest what it should do in order to eliminate unemployment.

(b) Referring to the LP_0 curve in exercise 3, what is the current equilibrium level of the interest rate?

(c) Given the interest rate, what is the level of desired investment expenditure according to the I^D schedule?

(d) What is the current equilibrium value of real national income? What is the value of the output gap?

(e) What is the value of the simple multiplier? What change in autonomous expenditure is required for the economy to achieve the potential national income level without creating any price increases?

Based on the information in (a) through (e), the research department is in a position to recommend policy changes for the central bank.

(f) Should the money supply be increased or decreased? Should the interest rate be increased or decreased?

(g) Changes in the money supply and the interest rate will change the level of investment. How much must investment be increased from its current level in order to achieve potential national income?

(h) To achieve this higher level of investment, what is the required level of the interest rate? (Refer to the I^D schedule.)

(i) Given the required level of the interest rate, what must the money supply be in order to achieve equilibrium in the money market at that interest rate? Refer to the LP_0 curve in exercise 3. What change in the current money supply is necessary?

Now suppose that the central bank is successful in lowering the interest rate and increasing investment by the appropriate magnitudes. It follows that real national income should increase by a multiple and attain a level of 1,600.

(j) Calculate the new level of consumption expenditure and calculate the aggregate level of expenditure at $Y = 1,600$. Is this an equilibrium situation?

6. *"Failures of the Transmission Mechanism"*

Question 5 was based upon many assumptions that affect the strength of the transmission mechanism to eliminate gap situations. We review some of them in separate cases in this question.

(a) Suppose that the liquidity preference curve was flat at an interest rate of 9 percent instead of that portrayed in exercise 3. What are the implications for the transmission mechanism's ability to eliminate the recessionary gap of 20?

(b) Now suppose that the LP_0 curve in question 3 holds, but that the I^D schedule [assumption (iii)] changes to one that indicates that investment expenditure remains at 200 regardless of the interest rate. Explain what this means and comment on the effectiveness of a monetary expansion to eliminate the recessionary gap of 20.

(c) Let's change assumption (vii). Suppose that lower interest rates created by the monetary expansion cause higher capital outflows. The exchange rate will appreciate (and the external value of the domestic currency will fall). Will this help or hinder the effectiveness of the transmission mechanism?

EXTENSION EXERCISE

E1. Read the appendix before attempting this exercise. The question focuses on the shape of the aggregate demand curve and the transmission mechanism. The following two tables show the effects of changes in the price level on desired investment.

LP Schedule

	Quantity of Money Demanded	
Interest Rate	P = 1	P = 2
4	80	100
6	70	90
8	60	80
10	50	70
12	40	60
14	30	50

I^D Schedule

Rate of Interest	Desired Investment Expenditure
10	180
11	179
12	177
13	174
14	170

Assume that the nominal supply of money is fixed at a value of 50.

(a) Assuming that the price level is 1.0, what is the equilibrium interest rate? What is the desired investment expenditure?

(b) Assume that the price level becomes 2.0. For a given level of real national income, what will happen to the demand for money? What will happen in the bond market? Explain.

(c) Using the LP schedule for P = 2, determine the new equilibrium interest rate.

(d) Given this change in the interest rate, what is the new level of desired investment expenditure?

The following table shows the effects of changes in desired investment (I) on real national income (Y).

Y	C	I ($i=10\%$)	AE ($i=10\%$)	AE ($i=14\%$)
340	170	180	350	_____
350	175	180	355	_____
360	180	180	360	_____
370	185	180	365	_____

(e) What is the equilibrium level of real national income (Y) associated with an interest rate of 10 percent and a price level of 1.0?

(f) The interest rate increase, because of a doubling of the price level, resulted in lower desired investment (from 180 to 170). Fill in the values for the new level of aggregate expenditure. What is the new equilibrium level of Y?

Now we synthesize the relationship between P and Y.

(g) Graph the AD curve in Figure 27-7, plotting the negative relationship between P and Y for this exercise. Use your answers to (e) and (f).

Figure 27-7

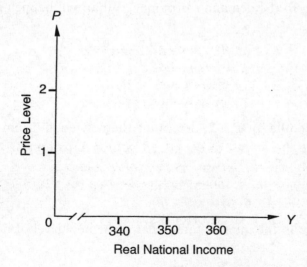

PRACTICE MULTIPLE CHOICE TEST

To answer questions 1 to 5, use Table 15.1 in the *Study Guide*.

1. A bond that promises to pay $100 one year from now and that has a constant annual interest rate of 5%, has a present value of
   (a) $105.   (b) $98.
   (c) $94.30.   (d) $78.40.
   (e) $95.20.

2. A bond that promises to pay $100 three years from now and that has a constant annual interest rate of 2 percent, has a current market value of
   (a) $98.   (b) $94.20.
   (c) $96.10.   (d) $97.10.
   (e) $288.40.

3. A perpetuity that pays $100 a year and has an annual interest rate of 15 percent, has a market value of
   (a) $115.   (b) $86.96.
   (c) $666.67.   (d) $15.
   (e) $100.

4. An asset that pays $100 after one year and $100 after two years and that has an annual interest rate of 10 percent, has a present value of
   (a) $200.   (b) $181.80.
   (c) $220.   (d) $173.50.
   (e) $77.20.

5. A bond that pays $100 three years from now and that currently sells for $88.90, has a annual interest rate of
   (a) about 13 percent.   (b) 12.5 percent.
   (c) 11.1 percent.   (d) 4 percent.
   (e) about 6 percent.

6. With a given stock of wealth, if bond holders attempt to sell bonds in order to increase their money holdings, then we would expect
   (a) the price of bonds and rate of return on them to increase.
   (b) the price of bonds and the interest rate to fall.
   (c) the price of bonds to fall and the interest rate to rise.
   (d) the price of bonds to rise and the interest rate to fall.
   (e) the exchange rate to appreciate.

7. With a constant money supply, a shift to the left of the *LP* function will cause
   (a) lower bond prices as money holders try to buy more bonds.
   (b) a reduction in the interest rate as money holders bid up the prices of bonds.
   (c) a reduction in bond prices as interest rates rise.
   (d) an increase in bond prices as interest rates rise.
   (e) real GDP to fall.

8. The *LP* function will shift down and to the left if
   (a) interest rates fall.
   (b) the money supply increases.
   (c) the money supply decreases.

(d) real GDP rises.

(e) the price level falls.

9. A steep *LP* curve

(a) reflects the fact that money holders are extremely responsive to interest rate changes.

(b) is consistent with the views of Keynesian economists.

(c) leads to very large changes in the interest rate when the money supply changes.

(d) reflects the fact that investment expenditures are extremely unresponsive to interest rate changes.

(e) would lead to a very small change in short-run real GDP if the money supply increased.

Questions 10 through 14 refer to Figure 27-8. An initial equilibrium at point *a* is changed by an increase in the money supply. The new short-run equilibrium is shown by point *b*.

Figure 27-8

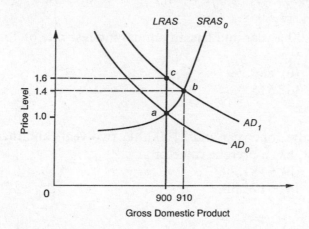

10. Point *b* represents

(a) an inflationary gap of 10, but constant factor prices.

(b) a recessionary gap of 10, but higher unit costs.

(c) a negative output gap of 10, but higher factor costs.

(d) long-run equilibrium, since input prices will never change.

(e) higher factor prices than at point *a*.

11. An increase in the money supply shifted the *AD* curve to the right because

(a) an excess demand for money was created in the money market; thus interest rates and investment expenditure will both increase.

(b) consumption expenditure increased as real GDP increased.

(c) real wealth decreased.

(d) a decline in interest rates stimulated more investment expenditures.

(e) the exchange rate depreciated.

12. An increase in the money supply is also likely to shift the *AD* curve to the right because

(a) lower interest rates lead to larger capital inflows and a depreciated exchange rate

(b) higher interest rates lead to lower net exports.

(c) an appreciation of the domestic currency and higher net exports.

(d) lower interest rates lead to higher capital outflows, an appreciated exchange rate, and increased net exports.

(e) None of the above are correct.

13. The gap situation depicted at point *b* is likely to cause further longer-term adjustments. Specifically, we would expect
    (a) factor prices to rise.
    (b) the *SRAS* curve to begin shifting leftward.
    (c) the price level to increase beyond 1.4.
    (d) a movement upward along AD_1.
    (e) All of the above.

14. As long as factor prices change completely to offset the price change, the long-run impact of the monetary expansion will be
    (a) at point *b*, since real wages do not change.
    (b) increases in both real GDP and the price level.
    (c) a price level of 1.6 and GDP of 900, or point *c*.
    (d) at point *a*, since price increases causes the *AD* curve to shift leftward to its initial position.
    (e) higher real and nominal GDP.

SOLUTIONS

Chapter Review

1. (a) 2. (e) 3. (a) 4. (b) 5. (a) 6. (b) 7. (b) 8. (a) 9. (a) 10. (d) 11. (d) 12. (c) 13. (e) 14. (c) 15. (b) 16. (c) 17. (e) 18. (d) 19. (e) 20. (c) 21. (e) 22. (e) 23. (c) 24. (d) 25.(e)

Exercises

1. (a) PV at 8 percent is $120/(1.08) = $111.11.
        PV at 10 percent is $120/(1.10) = $109.09.
        PV at 20 percent is $120/(1.20) = $100.00.
        PV at 25 percent is $120/(1.25) = $96.00.
        As the interest rate increased, the market price (present value) of bond A fell.
    (b) Other things being equal, the interest rate must have fallen.
    (c) PV at 10 percent is $120/(1.10)^2 = $99.17.
        PV at 20 percent is $120/(1.20)^2 = $83.33.
        PV at 25 percent is $120/(1.25)^2 = $76.80.
    (d) The price of bond A fell from $109.09 to $100.00, a 8.3 percent decrease. Bond B, having a longer maturity period, had a 16.0 percent decline in its price.
    (e) Bond A has the higher market price (compare $100.00 with $83.33). The further in the future that dollars are received, the lower the present value of those dollars, other things being equal. For bond A, $120 was received one year from now, whereas bond B paid $120 two years from now.
    (f) The person should be prepared to pay $105.26 for bond A, $92.34 for B.

2. (a) $1,000, $750, $250, $0.
    (b) $1,000/2 = $500.
    (c) $1,200/2 = $600.
    (d) $500/2 = $250.

3. (a) As the opportunity cost of money rises, people will tend to economize on their transactions demand for money. In addition, they are prepared to take more risk (and therefore buy more bonds) since the return on bonds has risen.

(b) Demand (either LP_1 or LP_0) equals supply at 9 percent. The supply of money curve is a vertical line at 500.

(c) At an interest rate of 9 percent, an excess demand for money exists. Households and firms would sell bonds to satisfy their excess demand for money. Hence bond prices would fall and interest rates would rise.

(d) As interest rates rise, the quantity demanded falls until demand equals the lower value of the money supply. Interest rates would equal 10.0 percent for LP_0 and 9.5 percent for LP_1.

(e) If LP_0 applies, the money supply must be 700. If LP_1 applies, the money supply must be 900.

4. (a) Excess demand for money at i; interest rates should rise to equilibrium at i_0 and E as individuals sell bonds, thereby driving down the price of bonds and raising the interest rate.

Figure 27-9

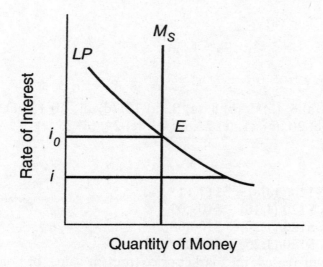

(b) Excess supply of money at i; interest rates should fall to equilibrium at i_0 and E as individuals buy bonds, thereby increasing bond prices and lowering the interest rate.

Figure 27-10

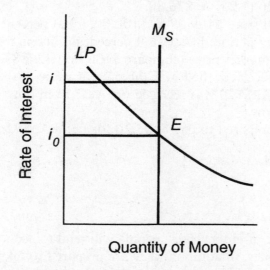

(c) Interest rate drops from i_0 to i_1; investment expenditures rise from I_0 to I_1.

Figure 27-11

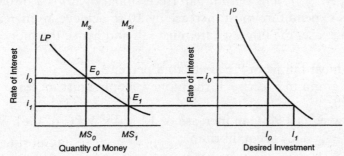

(d) Upward shift in *AE* caused by more desired investment expenditure, also shifting *AD* outward; equilibrium income rises from Y_0 to Y_1.

Figure 27-12

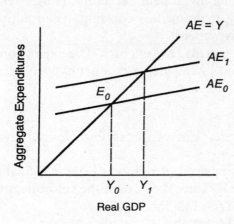
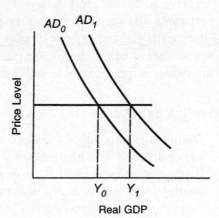

(e) An increase in the price level increases the nominal demand for money (for transactions purposes primarily) from LP_0 to LP_1; this raises interest rates from i_0 to i_1 and lowers investment from I_0 to I_1.

Figure 27-13

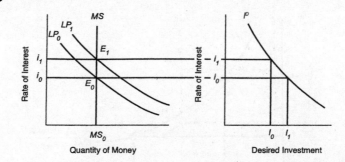

5. (a) Assumption (v) rules out an increase in the interest rate created by an increase in the demand for money because of a higher real GDP level. Assumption (vi) eliminates price level increases until potential real GDP has been reached. Hence, net exports are not affected and the *LP* curve does not shift since the price level is constant. Assumption (vii) rules out changes in net exports because of exchange rate changes. The exchange rate will not change if international capital flows are not affected.

(b) 9 percent, at which demand is equal to supply.

(c) 200.

(d) When $Y = 1,580$, $AE = Y$. The output gap (recessionary gap) is $1,580 - 1,600 = -20$.

(e) 2.0. Autonomous expenditure must increase by 10 to achieve an increase in Y of 20.

(f) Since AE must increase, the interest rate must fall and hence the money supply must rise.

(g) 10.

(h) The interest rate must fall from 9 percent to 8 percent.

(i) According to the graph in exercise 3, the money supply must increase from 500 to 700, an increase of 200.

(j) Consumption now equals 960, an increase of 12 ($20 \times MPC$ of 0.6). When $Y = 1,600$, $C = 960$ and $AE = Y$. This is equilibrium.

6. (a) The monetary transmission is totally ineffective since any change in the money supply has no effect on the interest rate. Since investment is not affected, the multiplier process does not come into play.

(b) The I^D is perfectly inelastic with respect to the interest rate. Presumably firms are not at all sensitive to the interest rate when making investment decisions. Thus, even though interest rates change with monetary policy, investment is constant. The multiplier process will not occur (including any change in investment).

(c) An appreciation of the exchange rate will increase net exports. The expansionary effects of the money supply increase will be helped by the increase in net exports.

Extension Exercise

E1. (a) Demand equals supply (50) at an interest rate of 10 percent. Desired investment expenditure is therefore 180.

(b) If price increases, the LP curve shifts upward or rightward (the nominal demand for money increases at every interest rate). Hence, bonds will be sold thereby lowering their price. As a consequence, the interest rate increases.

(c) The new equilibrium interest rate is 14 percent.

(d) The new level of investment is 170 for all levels of Y.

(e) $Y = AE$ at 360 (10 percent interest rate and $P = 1.0$).

(f) AE: 340, 345, 350, 355. The new equilibrium level of national income is 340.

(g) See Figure 27-14.

Figure 27-14

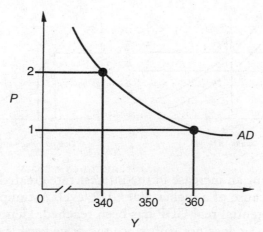

Practice Multiple Choice Test

1. (e) 2. (b) 3. (c) 4. (d) 5. (d) 6. (c) 7. (b) 8. (e) 9. (c) 10. (a) 11. (d) 12. (d) 13. (e) 14. (c)

CHAPTER 28

MONETARY POLICY IN CANADA

LEARNING OBJECTIVES

1 Explain the two methods by which the Bank of Canada changes the money supply.

2 Understand the difference between the Bank's policy variables and its policy instruments.

3 Recognize why the Bank of Canada cannot target the money supply and the interest rate independently.

4 Explain why monetary policy affects real GDP and the price level only after long lags.

5 Have a basic understanding of the main challenges that the Bank of Canada has faced over the past two decades.

CHAPTER OVERVIEW

This chapter concerns the policy instruments of monetary policy by the Bank of Canada that influence key macroeconomic variables and hence attempt to achieve certain **policy variables** (such as real national income and the price level). Certain **intermediate targets** (the money supply, the interest rate, and the **Monetary Conditions Index**) help guide the Bank when implementing monetary policy in the short run.

The Bank of Canada controls the supply of money by influencing the reserves of the commercial banks. Two **policy instruments** used by the Bank of Canada are **open-market operations** and **transfers of government deposits** between itself and the chartered banks. Purchases of bonds on the open market by the Bank of Canada or switching government deposits to the banks increase the reserves of the banking system. These policy stances increase the money supply, reduce interest rates, and shift the aggregate demand curve to the right.

The transmission mechanism may take a long time to influence policy variables such as real income and the price level. Changes in reserves are more-or-less immediate, but deposit creation (destruction), switching between assets, changes in investment plans, and the multiplier process all take time. Moreover, **shifts in the demand for money function** may counteract or thwart monetary policy. Hence, some economists believe that monetary policy involves long and **variable lags,** and its outcomes may be uncertain.

The chapter concludes by outlining 20 years of monetary policy in Canada. The appendix to the chapter discusses the relationship between the stock market and macroeconomic developments.

CHAPTER REVIEW

The Bank of Canada and the Money Supply

The two policy instruments of the Bank of Canada affect the money supply by influencing the reserve positions of banks. The following table which describes the appropriate policy stances by the Bank of Canada when dealing with different phases of the business cycle may be a helpful guide for you.

	Contraction of the Money Supply	Expansion in the Money Supply
Needed change in bank reserves	decrease	increase
Open market operations by the Bank of Canada	sell bonds to the public and the banks	buy bonds from the public and the banks
Switching government deposits	switch government deposits out of the banks	switch government deposits to the banks
Economic situation	inflationary gap	recessionary gap

When commercial banks find it necessary to borrow funds temporarily from the Bank of Canada, they are charged an interest rate on their loan. The **bank rate** is the interest rate at which the Bank of Canada lends to the commercial banks. You should read Applying Economic Concepts 28-1 to learn how the bank rate is related to the overnight rate.

1. Open-market operations are:
   (a) purchases and sales by the Bank of Canada of government securities in financial markets.
   (b) purchases and sales among the commercial banks of securities in financial markets.
   (c) sales of government securities by chartered banks to their customers.
   (d) total purchases and sales of government securities in the bond market.
   (e) switching government deposits between the banks and the Bank of Canada.

2. Which one of the following is *not* a policy instrument of the Bank of Canada?
   (a) Raising the tax rate on interest income received from government bonds.
   (b) Buying bonds from the commercial banks.
   (c) Switching government deposits between itself and the banking system.
   (d) Sale of bonds to the commercial banks.
   (e) Changes in the bank rate by influencing the level or range of the "overnight" rate.

3. If the Bank of Canada purchases bonds in the open market,
   (a) bank reserves will be reduced.
   (b) bank reserves will be increased.
   (c) the money supply will fall by a maximum of $1/v$ times the value of the purchase (v is the reserve ratio).
   (d) interest rates are likely to rise.
   (e) bond prices are likely to fall.

4. If the Bank of Canada sold $10 million of securities to the public in the open market,
   (a) reserves and securities in banks would each rise by $10 million.
   (b) deposits and reserves of banks would initially fall by $10 million.
   (c) the money supply would eventually increase by $1/v$ times the value of the sale (v is the reserve ratio).
   (d) deposits in the banking system would initially rise by $10 million.
   (e) the price of bonds would rise.

5. If the Bank of Canada purchases bonds in the open market, it is likely that
   (a) the price of bonds would fall and the interest rate would rise.
   (b) both the price of bonds and the interest rate would rise.
   (c) both the price of bonds and the interest rate would fall.
   (d) the price of bonds would rise and the interest rate would fall.
   (e) reserves in the banks would fall.

6. To eliminate an inflationary gap, the Bank of Canada might
   (a) sell bonds in the open market.
   (b) purchase bonds in the open market.
   (c) transfer government deposits into the banking system.
   (d) increase the monetary base.
   (e) lower the bank rate.

7. The bank rate is defined as the interest rate
   (a) charged on preferred-customer loans by a bank.
   (b) charged by banks for overdrafts of large corporations.
   (c) on credit card accounts.
   (d) on three-month treasury bills.
   (e) at which the Bank of Canada makes loans (advances) to the banks.

8. If the Bank of Canada transfers $10 million of government deposits from the banking system to itself,
   (a) reserves and government deposits in the banking system will increase by $10 million.
   (b) reserves and government deposits in the Bank will increase by $10 million.
   (c) reserves of the banks will fall by $10 million and government deposits in the Bank will increase by $10 million.
   (d) the money supply is likely to increase by $1/v$ times the amount of the transfer.
   (e) it is a signal to the financial system that the Bank is attempting to increase nominal national income.

9. Which of the following statements is *not* true in Canada?
   (a) A bank that has deficit reserves will borrow either from the Bank of Canada or from another institution.
   (b) An increase in the bank rate induces the commercial banks to hold more reserves in view of the higher cost of borrowing.
   (c) The Bank of Canada's assets include government securities.
   (d) The value of the exchange rate is excluded from the Monetary Conditions Index.
   (e) The Bank of Canada manages some government accounts in the banks.

10. If the Bank of Canada purchases government bonds in the open market,
   (a) an excess supply of money balances is created, higher bond prices will prevail, and aggregate expenditure will be higher than before.
   (b) an excess demand for money balances is created, higher bond prices will prevail, and aggregate expenditure will be lower than before.
   (c) an excess supply of money balances is created, lower bond prices will prevail, and aggregate expenditure will be lower than before.
   (d) an excess demand for money balances is created, lower bond prices will prevail, and aggregate expenditure will be higher than before.
   (e) None of the above.

11. If the Bank of Canada sells government bonds in the open market,
   (a) the aggregate demand curve will shift to the right.
   (b) the aggregate demand curve will shift to the left.
   (c) the aggregate expenditure curve will shift upward and to the left.
   (d) there will be a movement down the investment demand curve.
   (e) real GDP is likely to increase in the short run.

Policy Variables and Policy Instruments

Policy variables are real GDP and the price level. It is impossible for the Bank of Canada to set separate short-run targets simultaneously for the two policy variables. However, in the long run, the Bank of Canada can influence the price level which is associated with potential real GDP.

The Bank of Canada has typically used intermediate targets to guide it when implementing monetary policy in the very short run. The two most commonly used intermediate targets have been the money supply and the interest rate. It is critical that you understand that these two macroeconomic variables are not independent of each other. Thus, the central bank cannot use its instruments to influence both the interest rate and the money supply independently. The instability of the demand for money implies that the stance of monetary policy cannot be judged by money supply targets.

Change in the exchange rate can signal the need for changes in the stance of monetary policy. But care must be taken to identify the cause of the exchange-rate change. After reading Applying Economic Concept 28-2, you will understand the role of the exchange rate in influencing the **Monetary Conditions Index** (MCI) which is another intermediate target used by the Bank of Canada.

12. Which of the following has been considered an intermediate target by the Bank of Canada?
   (a) The interest rate.
   (b) Nominal GDP.
   (c) The price level.
   (d) Real GDP.
   (e) The inflation rate.

13. Which of the following events could explain an increase in the interest rate?
    (a) The Bank of Canada sells bonds in the open market.
    (b) The Bank of Canada transfers government deposits from the commercial banks to itself.
    (c) The *LP* curve shifts to the right.
    (d) All of the above.
    (e) None of the above.

14. An intermediate target of M1 control was found to be faulty because
    (a) the demand for M1 by the public was very stable.
    (b) the public rarely substituted between chequing deposits and savings deposits.
    (c) changes in M1 never affected the interest rate.
    (d) the public and firms found it relatively easy to switch between M1 and other forms of money such as savings deposits.
    (e) the demand for M1 depended only on interest rates and not real GDP.

15. When would it be appropriate for the Bank of Canada to use contractionary monetary policy?
    (a) During a recessionary gap.
    (b) When the Canadian dollar has appreciated because of a net export boom.
    (c) To prevent the Canadian dollar from appreciating because of an increase in the demand for Canadian assets.
    (d) To prevent the Canadian dollar from depreciating because of a decline in export sales.
    (e) If the Bank deems it desirable for the Canadian dollar to depreciate.

16. Which of the following is not a component of the Bank's Monetary Conditions Index?
    (a) The value of M1.
    (b) The value of short-term interest rates in a base year.
    (c) The value of the exchange rate.
    (d) The value of the exchange rate in a base year.
    (e) The value of short-term interest rates.

Lags in the Conduct of Monetary Policy

The role of lags in adjustment in the real sector to monetary shocks is a key component of the debate between Keynesians and Monetarists. Monetary policy used for stabilization purposes actually can be destabilizing if there are long and variable lags in adjustment. The text explains that changes to macroeconomic variables triggered by changes in the money supply potentially do not occur immediately because of the presence of execution lags.

17. An important implication of long and variable execution lags associated with monetary policy is that
    (a) national income can be easily fine-tuned with open-market operations.
    (b) monetary policy is never capable of eliminating an inflationary gap.
    (c) discretionary monetary policy may prove to be destabilizing.
    (d) a stable monetary rule, regardless of demand instability, guarantees monetary stability.
    (e) monetary policy does not have short-run effects on nominal GDP.

18. Which of the following is not an example of an execution lag?
    (a) The time interval between changes in bank reserves and the multiple impact on the money supply.
    (b) The time period during which business firms react to changes in interest rates with respect to investment intentions.
    (c) The time elapse between the Bank of Canada's diagnosis of the problem and its implementation of appropriate policy instruments.
    (d) The time taken for the full multiplier effect to affect real GDP.
    (e) Both (a) and (d).

20 Years of Canadian Monetary Policy

The section outlines the stances of the Bank of Canada and the underlying economic circumstances for the Bank's actions during various time intervals in the 1980s and 1990s. A key aspect for you to consider is the differences in the Bank's policies that were essentially short-term stabilization stances versus those that were focused on long-run price stability targets.

19. Which of the following did *not* occur in Canada during 1987–1990?
    (a) The inflation rate decreased.
    (b) The Bank of Canada's policy stressed long-term price stability.
    (c) The differential between Canadian and U.S. interest rates increased.
    (d) The Canadian dollar appreciated.
    (e) A "tight money" policy was pursued by the Bank of Canada.

20. The Asian Crisis beginning in 1997 produced a complicated combination of forces on the Canadian economy including
    (a) a positive *AD* effect from the increase in the demand for Canadian raw materials exports to Thailand and South Korea.
    (b) a positive *SRAS* effect from the lower-price inputs for Canadian manufacturing firms.
    (c) a negative *AD* effect from the decrease in the U.S. demand for Canadian goods.
    (d) an overall inflationary gap which caused an acceleration in the Canadian inflation rate.
    (e) a major increase in unemployment.

EXERCISES

1. Suppose that each bank in the banking system has achieved its target reserve position. Now the Bank of Canada transfers a total of $300 million of government deposits from the banking system to itself.

   (a) Show the effect of this transaction in the following balance sheets. Use + for an increase and – for a decrease.

Bank of Canada		Banking System	
	Government Deposits: Bank Reserves:	Reserves:	Government Deposits:

(b) Is the policy designed to combat a recessionary or an inflationary gap situation? Explain.

(c) If the target reserve ratio is 5 percent, what is the possible *final* change in the money supply? What would be the final change in the money supply if the target reserve ratio is 5 percent and the cash drain is 5 percent?

(d) Discuss the factors that determine the time it takes for the change in the money supply to eliminate the output gap problem.

2. Use Figure 28-1 to illustrate the effects of the following Bank of Canada monetary policies, and answer the questions.

Figure 28-1

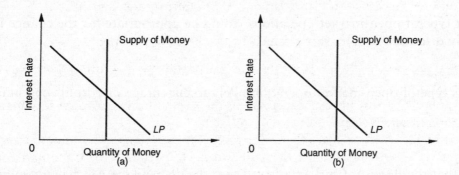

(a) Use graph (a) for this question. The Bank of Canada sells government securities.
Total reserves will (increase, decrease).
The money supply curve should shift to the _____.
This policy is (expansionary, contractionary).
The quantity of money demanded will (increase, decrease).
Interest rates will tend to _____.

(b) Use graph (b) for this question. The Bank of Canada transfers government deposits into the banks.
Excess reserves will initially (increase, decrease).
The money supply curve should shift to the _____.
This policy is (expansionary, contractionary).
The quantity of money demanded will (increase, decrease).
Interest rates will tend to _____.

(c) Use graph (a) for this question. The demand for money (*LP*) curve shifts farther to the left than the supply of money curve does.
Interest rates will tend to _____.
Investment expenditure will tend to _____.
National income will tend to _____.

3. Suppose that the demand for money (liquidity preference) function was $D_M = 300 - 20i$, where D_M is the quantity of money demanded and i is the rate of interest in percentage terms. The supply of money is 100.

    (a) What is the equilibrium value for the interest rate?

    (b) Suppose, because of expansion in the economy, that the demand curve for money becomes $D_M = 400 - 20i$, but the supply of money remains at 100. If the interest remained at 10 percent, what situation exists in the money market? What is likely to happen to the equilibrium level of the interest rate in the future? Be specific.

    (c) Given the circumstances described in (b) and assuming that the Bank of Canada was determined to maintain an interest-rate target of 10 percent, what change in the money supply would be required? Be specific.

    (d) What type of open-market operations would be appropriate for the change in the money supply discussed in (c)?

    (e) Is this type of open-market operation likely to encourage or curtail economic expansion?

4. Suppose that the Bank of Canada believed that the demand for M1 balances was given by the expression DM1 = 300 − 20i. Its previously announced money supply target was 200.

    (a) Assuming that Bank's view of the demand for M1 were correct, what would be the equilibrium interest rate?

    (b) Now, the Bank reduces its monetary base target from M1 = 200 to M1 = 150, but the interest rate does not change. Explain what may have happened.

    (c) Was the change in the policy stance of the Bank consistent with fighting high unemployment or high inflation? Comment on the effectiveness of the Bank's policy in terms of what actually occurred in the money and bond markets.

5. Suppose that you are an advisor to the Governor of the central bank of the country of Montand. The Governor has committed the Bank of Montand to a policy of zero inflation. The situation in the recent past is depicted by point *a* in Figure 28-2. Now, quite unexpectedly real national income and the price level rise to point *b*. Your research indicates that this situation is likely to prevail for some time. The Governor asks you to outline some of the policy options open to her.

Figure 28-2

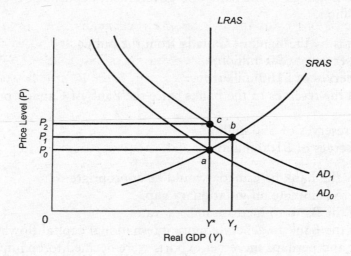

(a) **Policy Option I:** Reverse the trend and get the economy back to point *a*. What policy recommendations would you make? What reservations might you express to the Governor?

(b) **Policy Option II:** No central bank intervention. What arguments would you make to support this stance? If this "policy" is pursued, what reservations would you express to the Governor?

PRACTICE MULTIPLE CHOICE TEST

Answer questions 1 to 6 by assuming that the Bank of Canada decides to purchase $100 million of government securities from the non-commercial bank public. Assume that the public hold their all money balances in deposits, and that the target reserve ratio for all banks is 0.10.

1. The initial impact of this policy stance on the Bank of Canada's balance sheet will be recorded by
   (a) government deposits and bank reserves increasing both by $100 million.
   (b) only bond holdings by the Bank increasing by $100 million.
   (c) commercial bank reserves in the Bank of Canada and security holdings by the Bank increasing both by $100 million.
   (d) deposits of the public in the Bank of Canada and bond holdings by the Bank of Canada increasing both by $100 million.
   (e) only deposits of the public in the Bank of Canada increasing by $100 million.

2. The initial impact of this policy stance on the commercial banks' balance sheets will be
   (a) bond holdings of the banks and deposits of the public will increase both by $100 million.
   (b) increases in the deposits of the public in banks and the reserves of the banks both by $100 million.
   (c) deposits of the public in banks and bank reserves will decrease both by $100 million.
   (d) only an increase in banks' reserves by $100 million.
   (e) increases in bond holdings of the bank and government deposits at the commercial banks both by $100 million.

3. The purchase of bonds by the Bank of Canada from the public
   (a) creates excess reserves of $90 million.
   (b) creates deficit reserves of $100 million.
   (c) has no effects on the reserves of the banks since the Bank of Canada purchased bonds from the public.
   (d) creates deficient reserves of $90 million.
   (e) creates excess reserves of $100 million.

4. This policy stance by the Bank of Canada would be appropriate if
   (a) the Bank wishes to eliminate an inflationary gap.
   (b) it is the intent of the Bank to increase interest rates.
   (c) it is the intent of the Bank to generate more international capital flows into Canada.
   (d) more investment and perhaps more net exports were deemed to be important for increased economic activity.
   (e) Both (a) and (b) are correct.

5. If the target reserve ratio is 10 percent and there is no cash drain, the final change in deposits in the banking system generated by this policy change will be
   (a) +$100 million.   (b) −$110 million.
   (c) −$110 million.   (d) +$1 billion.
   (e) −$1 billion.

6. If the money supply did change by a predictable amount, we would expect
   (a) an initial excess supply of money in the money market and subsequent increases in the interest rates.
   (b) an initial excess supply of money in the money market and subsequent increases in bond prices.
   (c) an initial excess demand for money in the money market and subsequent increases in bond prices.
   (d) an initial excess demand for money in the money market and subsequent reductions in the interest rate.
   (e) banks to increase interest rates on loans to the public.

Answer questions 7 through 10 by referring to Figure 28-3

Figure 28-3

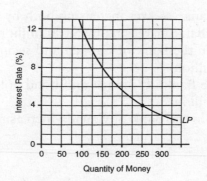

7. If the central bank chose an intermediate interest rate target of 12 percent,
   (a) both the money supply and the quantity of money demanded must be 100.
   (b) it can set the monetary base at whatever level it wishes.
   (c) a money supply of 150 would create an excess supply of bonds at an interest rate of 12 percent.
   (d) a money supply of 250 would create an equilibrium situation at 12 percent.
   (e) Both (a) and (c).

8. If the money supply were 150 and the central bank's interest rate target were 12 percent, the central bank
   (a) need do nothing since a money supply of 150 achieves its interest-rate target.
   (b) must sell bonds in the open market, thereby lowering bond prices.
   (c) will lower the bank rate to indicate its intentions to decrease the supply of money.
   (d) must increase government deposits in the banks in order to increase their reserves.
   (e) must buy bonds in the open market.

9. If the central bank set a monetary supply target of 150, then according to the *LP* (the demand for money) curve,
   (a) there would be an excess supply of money at an interest rate of 12 percent.
   (b) there would be an excess supply of bonds at an interest rate of 4 percent.
   (c) the equilibrium interest rate must be 8 percent.
   (d) All of the above.
   (e) None of the above.

10. If the central bank reduced its monetary supply target from 150 to 100,
    (a) it would have to increase its monetary base target.
    (b) the equilibrium interest rate would rise from 8 to 12 percent, provided that the *LP* (demand for money) curve did not shift.
    (c) it would have to increase the price of bonds by purchasing bonds in the bond market.
    (d) it must have agreed to assist the federal government in financing additional spending.
    (e) it should transfer government deposits from itself to the commercial banks.

Answer questions 11 through 14 by referring to Figure 28-4. The current situation is depicted at point *a*. Assume that both the *SRAS* and *LRAS* curves do not shift for the period under consideration.

Figure 28-4

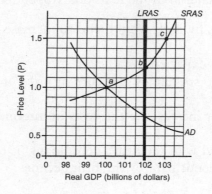

11. Which of the following combinations of policy objectives by a central bank are feasible in the short run?
    (a) A price level of 1.1 and real GDP of 100.
    (b) Potential GDP of 102 and a price level of 1.2.
    (c) Potential GDP of 102 and a price level of 1.0.
    (d) Real GDP of 99 and a price level of 1.0.
    (e) All of the above are feasible if appropriate monetary base policies were adopted.

12. Suppose that central bank policy is designed to eliminate the current output gap. Its monetary policy involves
    (a) a policy trade-off, since the elimination of the output gap is accompanied by an increase in the price level.
    (b) either an increase in its monetary base target or a decrease in its interest-rate target.
    (c) increasing the reserves of the banking system.
    (d) transferring government deposits from itself to the banks.
    (e) All of the above.

13. Information concerning the strength of the transmission mechanism indicates that every $500 million increase in the money supply increases real GDP by $1 billion. If the reserve ratio is 10 percent (and there is no cash drain), the output gap will be completely eliminated if the central bank
    (a) increases reserves in the banking system by $100 million.
    (b) increases the money supply by $500 million.
    (c) increases the reserves in the banking system by $10 billion.
    (d) increases the money supply by $2 billion.
    (e) None of the above.

14. Given the policy outlined in question 13, which of the following might explain why the economy might achieve a short-run equilibrium at point c rather than point b?
    (a) The central bank's policy is accompanied by an unexpected increase in household saving.
    (b) The government increased the tax rate to complement the central bank's policy.
    (c) The central bank's policy is accompanied by an unexpected decline in export sales.
    (d) Actual import purchases were lower than forecasted levels when the required change in the money supply was implemented.
    (e) High interest rates reduced investment expenditures more than was anticipated.

Questions 15 to 16 refer to the material in the textbook Appendix, "The Stock Market."

15. Which of the following events by itself would tend to increase the price of the stocks issued by a particular firm?
    (a) The firm's future sales are expected to fall.
    (b) A current shareholder who speculates that current price of the firm's stock is undervalued buys more.
    (c) The firm anticipates major increases in the costs of intermediate goods used to produce its product.
    (d) The interest rate associated with the firm's debt (loans) is expected to rise.
    (e) The present value of dividends paid by the firm declines.

16. In which of the following scenarios might the stock market be the cause rather than a consequence of a business cycle.
    (a) A decrease in stock prices causes consumers to permanently downsize the value of their total wealth.
    (b) A growing economy produces a "bull" stock market.
    (c) Increasing stock prices induce firms to finance additional investment by issuing more shares.
    (d) A recessionary gap causes stock prices to fall.
    (e) Both (a) and (c) are correct.

SOLUTIONS

Chapter Review

1. (a) 2. (a) 3. (b) 4. (b) 5. (d) 6. (a) 7. (e) 8. (c) 9. (d) 10. (a) 11. (b) 12. (a) 13. (d) 14. (d) 15. (b) 16. (a) 17. (c) 18. (c) 19. (a) 20. (b)

Exercises

1. (a) Bank of Canada: government deposits: + $300 million; bank reserves: –$300 million. Banking system: reserves –$300 million; government deposits: –$300 million.
   (b) Since the Bank of Canada's policy reduces reserves in the banking system, the policy is directed to decreasing economic activity, which is an anti-inflationary policy. Assuming a stable demand for money function, interest rates will rise and investment will fall.
   (c) A $6 billion reduction. This is equal to $300 million times 1/0.05, where the value 0.05 is the reserve ratio. With a cash drain of 5 percent, the decrease would be $3 billion.
   (d) A reduction in the money supply increases the interest rate. Firms would not necessarily revise their investment expenditures immediately. Moreover, when investment does decline, the effects on the induced components of aggregate expenditure may not be instantaneous; that is, the final effect of the multiplier process is achieved only after several time periods have elapsed.

2. (a) decrease; left; contractionary; decrease; rise.
   (b) increase; right; expansionary; increase; fall.
   (c) fall; increase; increase.

3. (a) Equating demand with supply, we obtain an equilibrium level of the interest rate of 10 percent.
   (b) At an interest rate of 10 percent, there would be an excess demand for money. Firms and households would sell their bonds, thereby reducing bond prices and increasing the interest rate on bonds. Equating the new demand function with the money supply, we find that the new equilibrium level of the interest rate is 15 percent.
   (c) Since an excess demand for money exists at $i = 10$ percent with the new demand for money function, it follows that the Bank of Canada must increase the money supply in order to prevent interest rates from rising. Using the function $D_M = 400 - 20i$ and the fact that i must be equal to 10 (percent), D_M must equal 200. Since the demand for money must equal the supply of money and since the demand for money with a 10 percent rate of interest is 200, it follows that the supply of money must be increased from 100 to 200, an increase of 100.

(d) The Bank of Canada should buy bonds in the open market to provide additional reserves for banks.

(e) Given the increase in the demand for money with a fixed supply of money, the resulting interest-rate increase would have reduced some investment expenditure, thereby curtailing some of the economic expansion. However, with the Bank of Canada's interest-rate target policy and the expansionary open-market operation, economic expansion would be sustained or perhaps increased.

4. (a) Equating demand to supply, the interest rate should be 5 percent.

(b) A lower monetary base target should have increased the equilibrium interest rate to 7.5 percent. If the interest rate did not change, the demand curve for M1 must have shifted leftward; i.e., the demand for M1 balances declined at every interest rate. In fact, assuming the new demand curve for M1 is parallel to the initial demand curve, the new equation must be $250 - 20i$ with a supply of 150.

(c) A reduction in the money supply and an intended increase in the interest rate are consistent with combatting inflation. Since the interest rate did not change, aggregate expenditures will not be reduced. Hence, the Bank's policy is likely to fail.

5. (a) The *AD* curve must be shifted leftward from point *b* back to point *a*. Such a change requires a contractionary monetary policy consisting of selling bonds in the open market or transferring government deposits from the commercial banks to the Bank of Montand. As a result, reserves of the commercial banks will fall. There are several reservations that you might express, but we discuss only three. First, the Governor must be warned that this policy stance involves reducing real national income. Some workers will lose their jobs and some firms will lose profits in the process. The Governor is bound to be criticized by these groups. Second, the transmission mechanism may be slow in achieving the Bank's goal. Will banks react by reducing loans; will interest rates rise; will firms and perhaps consumers downsize their expenditures; how long will the multiplier process take to reduce real national income by the value of the output gap? Third, you hope that neither the *SRAS* curve nor the *AD* curves shifts unexpectedly while the transmission mechanism is in operation. Otherwise, your recommended reduction in bank reserves may be an overkill or inadequate.

(b) Policy option II requires that the Bank of Montand does not change the nominal money supply and that private market forces eliminate the inflation gap. The inflationary gap should trigger factor price increases. Hence, the *SRAS* curve will shift upward until it reaches point *c*. Critics are sure to point out that the change in the price level is higher than before (compare $P_2 - P_0$ with $P_1 - P_0$). As real national income falls back to its potential level, the Governor must be warned to avoid the temptation to increase the nominal supply of money. Notice, that the movement from point *b* to point *c* involves rising prices and falling real output (stagflation). Critics are likely to notice the inactivity of the central bank. They may perhaps not appreciate that in time the inflationary gap will be eliminated ultimately by the reductions in real wealth, higher interest rates, and lower net exports (a movement up along AD_1).

Practice Multiple Choice Test

1. (c) 2. (b) 3. (a) 4. (d) 5. (d) 6. (b) 7. (a) 8. (b) 9. (d) 10. (b) 11. (b) 12. (e) 13. (a) 14. (d) 15. (b) 16. (e)

PART TEN

MACROECONOMIC PROBLEMS AND POLICIES

CHAPTER 29

INFLATION

LEARNING OBJECTIVES

1 Explain how wage changes are driven by both excess demand and inflationary expectations.

2 Show how constant inflation can be incorporated into the basic macroeconomic model.

3 Understand the effects of aggregate demand and supply shocks on inflation and real GDP.

4 Explain how the Bank of Canada may validate demand and supply shocks.

5 Explain the three phases of a disinflation.

6 Understand how the cost of disinflation can be measured by the sacrifice ratio.

7 Have a general understanding of Canadian inflation policy over the past two decades.

CHAPTER OVERVIEW

Inflation is triggered by a decrease in short-run aggregate supply (a negative supply shock) or an increase in aggregate demand (a demand shock). Actions by the central bank (validation) are especially important in determining whether inflation is **temporary** or **sustained**.

The *SRAS* curve shifts because of **demand conditions** (output gaps), **inflationary expectations,** and supply shocks from non-wage factor price changes. Wage rate demands can be conditioned by expected inflation, and the chapter discusses two alternative ways that expectations are formed: **backward-looking expectations** and **forward-looking expectations** (a strong version is **rational expectations**).

Inflationary shocks that are not validated by the central bank increasing the money supply tend to be self-correcting, although the time of adjustment may be long. By way of contrast, inflationary shocks that are validated can create sustained inflation. Validated inflation may also trigger expectations of sustained inflation, including **accelerating inflation**.

The process by governments, particularly the monetary authority, to eliminate **sustained inflation** is extremely difficult. There are no quick fixes. The text outlines three important phases that are required to eliminate a sustained (or entrenched) inflationary situation.

The consequences of inflation are both real and monetary. The textbook introduces a measure of the real costs of disinflation; the **sacrifice ratio**. In the short run, demand-shock inflation tends to increase real income above its potential level whereas supply-shock inflation is accompanied by a decrease in real income below its potential level. In the long run, inflation is a purely monetary phenomenon.

The chapter concludes by describing Canada's inflationary experience in the 1980s and 1990s.

CHAPTER REVIEW

Adding Inflation to the Model

Previous chapters examined how temporary inflationary periods were explained in the *AD-SRAS* framework. By introducing inflationary expectations in this chapter, the *AD-SRAS* model is able to explain the existence of sustained inflation. The expectation of some specific inflation rate creates pressure for wages to rise by that rate. Hence, the *SRAS* curve shifts up and to the left. Learn the differences between backward- and forward-looking expectations models. In order for a purely expectational inflation to continue, the central bank must be **validating** the expectations by constantly increasing the money supply.

1. When the measured unemployment rate is below the *NAIRU* rate,
   (a) current national income is less than potential national income.
   (b) there is a recessionary gap.
   (c) frictional and structural unemployment are zero.
   (d) there will be pressure for factor prices to increase.
   (e) the Phillips curve analysis predicts negative percentage changes in wage rates.

2. Expectations of inflation will influence workers' demands for money wage changes. Hence, an expectation of future inflation will cause
   (a) the *AD* curve to shift up and to the right.
   (b) the *SRAS* curve to shift down and to the right.
   (c) the *AD* curve to shift down and to the left.
   (d) an inflationary gap in which measured unemployment is less than the *NAIRU*.
   (e) a recessionary gap as the *SRAS* curve shifts up and to the left and away from potential GDP.

3. Which of the following is not a characteristic or implication of backward-looking expectations?
   (a) Backward-looking expectations tend to change slowly.
   (b) If inflation has been 5 percent for several years in the past, people will expect it to be 5 percent next year.
   (c) People revise their expectations in light of the mistakes that they made in estimating inflation in the past.
   (d) People will not continue to make persistent, systematic errors in forming expectations.
   (e) None of the above.

4. If there is no supply-shock inflation, expectations of future inflation are 1.5 percent, and excess-demand inflation is 4 percent then the predicted overall change in actual wages and prices is
   (a) 1.5 percent.
   (b) 4.0 percent.
   (c) 5.5 percent.
   (d) 2.5 percent.
   (e) 62.5 percent.

5. An inflationary process is said to be *validated* when
   (a) at least two federal government departments agree on the magnitude of price increases.
   (b) the initial cause of the inflation was an expansion of government expenditure.
   (c) the Bank of Canada maintains a constant nominal money supply during the inflationary process.
   (d) the central bank increases the money supply at such a rate that the expectations of inflation end up being correct.
   (e) the *SRAS* curve shifts leftward because of inflationary expectations.

6. A constant inflation rate is produced when
   (a) actual inflation is equal to a constant expectation of inflation.
   (b) excess-demand inflation is zero.
   (c) the economy operates at its potential level of GDP.
   (d) the central bank increases the money supply at the same rate as the expected and actual inflation rates.
   (e) All of the above are correct.

Shocks and Policy Responses

This section identifies four different inflation cases; demand shocks with and without monetary validation and supply shocks with and without monetary validation. Without validation, demand and supply shocks produce only temporary inflation. With continuing monetary validation, inflation initiated by either supply demand shocks can continue indefinitely. Hence, in the long run inflation is a monetary phenomenon.

The **acceleration hypothesis** states that when the central bank engages in whatever rate of monetary expansion is needed to hold the inflationary gap constant, the actual inflation rate will accelerate because of the development of inflationary expectations. The effects of introducing inflationary expectations into the Phillip's curve framework are discussed in Extensions to Theory, 29-1.

7. Which one of the following could not be the initiating cause of a demand shock inflation?
   (a) An increase in the prices of imported goods and services.
   (b) An increase in exports.
   (c) An increase in the supply of money.
   (d) A decrease in tax rates.
   (e) An increase in investment expenditures.

8. Which of the following does not describe the effects of a positive demand shock without monetary validation or expectational effects?
   (a) At the initial stage, Y rises above Y* and the price level increases.
   (b) When an inflationary gap is created, the *SRAS* curve shifts rightward.
   (c) As the *SRAS* curve shifts upward and to the left, Y begins to fall back to Y*.
   (d) As the *SRAS* curve shifts upward, P rises further.
   (e) In the long-run, real income will not change and the price level, although higher than before, will be stable.

9. Which of the following does not describe the effects of a positive demand shock with monetary validation but without expectational effects?
   (a) At the initial stage, Y rises above Y^* and the price level increases.
   (b) Money wages increase because of the excess-demand inflation.
   (c) As the *SRAS* curve shifts upward, the monetary authority increases the money supply to prevent real GDP from decreasing.
   (d) With monetary validation, the excess-demand inflation is maintained and hence the *SRAS* curve continues to shift upward.
   (e) In the long-run, real income is restored at Y^* and stable prices will be obtained even though monetary validation continues.

10. A negative supply-shock inflation could be caused by
    (a) a rise in the price of imported raw materials.
    (b) an increase in government purchases.
    (c) an opening up of a new source of imported materials.
    (d) a decrease in the GST and/or provincial sales tax.
    (e) an increase in the money supply.

11. Which of the following does not describe a negative supply shock inflation without validation or expectational effects?
    (a) As the *SRAS* curve shifts upward, prices rise.
    (b) As the *SRAS* curve shifts upward, the actual unemployment rate decreases below the *NAIRU*.
    (c) Initially output falls, but as wages fall in response to the recessionary gap, output begins to increase back to its potential level.
    (d) The initial phase is described as stagflation.
    (e) In the initial phase, there is a movement along the *AD* curve as interest rates increase with prices.

12. The reason why the central bank may choose to counteract a negative supply shock by increasing the money supply is
    (a) to avoid a prolonged recessionary gap situation.
    (b) to reward workers whose productivity has risen because of the supply shock.
    (c) to reduce expectational inflation.
    (d) to counteract the leftward shift in the *AD* curve that will occur when prices rise.
    (e) Both (b) and (c) are correct.

13. Which one of the following statements about inflation is true?
    (a) Price level increases must eventually come to a halt, unless monetary expansion occurs.
    (b) Inflations that are not validated are always of short duration.
    (c) A temporary inflation occurs only with a monetary expansion.
    (d) Assuming that actual national income was initially at its potential level, demand-shock inflation never can have short-run effects on real national income.
    (e) From the point of view of long-run equilibrium, inflation is never sustained.

14. The acceleration hypothesis holds that
    (a) inflation will accelerate even if the central banks do not engage in validation.
    (b) inflation rates will increase without expectational inflation.
    (c) the *AD* and *SRAS* curves shift by a constant amount over time.
    (d) when the central bank engages in whatever rate of monetary expansion is needed to hold the inflationary gap constant, the rate of actual inflation will accelerate.
    (e) the percentage change in nominal wealth must be equal to the inflation rate.

Reducing Inflation

Disinflation means a reduction in the rate of inflation when an inflationary process has been sustained. The policy associated with disinflation imposes costs (reduced real GDP and cyclical unemployment). The textbook delineates three critical phases involved in disinflation. Economists have derived a simple measure of the costs of disinflation on the depth and length of recession and on the amount of disinflation. This measure is called the sacrifice ratio.

15. Which of the following is a characteristic of Phase 1 of breaking a sustained inflation?
    (a) The *SRAS* curve continue to shift downward and to the right.
    (b) The inflationary gap increases in size.
    (c) The central bank stabilizes the *AD* curve.
    (d) A recessionary gap is generated.
    (e) Expectations of future inflation increase.

16. Which of the following does the textbook identify as Phase 2 of breaking a sustained inflation?
    (a) Slowing the rate of monetary expansion below the current rate of inflation.
    (b) An initial demand and expectational inflation becomes a pure expectational inflation.
    (c) Productivity rises more than wages.
    (d) At the end of the stagflation, unit costs fall, thus shifting the SRAS curve downward.
    (e) At the end of the stagflation, the central bank may increase the money supply to shorten the recessionary gap phase.

17. The duration of the recession that develops when a central bank stops validating a sustained inflation
    (a) depends on inflationary expectations and wage momentum.
    (b) is determined by coincidental leftward shifts of the *AD* curve.
    (c) will typically be very short according to Keynesians.
    (d) will typically be very long according to monetarists.
    (e) must be extremely short if expectations are backward looking.

18. The cost of disinflation
    (a) is the cost of the recession that is needed to dampen inflationary tendencies.
    (b) depends on the size and duration of the recession that is generated.
    (c) is greater the more backward looking are expectations.
    (d) depends on the extent to which inflation must decrease.
    (e) All of the above are correct.

19. The sacrifice ratio is defined as
    (a) the extent to which inflation redistributes income from the poor to the rich.
    (b) the cumulative loss in real GDP due to inflation.
    (c) the extent to which potential GDP declines because of inflation.
    (d) the cumulative loss in real GDP expressed as a percentage of potential GDP divided by the number of percentage points by which inflation has fallen.
    (e) the number of percentage points by which inflation has fallen divided by the cumulative loss in GDP.

Inflation in Canada

Although inflation in the last five years of the millennium has been less than 2 percent, Canada has experienced periods of double-digit inflation in the middle and late 1970s and lower but still sustained inflation during the 1980s. The double-digit inflation was broken by a highly restrictive monetary policy which resulted in a major recession with all its attendant costs. A sustained inflation rate of 4 percent was probably fuelled by inflationary expectations and random shocks. During this period, the Bank of Canada reacted once again by adopting a restrictive monetary policy which drove up interest rates.

In the early 1990s, the Bank of Canada announced a controversial series of inflation-control targets despite the existence of a recessionary gap. The target range was gradually reduced to 1–3 percent. By 1993–94, the economy began to grow and overall unemployment fell. The Bank's inflation targets were achieved between 1995 and 1996.

20. In which of the following periods did the Bank of Canada's anti-inflationary policy contribute to the creation of a recessionary gap?
(a) 1975–1980.
(b) 1981–1984.
(c) 1985–1990.
(d) 1991–1992.
(e) Both (b) and (d).

EXERCISES

1. Briefly explain each concept and illustrate it on the graph. Assume no expectational effects.

(a) a negative supply shock that is validated thereafter.

Figure 29-1

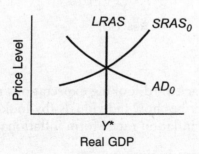

(b) a negative supply shock with no monetary validation.

Figure 29-2

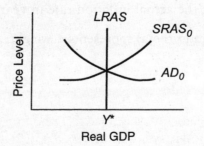

(c) a positive demand shock with no monetary validation.

Figure 29-3

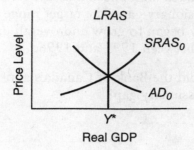

(d) a positive demand-shock inflation that is validated thereafter.

Figure 29-4

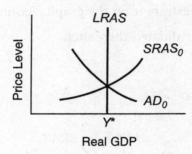

2. This exercise illustrates how backward-looking expectations might be generated. A simple equation is presented that describes how individuals (by looking at the central bank's inflation target and current, actual inflation rates) form inflationary expectations for next year.

The expectation of inflation equation is given by

$$\Pi^*_{t+1} = \Theta\Pi^T + (1 - \Theta)\Pi_t, \text{ where}$$

Π^*_{t+1} is the expected inflation rate for year t + 1 as estimated in year t.

Π^T is the central bank's announced target rate.

Π_t is the actual inflation rate in year t.

Θ (Greek letter theta) represents a weight; $0 < \Theta < 1$.

Expectations are estimated over an eight-year period. The table below shows values for both the central bank's target inflation and actual inflation.

Year (t)	Π_t	Π^T	Π^*_{t+1} $\Theta = 0.4$	Π^*_{t+1} $\Theta = 0.9$
1	10	2		
2	9	2		
3	6	2		
4	3	2		
5	2	2		
6	2	2		
7	2	2		
8	2	2		

(a) Assuming that $\Theta = 0.4$, estimate the values of expected inflation for each year.

(b) If Θ had been equal to 0.9, what would have been the values of Π^*_3 and Π^*_4?

(c) Which of the two weights represents "more" backward-looking expectations? Explain.

(d) Given the different speed of adjustment of inflationary expectations, predict which disinflation is more costly in terms of lost output— $\Theta = 0.4$ or $\Theta = 0.9$. Remember, the textbook makes the point that the costs of disinflation depend on the size and duration of recessionary gaps that are needed to eliminate inflationary expectations.

3. This exercise focuses on eliminating sustained inflation. Suppose that an economy has for some time been experiencing inflation that has been validated by monetary policy. The starting point for this example is point A in Figure 29-5.

(a) If the central bank stops expanding the money supply, what do you predict will happen during phase 1 to the levels of real national income and the price level? What will happen to the SRAS curve? Draw the new SRAS curve and label it SRAS₁.

(b) During phase 2, inflationary expectations are still present such that the SRAS curve shifts to SRAS₂. Indicate the new (temporary) equilibrium point on the graph. What is the value of the recessionary gap? What are the values for real national income and the price level?

Figure 29-5

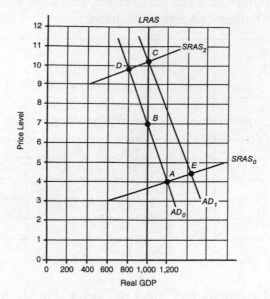

(c) After expectations are reversed, and assuming no changes in the money supply (*AD* remains at AD_0), what are your predictions for the equilibrium levels of real national income and price?

(d) Suppose in phase 3 that expectations are reversed but the central bank increases the money supply sufficiently to shift the *AD* curve to AD_1. What will be the equilibrium levels of real national income and price?

4. Figure 29-6 illustrates an initial equilibrium at point *E* with real national income Y_0 and price level *P*. Y^* is potential national income.

Figure 29-6

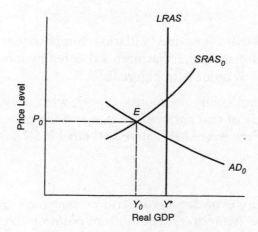

(a) If an increase in the money supply stimulated demand enough to achieve potential national income, draw the new aggregate demand curve and indicate the new price level.

(b) Suppose that the resulting rise in the price level in (a) caused expectations that inflation would occur in the future, and as a result, wages rose throughout the economy. Show on the graph what would happen to the *SRAS* curve. What will be the immediate consequence for real national income and the price level?

(c) If the supply shock that occurred in (b) was fully validated, what would happen to the aggregate demand curve? Illustrate on the graph.

5. A country has been experiencing sustained inflation and an increasing unemployment rate above the *NAIRU*. Mario Marchese, the finance critic of the major opposition party in parliament rises in his place and asks the finance minister, Yves Moreau, to explain the situation and to indicate what the government intends to do about the situation. The minister responds that the problem has been caused initially by continual supply shocks of higher prices of imported manufacturing goods that the domestic economy cannot produce. Moreau is pleased to announce that no further supply shocks are anticipated and assures Marchese that his government has been quite responsible by keeping its expenditures and the nominal money supply increases at modest levels. To be fair, he does express concern that wages have been rising because of the supply shocks.

Marchese, an avid monetarist, jumps to his feet once again and demands that Moreau instruct the central bank to decrease the nominal stock of money. The minister responds that he is not prepared to do any such thing. Hopefully, with the elimination of these supply shocks, the economy will adjust back to full employment with price stability. He also alludes to the fact that he is prepared to consider increasing the money supply to speed up the process to full employment.

From across the floor of parliament, Marchese yells to Moreau, "Shame, resign."

(a) Explain why wages are rising.

(b) Comment on why Marchese believes that a decrease in the nominal money supply is an appropriate policy stance.

(c) Provide some economic reasons for Moreau's policy stance.

PRACTICE MULTIPLE CHOICE TEST

Questions 1 through 4 refer to Figure 29-7.

Figure 29-7

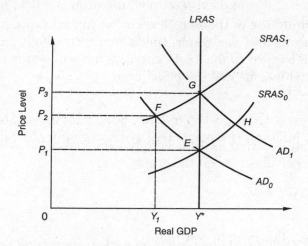

1. Starting from equilibrium at point *E*, if a supply shock shifts the *SRAS* curve from *SRAS*₀ to *SRAS*₁ and there is no monetary validation,
   (a) the recessionary gap puts downward pressure on wages and prices, slowly shifting *SRAS* back downward to *SRAS*₀.
   (b) aggregate demand will increase from *AD*₀ to *AD*₁.
   (c) the long-run equilibrium will be at point *G*.
   (d) the long-run equilibrium will be at point *F* as long as wages rise less than productivity.
   (e) the long-run equilibrium will be at point *F* since the *LRAS* must shift leftward.

2. Starting from equilibrium at point *E*, if the short-run aggregate supply curve shifts from *SRAS*₀ to *SRAS*₁ and there is complete monetary validation,
   (a) real national income would temporarily fall to *Y*₁, then be restabilized at *Y**.
   (b) the aggregate demand curve will shift to the right to pass through point *G*.
   (c) the price level will rise to *P*₃, assuming that no inflationary expectations are generated.
   (d) in the long run, inflation is a monetary phenomenon.
   (e) All of the above will occur.

3. Starting from equilibrium at point *E*, the aggregate demand curve shifts from *AD*₀ to *AD*₁. If there is no monetary validation, long-run equilibrium will be at
   (a) point H, if no inflationary expectations are generated.
   (b) point E, because the *AD* curve shifts leftward when the price level rises.
   (c) point G, if no inflationary expectations are generated.
   (d) point F, because the *AD* curve shifts leftward if inflationary expectations are generated.
   (e) point H, where actual output exceeds potential output.

4. Starting from equilibrium at point *E*, the aggregate demand curve shifts from *AD*₀ to *AD*₁. If there is no monetary validation,
   (a) the price level may temporarily increase to more than *P*₃ because of inflationary expectations.
   (b) a recessionary gap may be temporarily created because of inflationary expectations.
   (c) long-run equilibrium will be at point G, even though short-run inflationary expectations have been created.

(d) the actual unemployment rate may be above the *NAIRU* price temporarily if expectations cause a recessionary gap.

(e) All of the above.

5. If supply-shock inflation is –2.6% and expectational inflation is 3.0%, then
   (a) the *SRAS* curve will shift up and to the left.
   (b) the *SRAS* curve will shift down and to the right.
   (c) actual inflation will be 0.4%.
   (d) an inflationary gap situation will be created.
   (e) Both (a) and (c) are correct.

6. If the accumulated loss in real GDP is $120 million, potential GDP is $600 million, and the needed reduction in price inflation is 4 percentage points, what is the value of the sacrifice ratio?
   (a) 4.   (b) 30.
   (c) 5.   (d) 150.
   (e) 1.25.

7. The interpretation of a sacrifice ratio of 3 is that
   (a) the central bank' inflation target must have been 3 percent.
   (b) the Lorenz curve must have shifted out by 3 percent.
   (c) the output gap must have been 3 percent of the nation's potential GDP.
   (d) it costs 3 percent of real GDP for each percentage point of inflation that is reduced.
   (e) real GDP will fall by a multiplier effect of 3 if inflation is reduced by 1 percentage point.

8. Expectations will be more backward looking if decision makers
   (a) weight current inflation more heavily in their formulation of expected inflation.
   (b) weight the central bank's target inflation rate more heavily in their formulation of expected inflation.
   (c) ignore the role of current, actual inflation in their formulation of expected inflation.
   (d) base their expectations of future inflation on what they think will happen in the economy in the future.
   (e) None of the above are correct.

9. According to the material in Extensions to Theory 29-1 an "augmented" Phillips curve
   (a) is one which incorporates the level of the government's budget surplus.
   (b) is identical to the *LRAS*.
   (c) demonstrates how the Phillips curve's position is determined by various levels of inflation expectations.
   (d) illustrates that changes in price expectations have no role in determining the rate at which money wages (and prices) change.
   (e) shows clearly that the *NAIRU* is influenced by inflationary expectations.

10. The key point about constant, purely expectational inflation is that
    (a) there is no excess-demand effect.
    (b) wages rise at the expected rate of inflation.
    (c) the labour shortages that accompany an inflationary gap are absent.
    (d) the labour surpluses that accompany a recessionary gap are absent.
    (e) All of the above are correct.

SOLUTIONS

Chapter Review

1. (d) 2. (e) 3. (d) 4. (c) 5. (d) 6. (e) 7. (a) 8. (b) 9. (e) 10. (a) 11. (b) 12. (a) 13. (a) 14. (d) 15. (c) 16. (b) 17. (a) 18. (e) 19. (d) 20. (b)

Exercises

1. (a) Monetary validation of a single supply shock causes costs, the price level, and the money supply all to move in the same direction. The supply shock is represented in the leftward shift of the $SRAS$ curve; monetary validation shifts the AD curve rightward. Equilibrium shifts from E_0 to E_2.

    Figure 29-8

    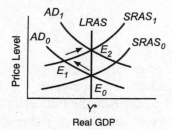

    (b) The supply curve shifts to the left as a result of the supply shock, but without monetary validation, unemployment puts downward pressure on wages and costs, shifting the $SRAS$ curve back to $SRAS_0$.

    Figure 29-9

    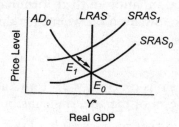

    (c) The demand shock shifts the AD curve and creates an inflationary gap; this causes wages to rise, shifting the $SRAS$ curve to the left. The monetary adjustment mechanism causes movement along the AD curve, with the rise in price level eliminating the inflationary gap (at E_2).

    Figure 29-10

    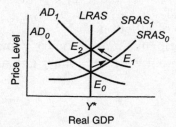

(d) The adjustment process in (c) is frustrated with monetary validation; increases in the money supply shift the *AD* curve to the right, and inflation is sustained. The economy moves along the vertical path indicated by the arrow.

Figure 29-11

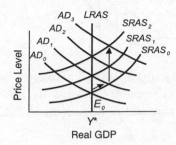

2. (a) Π^*_{t+1} (Θ =.4) = 6.8, 6.2, 4.4, 2.6, 2.0 2.0, 2.0, 2.0.
   (b) Π^*_3 = .9 (2) + .1 (9) = 2.7.
   Π^*_4 = .9 (2) + .1 (6) = 2.4.
   (c) Θ = 0.4 is the more backward-looking expectation. It puts more weight on this year's inflation rate and less weight on the central bank's target.
   (d) When Θ = 0.9, expected inflation approaches the central bank's target much faster. Hence, the recession's duration will be shorter. It follows that the costs of disinflation will be higher for Θ = 0.4 than for Θ = 0.9.

3. (a) Under the combined influence of an inflationary gap and expectation of continued inflation, wages continue to rise, and the *SRAS* curve thus continues to shift. In terms of the graph, the *SRAS* curve shifts leftward to *SRAS*₁ and intersects the *LRAS* curve at point *B*. At this point, real national income is at its potential level (1,000) and the price level is 7.
   (b) Continuing price expectations shift the *SRAS* curve up to *SRAS*₂. This curve intersects *AD*₀ at point *D*. A recessionary gap of 200 has been created. Real national income is 800, and the price level is approximately 10.
   (c) The recessionary gap is likely to reduce inflationary expectations and therefore wage rates. Hence the *SRAS* curve will tend to shift rightward (slowly) to point *B* (*SRAS*₁). There will be a movement along *AD*₀ from point *D* to point *B*, at which the price level is 7 and the economy is producing at its potential level.
   (d) This question differs from (c) in that the central banking authority increases the money supply, perhaps to speed up the process of attaining potential national income. The *AD* curve shifts rightward with monetary expansion. The new equilibrium point is point *C*, at which the price level is approximately 10 and real national income is 1,000.

4. (a) The new *AD* curve is *AD*₁ and the price level is *P*₁. (See Figure 29-12.)
   (b) The *SRAS* would shift to the left, for example, *SRAS*₁ in the graph, and the price level would rise further (along *AD*₁) to *P*₂. Real national income would decline to *Y*₁.
   (c) The aggregate demand curve would shift to *AD*₂. (See Figure 29-12.)

Figure 29-12

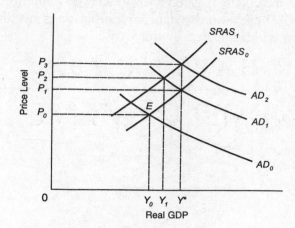

5. (a) The repeated supply shocks that increased domestic prices likely have generated cost of living increases and possibly expectations of future inflation. To protect the level of real wages, workers have been demanding higher money wages.

(b) We suspect that Marchese believes that a decreased money supply will dampen inflationary expectations at a faster rate. Moreover, the contractionary money policy would certainly increase the value of the recessionary gap and workers might be more prone to lower their wages. Thus, although unemployment would be higher than before, the speed at which the economy adjusts back to price stability at potential output may be increased. In the long run, inflation is a monetary phenomenon.

(c) Moreau does not want to increase the recessionary gap as Marchese suggests. Perhaps, he believes that prices will soon fall as workers lower their wage demands as supply shocks cease to occur. Alternatively, when he is convinced that inflationary expectations have subsided and that wages are falling, he may be prepared to speed up the process to full employment by increasing the money supply. During the monetary expansion, prices will rise as the *AD* curve shifts to the right. Hopefully, the price increases will not rekindle inflationary expectations.

Practice Multiple Choice Test

1. (a) 2. (e) 3. (c) 4. (e) 5. (e) 6. (c) 7. (d) 8. (a) 9. (c) 10. (e)

CHAPTER 30

UNEMPLOYMENT

(LO) LEARNING OBJECTIVES

1 Understand how employment and unemployment change over the short and long runs.

2 Explain the difference between the New Classical and New Keynesian views of cyclical unemployment.

3 Understand the causes of frictional and structural unemployment.

4 Explain the various forces that cause the *NAIRU* to change.

5 Understand how various policies might be used to reduce unemployment.

CHAPTER OVERVIEW

This chapter examines employment and unemployment in Canada. In the short run there can be large gross flows into and out of employment and unemployment. Several kinds of unemployment are discussed. **Cyclical unemployment** occurs during short-run recessionary gap situations. **Structural unemployment**, which results from the need to reallocate resources due to changing patterns of demand and supply, and **frictional unemployment**, which occurs as people move from job to job as a normal part of labour turnover, are long-run determinants of the *NAIRU*. These distinctions are important in deciding what policies should be used to reduce the unemployment rate.

The chapter outlines the opposing views of the **New Classical** and **New Keynesian** schools concerning the flexibility of wages and the existence of involuntary unemployment. The efficiency wage theory also explains why firms might choose to pay wages higher than the minimum amount that would induce workers to work for them.

The components of the *NAIRU* are outlined, and the economic and demographic factors that cause it to change are discussed.

CHAPTER REVIEW

Employment and Unemployment

The importance of stocks and flows in the labour market is outlined in the box, *Applying Economic Concepts* 30-1. To better understand the issues related to flows and stocks among three "states" of the labour force (employed *E*, unemployed *U*, and not in the labour force *N*) and between two time periods, *t* and *t* + 1, you might find the following matrix helpful. There are questions in the Practice Multiple Choice Test section that test further your comprehension of labour market flows and stocks.

	E_{t+1}	U_{t+1}	N_{t+1}
E_t	EE	EU	EN
U_t	UE	UU	UN
N_t	NE	NU	NN

The element *UE* is the flow of persons who were unemployed in period *t* and who became employed in period *t* + 1. The element *NU* is flow of individuals who were not in the labour force in period *t* but who entered the labour force in period *t* + 1 but who did not find work.

Questions 1 to 7 refer to the above matrix.

1. Which element of the matrix represents cases where employed workers lost their jobs or quit their jobs and became unemployed between *t* and *t* + 1?
   (a) *UE*.   (b) *NU*.   (c) *EU*.   (d) *UU*.   (e) *EE*.

2. The elements *NU* and *NE* represent flows of individuals between *t* and *t* + 1 who are
   (a) entering the labour force in *t* + 1.
   (b) leaving the labour force in *t* + 1.
   (c) entering the labour force in *t*.
   (d) leaving the labour force in *t*.
   (e) unemployed individuals finding jobs in *t* + 1.

3. The flow of new entrants to the labour force between the two time periods who do not find work in *t* + 1 would appear in element
   (a) *UE*.   (b) *UN*.   (c) *EN*.   (d) *NU*.   (e) *UU*.

4. The flows out of unemployment between the two time periods are represented by the elements
   (a) *UN* and *UE*.   (b) *UU* and *EE*.
   (c) *NU* and *EU*.   (d) *UU*.
   (e) *EU*.

5. The flows *into unemployment* between the two time periods consist of
   (a) individuals who were employed and who become unemployed.
   (b) workers who were employed and who exited from the labour force.
   (c) workers who entered the labour force and became employed immediately.
   (d) the element *NU*.
   (e) Both (a) and (d) are correct.

6. If the flows *into unemployment* exceed the flows *out of unemployment*, the stock of unemployed workers will
   (a) not be affected.
   (b) increase.
   (c) equal the stock of employed workers.
   (d) decrease.
   (e) decrease because the labour force increases.

7. The total stock of unemployed persons in period t is
   (a) $UE + UU + UN$.
   (b) UU.
   (c) $EU + UU + NU$.
   (d) UN.
   (e) $NN + EE$.

8. The measured unemployment rate will rise if
   (a) the percentage increase in employment is greater than the percentage increase in the labour force.
   (b) the percentage increase in total unemployment is less than the percentage change in the labour force.
   (c) with a constant labour force, the number of new jobs created is less than the number of jobs lost.
   (d) actual income rises temporarily from its potential level.
   (e) more discouraged, unemployed workers leave the labour force.

9. Which of the following is a potential cost of unemployment?
   (a) The potential output of valuable resources is wasted.
   (b) Workers who would like to work at prevailing wages may stay out of the labour force.
   (c) The unemployed contribute to social unrest in some societies.
   (d) Workers who are unemployed for prolonged periods miss job training opportunities.
   (e) All or any of the above.

Cyclical Unemployment

Cyclical unemployment occurs when there are supply and demand shocks and wages are not flexible. If wages were flexible, then employment and real wages would be procyclical, but there would no change in unemployment. Hence, the key issues around the creation of involuntary unemployment are the reasons why wages may decline slowly during recessionary gap situations. Although New Classical theories can explain the procyclical movement of employment, they cannot explain the existence of cyclical unemployment. New Keynesians offer the theoretical framework of long-term employment relationships and **efficiency wages** to explain slow reactions of wages to macroeconomic shocks and the creation of involuntary unemployment during short-term recessionary gaps.

10. Involuntary unemployment
    (a) occurs when there is a job available but the unemployed person is unwilling to accept it at the existing wage.
    (b) will tend to increase during booms.
    (c) will tend to increase as the costs of searching for a job increase, other things equal.
    (d) occurs when a person is willing to accept a job at the going wage rate but no such job can be found.
    (e) occurs when highly skilled jobs are available but an unskilled worker is not qualified to be hired.

Answer questions 11 through 13 by referring to Figure 30-1 which depicts aggregate labour demand and supply in an economy: The initial equilibrium situation is point *a*.

Figure 30-1

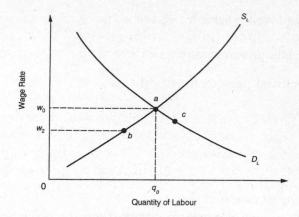

11. Which of the following statements is true?
    (a) At wage rates above w_0, there is an excess demand for labour.
    (b) Unemployment at point *a* consists of structural and frictional unemployment.
    (c) If the wage rate is fully flexible, involuntary unemployment occurs when the wage is below w_0.
    (d) At wage rates less than w_0, there is an excess supply of labour.
    (e) All of the above.

12. If the labour demand curve shifts leftward and intersects the labour supply curve at point *b*,
    (a) all of the laid-off workers are involuntarily unemployed when the wage rate falls to w_2.
    (b) there will be involuntarily unemployed workers if the wage rate remains at w_0.
    (c) providing the wage rate falls to w_2, employment falls but there are no involuntarily unemployed workers.
    (d) the economy is currently encountering an inflationary gap situation.
    (e) Both (b) and (c).

13. Assuming that the real wage rate is fully flexible and that the labour supply curve shifts rightward and intersects the labour demand curve at point *c*, then
    (a) both employment and involuntary unemployment increase.
    (b) both employment and involuntary unemployment decrease.
    (c) both employment and involuntary unemployment remain constant.
    (d) employment increases, but there is no involuntary unemployment at point *c*.
    (e) voluntary unemployment decreases and employment increases.

14. New Keynesian theories about the persistence of involuntary unemployment
    (a) stress the importance of adverse supply shocks.
    (b) start with the observation that wage rates do not respond quickly to changes in demand and supply in labour markets.
    (c) imply that most unemployment is caused by fluctuations in the willingness of people to supply labour.
    (d) are based on the premise that all unemployment workers cannot be retrained.
    (e) None of the above are correct.

15. Efficiency wage theories suggest that
    (a) wages readily fall in response to excess supply in labour markets.
    (b) employers may get a more efficient work force when labour is paid more than the competitive wage rate.
    (c) wages must be competitively determined for workers to be efficient.
    (d) workers are paid primarily on the basis of the efficiency of management and supervisors.
    (e) workers are paid primarily on the basis of their annual productivity increases.

The *NAIRU*

The *NAIRU* is the unemployment rate that holds when the economy's national income is at its potential level. The NAIRU consists only of structural and frictional unemployment. Make sure you understand the factors that can cause the *NAIRU* to change over time. Also, you should understand the term **hysteresis**; the size of the *NAIRU* can be influenced by the the size of the actual current rate of unemployment.

16. Unemployment that occurs as a result of the normal turnover of labour as people move from job to job is called
    (a) involuntary unemployment.
    (b) structural unemployment.
    (c) cyclical unemployment.
    (d) frictional unemployment.
    (e) real-wage unemployment.

17. The existence of structural unemployment means that
    (a) there is an inadequate number of jobs in the economy.
    (b) the building trades workers, particularly those in structural steel, are suffering high rates of unemployment.
    (c) the composition of the demand for labour does not match the composition of available supply.
    (d) cyclical unemployment must also be present.
    (e) all unemployment is voluntary.

18. Search unemployment
    (a) may be a form of voluntary frictional unemployment.
    (b) will tend to increase if search costs are low.
    (c) occurs when members of the labour force look for more suitable jobs.
    (d) occurs because workers do not have perfect knowledge of job availability.
    (e) All of the above.

19. Which of the following does *not* usually explain the creation of structural unemployment?
    (a) Economic adjustments created by changes in input mixes.
    (b) Changes in the composition of the labour force.
    (c) The pattern of the demand for goods changes.
    (d) Contractionary monetary policy.
    (e) New labour force entrants having inadequate training or skills for available jobs.

20. If an economy has achieved its *NAIRU*, it follows that
    (a) the measured unemployment rate is necessarily zero.
    (b) the economy operates in a recessionary gap.
    (c) the value of the output gap is zero.
    (d) there is neither structural nor frictional unemployment in the economy.
    (e) all unemployment is involuntary.

21. Which of the following will increase the *NAIRU*?
    (a) An improvement in the educational attainment of the labour force.
    (b) A slowdown in the pace at which the structural demand for labour is changing.
    (c) Less barriers to the flow of labour from a declining to an expanding labour sector.
    (d) A decrease in the speed at which labour adapts to structural changes in labour demand.
    (e) The Bank of Canada buys bonds in the open market.

22. Which of the following is *not* correct?
    (a) Unemployment insurance (now called employment insurance) likely increases search unemployment.
    (b) Trying to reduce the unemployment rate to zero is both impractical and undesirable.
    (c) Frictional unemployment in an economy such as Canada's is inevitable.
    (d) Long-term relationships between employers and workers help to explain the lack of wage adjustments during economic downturns.
    (e) The *NAIRU* in Canada has not changed over the last half century.

23. *Hysteresis* means that an increase in cyclical unemployment may
    (a) decrease the level of frictional and structural unemployment.
    (b) increase the probability that new labour force participants will receive job training during and after a recession.
    (c) increase the level of the *NAIRU*.
    (d) Both (a) and (b).
    (e) lead to the creation of new jobs in certain economic regions.

Reducing Unemployment

Different economic factors determine the three types of unemployment discussed in the textbook. It follows that policy selection should be centred on the causes of each.

24. Which of the following policies would be appropriate for reducing the level of cyclical unemployment?
    (a) The Bank of Canada sells large volumes of government bonds in the open market.
    (b) The federal government increases personal income taxes.
    (c) The province of Alberta cuts back on its expenditures to education.
    (d) The city of Moncton increases its expenditures on public housing construction.
    (e) The Bank of Canada transfers government deposits from the banks to itself.

25. Which of the following would be appropriate for reducing structural unemployment in the long run?
    (a) More effective job training programs.
    (b) Increases in the minimum wage in all provinces.
    (c) Policies designed to promote more labour-saving technological change.
    (d) Strongly enforced interprovincial agreements to restrict labour migration.
    (e) Increasing government subsidies to declining industries.

EXERCISES

1. Classify the following situations as frictional unemployment, structural unemployment, search unemployment, or cyclical unemployment, and briefly explain your choice.

   (a) An auto assembly worker is laid off because auto sales decrease during a slowdown in economic activity.

   (b) An engineer refuses a job offer and decides to look for another job that has a higher rate of remuneration.

   (c) A social worker is laid off because the city of Toronto cancels one of its social welfare programs.

   (d) A brewery worker in Regina is laid off when the firm relocates its production to Saskatoon.

   (e) Bookkeepers are laid off as Vancouver firms introduce computerized accounting software packages into their office operations.

   (f) Systems analysts lose their jobs as firms curtail projects due to slumping sales.

2. What specific government policy would you recommend for each of the following causes of unemployment? Explain briefly.

   (a) Structural unemployment caused by sectoral shifts in demand.

   (b) Cyclical unemployment.

   (c) Longer search unemployment caused by generous unemployment insurance benefits.

(d) Frictional unemployment.

Practice Multiple Choice Test

Questions 1 to 8 refer to the following labour-market-status matrix for a hypothetical economy. The entries represent flows between two time periods, say 1990 and 1991. The columns refers to 1991 and the rows refer to 1990.

	E_{91}	U_{91}	N_{91}
E_{90}	260	15	5
U_{90}	22	20	8
N_{90}	3	10	20

1. What is the value of the labour force in 1990?
   (a) 200.   (b) 280.   (c) 220.   (d) 330.   (e) 317.

2. What is the unemployment rate in 1990?
   (a) 15.2 percent.   (b) 14.3 percent.
   (c) 13.6 percent.   (d) 12.7 percent.
   (e) None of the above.

3. What is the participation rate in 1990?
   (a) 87.3 percent.   (b) 96.1 percent.
   (c) 90.9 percent   (d) 100 percent.
   (e) 83.3 percent.

4. What was the total new flow into unemployment from 1990 to 1991?
   (a) 20.   (b) 25.   (c) 15.   (d) 20.   (e) 10.

5. What was the total new flow out of unemployment from 1990 to 1991?
   (a) 22.   (b) 8.   (c) 10.   (d) 30.   (e) 20.

6. On the basis of your answers to questions 4 and 5, you can predict that the stock of unemployment in 1991 is
   (a) higher than 1990.
   (b) is lower than 1990.
   (c) equal to 50.
   (d) equal to the 1990 stock of unemployment.
   (e) equal to 20.

7. Comparing the 1990 flows of employed and unemployed workers who moved out of the labour force in 1991 to those who moved into the labour force in 1991, we observe that
   (a) the inflow was greater than the outflow.
   (b) the outflow was greater than the inflow.
   (c) the labour force increased over the one-year span.
   (d) the labour force decreased over the one-year span.
   (e) the labour forces were the same in the two years.

8. The unemployment rate in 1991 is
   (a) 15.2 percent.   (b) 10.6 percent.
   (c) 13.6 percent.   (d) 12.9 percent.
   (d) 10 percent.

9. Which of the following are aspects of the New Keynesian theory of long-term employment relationships?
   (a) Wages rates adjust quickly in excess labour demand and excess labour supply situations.
   (b) Any market clearing that occurs during short-term fluctuations focuses on the volume of employment rather than on wages.
   (c) As the productivity of older workers falls over time, wages for them are adjusted downward.
   (d) Long-term labour contracts provide a great deal of flexibility to firms that wish to lower or increase wage rates.
   (e) Fringe benefits with one firm are easily transferred to another firm when a worker moves from one job to another.

10. One aspect of the efficiency wage hypothesis is
    (a) firms pay a wage premium so that workers are reluctant to shirk their responsibilities and duties.
    (b) it is relatively easy for employers to monitor workers' performance.
    (c) wage premiums paid by one firm are easily transferred to another firm.
    (d) paying a wage premium to workers will increase the incidence of quit rates and absenteeism.
    (e) unions demand payment-for-performance for their members.

11. New Keynesian economists
    (a) believe that wages adjust quickly to short-run gap situations.
    (b) argue that short-run recessionary gaps cannot last for long.
    (c) stress wage adjustments rather than employment adjustments.
    (d) agree with New Classical economists that the actual unemployment rate is equal to the *NAIRU* in the long run.
    (e) reject the concept of search unemployment.

Questions 12 to 15 refer to Figure 30-2. The economy begins at E_0 where real GDP equals potential GDP (Y^*). The unemployment rate at Y^* is assumed to be 7%.

Figure 30-2

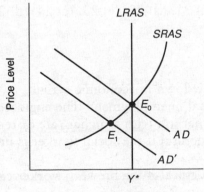

12. At E_0, what type of unemployment exists?
    (a) Cyclical unemployment of 7 percent.
    (b) Involuntary unemployment of 7 percent.
    (c) There is no unemployment since the economy operates at its potential level.
    (d) Structural and frictional unemployment equal to 7 percent.
    (e) Only frictional unemployment since structural unemployment is only a concern during economic slumps.

13. A negative aggregate demand shock now shifts the AD curve to AD'. At E_1 the measured unemployment rate is 8.7 percent. What is the level of cyclical unemployment?
    (a) 1.7 percent.   (b) 7 percent.
    (c) 15.7 percent.   (d) 8.7 percent.
    (e) It cannot be determined because the combined levels of structural and frictional unemployment have not been provided.

14. Assuming the $SRAS$ curve does not change, which of the following would be appropriate stabilization policies to eliminate the output gap?
    (a) Shift the AD curve by selling government bonds in the open market.
    (b) Increasing income-tax rates.
    (c) Shift the AD curve to the right by transferring government deposits from the central bank to the commercial banks.
    (d) Use monetary policy to quickly reduce structural unemployment.
    (e) Increase the government's budget surplus.

15. If monetary and fiscal policy are not used, market adjustments would eliminate the output gap in the long run by
    (a) shifting the $SRAS$ curve to the left as wage rates fall.
    (b) shifting the AD curve to the left as the price level falls.
    (c) shifting the AD curve to the right as the price level falls.
    (d) shifting the $SRAS$ curve to the right as wage rates fall.
    (e) shifting the $LRAS$ curve to the left.

SOLUTIONS

Chapter Review

1. (c) 2. (a) 3. (d) 4. (a) 5. (e) 6. (b) 7. (a) 8. (c) 9. (e) 10. (d) 11. (b) 12. (e) 13. (d) 14. (b) 15. (b) 16. (d) 17. (c) 18. (e) 19. (d) 20. (c) 21. (d) 22. (e) 23. (c) 24. (d) 25. (a)

Exercises

1. (a) Cyclical, because of the slowdown in economic activity.
    (b) Search or voluntary frictional unemployment. The engineer refused a job because of the expectation of finding another job with a higher rate of remuneration.
    (c) Frictional if short-term, structural if the social worker is unable to find work after a prolonged search.
    (d) Frictional if short-term, structural if the brewery worker cannot find work in Regina or refused to move to Saskatoon.
    (e) Structural if bookkeepers have to undergo retraining in order to acquire skills required for computerized accounting software or for other types of occupations. It would be frictional if the bookkeepers could find non-computerized office work elsewhere.

(f) If the reduction in sales is a result of a general economic recession, cyclical unemployment exists. Conversely, the sales reduction may be due to a sectoral shift away from these firms, in which case the unemployment is frictional if the system analysts find work elsewhere easily, or structural if their unemployment is of long duration.

2. (a) Retraining and relocation grants to make movement of labour easier; policies to improve information about existing and (possibly) future employment opportunities.
   (b) Expansionary fiscal and monetary policies.
   (c) Any policy changes are bound to be controversial. Current provisions may be enforced more strictly, or you may recommend changes in unemployment provisions such as reduced weeks or lower weekly benefits.
   (d) Increasing knowledge that workers have about market opportunities would reduce frictional unemployment. Also, the government may wish to provide workers with relocation subsidies.

Practice Multiple Choice Test
1. (d) 2. (a) 3. (c) 4. (b) 5. (d) 6. (b) 7. (e) 8. (c) 9. (b) 10. (a) 11. (d) 12. (d) 13. (a) 14. (c) 15. (d)

CHAPTER 31

BUDGET DEFICITS AND SURPLUSES

LEARNING OBJECTIVES

1 Understand how the government's annual budget deficit (or surplus) is related to its stock of debt.

2 Explain the difference between the overall budget deficit and the primary budget deficit.

3 Explain the meaning of the cyclically adjusted budget deficit, and how it can be used to measure the stance of fiscal policy.

4 Understand Ricardian equivalence.

5 Explain how deficits crowd out investment and net exports.

6 Explain why a high stock of debt may hamper monetary and fiscal policy.

7 Discuss several different proposals for balancing the budget.

CHAPTER OVERVIEW

The **government's budget constraint** means that government expenditures must be equal to tax revenue plus borrowing. The government's budget deficit is equal to total government expenditure (including **debt-service payments**) minus total government revenue. Since the government must borrow to finance any shortfall in its revenues, the annual deficit is equal to the amount borrowed by the government during the course of a year. Whenever the deficit is positive, the stock of government debt is growing. Conversely, a budget surplus reduces the stock of debt.

There are three components of government expenditure; purchases of goods and services (G), transfer payments (TR) and debt-service payments ($i \times D$) where D is the outstanding stock of government debt and i is the interest rate. The **primary budget deficit** is equal to the excess of the government's program spending over total tax revenues. The difference between the total budget deficit and the primary deficit is the debt-service payments. The primary deficit shows the extent to which tax revenues are able to finance the discretionary part of total expenditures (purchases and transfer payments).

The actual value of the budget deficit is a poor measure of the stance of fiscal policy since its value fluctuates during various phases of the business cycle. Changes in the value of the **cyclically-adjusted deficit** (*CAD*) reflect changes in the stance of fiscal policy. A rise in the cyclically-adjusted budget deficit reflects expansionary fiscal policy.

Changes in the **debt-to-GDP** ratio depend on the real interest rate, the growth rate of real GDP, and the size of the primary budget deficit. If the real interest rate exceeds the growth rate of real GDP, then stabilizing the debt-to-GDP ratio requires that the government run a primary budget surplus.

Three possible effects of government debt and deficits are discussed: "**crowding out**" effects; the potential harm of government debt to future generations; and limitations that debt puts on the conduct of economic policy. There are two possible crowding out effects in an open economy: private-sector investment is reduced if government borrowing increases the interest rate and net exports are reduced if increased domestic interest rates cause an increase in the external value of the domestic currency.

The chapter concludes by discussing different concepts of balanced budgets; **annually balanced budgets** and **cyclically balanced budgets**.

CHAPTER REVIEW

Facts and Definitions

Any excess of total government spending over tax revenues must be financed by government borrowing which adds to the stock of outstanding government debt. Alternatively, any excess of tax revenues over total government spending might be used to retire debt. The distinction between overall and primary budget deficits is important for you to understand. And, it would be useful for you to have a general idea of the recent record of budget deficit policies and trends in the debt-to-GDP ratio both at the federal and provincial levels in Canada.

1. The value of the Canadian federal (government net) debt as a share of GDP in the 1990s was
   (a) somewhere between 60 and 70 percent.
   (b) lower than its value in the 1960s.
   (c) greater than its value during World War II.
   (d) equal to the value of the federal government deficit as a share of GDP.
   (e) slightly less than 90 percent.

2. Which one of the following statements is true?
   (a) An overall budgetary deficit implies a primary budget deficit.
   (b) A budgetary deficit means that government borrowing does not change.
   (c) Higher real interest rates imply lower debt-service payments.
   (d) A budgetary deficit necessitates an increase in government borrowing.
   (e) Transfer payments are excluded from the category program spending.

3. The primary federal deficit is defined as
   (a) the total federal deficit minus the value of outstanding debt.
   (b) the total federal deficit generated by transfer payments to primary industries.
   (c) the total federal deficit excluding debt-service payments.
   (d) the deficit that exists at potential national income.
   (e) the federal deficit attributable to debt-service payments.

4. Which of the following equations is correct?
   (a) $\Delta D = T + (G + TR + i \times D)$.
   (b) Primary Budget Deficit: $G + TR + i \times D$.
   (c) Government Budget Constraint: $G - T = $ Borrowing.
   (d) Primary Budget Deficit: $(G + TR) - T$.
   (e) $\Delta D = G + TR - T$.

5. In the fiscal year 1996–97, the federal government had an overall budget deficit of $13.7 billion while debit-service payments were $45.2 billion. Hence, in that year
   (a) the primary budget deficit was $58.9 billion.
   (b) the government did not need to borrow.
   (c) the primary budget deficit was $31.5 billion.
   (d) tax revenues were more than sufficient to cover program expenditures.
   (e) the primary budget surplus was $31.5 billion.

Some Analytical Issues

The stance of fiscal policy (contractionary or expansionary) is best judged by changes in the value of the cyclically-adjusted deficit (CAD) since some changes in budget deficits (surpluses) occur even when there has been no change in fiscal policy. The key to this issue is the budget deficit function. Changes in deficits caused by changes in real GDP are represented by movements along a budget deficit function. Shifts in the budget deficit function are caused by changes in tax rates and government spending. For **each** budget deficit function, the value of the cyclically-adjusted deficit is measured at potential real GDP (Y^*).

To fully understand the equation that explains changes in the debt-to-GDP ratio, it would be useful to reread Extensions in Theory 31-1. The change in the debt-to-GDP ratio (Δd) depends on the value of the primary deficit as a percentage of GDP (x), the real rate of interest (r), the growth in real GDP (g), and d, the debt-to-GDP ratio. Using this equation, it is then possible to determine the conditions that are needed to stabilize the debt-to-GDP ratio.

The link between government deficits and private saving is associated with the idea of **Ricardian Equivalence**. The central idea here is, do consumers faced with a decrease in taxes (because of an increase in the budget deficit) increase their current consumption? "Ricardian" consumers believe that all deficits must be eventually paid for in higher future taxes. Therefore, they increase private saving not consumption. "Non-Ricardian" consumers believe that not all of the increase in the budget deficits will be paid for by future taxes. Hence, they distribute their increase in wealth between saving and consumption.

Questions 6 to 9 are based on Figure 31-1.

Figure 31-1

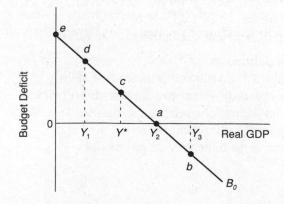

6. Referring to the budget deficit function labelled B_0, which of the following points represents a budget surplus?
   (a) *e.*   (b) *a.*   (c) *b.*   (d) *c.*   (e) *d.*

7. A movement from point *a* to point *d*
   (a) represents an increase in the budget deficit because either government expenditures have increased or tax rates have been reduced.
   (b) represents the creation of a budget surplus because government expenditures have been cut or tax rates have been increased.
   (c) illustrates the creation of a budget surplus since tax revenues have fallen with the decline in real GDP.
   (d) indicates that a budget deficit has been created as tax revenues fall with declines in real GDP.
   (e) indicates that a budget surplus has been created as tax revenues fall with declines in real GDP.

8. The cyclically-adjusted deficit for budget deficit function B_0 is a
   (a) deficit of the distance Y^* *c*.
   (b) deficit of the distance $0e$.
   (c) a balance at point *a*.
   (d) a surplus of the distance Y_3 *b*.
   (e) a deficit of the distance Y_1 *d*.

9. If at every level of real GDP the budget deficit function shifted up, then
   (a) the value of the CAD would increase.
   (b) the stance of fiscal policy was expansionary.
   (c) the stance of fiscal policy was contractionary.
   (d) the value of the CAD would decrease.
   (e) both (a) and (b) are correct.

10. Which of the following events by itself will increase the debt-to-GDP ratio?
    (a) The real interest rate exceeds the growth rate of real GDP.
    (b) The government runs a primary budget surplus.
    (c) The real interest rate is equal to the real growth rate of GDP and the government runs a primary budget surplus.
    (d) Tax rates increase.
    (e) Both (c) and (d) are correct.

11. If the real interest rate exceeds the growth rate in real GDP, then the goal of a stable debt-to-GDP ratio requires
    (a) a constant value of outstanding debt even though real GDP is growing.
    (b) a primary budget deficit.
    (c) budget deficits so that debt grows at the same rate as GDP.
    (d) a primary budget surplus.
    (e) annually balanced budgets.

12. Which of the following statements about the relationship between national saving and government budget deficit are correct?
    (a) National saving is equal to private saving minus the government budget deficit.
    (b) The link between budget deficits and private saving determines the effect of budget deficits on the level of national saving.
    (c) If an increase in the budget deficit of $5 million causes private saving to increase by $5 million, the national saving does not change.
    (d) If an increase in the budget deficit of $10 million causes private saving to increase by $8 million, national saving will decline by $2 million.
    (e) All of the above are correct.

13. Ricardian equivalence states that if the government decides to borrow $7 million dollars to finance a tax cut of $7 million, then
    (a) current taxpayers do not believe that current borrowing will affect their future tax liabilities.
    (b) financing government deficits with foreign capital is equivalent to financing the deficits domestically.
    (c) private saving will increase by $7 million since consumers believe that the current borrowing will translate into future increased tax liabilities of $7 million.
    (d) national saving must increase.
    (e) the growing public debt always increases permanent disposable income.

The Effects of Government Debt and Deficits

This section deals with the potential effects of government deficits (and surpluses). Two crowding-out effects are identified, the debate regarding the redistribution of resources away from future generations to current generations is outlined, and the efficacy of fiscal and monetary policy with lower or higher debt levels is discussed.

14. With a decrease in current taxes, "non-Ricardian" consumers are likely to
    (a) cause the *AD* curve to shift up and to the right in the short run since national saving decreases.
    (b) have no effect on the *AD* curve since national saving is unaffected.
    (c) cause the *AD* curve the shift down and to the left as they increase private saving by more than the decrease in government saving.
    (d) have no effect on either the *AD* curve or real interest rates.
    (e) cause the *SRAS* curve to shift down and to the right.

15. The "crowding out" effect of a larger government budget deficit in a closed economy refers to the outcome of
    (a) higher interest rates and less private investment.
    (b) higher interest rates and more saving.
    (c) lower interest rates and more investment.
    (d) lower interest rates and less saving.
    (e) no change in national saving.

16. The "crowding out" of a larger government budget deficit in an open economy refers to the outcome of
    (a) higher interest rates, an appreciation of the domestic currency, and increased net exports.
    (b) higher interest rates, lower capital inflows and net exports.
    (c) lower interest rates, more capital inflows, lower net exports.
    (d) a depreciation of the domestic currency and an increase in net exports.
    (e) higher interest rates, an appreciation of the domestic currency, and reduced net exports.

17. If a larger government budget deficit reduces the capital stock in the long run, then
   (a) the current standard of living is likely to decline, but the future standard of living will improve.
   (b) the future standard of living is likely to decline.
   (c) the current generation bears the burden of the debt.
   (d) the concept of Ricardian "equivalence" holds.
   (e) future generations will be unaffected so long as consumption expenditure increases offset the effects of the deficit.

18. Some economists are concerned that policies that result in a large and growing budget deficit
   (a) reduce the government's flexibility to use fiscal policy as a stabilization tool.
   (b) create high interest payments, leaving less revenue for other public needs.
   (c) may lead to a growing foreign indebtedness.
   (d) will erode the competitiveness of the export sector as the exchange rate depreciates.
   (e) All of the above.

Balanced Budgets

This section deals with two balanced-budget proposals. One requires governments to balance their budgets annually. Under this scheme, a predicted budget surplus would require governments to spend more or lower taxes. The second scheme requires governments to balance their budgets over the full course of a business cycle. In a growing economy, it is more sensible to focus on changes in the debt-to-GDP ratio than on balancing the budget annually or over the duration of a business cycle.

19. An annually balanced budget would be destabilizing because
   (a) it would lead to too large a government sector and greater economic inefficiency.
   (b) it would lead to too small a government sector and inadequate provision of public goods.
   (c) aggregate demand would grow faster at all stages of the business cycle.
   (d) government expenditure (hence, aggregate demand) would be increased in expansions and reduced in contractions.
   (e) the debt to GDP ratio must increase through time.

EXERCISES

1. You are given the following data about the planned 1999 fiscal activity of a government in a hypothetical economy. All data are in billions of the domestic currency.

   Real GDP in 1998 and 1999 is 200.
   Government expenditure on goods and services in 1999 is 20.
   Transfer payments in 1999 are 5.
   Outstanding government debt at the beginning of 1999 is 100.
   Taxation revenue in 1999 is 30.
   Interest rate paid on outstanding debt is 10 percent.

   (a) Calculate the value of debt-service payments in 1999, assuming that the interest on any newly created debt in 1999 is not paid until 2000.

   (b) Calculate the value of program spending in 1999.

(c) Calculate the value of the primary budget deficit. The value of the overall budget deficit.

(d) What is your estimate of the level of government borrowing required in 1999?

(e) Estimate the debt-to-GDP ratio at the beginning of 1999. At the end of 1999.

(f) What is the deficit-GDP ratio at the end of 1999?

2. The Minister of Finance tables her 2000 budget forecast in the House of Commons. The budget includes a graph of the budget deficit function labelled B_{2000}; see Figure 31-2. Reluctantly, she reveals an anticipated downturn in the economy such that the 2000 real income level will fall by $10 billion from the 1999 level of $160 billion (which is equal to potential GDP). The government's 2000 fiscal policy measures, that will be outlined in detail at a later date, will not change the 1999 federal debt-to-GDP ratio of 60 percent.

Karmit Singh, an energetic member of one of the opposition parties, decides to do some serious homework to understand the 2000 budget and its relationship with last year's budget.

(a) He prepares the following checklist for the 2000 budget. Calculate the 2000 magnitudes for him and fill in the missing entries.

The forecasted level of real national income _____.
The value of the output gap _____.
The forecasted deficit-to-GDP ratio _____.
The tax rate as a percentage _____.
The estimated value of federal debt outstanding _____.
Best estimate of the level of government expenditure _____.
The value of the cyclically-adjusted deficit _____. (Use the formula, $B = 30 - 0.2Y^*$, where Y^* is potential GDP.)

Figure 31-2

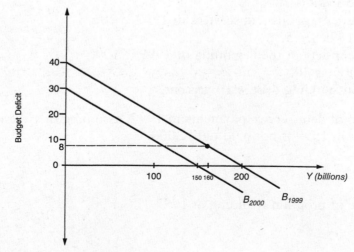

(b) Next, Singh retrieves 1999 budget information that includes a graph of the budget deficit function labelled as B_{1999} in Figure 31-2. Assuming that the function depicts actual values, calculate the 1999 values below and fill in the 1999 missing entries.

The level of real national income _____.
The value of the output gap _____.
The deficit-to-GDP ratio _____.
The tax rate as a percentage _____.
The value of federal government debt outstanding _____.
Best estimate of the level of government expenditure _____.
The value of the cyclically-adjusted deficit. _____. (Use the formula, $B = 40 - 0.2Y^*$.)

(c) By comparing 2000 and 1999 figures, what should Singh conclude about the change in the fiscal policy stance of the government?

(d) During a question period, Singh asks the Minister why government policy for 2000 appears to be procyclical rather than countercyclical. The Minister acknowledges that Singh's analysis is correct. However, she replies that, although her policies are painful in the short term, the economy will be better off in the long run. Discuss this statement.

3. *The Mathematics of the Change in the Debt-to-GDP Ratio*

Suppose that a hypothetical economy has a real interest of 4 percent, a growth rate of real GDP of 2 percent, a debt-to-GDP ratio of 50 percent and a primary budget deficit-to-GDP ratio of 1 percent.

(a) Calculate the change in the debt-to-GDP ratio. What does this value imply about government borrowing?

(b) Calculate the value of the primary budget deficit-to-GDP ratio that would be required to keep the debt-to-GDP ratio constant.

(c) Assuming a zero inflation rate, what annual budget deficit-to-GDP ratio is required to have a constant debt-to-GDP ratio of 50 percent?

(d) Recalculate your answers to parts (a), (b), and (c), assuming that the economy had a debt-to-GDP ratio of 60 percent; all other variables remain the same. What policy issues arise because of the higher debt-to-GDP ratio?

4. Can an annually balanced budget be a short-run destabilizing force in the economy? The proof to this proposition involves showing that private-sector shocks have a greater multiplier effect with a balanced budget requirement than without it. Consider the following behavioural equations for the economy of Soo.

$C = 50 + 0.8(Y - T)$ $I = 100$
Government expenditure $= G$ $(X - IM) = 10 - 0.04Y$
$T = 0.2Y$ Potential GDP $(Y^*) = 800$

(a) If $G = 160$, what is the current equilibrium level of Soo's real national income? What is the current budget balance for Soo's government? What is the current value of the output gap?

(b) Now assume that Soo's exports fall by 2 such that the new net export function is $8 - 0.04Y$. Assume also that the price level, the exchange rate, and the interest rate in Soo are unaffected by this change. Determine the new equilibrium levels of Y and the government's budget position. What was the value of the (simple) multiplier? What is the value of the output gap?

(c) Suppose that the conservative forces in Soo's government had been successful in implementing an annually balanced budget requirement before exports fell. Hence, in each year G must equal $0.2Y$ (spending equals taxation revenue). Prove that the equilibrium level of Y is 800.

(d) As before, exports fall by 2 such that the net export equation becomes $8 - 0.04Y$. Using the fact that $G = 0.2Y$, solve for the equilibrium level of Y. What is the value of G at the new equilibrium level of Y? What is the multiplier value now? What is the value of the output gap? How does this value compare with that of having no annually balanced budget requirement? Why are they different?

EXTENSION EXERCISE

E1.   This exercise focuses on the crowding-out effect in a closed economy. The country of Zed has a domestic market for financial funds (denominated in zeds, abbreviated z). At present, all borrowing and lending occurs in the private sector. The government of Zed plays a completely passive role; it has no expenditures, owes no debt, and collects no tax. The supply of funds (S) arising from private saving in the private sector is given by the equation $S = 30 + i$. The private-sector demand for funds for investment purposes (D) is $D = 60 - 5i$. Both curves represent demand and supply conditions each year; thus they are flow equations. Current GDP is 1,000 and i (= r) is the real rate of interest.

(a)   Plot the two curves in Figure 31-3 and determine the current equilibrium levels of the interest rate (i) and the total amount of private borrowing (in zeds) and saving.

Figure 31-3

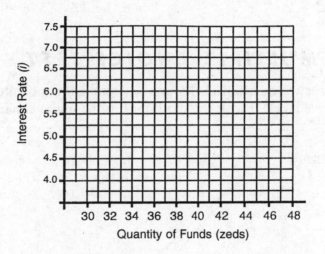

(b)   Zed's government introduces, at the beginning of the year, some public spending programs that will cost 12 zeds. This program will be financed entirely by issuing $12z$ of long-term government bonds and selling them in the financial funds market. Hence the new demand for funds is $D = 72 - 5i$, which is the sum of private and public borrowing. No taxes are planned. Suppose that the spending program has no effect on either real GDP or the price level. If the private-sector supply curve for funds remains stable, determine the new equilibrium levels for i and total borrowing either by plotting the new demand curve or by solving algebraically.

(c)   At the new equilibrium, what is the level of private-sector borrowing? How does this compare with private-sector borrowing before the increase in government borrowing? What has happened to the level of national saving? Can savers in Zed be characterized as "Ricardian" consumers?

(d) How much investment (borrowing) has been crowded out?

(e) At the beginning of the year, what is the deficit-to-GDP ratio? What is the debt-to-GDP ratio? If no debt is redeemed at the end of the year, what debt service payments will the government of Zed owe? What is its total deficit at the end of the year?

PRACTICE MULTIPLE CHOICE TEST

Use Figure 31-4 to answer questions 1 through 3. Assume that potential real national income is 600 and that the curve labelled with the subscript 0 is the initial situation.

Figure 31-4

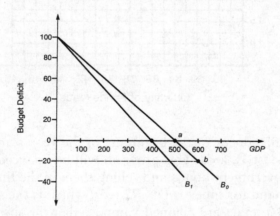

1. Which one of the following statements is *not* true for the deficit function, B_0?
   (a) The tax rate is equal to 20 percent.
   (b) The cyclically adjusted deficit is 20.
   (c) There is a balanced budget at $Y = 500$.
   (d) The cyclically adjusted deficit is –20; i.e., a surplus.
   (e) When $Y = 0$, the budget deficit is 100.

2. For the curve B_0, which one of the following statements is true?
   (a) A movement from point a to point b represents an increase in tax rates.
   (b) The decrease in the budget deficit depicted by a movement from point b to point a must have been caused by an increase in government expenditure.
   (c) Since the budget deficit increased when national income fell from 500 to 400, the government must have increased its discretionary spending.
   (d) Changes in discretionary fiscal policy are shown by movements along the budget deficit function.
   (e) Movements along the function represent the automatic stabilizing influence of the tax system.

3. If the budget deficit function changes to B_1, then
   (a) the cyclically-adjusted deficit increases to 50.
   (b) the tax rate increased from 20 to 25 percent.
   (c) the tax rate decreased from 20 to 15 percent.
   (d) government expenditures must have decreased at every level of national income.
   (e) the budget deficit decreases at every level of national income because the private saving ratio has increased.

Answer questions 4 to 9 by referring to the following table which shows hypothetical data from year 1998 to 2000. The symbols used are as defined in the textbook.

Year	x	r	g	d	Δd
1998	0	.030	.025	.600	
1999	−.010	.028	.025		
2000	−.020	.025	.025		

4. The symbol g denotes
   (a) the primary budget as a percentage of GDP.
   (b) the debt-to-GDP ratio.
   (c) the growth rate of real GDP.
   (d) the rate of inflation.
   (e) the real rate of interest.

5. Between 1998 and 2000, which of the following statements is true?
   (a) The growth in real GDP increased.
   (b) Real interest rates decreased.
   (c) The primary budget balance became a budgetary deficit.
   (d) The primary budget balance became a budgetary surplus.
   (e) Both (b) and (d) are correct.

6. The three-digit value of Δd for 1998 is
   (a) .033.   (b) −.055.
   (c) −.005.   (d) +.003.
   (e) .055.

7. Since d in 1999 is equal to d in 1998 plus Δd in 1998, what is the three-digit value for d in 1999?
   (a) .603.   (b) .595.
   (c) .597.   (d) .545.
   (e) .595.

8. The three-digit values of Δd for 1999 and of d for 2000 are
   (a) 0, .600.   (b) −.02, .595.
   (c) −.008, .595.   (d) −.007, .589.
   (e) None of the above.

9. Which of the following statements is true? Between 1999–2000,
   (a) the budget surplus fell.
   (b) the debt-to-GDP ratio fell.
   (c) the real rate of interest increased.
   (d) the change in the debt-to-GDP (Δd) ratio became positive.
   (e) All of the above are correct.

Questions 10 to 11 refer to Figure 31-5. The initial situation for a closed economy is point E_0. Now suppose that the government increases its expenditures but keeps its tax rates unchanged.

Figure 31-5

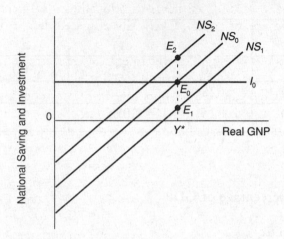

10. In the short run, we would expect this policy stance to
    (a) create a budget surplus and a reduction in government borrowing.
    (b) create an inflationary gap by shifting the national saving curve to NS_1.
    (c) create a recessionary gap by shifting the national saving curve to NS_2.
    (d) increase the measured unemployment beyond the $NAIRU$.
    (e) shift the budget deficit function down and to the right.

11. In the long run the effects of this policy stance are
    (a) the restoration of potential real GDP and a higher price level.
    (b) higher interest rates triggered by increased demand for nominal money balances.
    (c) a downward shift in the investment curve intersecting NS_1 at point E_1.
    (d) upward shifts in the $SRAS$ curve as money wages are bid up.
    (e) All of the above.

SOLUTIONS

Chapter Review

1. (a) 2. (d) 3. (c) 4. (d) 5. (e) 6. (c) 7. (d) 8. (a) 9. (e) 10. (a) 11. (d) 12. (e) 13. (c) 14. (a) 15. (a) 16. (e) 17. (b) 18. (e) 19. (d)

Exercises

1. (a) 10 = (.10 × 100).
   (b) 25 = (government spending on goods and services plus transfer payments).

(c) A primary budget deficit of –5 (a surplus of 5). This value is obtained by subtracting 30 from 25. An overall budget deficit of 5 = (a primary deficit (surplus) of –5 plus debt-service payments of 10).

(d) The overall budgetary deficit of 5 must be financed by borrowing.

(e) Fifty percent = (100 ÷ 200 × 100%). 52.5 percent = (105 ÷ 200 × 100%).

(f) Two and a half percent = (5 ÷ 200 × 100%).

2. (a) $150 billion; –10 (recessionary gap); 0; 20 percent; $90 billion (60 percent of $150 billion); $30 billion (the vertical intercept value); $2 billion surplus = (30 – 0.2 × 160).

   b) $160 billion; 0; 5 percent (8 ÷ 160); 20 percent; $96 billion (60 percent of $160 billion); $40 billion (the vertical intercept value); Cyclically-adjusted deficit of $8 billion (40 – 32).

   (c) Although the tax rate has not changed, government expenditures have fallen by $10 billion from 1999 to 2000. This change in fiscal policy is best seen by noting that the government plans a cyclically-adjusted surplus in 2000 (and reducing outstanding debt), while it ran a cyclically-adjusted deficit in 1999. Also note that the change in fiscal policy stance is at a time when real national income is falling; i.e., fiscal policy is procyclical.

   (d) The government appears to want to stabilize the debt-to-GDP ratio. Notice that the government ran a budget deficit in 1999 when the economy was at its potential level of output. With the downturn in the economy in 2000, tax revenues will be lost. If the government had continued its 1999 level of expenditures at $40 billion in 2000, the deficit would have grown and the government would have had to increase the debt-to-GDP ratio. Future tax liabilities will be higher and possibly some of the crowding-out effects discussed in the text may cause declines in investment and exports.

3. (a) The change in the debt-to-GDP ratio is given by the formula $\Delta d = x + (r - g)d$. In this case, the change in the debt-to-GDP ratio is 2 percent = $[0.01 + (0.04 - 0.02) \times 0.50]$. Since this value is positive, government borrowing increased.

   (b) To obtain $\Delta d = 0$, then a primary surplus of 0.01 (a primary deficit of –0.01) is required to offset the growth in real debt-service payments of 0.01.

   (c) The formula is given by deficit/GDP = $(\pi + g)$ times (debt/GDP). Since $\pi = 0$, then the deficit/GDP ratio is 1 percent = 0.02 times 0.50.

   (d) The change in the debt-to-GDP ratio is 2.2 percent. The primary surplus required to keep $\Delta d = 0$ is 0.012. The new deficit/GDP ratio is 1.2 percent. One policy implication is that program spending must be reduced more than before because of a higher debt-to-GDP ratio. Hence, the flexibility in conducting counter-cyclical fiscal policy has been diminished.

4. (a) $AE = 50 + 0.8(Y - 0.2Y) + 100 + 160 + 10 - 0.04Y$. Using the equilibrium condition $Y = AE$, we obtain $Y = 800$. There is no output gap. The budget is balanced since total government spending equals total taxation revenue of 160.

   (b) The new equilibrium GDP is 795. An export decline of 2 generated a decline in GDP of 5; hence the multiplier is 2.5. There is an output (recessionary) gap of –5 and the government deficit is 1.0.

   (c) The expression for aggregate expenditure is now $50 + 0.8(Y - 0.2Y) + 100 + 0.2Y(= G) + 10 - 0.04Y$. As before, $Y = 800$.

   (d) With the decline in net exports of 2, the new equilibrium GDP is 790. Since total taxation revenue is 158, G must also be 158. The multiplier value is 5 since a decline in net exports of 2 created a reduction of 10 in GDP. The output gap is now –10, which is greater than in part (b), which required no balanced budget. The multiplier with an annually balanced budget requirement is larger because the recessionary gap automatically reduces tax revenue, which must be matched by an equal reduction in government spending. Thus, as the text suggests, an annually balanced budget serves as a *built-in destabilizer*.

Extension Exercise

E1.   (a) i = 5 percent and total private saving borrowing (investment) = 35 zeds.

Figure 31-6

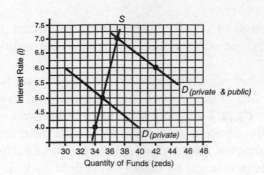

(b) i = 7 percent and total private saving (= borrowing) is 37 zeds. $72 - 5i = 30 + i$; i = 7 percent.

(c)   With the original demand curve for funds, private-sector borrowing at an interest rate of 7 percent would have been 25. We know that total borrowing at 7 percent is 37, 12 of which is government borrowing. National saving is equal to private saving at 7 percent minus the budgetary deficit, or $37 - 12 = 25$. Notice that private savings increased by 2 with the increase in the interest rate. Since private saving did not increase by the value of the budget deficit, national saving fell with the result that savers in this economy cannot be characterized as "Ricardian" consumers.

(d) $10 = (35 - 25)$.

(e)   The deficit-to-GDP and debt-to-GDP ratios are both 1.2 percent. Since the interest rate is 7 percent, debt service payments are 0.84 zees. The total deficit is therefore 12.84 zeds.

Practice Multiple Choice Test

1. (b) 2. (e) 3. (b) 4. (c) 5. (e) 6. (d) 7. (a) 8. (c) 9. (b) 10. (b) 11. (e)

CHAPTER 32

ECONOMIC GROWTH

LEARNING OBJECTIVES

1 Understand how small differences in growth rates can generate large differences in income over many years.

2 Explain the costs and benefits of economic growth.

3 List the four fundamental determinants of growth in real GDP.

4 Understand the main elements of Neoclassical growth theory.

5 Have a general knowledge of the new growth theories based on endogenous technical change and increasing returns.

6 Explain why resource exhaustion provides society with incentives for technological improvements.

CHAPTER OVERVIEW

This chapter considers economic theories of how and why economies grow and living standards increase over time. Factors that affect the rate of economic growth include the quantity of labour and capital; the stock and quality of human capital; and technological improvement. The importance of ideas, knowledge, and new technology is the focus of other theories of economic growth.

The chapter discusses the **costs and benefits of economic growth**. One of the potential costs of economic growth is that current consumption might be diverted to capital formation. The distinction between economic growth and living standards (measured by *per capita* output) is discussed.

Neoclassical growth theory, using an **aggregate production function** stresses, **diminishing returns** to a variable factor, **constant returns to scale**, **balanced growth**, and **embodied technological change**. Other growth theories emphasize the possibility of historical **increasing returns to investment** because of fixed costs, knowledge, and **endogenous technological change**. The chapter concludes by discussing the limits to economic growth (resource depletion and pollution).

CHAPTER REVIEW

The Nature of Economic Growth

This section demonstrates the powerful and **cumulative effect** of constant growth rates on the level of real GDP over time. You would profit by learning two equations. The first calculates the value of real GDP after N years when real GDP grows at a constant rate. Specifically, real GDP after N years equals $Y_0(1 + g)^N$, where Y_0 is the initial value of GDP and g is the constant rate of growth. This formula will also be helpful in understanding the opportunity costs of growth. The second equation is the famous *Rule of 72*. The time taken for a variable to double in value is approximated by dividing 72 by the growth rate (if the growth rate = 10%/year, you divide by 10).

1. Economic growth is best defined as
   (a) a rise in real national income as unemployment is reduced.
   (b) fluctuations of GDP around its potential level.
   (c) a rise in real per capita GDP (living standard) over time.
   (d) increases in current real GDP as structural unemployment decreases.
   (e) a reduction in the inequality of income distribution.

2. Theories of economic growth stress
   (a) ways of reducing income inequalities.
   (b) the elimination of short-term inefficiencies.
   (c) the factors that increase potential real GDP over time.
   (d) the need to increase consumption and decrease saving over time.
   (e) the need for countries to become self-sufficient in food production.

3. According to the "rule of 72," a growth in population of 2 percent per year means that population will double in approximately
   (a) 2 years.   (b) 144 years.
   (c) 72 years.   (d) 260 years.
   (e) 36 years.

4. What is the value of $100 that grows at 5 percent per year after 6 years?
   (a) $130.   (b) $105.
   (c) $134.01   d) $630.
   (e) None of the above.

5. A contemporary view of the relationships among economic growth, reducing efficiency, and improving equity is that
   (a) all three are interrelated.
   (b) by necessity, economic growth always eliminates inefficiencies and inequities among socio-economic groups.
   (c) achieving one of them can have detrimental effects on the others.
   (d) All of the above.
   (e) None of the above.

6. Which of the following would normally not be considered a beneficial result of economic growth?
   (a) higher living standards.
   (b) more wealth concentrated in the hands of a few citizens.
   (c) ease in achieving some types of income redistribution.
   (d) technological changes that produce substitutes for dwindling resource stocks.
   (e) a higher quality of life.

7. For the economy as a whole, the primary opportunity cost of economic growth is
   (a) the reduction in GDP per capita in future time periods.
   (b) the widespread environmental deterioration that inevitably results from economic growth.
   (c) the loss of current consumption opportunities.
   (d) increased unemployment in the short run.
   (e) a greater inequality of income within a country that inevitably results from economic growth.

Theories of Economic Growth

The four fundamental determinants of growth of total output are (1) *growth in the labour force*; (2) *growth in human capital*; (3) *growth in physical capital*; and (4) *technological improvement*. **The short-run and long-run effects of increased investment and saving** are noted.

Neoclassical growth theory connects the four forces of economic growth by the aggregate production function which has three major properties: (1) diminishing marginal productivity of a variable factor, (2) constant returns to scale, and (3) embodied technological change. (*Note:* Students who have not taken microeconomics may wish to attempt Exercise 2 before attempting the multiple-choice questions in this section.) The implications of these properties on growth in GDP and on living standards are also explained.

Other growth theories stress the endogenous nature of technological change with economic causes and the possibility of increasing returns to investment.

8. In terms of aggregate demand and aggregate supply, economic growth refers to
   (a) rightward shifts of the *LRAS* curve.
   (b) rightward shifts of the *AD* curve.
   (c) leftward shifts of the *SRAS* curve.
   (d) simultaneous rightward shifts of the *AD* curve and the *SRAS* curve.
   (e) the elimination of a recessionary gap.

9. In the long run, all else equal, an increase in saving in a country is likely to
   (a) cause the aggregate demand curve to shift to the left.
   (b) cause real national income to fall because of inadequate aggregate demand.
   (c) increase economic growth because more investment expenditure can be financed from these funds.
   (d) reduce structural unemployment and therefore increase potential GDP.
   (e) increase the reliance on foreign capital to finance investment.

10. In neoclassical theories of growth which assume unchanging technology, capital accumulation
    (a) decreases living standards as measured by real per capita output.
    (b) generates a constant rate of growth in GDP per capita.
    (c) increases output per worker subject to the law of diminishing returns.
    (d) has no effect on GDP in the short run or the long run.
    (e) has no effect on the standard of living in the long run.

11. The neoclassical assumption of constant returns to scale means that
    (a) economic growth occurs with increased GDP per capita.
    (b) GDP per capita increases with economic growth.
    (c) living standards must decrease with economic growth.
    (d) living standards must decrease if technological change is labour augmenting.
    (e) None of the above are correct.

12. Which of the following is *not* a feature of the increasing returns theory of economic growth?
    (a) Firms that first develop new investment opportunities receive low initial rates of return because of high fixed costs.
    (b) Investors who follow "pioneer" investors face higher investment costs and therefore decreasing rates of return.
    (c) Once a technological breakthrough has been made, new investors garner high rates of return since this technology is usually available to them.
    (d) The acceptability of new products takes a learning-by-using process by consumers.
    (e) Both (b) and (d).

13. Which of the following is *not* a feature of the endogenous technological change theories?
    (a) Technological change is viewed as exogenous.
    (b) The diffusion of technology is not costless.
    (c) Innovation is encouraged by a strongly competitive environment and discouraged by monopoly practices.
    (d) Shocks can sometimes provide a spur to innovation.
    (e) Technological change is responsive to such economic signals as prices and profits.

Are There Limits to Growth?

Although resource exhaustion is a general concern, modern growth theory stresses the historical record of continual technological change and increasing resource stocks. However, the management of pollution has become a pressing matter.

14. Which of the following statements accurately reflects an issue related to economic growth?
    (a) There is no evidence that technological change may require less inputs to produce a given level of output.
    (b) The capacity of the earth's natural processes to cope with the pollution created by a growing population cannot be sustained.
    (c) The benefits of technological advances are distributed across all nations too quickly.
    (d) All nations share equally in the benefits of economic growth.
    (e) Sustainable growth is best generated by using natural resources at a faster rate.

EXERCISES

1. Suppose that an economy's current GDP is 100. Economists have estimated that the country's potential national income could grow by either 1 percent, 2 percent, or 6 percent, depending on its policies with respect to promoting savings and investment, providing education, allowing free international trade, and protecting the environment. You are asked to determine the economic implications of the alternative growth scenarios.

    (a) Calculate, to one decimal, the missing values in the following table. Use the compound growth formula, $Y_0(1 + g)^N$, where Y_0 is current GDP, g is the annual rate of growth, and N is the number of compounding periods.

Estimated GDP at various growth rates

Year	1%	2%	6%
0	100	100	100
1	____	____	____
10	____	____	____
12	____	____	____
36	____	____	____
72	____	____	____
100	____	____	____

(b) What is the effect on GDP of a doubling of the annual growth rate from 1 percent to 2 percent after 1 year? After 10 years? After 100 years?

(c) What is the effect of GDP of a trebling of the annual growth rate from 2 percent to 6 percent after 1 year? After 10 years? After 100 years?

(d) Use your calculations to illustrate the *rule of 72* by filling in the following blanks. Refer to the Mathematical Note at the back of the textbook. At 1 percent annual growth, GDP doubles after about _____ years; at 2 percent annual growth, GDP doubles after about _____ years; at 6 percent annual growth, GDP doubles after about _____ years.

(e) What additional information would you need to determine how living standards change in the three scenarios?

2. Consider the following aggregate production function, $Y = T \times (KL)^{1/2}$, where

Y is real GDP
T is the state of technology
K is the capital stock
L is the amount of labour
The term $(KL)^{1/2}$ is the square root of the product KL

For parts (a) to (c), we assume that the aggregate production function takes on a specific functional form:

$$Y = 3(KL)^{1/2}.$$

(a) The table below represents the case where labour use changes but all other factor supplies and technology are constant. Fill in the missing values in the table for values of real GDP.

Labour (L)	Capital (K)	Technology (T)	Real GDP (Y)
10	20	3	42.4
15	20	3	
20	20	3	
25	20	3	

(b) The marginal productivity of labour is defined as the change in real GDP divided by the change in labour use. What is the marginal productivity when labour use increases from 10 to 15? From 15 to 20? From 20 to 25? What do you observe?

(c) As labour use increases, what happens to the living standard as measured by the value of real output per worker?

Parts (d) and (e) have the same functional form for the aggregate production function but different data. Specifically, labour and capital increase by the same proportion 50 percent, and technology continues to remain constant at 3.

Labour (L)	Capital (K)	Technology (T)	Real GDP (Y)
10	20	3	42.4
15	30	3	
20	40	3	
25	50	3	

(d) Fill in the missing value for Y. What do you observe happens to changes in Y for successive, proportional increases in labour and capital?

(e) What happens to the standard of living as measured by real output per worker?

Part (f) assumes that technology changes. The value of T increases from 3 to 4, but factor use remains constant.

Labour (L)	Capital (K)	Technology (T)	Real GDP (Y)
20	20	4	

(f) Calculate the value of real GDP for this case. Compare this value with the value in row 3 for part (a). What do you conclude?

3. This exercise focuses on the opportunity costs of growth. Suppose that real GDP of an economy was 100 in year 0, consumption expenditure was 85, and investment expenditure was 15. The growth of real national income on an annual basis is expected to be 2 percent. The current government urges the citizens of this nation to pursue policies to increase the growth rate to 4 percent on an annual basis.

Its economic forecasters suggest that by reducing consumption to 70 (increasing saving by 15) and by increasing investment expenditure to a level of 30, (1) consumption expenditure 7 years hence will be equal to that level of consumption without these policies (with the economy growing at 2 percent), and (2) the aggregate level of consumption in 20 years will be *double* the level associated with a 2 percent growth rate.

| | Annual Level of Consumption | | |
In Year	2 Percent Growth	4 Percent Growth	Cumulative (Loss) or Gain
0	85.0	70.0	(15.0)
1	86.7	72.8	(28.9)
2	88.4	75.7	(41.6)
3	90.2	78.7	(53.1)
4	92.0	81.9	(63.2)
7	97.6	92.1	(84.4)
8	99.6	95.8	(88.2)
9	101.6	99.6	(90.2)
10	103.6	103.6	(90.2)
17	119.0	136.4	(23.7)
18	121.4	141.8	(3.3)
20	126.3	153.4	47.8
30	154.0	227.0	
40	187.7	336.1	
50	228.8	497.5	

Your task is to confirm the accuracy of the government's economic forecasts by answering the following questions.

(a) Prove that the value of consumption after 10 years is equal to 103.6 for both a growth rate of 2 percent and for 4 percent. Use the formula, $C = C_0(1 + g)^N$.

(b) What is the loss in consumption in year 4 because of the government's growth policy? What is the cumulative loss after four years?

(c) In what year will the level of consumption with a 4 percent growth rate equal the level of consumption with a 2 percent growth rate? Compare your answer with the government's assertion.

(d) In what year does this economy recoup all of the cumulative losses in forgone consumption? This is called the "break-even" year.

(e) Is the government's assertion that this society will double its consumption level in 20 years correct?

PRACTICE MULTIPLE CHOICE TEST

Questions 1 through 4 refer to the following data for an economy with a constant technology:

Labour	Capital	Output
10.0	10	10.0
10.0	15	11.8
10.0	20	13.2
15.0	15	15.0
22.5	15	19.1

1. The marginal product of capital (extra output per extra unit of capital input, other inputs unchanged)
   (a) is 1.8 when capital rises from 10 to 15.
   (b) is .14 when capital rises from 15 to 20.
   (c) rises when progressively more capital is used.
   (d) demonstrates the principle of increasing returns to scale.
   (e) is 0.36 when capital rises from 10 to 15.

2. The marginal product of labour (extra output per extra unit of labour input, other inputs unchanged)
   (a) is 0.55 (approximately) when labour rises from 15 to 22.5.
   (b) is 4.1 when labour rises from 15 to 22.5.
   (c) is 1.8 when labour rises from 10 to 15.
   (d) cannot be estimated in this table.
   (e) demonstrates the principle of increasing returns to scale.

3. This economy operates under constant returns to scale because
   (a) increasing capital inputs has a constant positive effect on output.
   (b) increasing labour and capital inputs by 50 percent increases output by 50 percent.
   (c) increasing labour inputs has a constant positive effect on output.
   (d) both marginal productivities are positive and constant.
   (e) of the law of diminishing returns.

4. When labour (workers) increases from 15.0 to 22.5 and capital remains at 15,
   (a) living standards per worker increase because marginal productivity is positive.
   (b) output per worker stays constant because capital is constant.
   (c) living standards per worker decrease even though marginal productivity is positive.
   (d) the average productivity of labour (workers) is 0.55 approximately.
   (e) living standards per worker increase because average productivity of labour increases.

5. Suppose that two countries have the same per capita output. Country A has an annual economic growth rate of 6 percent, while country B grows at 3 percent per year. According to the rule of 72, country A will have a per capita output four times as large as country B's in
   (a) 12 years.   (b) 36 years.
   (c) 24 years.   (d) 48 years.
   (e) 72 years.

6. Ken and Bill begin the same job with a first year salary of $18,000. If Ken's salary grows at 3 percent each year and Bill's grows at 2 percent per year, then after 8 years
   (a) Ken's yearly salary will be about $1,710 more than Bill's.
   (b) Ken's yearly salary will be about $21,100.
   (c) Ken's yearly salary will be about $1,440 more than Bill's.
   (d) Ken's yearly salary will be about $22,320.
   (e) Both (c) and (d).

7. Which of the following cases associated with the Neoclassical theory would increase a country's standard of living?
   (a) Capital accumulates over time, but other factor uses are constant.
   (b) Labour supply increases over time, but other factor uses are constant.
   (c) All factors increase over time by the same proportion.
   (d) Technological improvements result in increased production with less or the same amounts of all inputs.
   (e) All factor supplies decrease over time with technology constant.

Questions 8 to 11 assume an aggregate production function of $Y = K \times L^{1/2}$.

8. What is the value of Y when $K = 2$ and $L = 4$?
   (a) 4.   (b) 8.
   (c) 2.8.   (d) 5.7.
   (e) None of the above.

9. What is the value of K when $Y = 7.35$ and $L = 6$?
   (a) 1.23.   (b) 10.4.
   (c) 4.2.   (d) 1.73
   (e) 3.

10. What is the value of L when $K = 4$ and $Y = 11.31$?
   (a) 32.   (b) 5.66
   (c) 2.38.   (d) 8.
   (e) 2.83.

11. Comparing your answers to questions 9 and 10, you conclude that this production function conforms to that suggested by
    (a) the Neoclassical theory which features constant returns to scale.
    (b) recent growth theories that emphasize increasing returns to scale.
    (c) recent growth theory that stresses endogenous technological change.
    (d) the Neoclassical theory which features exogenous technological change.
    (e) Professor Solow's measure of technological change.

SOLUTIONS

Chapter Review

1. (c) 2. (c) 3. (e) 4. (c) 5. (a) 6. (b) 7. (c) 8. (a) 9. (c) 10. (c) 11. (b) 12. (b) 13. (a) 14. (b)

Exercises

1. (a)

Year	1%	2%	6%
1	101.0	102.0	106.0
10	110.5	121.9	179.1
12	112.7	126.8	201.2
36	143.1	204.0	814.7
72	204.7	416.1	6,637.8
100	270.5	724.5	33,930.2

(b) After 1 year, GDP is about 1 percent more; after 10 years, GDP is 11.4 more or about 10 percent more; after 100 years, GDP is 168 percent greater (454 more).

(c) After 1 year, GDP is 4 percent more; after 10 years, GDP is about 47 percent more (57.2 more); after 100 years, GDP is almost 46 times more.

(d) 72 years; 36 years; 12 years.

(e) Most importantly, we would need population information because if we are interested in improved living standards, we are concerned with increasing GDP per person. If we are concerned with a broader definition of economic welfare, factors such as health and environmental standards might also be considered. The actual distribution of income, rather than its average value per person, may also interest us.

2. (a) Real GDP = 52.0, 60.0, 67.2.
    The value 67.2 is obtained by taking the square root of 25 times 20 which is equal to 22.4 and multiplying by 3.

(b) When labour increases from 10 to 15, output increases by 9.6. Hence MP_L = 1.9
    When labour increases from 15 to 20, output increases by 8.0. Hence MP_L = 1.6.
    When labour increases from 20 to 25, output increases by 7.2. Hence MP_L = 1.4.
    There are diminishing returns to labour.

(c) Real per worker output continually falls; Average output per worker = 4.2, 3.5, 3.0, 2.7.

(d) Y = 63.6, 84.9, 106.1. Output increased by 50 percent which is the same proportionate increase as occurred to labour and capital. Take for example the effect on output when labour increased from 10 to 15 and capital increased by 20 to 30. Both of these represent 50 percent increases. Output increased from 42.4 to 63.6. This also represents a 50 percent increase.

(e) GDP per worker remains constant at 4.2. Hence, the standard of living has not changed.

(f) Real GDP is 80. The equivalent case is in part (a) where GDP was 60.0. Hence, a technological improvement increases output by 20 units without any increased usage of labour or capital.

3. (a) C after 10 years at $g = .02$ is $85(1.02)^{10} = 103.6$. C after 10 years at $g = .04$ is $70(1.04)^{10} = 103.6$.

(b) The loss in consumption is 10.1 (92.0 – 81.9); 63.2 is the cumulative loss.

(c) According to the schedule, consumption (C) at 4 percent growth will equal C at 2 percent growth in year 10. This is substantially longer than suggested by the government.

(d) Sometime between the eighteenth and nineteenth years. Note that we have treated all gains and losses the same, regardless of the year in which they occur.

(e) No; it is much later. According to the schedule, C at 4 percent growth is double C at 2 percent growth in approximately 45 years.

(*Note:* All calculations assume annual compounding.)

Practice Multiple Choice Test

1. (e) 2. (a) 3. (b) 4. (c) 5. (d) 6. (a) 7. (d) 8. (a) 9. (e) 10. (d) 11. (b)

CHAPTER 33

CHALLENGES FACING
THE DEVELOPING COUNTRIES

LO LEARNING OBJECTIVES

1　Gain a general knowledge of the extent of world income inequality.

2　Understand some of the main challenges facing developing countries.

3　Understand the emergence of a new view of development, known as the "Washington consensus."

4　Understand the current debates about development policies.

CHAPTER OVERVIEW

About one-quarter of the world's population still exists at a level of bare subsistence, and nearly three-quarters are poor by Canadian standards. Although some poorer societies have grown rapidly, the **development gap** between the very richest and very poorest remains large and appears to be increasing.

　Impediments to economic development include excessive population growth; resource limitations; inefficient use of resources; inadequate infrastructure; excessive government intervention; lack of property rights; and institutional and cultural patterns that make economic growth difficult.

　The older model for development policies included heavy tariff barriers; hostility to **foreign direct investment**; controls and subsidization of local activities; and exchange rates pegged at excessively low values.

　The new view, the so-called "**Washington consensus**," describes the conditions that may be necessary and sufficient for a poorer country to get itself on a path of sustained development.

CHAPTER REVIEW

The Uneven Pattern of Development

Some readers will be shocked to learn that citizens of the 63 so-called low income countries earn on average less than $2.00 American a day; in some of these countries the daily earnings are less than 50 U.S. cents. The gap between these countries and the high income countries such as Switzerland, Japan, the United States, France, and Canada appears to be growing. Between the "developed" countries and "developing" countries, there is another group of nations, called the **newly industrialized countries (NICs)**.

1. The development gap is defined as
   (a) the discrepancy between the standards of living in countries at either end of the world income distribution.
   (b) the difference between output growth rates in developed and developing countries.
   (c) the difference in the degree of allocative efficiency in developed countries and developing countries.
   (d) the discrepancy between the savings rates in developed countries compared with those in developing countries.
   (e) None of the above.

2. The group of nations, called the newly industrialized countries (NICs),
   (a) grew rapidly in terms of real per capita GDP rapidly in the three decades after 1960.
   (b) typically have per capita incomes close to 50 percent of those found in developed nations.
   (c) include countries such as South Korea and Singapore.
   (d) generally followed outward-looking and market-based policies.
   (e) All of the above are correct.

Impediments to Economic Development

Developing countries face many impediments to improvements in living standards. Several barriers to growth are discussed in this chapter. There is an exercise that illustrates the **vicious circle of poverty** faced by various African countries.

3. Increases in real GDP in developing countries do not necessarily lead to economic advancement if
   (a) growth in productivity is greater than real GDP growth.
   (b) population growth exceeds real GDP growth.
   (c) market-oriented processes replace command-economy decision making.
   (d) foreign capital is the major source of the expansion in real GDP.
   (e) None of the above.

4. Which one of the following would *not* be considered a barrier to economic development of particular countries?
   (a) Rapid population growth.   (b) Inefficient use of resources.
   (c) International trade.   (d) Inadequate human resources.
   (e) Inadequate services such as communications and transportation.

5. Which of the following is the best example of *allocative inefficiency*?
   (a) Some productive processes use too much labour relative to capital.
   (b) Society is at the "wrong" point on its production possibility boundary.
   (c) Firms do not seek to maximize their profits.
   (d) Owners of factors of production do not seek to maximize their material welfare.
   (e) Some productive processes use too much capital relative to labour.

6. The vicious circle of poverty
   (a) refers to insufficient domestic savings generated at low levels of income to finance economic growth.
   (b) applies to countries that borrow from abroad and spend the proceeds on consumer goods.
   (c) results from the failure of policies in developing countries to hold population growth to zero percent.
   (d) describes a situation in which savings out of domestic income are invested abroad, lowering the domestic rate of capital accumulation.
   (e) implies that a widening of income-distribution inequality is an inevitable aspect of economic development.

7. What factors contributed to the growth of external debt of many developing nations?
   (a) OPEC substantially increased oil prices in 1973 and 1979.
   (b) Increases in real interest rates in the 1980s increased debt-servicing charges for governments in these countries.
   (c) High export sales of developing nations were financed by large capital outflows.
   (d) High saving rates in these countries translated into large capital inflows from developed countries.
   (e) Both (a) and (b) are correct.

Development Policies

The evolution of development policies has gone from highly protectionist and inward-looking policies to market-oriented policies that emphasize trade, investment in essential infrastructure, acceptance of the advantages of foreign direct investment (**FDI**), organizational structures which span national borders (transnational corporations, **TNCs**), the diffusion of foreign technologies to domestic firms, and the importance of human capital investments and having a qualified and competent cadre of management.

8. Which of the following was *not* a feature of the *older view* of development policies?
   (a) Import substitution.
   (b) Fixed exchange rates and exchange controls.
   (c) Governments were receptive to foreign investment.
   (d) Investment policies were focused on government-owned industries.
   (e) Heavy subsidization of private local firms.

9. Which of the following considerations contributed to a reappraisal of the older view of development policies?
   (a) Growth rates in countries that had followed interventionist approaches were high.
   (b) Many of the NIC (New Industrialized Countries) nations were lagging beyond in terms of their economic growth.
   (c) Countries that had successfully resisted the presence of multinational corporations within their boundaries had made major strides in living standard improvements.
   (d) Countries that had adopted collectivized agriculture programs had all become self-sufficient in food.
   (e) None of the above are correct.

10. One of the important implications of modern growth theory, as it applies to developing countries is
    (a) some industries must be subsidized as long as they cannot compete with global companies.
    (b) the costs of foreign direct investment (FDI) usually outweigh the benefits for most traditionally based economies.
    (c) adopting someone else's technology, for the most part, is a costless task.
    (d) the new technologies brought by transnational companies must be diffused into the local economy.
    (e) population growth will continue to be the most important source of economic growth.

11. The Washington Consensus regarding the appropriate policies for developing countries to pursue includes all but which of the following items?
    (a) Limiting government budget deficits in order to avoid the need for inflationary finance or higher interest rates.
    (b) Relying on market-determined exchange rates.
    (c) Applying protection to infant industries in selected cases for a limited period of time.
    (d) Maximizing economic growth without regard to its effect on the distribution of income.
    (e) Education, health, and infrastructure investment are desirable forms of public expenditure.

12. Which of the following is a potential cost of economic development?
    (a) Some traditional ways of doing things may have to be altered.
    (b) Current consumption may have to be sacrificed in order to generate economic development.
    (c) The inequality of income distribution may increase in the absence of redistributive policies.
    (d) Governments may have to increase their expenditures to improve economic infrastructures.
    (e) All of the above.

13. Some economists argue that active government policies that go beyond the Washington consensus may be needed because
    (a) a country is best served by protecting industries regardless of their long-term comparative advantage prospects.
    (b) income needs to be transferred to the rich in order to finance greater investment.
    (c) innovation can be encouraged by wise government policies.
    (d) domestic firms should not share in technology transfers by transnational corporations without paying sufficiently high licence fees.
    (e) None of the above are correct.

EXERCISES

1. Is there an association between a country's standard of living and its population growth? The data for seven selected countries are taken from the United Nation's website.

Country	Per Capita GDP ($U.S.), 1997	Av. Annual Rate of Population Change (%)
Chile	5,271	1.36
Brazil	4,930	1.24
Zimbabwe	802	2.09
Nigeria	1,376	2.84
Senegal	519	2.66
Pakistan	466	2.71
Mexico	4,265	1.63

(a) Using the Union Nation's categories, which of the seven countries are low income? Which are considered to be upper middle income? Which are in the lower middle income category? (*Hint:* Check Table 33-1 in the textbook for the categorizations of countries by income levels.)

(b) Plot the relationship between standard of living and population growth. What do you observe generally? Provide some explanation for your observation.

Figure 33-1

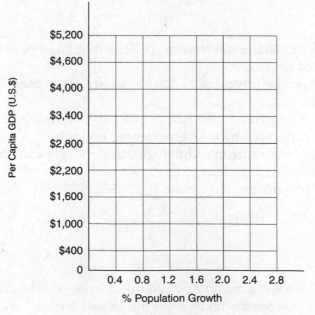

2. The textbook explains the concept of the *vicious circle of poverty*. If more domestic capital is to be created at home by a country's own efforts, resources must be diverted from the production of goods for current consumption. This reallocation of resources implies a reduction in current living standards, and if living standards are already at or near the subsistence level, such a diversion will be difficult.

The data for various African countries are obtained from the websites for the United Nations and the World Bank. You might wish to browse the websites for other countries; see (www.un.org), "Indicators on Income and Economic Activity" and (www.worldbank.org), Table 4.9, "Structure of Demand."

Country	Saving Rate as a % of GDP, 1997	Per Capita GDP (U.S. dollars), 1997
Botswana	45	$3,209
Central African Republic	7	$364
Chad	1	$149
Ethiopia	9	$104
Ghana	10	$398
Kenya	11	$356
Nigeria	22	$1,376
Rwanda	−7	$170
South Africa	17	$3,331
Uganda	8	$313

(a) The vicious circle of poverty implies a negative relationship between the domestic saving rate and the level of per capita GDP. Are the data for these 10 African countries consistent with this hypothesis?

(b) Go to the World Bank's website and find Table 4.9. (If you can't find the website, refer to the **Solutions Section** and then answer the rest of the question.) For each of the ten countries listed above, find gross domestic investment and the difference between exports and imports of goods and services for 1997. Can countries finance some domestic investment by running deficits on their current accounts?

3. Briefly explain the advantages and drawbacks of the following development policies.

(a) A policy of developing a strong agriculture-based economy.

(b) Specialization in producing a single commodity.

(c) Development of domestic industries that produce substitutes for imported products.

(d) Encouraging foreign direct investment to finance economic development.

PRACTICE MULTIPLE CHOICE TEST

Questions 1 to 6 are based on two hypothetical economies, *A* and *B*, both of which are less developed in terms of advanced country standards.

Both countries have *x* units of working labour and *y* units of land, but very little capital. Country *A* has a population of 8 and country *B* has a population of 10. Assume that either country produces and consumes only wheat and peanuts. The production possibilities (in bushels) are given in the schedules below. Students who have not taken microeconomics should review the material in Chapter 1.

Country A		Country B	
Wheat	Peanuts	Wheat	Peanuts
100	0	200	0
90	10	180	18
80	19	160	35
70	27	140	51
60	34	120	66
50	40	100	80
40	45	80	93
30	49	60	105
20	52	40	116
10	54	20	126
0	55	0	135

1. What are *A*'s opportunity costs (in terms of peanut production) of increasing wheat production from 20 to 30?
   (a) 52.   (b) 49.
   (c) 3.   (d) 101.
   (e) 10.

2. What are *B*'s opportunity costs (in terms of peanut production) of increasing wheat from 20 to 40?
   (a) 10.   (b) 126.
   (c) 146.   (d) 242.
   (e) 20.

3. What are *A*'s opportunity costs of increasing wheat production from 30 to 40?
   (a) 4.   (b) 49.
   (c) 45.   (d) 94.
   (e) 10.

4. What are *B*'s opportunity costs of increasing wheat production from 40 to 60?
   (a) 221.   (b) 116.
   (c) 105.   (d) 11.
   (e) 20.

5. Comparing your answers to (1) and (3) for country A and to (2) and (4) for country B, you can conclude that the opportunity cost for successive increases in wheat production
   (a) remains constant.
   (b) decreases.
   (c) is zero for all ranges of increases.
   (d) increases.
   (e) is equal for both countries.

6. Suppose that production and consumption in country A are 16 bushels of peanuts and 80 bushels of wheat. What situation exists in A?
   (a) Country A operates on its production possibility boundary.
   (b) This combination lies outside A's production possibility boundary.
   (c) Country A is incurring productive inefficiency.
   (d) Country A's national income is valued at 96 bushels.
   (e) Both (b) and (c) are correct.

SOLUTIONS

Chapter Review

1. (a) 2. (e) 3. (b) 4. (c) 5. (b) 6. (a) 7. (e) 8. (c) 9. (e) 10. (d) 11. (d) 12. (e) 13. (c)

Exercises

1. (a) Upper middle income ($3,126 to $9,655): Brazil, Chile, and Mexico. Lower middle income ($786 to $3,125): Nigeria and Zimbabwe. Low income ($785 or less): Pakistan and Senegal.
   (b) In general terms, there appears to be a negative relationship. The Neoclassical growth theory predicts diminishing marginal productivity with an increasing labour force applied to a constant stock of other factors. Average product will also decrease through time.

2. (a) Yes. The two countries with the highest per capita GDPs (Botswana and South Africa) have high saving rates. The countries with the lowest per capita GDPs, (Chad, Ethiopia, Rwanda) tend to have low saving rates.
   (b)

Country	Domestic Investment as a % of GDP, 1997	Current Account Balance as a % of GDP, 1997
Botswana	26	+18
Central African Republic	9	–2
Chad	19	–18
Ethiopia	19	–10
Ghana	24	–14
Kenya	19	–8
Nigeria	15	+7
Rwanda	11	–18
South Africa	16	+1
Uganda	15	–7

Notice that the Central African Republic, Chad, Ethiopia, Rwanda, and Uganda had very low saving rates. It would appear that international capital inflows (created by current account deficits) allowed them to finance more domestic investment than would have been possible from domestic saving. On the other hand, Botswana, Nigeria, and South Africa ran current account surpluses.

3. (a) Advantages: It meets the fundamental needs of its population and may allow a surplus for export; technical training requirements are low; the congestion of urban areas is avoided.
    Disadvantages: Agricultural commodities have faced worsening terms of trade in the past, because price and income elasticities in world markets are low; countries able to expand output in areas where they account for a small share of world production (and thus face a nearly horizontal demand curve) will benefit most. Moreover, the government should be confident that agricultural producers will be able to compete globally.

   (b) Advantages: Stresses specialization in commodities with the greatest comparative advantage and possibly leads to the highest immediate growth and standard of living.
    Disadvantages: Subjects country to short-term fluctuations in demand and supply and long-term secular risk of resource exhaustion or technological obsolescence.

   (c) Advantages: Easy to start by establishing a tariff, giving subsidies to import-competing industries, or import licensing; may lead to diversification and less reliance on foreign supplies for domestic consumption.
    Disadvantages: Greater risks of long-term inefficiencies relative to global competition; long-term growth jeopardized. Also, consumers pay higher prices unless protection generates scale efficiencies.

   (d) Advantages: Lessens the pressure for domestic saving to finance economic growth. State of the art technology is available immediately. Provides the opportunity for the diffusion of technology and managerial techniques over sectors of the economy. Increases employment and may result in more efficient labour use.
    Disadvantages: Foreign technology and managerial techniques may not be easily adaptable to domestic economy. Once resources have been exhausted, foreign companies may pull out. Some have argued that "branch-plant" economy may breed inefficiencies particularly if companies do not invest in R & D and demand tariff protection in the host economy.

Practice Multiple Choice Test

1. (c) 2. (a) 3. (a) 4. (d) 5. (d) 6. (c)

PART ELEVEN

INTERNATIONAL
ECONOMICS

CHAPTER 34

THE GAINS FROM INTERNATIONAL TRADE

LO LEARNING OBJECTIVES

1 Understand why the gains from trade depend on comparative advantage and not on absolute advantage.

2 Explain the gains from trade due to economies of scale and learning by doing.

3 Understand how factor endowments and climate can influence a country's comparative advantage.

4 Explain the law of one price.

5 Explain why countries export some goods and import other goods.

6 Understand what is meant by a country's term of trade.

CHAPTER OVERVIEW

This chapter explains how international trade makes possible a higher average standard of living for a country. A country benefits from buying goods abroad at a lower cost. A country is said to have an **absolute advantage** in the production of a particular commodity when it can produce more of the good with a given amount of resources than can other countries. A country has a comparative advantage in producing a particular good when it has a lower opportunity cost in production than other countries. The **gains from trade** do not depend upon absolute advantage, but rather upon comparative advantage. Even if a country has an absolute advantage in the production of all goods, both trading partners can share in the gains from trade.

Comparative advantage can be attributed to differences in exogenous considerations such as factor endowments and climate. Today, there is widespread acceptance by economists that comparative advantage may also be acquired. International trade encourages countries to specialize production in the products where they have a comparative advantage as opposed to the costly product diversification associated with self-sufficiency. The gains from trade are likely to be even greater when countries can achieve economies of scale, or benefit from **learning-by-doing**.

When transportation costs are insignificant, a traded good will sell at the same price in all countries—this is the so-called *law of one price*. This price is referred to as the world price.

The division of the gains from trade between two countries depends upon the **terms of trade** which refers to the ratio of the price of exported goods to the price of imported goods. The terms of trade determine the quantity of imported goods that can be obtained per unit of exported good.

CHAPTER REVIEW

Sources of the Gains from Trade

After studying this section, you should recognize that international trade among countries involves basically the same principles of exchange that apply to trade among individuals. You will also learn that although gains from trade can occur even when production is fixed, further gains arise when nations specialize production in goods for which they have a comparative advantage. Comparative advantage arises from differences in production opportunity costs which are determined by factor endowments and climate but also by changing human skills and experience in production.

1. Country X has an absolute advantage over country Y in the production of widgets if
   (a) fewer resources are required in X to produce a given quantity of widgets than in Y.
   (b) a given amount of resources in X produces more widgets than the same amount of resources in Y.
   (c) relative to Y, more widgets can be produced in X with fewer resources.
   (d) All of the above.
   (e) None of the above.

2. If, given the same amount of inputs, Canadian farmers produce 2 tons of rice per acre while Japanese farmers produce 1 ton of rice per acre, we can be certain that
   (a) Canada should export rice to Japan.
   (b) Canada has a comparative advantage in rice production.
   (c) Canada has an absolute advantage in rice production.
   (d) Japanese rice farmers must be paid twice as much as Canadian farmers.
   (e) Both (a) and (b) are correct.

3. Comparative advantage is said to exist whenever
   (a) one country can produce a given level of output with fewer resources compared to another country.
   (b) a given amount of resources produces more output in one country compared to another.
   (c) one country has an absolute advantage over another country in the production of all goods.
   (d) different countries have different opportunity costs in production.
   (e) two countries are of different sizes.

4. If there are two countries A and B, and two goods X and Y, and if A has a comparative advantage in the production of X, it necessarily follows that
   (a) A has an absolute advantage in the production of X.
   (b) B has an absolute advantage in the production of X.
   (c) A has a comparative disadvantage in the production of Y.
   (d) B has an absolute advantage in the production of Y.
   (e) B has a comparative disadvantage in the production of Y.

5. Which of the following is *not* a source of comparative advantage?
   (a) Factor endowments.
   (b) Climate.
   (c) Country size.
   (d) Acquiring human capital.
   (e) None of the above.

6. Gains from specialization can arise when
   (a) countries have different opportunity costs in production.
   (b) there are economies of scale in production.
   (c) experience gained via specialization lowers cost through learning by doing.
   (d) trading partners have a different comparative advantage.
   (e) All of the above.

7. Free trade within the European Community led to
   (a) each member country specializing in specific products (e.g., furniture, cars, etc.).
   (b) a large increase in product differentiation, with countries tending to specialize in subproduct lines (e.g., office furniture, household furniture, etc.).
   (c) no perceptible alteration in production patterns.
   (d) less trade among EC members.
   (e) less product diversity.

8. Economies of scale and learning by doing are different because
   (a) one refers to an increase in variable costs and the other to a decrease.
   (b) economies of scale refer to a movement along the average cost curve, whereas learning by doing shifts the average cost curve.
   (c) economies of scale affect variable costs, but learning by doing affects only fixed costs.
   (d) learning by doing affects profits but not costs.
   (e) economies of scale affect costs, whereas learning by doing affects revenue.

9. According to the Hecksher-Ohlin theory,
   (a) resource-rich countries benefit the most from trade.
   (b) different opportunity costs across countries can be explained by differences in factor endowments.
   (c) different opportunity costs across countries can be explained by differences in production functions.
   (d) low wage countries gain the most from trade.
   (e) countries with similar opportunity costs can gain the most from trade.

10. The concept of dynamic comparative advantage is best characterized by
    (a) the importance of factor endowments in determining trade patterns.
    (b) changes in a country's terms of trade due to depletion of natural resources.
    (c) acquiring new areas of specialization through investment in human capital.
    (d) changes in a country's variable costs due to economies of scale.
    (e) Both (a) and (b) are correct.

The Determination of Trade Patterns

After reading this section you will understand the law of one price and its implications for a country's imports and exports. Make certain that you understand the relationship between a country's comparative advantage and its no trade price.

11. The *law of one price* refers to
   (a) the idea that international cartels will collude to charge a single price.
   (b) federal statutes that regulate firms to charge the same price domestically as internationally.
   (c) the idea that when transportation costs are insignificant, a product will tend to have the same price worldwide.
   (d) the international trade principle that export products cannot be subject to price discrimination.
   (e) None of the above.

12. A single world price of oil is likely to exist if
   (a) oil can be transported easily from one country to another.
   (b) each country produces all of its domestic consumption.
   (c) all governments restrict exports of oil.
   (d) demand is the same in all countries.
   (e) the cost of producing oil is the same in each country.

13. Canada is a major exporter of nickel because at the world price
   (a) Canadian quantity demanded exceeds Canadian quantity supplied.
   (b) Canadian quantity supplied exceeds Canadian quantity demanded.
   (c) the quantity of nickel demanded by Canadians exceeds domestic production.
   (d) Canada mines more nickel than any other country.
   (e) domestic consumption and production are the same as they would be in the "no trade" equilibrium.

The Terms of Trade

After studying this section you should be able to explain that the terms of trade, defined as the ratio of export prices to import prices, indicate how the gains from trade are divided between buyers and sellers. You will also be able to distinguish an improvement in the terms of trade from a deterioration.

14. The terms of trade
   (a) refer to the quantity of imported goods that can be obtained for each unit of an exported good.
   (b) are measured by the ratio of the price of exports to the price of imports.
   (c) determine the division of the gains from trade.
   (d) All of the above.
   (e) None of the above.

15. A rise in export prices as compared to import prices is considered a favourable change in the terms of trade since
   (a) one can export more per unit of imported goods.
   (b) employment in export industries will increase.
   (c) one can acquire more imports per unit of exports.
   (d) total exports will increase.
   (e) All of the above.

EXERCISES

1. **Comparative and Absolute Advantage**

This exercise provides basic production data and requires you to calculate the opportunity cost of production. It then draws out the distinction between absolute and comparative advantage and the implications for trade.

For each of the following scenarios, determine the opportunity costs of producing each good in each country, and indicate in which commodity each country should specialize its trade production.

(a) One unit of resources can produce:

The opportunity costs are:

	Radios	Cameras		1 Radio	1 Camera
Japan	2	4	Japan	_____	_____
Korea	3	1	Korea	_____	_____

Japan should specialize in the production of _____.
Korea should specialize in the production of _____.

(b) One unit of resources can produce:

The opportunity costs are:

	Radios	Cameras		1 Radio	1 Camera
Japan	2	4	Japan	_____	_____
Korea	1	3	Korea	_____	_____

Japan should specialize in the production of _____.
Korea should specialize in the production of _____.

(c) One unit of resources can produce:

The opportunity costs are:

	Radios	Cameras		1 Radio	1 Camera
Japan	2	4	Japan	_____	_____
Korea	1	2	Korea	_____	_____

Japan should specialize in the production of _____.
Korea should specialize in the production of _____.

(d) Which scenario represents reciprocal absolute advantage?

(e) Which scenario demonstrates that absolute advantage is not a sufficient condition for trade to occur? Explain.

(f) Which scenario suggests why a nation as technologically advanced as Japan can gain from trading with other countries with lower wages? Explain.

2. Countries *A* and *B* each currently produce both watches and dairy products. Assume that country *A* gives up the opportunity to produce 100 litres of dairy products for each watch it makes, and *B* could produce one watch at a cost of 200 litres of dairy products.

   (a) The opportunity cost of making watches (in terms of dairy products) is lower in country _____.

   (b) The opportunity cost of making dairy products (in terms of watches) is lower in country _____.

   (c) Country *B* should specialize in _____ and let country *A* produce _____.
   (d) The terms of trade (the price of one product in terms of the other) would be somewhere between _____ and _____ litres of dairy products for one watch.

3. **The Terms of Trade**

   The following table provides (hypothetical) data on the index of merchandise export prices and the index of merchandise import prices during the 1990s in Canada.

Year	Index of Export Prices	Index of Import Prices	Terms of Trade
1990	100.6	98.6	_____
1992	103.3	102.3	_____
1994	157.1	135.6	_____
1996	176.6	157.9	_____
1998	205.4	200.7	_____

   (a) Using the definition of the terms of trade that involves indexes, complete the table by calculating the terms of trade to one decimal place.

   (b) What does an increase in the terms of trade signify?

   (c) Would you classify the change in the terms of trade during the period 1992 to 1994 as favourable to Canada? Explain.

4. **The Production Possibility Curve and Trade**

   The following table provides data on the productivity of a single unit of resource in producing wheat and microchips in both Canada and Japan.

One Unit of Resources Produces		
	Wheat (tons)	Microchips
Canada	50	20
Japan	2	12

(a) Which country has an absolute advantage in the production of wheat? Of microchips?

(b) What is the opportunity cost of producing a ton of wheat in Canada? In Japan?

(c) Which country has a comparative advantage in the production of wheat? Of microchips?

(d) Suppose that Canada is endowed with 2 units of this all-purpose resource while Japan is endowed with 10 units. Draw each country's production possibility boundary on the following grids. (Assume constant productivity).

Figure 34-1

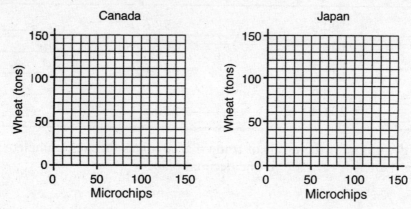

(e) Suppose that prior to trade, each country allocated half of its resource endowment to production of each good. Indicate the production and consumption points of each country in the graphs (for simplicity, assume that these are the only two countries in the world).

(f) What is world output of each good?

(g) Indicate the production points of each country after trade, and determine world production levels.

(h) Suppose that the terms of trade are one microchip for one ton of wheat and that Canada consumes as much wheat after trade as it did before trade. Indicate the post-trade consumption points of each country and each country's imports and exports.

(i) If the terms of trade changed to two microchips for one ton of wheat, which country would benefit? Explain.

5. **Imports and Exports**

Figure 34-2 depicts Canadian domestic supply and demand curves, S_c and D_c, respectively, for a commodity in a market for which Canada is assumed to face a fixed world price.

Figure 34-2

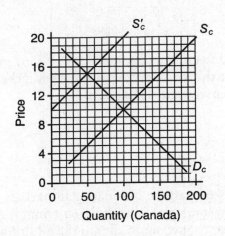

(a) At a world price of $5, Canadian producers sell _____ units, while Canadian consumers purchase _____ units. Canada therefore (imports/exports) _____ units of this commodity.

(b) Suppose a tariff of $2 per unit is imposed. Canadian production would change to _____ units, while Canadian consumption would change to _____ units. Canada would then (import/export) _____ units. The government's tariff revenue would be _____. Revenue of domestic producers would (increase/decrease) by _____, while expenditure of domestic consumers would (increase/decrease) by _____.

(c) If the world price increased from $5 to $12 per unit (assuming there were no tariff), Canadians would consume _____ units but produce _____ units. Thus Canada would (import/export)_____ units.

(d) Should domestic supply shift to S'_c while the world price remains at $12, domestic production would now be _____ units and domestic consumption _____ units. Canada would therefore be an (importer/exporter) of _____ units.

EXTENSION EXERCISES

E-1. The following exercise examines the tendency towards specialization with trade when production is characterized by increasing opportunity costs (i.e., production possibility curve is concave). A review of Extensions in Theory 34-1 entitled *The Gains From Trade More Generally* will help you answer this exercise (see pages 828–9 of the text).

The graph in Figure 34-3 depicts a country's production possibility curve between wool and lumber. Prior to trade, the country is producing and consuming at point R, which involves 10 units of wool and 10 units of lumber. Due to large increases in construction activity in this economy, the country now decides that it wishes to consume 14 units of lumber.

Figure 34-3

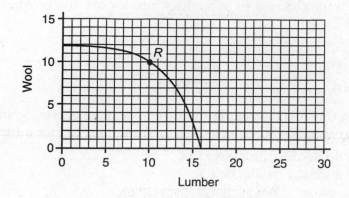

(a) How much wool must this country give up to obtain the additional four units of lumber in a no-trade environment. Explain.

(b) Suppose that the terms of trade in international markets are one unit of wool for two units of lumber. Assuming that production remains at R, how much wool would the country have to give up to obtain the additional four units of lumber if it engages in international trade? Explain.

E-2. This exercise addresses the efficiency gain from free trade by measuring the impact on consumer and producer surplus in moving from a no-trade situation to free trade for an imported good in part (a) and an exported good in part (b) (the same analysis can be applied to the removal or reduction of tariffs).

In what follows, assume that Canadian demand is a small part of world demand so that the world price P_W is independent of both Canadian demand D_C and supply S_C. Thus foreign supply is perfectly elastic at P_W. In the no-trade situation, the equilibrium price and quantity are P_E and Q_E.

(a) In Figure 34-4, P_W is less than P_E, so trade will result in imports of this good.

Figure 34-4

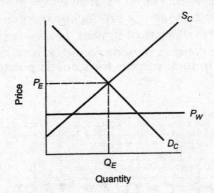

Once trade is permitted,
(i)   label domestic consumption D_D.
(ii) label domestic production S_D.
(iii) What is the change in consumer surplus in Canada?

(iv) What is the change in producer surplus of Canadian firms?

(v)   Is the net change in total surplus for Canada positive or negative? And, how much is it?

(b) In Figure 34-5, P_W is greater than P_E, so trade will result in exports of this commodity.

Figure 34-5

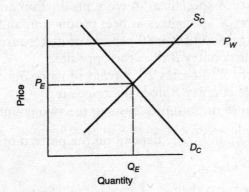

Once trade is permitted,
(i)   label domestic consumption D_D.
(ii) label domestic production S_D.
(iii) What is the change in consumer surplus in Canada?

(iv) What is the change in producer surplus of Canadian firms?

(v) Is the net change in total surplus for Canada positive or negative? And, how much is it?

PRACTICE MULTIPLE-CHOICE TEST

1. In a two-country and two-good model, gains from trade would not exist if
   (a) one country had an absolute advantage in the production of both goods.
   (b) a given amount of resources produced more of both goods in one country.
   (c) one country was endowed with far more resources than the other.
   (d) the countries had the same opportunity costs in the production of both goods.
   (e) only one country had a comparative advantage in the production of one good.

2. Which of the following statements is not true about opportunity cost?
   (a) Equal opportunity costs for pairs of commodities between two countries lead to gains from trade.
   (b) Opportunity costs depend on relative production costs.
   (c) Differences in opportunity costs across countries can enhance total output of both goods through trade and specialization.
   (d) Comparative advantage can be expressed in terms of opportunity costs.
   (e) Opportunity cost can be read as the slope of a tangent to a country's production possibility curve.

3. If production of each unit of wool in country A implies that beef production must be decreased by four units, while in country B each additional unit of beef decreases wool output by four units, the gains from trade
   (a) are maximized if country A specializes in wool production and country B in beef.
   (b) are maximized if country A specializes in beef production and country B in wool.
   (c) are maximized if country A allocates 80 percent of its resources to wool and the remainder to beef, while country B does the opposite.
   (d) are maximized if country A allocates 20 percent of its resources to wool and the remainder to beef, while country B does the opposite.
   (e) cannot be realized because opportunity costs in the two countries are the same.

4. The gains from specialization and trade depend on the pattern of _____ advantage, not _____ advantage.
   (a) absolute, comparative.
   (b) monetary, nonmonetary.
   (c) absolute, reciprocal.
   (d) comparative, absolute.
   (e) size, cost.

5. By trading in international markets, countries
   (a) can consume beyond their production possibility boundary.
   (b) will always produce the same commodity bundle as before trade.
   (c) can produce outside of their production possibility boundary.
   (d) must choose one of the intercepts on the production possibility boundary, indicating complete specialization.
   (e) always produce and consume the same bundle of commodities.

Questions 6 to 9 refer to the data in the following table. You will find it useful to first calculate the opportunity costs of production for each commodity in each country.

	One Unit of Resource Can Produce	
Country	**Lumber (bd m)**	**Aluminum (kg)**
Australia	4	9
Canada	9	3
Brazil	3	2

6. Considering just Australia and Canada,
   (a) Australia has an absolute advantage in lumber.
   (b) Australia has an absolute advantage in aluminum.
   (c) There are no possible gains from trade.
   (d) Canada should specialize in aluminum production.
   (e) Australia has a comparative advantage in lumber.

7. Considering just Canada and Brazil,
   (a) Brazil has an absolute advantage in lumber.
   (b) Brazil has a comparative advantage in aluminum.
   (c) Canada has an absolute advantage in only one commodity.
   (d) There are no possible gains from trade.
   (e) None of the above.

8. In Australia, the opportunity cost of 1 board metre (bd m) of lumber is
   (a) 2.25 kg of aluminum.   (b) 0.44 kg of aluminum.
   (c) 0.36 kg of aluminum.   (d) 3.60 kg of aluminum.
   (e) 3.00 kg of aluminum.

9. In Canada, the opportunity cost of 1 kilogram of aluminum is
   (a) 0.33 bd m of lumber.   (b) 2.70 bd m of lumber.
   (c) 3.0 bd m of lumber.   (d) 3.33 bd m of lumber.
   (e) 1.50 bd m of lumber.

10. For a country with one important export commodity such as coffee or oil,
    (a) a rise in the commodity's price will improve the country's terms of trade.
    (b) a fall in the commodity's price is a favourable change in its terms of trade.
    (c) its terms of trade will improve only if it is able to increase the quantity of exports.
    (d) its terms of trade will improve only if world demand for its exports is inelastic.
    (e) its terms of trade improve only if the price of imports decrease.

Use the following diagram to answer questions 11 and 12.

Figure 34-6

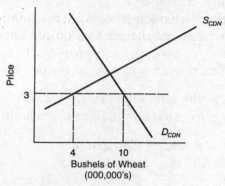

11. At a world price of $3, Canada will
    (a) produce 4 million bushels of wheat.
    (b) consume 10 million bushels of wheat.
    (c) import 6 million bushels of wheat.
    (d) consume more wheat than it produces.
    (e) All of the above are correct.

12. If the world price remains at $3, while the Canadian demand for wheat increases, the primary result would be
    (a) an increase in Canadian production of wheat.
    (b) an increase in the price of wheat in Canada.
    (c) a decrease in wheat exports.
    (d) an increase in wheat imports.
    (e) a decrease in quantity supplied by Canadian producers.

SOLUTIONS

Chapter Review

1.(d) 2.(c) 3.(d) 4.(c) 5.(c) 6.(e) 7.(b) 8.(b) 9.(b) 10.(c) 11.(c) 12.(a) 13.(b) 14.(d) 15.(c)

Exercises

1. (a) Japan: 1 radio costs 2 cameras; 1 camera costs 1/2 radio.
        Korea: 1 radio costs 1/3 camera; 1 camera costs 3 radios.
        Japan should produce cameras. Korea should produce radios.
    (b) Japan: 1 radio costs 2 cameras; 1 camera costs 1/2 radio.
        Korea: 1 radio costs 3 cameras; 1 camera costs 1/3 radio.
        Japan should produce radios. Korea should produce cameras.
    (c) Japan: 1 radio costs 2 cameras; 1 camera costs 1/2 radio.
        Korea: 1 radio costs 2 cameras; 1 camera costs 1/2 radio.
        Japan should produce both and Korea should produce both. There would be no gains from trade.
    (d) Case (a) represents reciprocal absolute advantage; Japan has an absolute advantage in cameras, and Korea has an absolute advantage in radios.

(e) Case (c) shows that even though Japan has an absolute advantage in producing both goods, no trade will occur because relative prices (or opportunity costs of production) are identical to those in Korea.

(f) Case (b) shows that even though Japanese workers are more productive in both industries (and therefore can expect to earn more than Korean workers), mutually beneficial trade can still occur if each country exports the good for which it has a comparative advantage.

2. (a) *A*.
   (b) *B*.
   (c) dairy products, watches.
   (d) 100, 200.

3. (a) 102.0, 101.0, 115.9, 111.8, 102.3.
   (b) An increase in the terms of trade means that fewer exports are required to pay for a given amount of imports.
   (c) The terms of trade changed from 101.0 to 115.6; this was a favourable change in our terms of trade. It cost us fewer exports to buy the same imports, or for the same exports we received more imports.

4. (a) Canada has an absolute advantage in both goods.
   (b) 0.4, 6.0.
   (c) Canada, Japan.
   (d) **Figure 34-7**

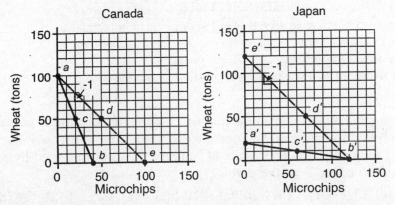

Canada's production possibility boundary is denoted *ab*, and Japan's is *a'b'*.

(e) Canada would be producing and consuming 50 tons of wheat and 20 microchips (point *c* in the diagram), and Japan would be producing and consuming 10 tons of wheat and 60 microchips (point *c'*).

(f) Assuming that these are the only countries making up the world, total output of wheat is 60 tons and world production of microchips is 80 units.

(g) Each country specializes in the commodity in which it has a comparative advantage. Thus Canada specializes completely in wheat production (see point *a*), and Japan specializes completely in microchip production (see point *b'*). World output is now 100 tons of wheat and 120 microchips.

(h) Terms of trade equal to one ton of wheat for one microchip mean that Canada can trade from its production point *a* to any point on its consumption possibility curve *ae* which has a slope of –1, representing the terms of trade. Similarly, Japan can trade from point *b'* to any point on its consumption possibility curve *b'e'*. Since it was assumed that Canada consumes the same amount of wheat both before and after trade, its consumption bundle is represented by point *d*, which contains 50 units of each good. Therefore,

Canada is exporting 50 tons of wheat in return for imports of 50 microchips. Japan, having exported 50 microchips to Canada, has 70 remaining for its own consumption. When this is combined with its 50 tons of wheat imports, Japan consumes at point d'.

(i) The terms of trade lines in the graphs would become flatter with a slope of $-1/2$. Thus Canada's consumption possibilities would increase (the dashed line rotates outward on point a), while Japan's decrease (the dashed line rotates inward on point b'). Thus Canada would get a larger share of the gains from trade.

6. (a) 50; 150; imports; 100.
   (b) 70; 130; import; 60; $120; increase; $240; increase; $160.
   (c) 80; 120; exports; 40.
   (d) 20; 80; importer; 60.

Extension Exercises

E-1. Five units. This requires a movement along the production possibility boundary from point R to point A on the following graph.

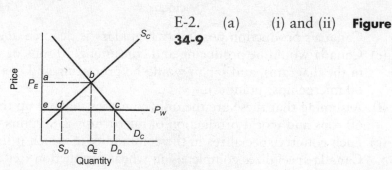

Figure 34-8

(b) Two units. The terms of trade line has a slope of $-1/2$ and is tangent to the production possibility curve at R. Thus the economy can export two units of wool in return for imports of four units of lumber; this is represented by a movement from point R to point T on the graph.

E-2. (a) (i) and (ii) **Figure 34-9**

(iii) Canadian consumer surplus increases by area $abce$.
(iv) Canadian producer surplus decreases by area $abde$.
(v) Positive. The increase in consumer surplus outweighs the loss in producer surplus; Canada receives a net gain in efficiency equal to area bcd.

(b) (i) and (ii) **Figure 34-10**

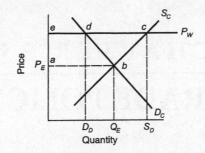

(iii) Canadian consumer surplus decreases by area *abde*.

(iv) Canadian producer surplus increases by area *abce*.

(v) Positive. The increase in producer surplus outweighs the loss in consumers surplus; Canada receives a net gain in efficiency equal to area *bcd*.

Practice Multiple Choice Test

1.(d) 2.(a) 3.(b) 4.(d) 5.(a) 6.(b) 7.(b) 8.(a) 9.(c) 10.(a) 11.(e) 12.(d)

CHAPTER 35

TRADE POLICY

LEARNING OBJECTIVES

1 Understand the various situations in which a country may rationally choose to protect some industries.

2 Recognize the most common fallacious arguments in favour of protection.

3 Explain the effects of placing a tariff or a quantity restriction on an imported good.

4 Recognize that trade-remedy laws are sometimes just thinly disguised protection.

5 Explain the difference between trade creation and trade diversion.

6 Know the main features of the North American Free Trade Agreement.

CHAPTER OVERVIEW

This chapter examines the ways in which a government may intervene in markets to restrict international trade and the resulting consequences. **Protectionist trade policy** usually takes one of two forms: **tariffs** that serve to raise import prices, and **nontariff barriers**—such as **import quotas** or **voluntary export restrictions**—that serve to reduce import quantities.

Free trade maximizes world output and living standards. Arguments for protection may rest on objectives other than maximizing living standards such as reducing fluctuations in national income or economic diversification. Protectionism may also be advanced by a large country as a means of gaining a favourable improvement in the terms of trade, and thereby increase national income. Several fallacious but widely employed arguments for protection are also discussed.

Since its inception in 1947, The General Agreement on Trade and Tariffs (GATT) has served to substantially reduce tariffs through a series of multilateral negotiations. The most recent set of negotiations, the Uruguay Round, concluded an agreement in several important areas that will serve to promote more liberal trade. It also saw the replacement of the GATT with the World Trade Organization (WTO).

Recently, there has been a sharp increase in the number and extent of regional trade-liberalizing agreements such as **free trade areas** and **common markets**. The North American Free Trade Agreement (NAFTA) is the world's largest and most successful free trade area and the European Union is the world's largest and most successful common market. These regional agreements bring about efficiency gains through **trade creation**, but may also lead to efficiency losses from **trade diversion**.

CHAPTER REVIEW

Free Trade or Protection?

After reading this section, you should be able to discuss the benefits and costs of expanding international trade; understand how tariffs and quotas influence trade patterns and affect a nation's standard of living; and, recognize fallacious arguments for protection.

1. Which of the following statements is *not* true of free trade?
   (a) Free trade leads to a maximization of world output.
   (b) Free trade maximizes world living standards.
   (c) Free trade always makes each individual better off.
   (d) Free trade can increase the average income in a country.
   (e) Free trade encourages countries to specialize in production.

2. The infant industry argument for tariffs is
   (a) only appropriate for industries where there are no economies of scale.
   (b) an example of dynamic comparative advantage.
   (c) theoretically valid if a new producer can sufficiently reduce average costs as output increases.
   (d) a proposal to earmark tariff revenues to finance day care facilities.
   (e) most applicable in developing countries because of their relative abundance of labour.

3. Protection against low-wage foreign labour is a fallacious protectionist argument because
   (a) free trade benefits everyone.
   (b) the gains from trade depend on comparative, not absolute, advantage.
   (c) when the foreign country increases its exports to us, their wages will rise.
   (d) the terms of trade will equalize for low- and high-wage countries.
   (e) low-wage labourers are necessarily less productive.

4. If the objective of a government is to maximize national income, which of the following is the *least* valid reason for using tariff protection?
   (a) To protect against unfair subsidization of foreign firms by their governments.
   (b) To protect against unfair low wages paid to foreign labour.
   (c) To protect newly developing industries.
   (d) To protect against dumping of foreign produced goods.
   (e) To alter the terms of trade.

5. Strategic trade policy
   (a) involves government assistance for key growth industries by protecting domestic markets and/or providing subsidies.
   (b) involves erecting higher tariff and nontariff barriers across the board to protect domestic industry.
   (c) means that the government negotiates special trade agreements with its important defence partners.
   (d) is designed to encourage the migration of certain industries to other countries to better exploit domestic comparative advantage.
   (e) attempts to encourage investment for domestic production in those markets that a country currently imports.

6. Which of the following is *not* a fallacious protectionist argument?
   (a) Buy Canadian, and both the money and the goods stay at home.
   (b) Trade cannot be mutually advantageous if one of the trading partners is much larger than the other.
   (c) Too many imports lower Canadian living standards as our money is shipped abroad.
   (d) A foreign firm, temporarily selling in Canada at a much lower price than in its own country, threatens the Canadian industry's existence.
   (e) A high wage country such as Canada cannot effectively compete with a low wage country such as Mexico.

Methods of Protection

This section discusses protectionist trade policies that directly raise the price of imports or directly reduce the quantity of imports. It also provides a review of the various trade policy remedies and procedures available in major trading countries.

7. Countervailing duties are attempts to maintain "a level playing ground" by
   (a) retaliating against foreign tariffs.
   (b) raising or lowering tariffs multilaterally.
   (c) establishing a common tariff wall around a customs union.
   (d) assessing tariffs that will offset foreign government subsidies.
   (e) subsidizing exports.

8. Which of the following statements about nontariff barriers to trade (NTBs) is *incorrect*?
   (a) The use of NTBs has been declining worldwide for the last 50 years.
   (b) The misuse of antidumping and countervailing duties unilaterally constitutes an increasingly important NTB.
   (c) Voluntary export restraints, negotiated agreements, and quotas are examples of NTBs.
   (d) Most NTBs are ostensibly levied for trade relief purposes but end up being protectionist.
   (e) Environmental and labour standards can be used as disguised NTB's.

9. Which of the following motivations for dumping can be of permanent benefit to the buying country?
   (a) Predatory pricing.
   (b) Cyclical stabilization of sales.
   (c) Enabling foreign producers to achieve lower average costs and therefore price.
   (d) Altering the terms of trade.
   (e) All of the above.

Current Trade Policy

After reading this section you will have a better appreciation of the issues in multilateral, regional, and bilateral trade negotiations, and be able to discuss the important highlights of the NAFTA and its impact on the Canadian economy.

10. Which of the following is an example of trade diversion?
    (a) A government promotes diversification of a country's industries.
    (b) Liberalized trade encourages industries to specialize in subproduct lines.
    (c) The NAFTA encourages more trade between low and high wage countries.
    (d) The NAFTA encourages Canada to switch imports from low wage nonmember countries to Mexico.
    (e) Publicized trade disputes divert attention from the gains from trade.

11. A common market includes all but which of the following?
    (a) tariff-free trade among members.
    (b) a common trade policy with the rest of the world.
    (c) rules of origin.
    (d) free movement of labour.
    (e) free movement of capital.

12. The countries in a free trade area
    (a) impose no tariffs on each other's goods.
    (b) each have an independent tariff structure with the rest of the world.
    (c) do not permit the free movement of labour across their borders.
    (d) do not have a common monetary policy.
    (e) All of the above.

13. Which of the following was *not* one of the features of the NAFTA?
    (a) "Sunset" elimination of all tariffs within 15 years.
    (b) Elimination of countervailing duties between the two countries.
    (c) Exemption of cultural industries.
    (d) Continuance of quotas to support provincial supply management schemes.
    (e) Provision for national treatment for most service industries.

14. Which of the following was *not* an outcome of the Uruguay Round of GATT negotiations?
    (a) Major trade liberalization in agriculture.
    (b) Repacement of the GATT with the World Trade Organization (WTO).
    (c) A new dispute settlement mechanism.
    (d) Reduction in world tariffs by approximately 40 percent.
    (e) All of the above.

EXERCISES

1. **Import Quotas and Tariffs**

   (a) The three graphs in Figure 35-1 illustrate the demand and supply of an imported commodity Z in a free trade environment. Revise these graphs according to the protectionist policy outlined below each panel, and indicate the new price P^* and the new quantity as Q^*.

   Figure 35-1

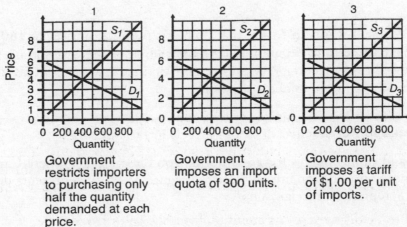

Government restricts importers to purchasing only half the quantity demanded at each price.

Government imposes an import quota of 300 units.

Government imposes a tariff of $1.00 per unit of imports.

(b) Instead of the above graphs, suppose the demand for Z were highly inelastic. Which policy would the government be least likely to choose if it wanted to minimize imports? Why?

2. **Tariffs and Quotas, Again**

The hypothetical market for canned tuna is described in Figure 35-2, where the foreign supply curve (S_f) is drawn as perfectly elastic (i.e., horizontal) and the domestic demand and supply curves are denoted D_C and S_C, respectively.

Figure 35-2

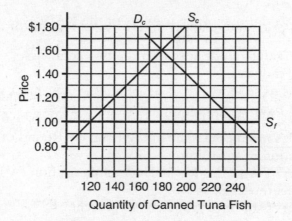

(a) Under free trade, what is the quantity of tuna consumed in Canada, the quantity supplied by Canadian producers, and the quantity supplied by foreign producers to Canadian consumers?

(b) If a 20 percent tariff is imposed, by how much does the foreign supply curve shift upward? Draw the new foreign supply curve, and calculate the consequent changes in domestic consumption, domestic production, and imports. Why is the change in imports greater than the change in domestic production?

(c) If the government wants to ensure that domestic production rises to 160, how large a quota for imported tuna should it allow? Explain.

3. **Tariffs, Quotas and Revenue**

The demand and supply curves for an imported good in a market where Canada does not have any domestic production are presented in Figure 35-3. D_C represents demand in Canada, and S_f represents foreign supply.

Figure 35-3

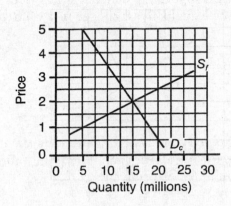

(a) What are equilibrium price and quantity and the total revenue of foreign firms?

(b) Suppose that the government imposes a specific tariff on this commodity equal to $2 per unit. What are the resulting equilibrium price Canadian consumers pay and the quantity they import? Illustrate this on the graph.

(c) What are the revenues of foreign firms and the Canadian government?

(d) Instead of the tariff, suppose that the Canadian government imposed an import quota on this good equal to 10 million units. What is the new supply curve that Canadian consumers effectively face?

(e) What would be the resulting market price and revenue of both foreign firms and the government under the quota scheme?

4. **Improving the Terms of Trade**

Suppose a country constitutes a significant proportion of world demand for widgets—for simplicity, we shall assume its represents all of world demand. Production, however, takes place by both domestic and foreign firms. The domestic supply curve of widgets is denoted S_D in Figure 35-4, and the foreign supply curve as S_F. The domestic (and, by assumption, world) demand curve is denoted D.

(a) Draw the total (i.e., world) supply curve for widgets. (*Hint:* world supply is the horizontal summation of domestic and foreign supply curves)

Figure 35-4

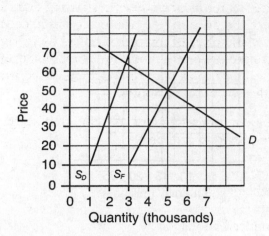

(b) Determine the world price of widgets. What is the level of domestic consumption, imports and domestic production?

(c) The domestic government seeks to improve its terms of trade by imposing a tariff on imports of widgets. Suppose it levies a tariff of $20 per imported widget. Using a broken line, draw the after-tariff supply curve for foreigner firms and the new world supply curve. What are the new price and quantity? Label them P_1 and Q_1, respectively.

(d) What effect has the tariff had on the price received by foreign firms?

(e) What effect has the tariff had on imports and domestic production?

PRACTICE MULTIPLE CHOICE TEST

1. Which of the following trade practices is *not* specifically designed as a device to promote protectionism?
   (a) Tariffs. (b) Voluntary export restrictions.
   (c) Countervailing duties. (d) Import quotas.
   (e) Costly customs procedures.

2. Which of the following national objectives is a valid argument for some degree of protectionism?
   (a) Concentration of national resources in a few specialized products.
   (b) Increases in average incomes.
   (c) Diversification of a small economy in order to reduce the risk associated with cyclical fluctuations in price.
   (d) Ability of domestic firms to operate at minimum efficient scale.
   (e) Maximization of the national standard of living.

3. A country may favourably alter its terms of trade by restricting domestic
   (a) demand and thereby reduce the price of imports for domestic consumers.
   (b) demand and thereby reduce the price of imports received by foreign producers.
   (c) supply and thereby reduce the price of imports for domestic consumers..
   (d) supply and thereby reduce the price of imports for domestic consumers.
   (e) demand and supply and thereby reduce imports.

4. _____ serve to raise a country's standard of living only to the extent that they raise
   national income to permit the purchase of more _____.
   (a) Tariffs; imports.
   (b) Exports; imports.
   (c) Imports; strategic subsidies.
   (d) Imports; non-traded goods.
   (e) Exports; domestically produced goods.

5. A large country, accounting for a significant share of world demand for an imported product,
   can increase its national income by
   (a) encouraging domestic production.
   (b) restricting domestic demand for the product, thereby decreasing its price and improving
       the terms of trade.
   (c) imposing import quotas on the product.
   (d) subsidizing imports of the good and thereby monopolize world consumption.
   (e) negotiating voluntary export restrictions.

6. The problem with restricting imports as a means of reducing domestic unemployment is that
   (a) it merely redistributes unemployment from import-competing industries to our export
       industries when trading partners retaliate.
   (b) Canadians would rather do without than have to buy Canadian-produced goods.
   (c) Our import-competing industries are not labour-intensive.
   (d) Our import-competing industries are always fully employed.
   (e) Both (c) and (d) are correct.

7. A central difference in the effects of a tariff and a voluntary export restriction (VER)—set at
   the same quantity as under the tariff—is that
   (a) the VER yields a higher price for consumers than the tariff.
   (b) the tariff pushes the consumer price beyond the price associated with the VER.
   (c) government tariff revenue becomes suppliers' revenue with a VER.
   (d) as the quantity sold decreases under the VER, the revenue of producers decreases.
   (e) Both (a) and (c) are correct.

8. Opponents of strategic trade policy have argued that
   (a) it is nothing more than a modern version of old justifications for protection.
   (b) governments are not necessarily good at picking winners.
   (c) it is best to let other countries engage in export subsidization.
   (d) All of the above.
   (e) None of the above.

9. Which of the following is *not* true of the EU's Common Agricultural Policy (CAP)?
   (a) The CAP has led to agricultural surpluses in the EU.
   (b) The CAP has turned the EU from a net importer of many agricultural products to self-sufficiency.
   (c) The CAP leads the EU to heavily subsidize its agricultural exports.
   (d) The CAP benefits agricultural producers in less developed countries.
   (e) Quotas that support the CAP are being replaced with tariff equivalents.

10. The principle of national treatment that is embedded in the NAFTA means that Canada could, for example, introduce any product standards it likes, so long as
    (a) they apply only to Canadian-produced goods.
    (b) the standards are no more stringent than those existing in either Mexico or the United States.
    (c) they apply equally to Canadian-, Mexican-, and American-produced goods sold in Canada.
    (d) they apply only to Canadian exports.
    (e) they apply only to Canadian imports.

11. A major effect of a tariff is to
    (a) redistribute income from consumers to domestic producers and the government.
    (b) allow consumers to benefit at the expense of domestic producers.
    (c) discourage domestic production.
    (d) encourage consumers to buy more of the good.
    (e) reduce government revenues.

12. A free trade agreement
    (a) must include rules of origin.
    (b) eliminates the need for customs controls on the movement of goods.
    (c) allows for free cross-border movement of labour.
    (d) erects a common tariff wall against nonmember countries.
    (e) Both (a) and (d) are correct.

13. Which of the following is *not* a feature of the NAFTA?
    (a) A common regime for antidumping and countervailing duties.
    (b) The principle of national treatment.
    (c) A dispute-settlement mechanism.
    (d) Accession clause whereby other countries may join.
    (e) Reduction in the barriers to trade in both goods and services among member countries.

Questions 14 to 17 refer to Figure 35-5 which gives the domestic demand and supply curves for a commodity as well as the world price.

Figure 35-5

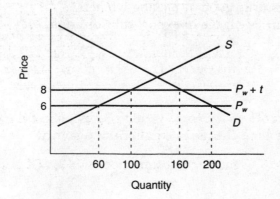

14. At a world price of $6, imports of this commodity are
    (a) 200.
    (b) 160.
    (c) 140.
    (d) 60.
    (e) 40.

15. If a tariff of $2 is levied against imports of this commodity, domestic **consumption and** production would be
    (a) 200 and 60, respectively.
    (b) 160 and 60, respectively.
    (c) 200 and 100, respectively.
    (d) 160 and 100, respectively.
    (e) 160 and 40, respectively.

16. Given a tariff of $2, government tariff revenue would be
    (a) $120.
    (b) $320.
    (c) $200.
    (d) $1280.
    (e) $800.

17. The tariff has _____ imports of this commodity by _____ units.
    (a) reduced; 80.
    (b) reduced; 40.
    (c) reduced; 100.
    (d) increased; 40.
    (e) increased; 60.

SOLUTIONS

Chapter Review

1.(c) 2.(c) 3.(b) 4.(b) 5.(a) 6.(d) 7.(d) 8.(a) 9.(c) 10.(d) 11.(c) 12.(e) 13.(b) 14.(a)

Exercises

1. (a) **Figure 35-6**

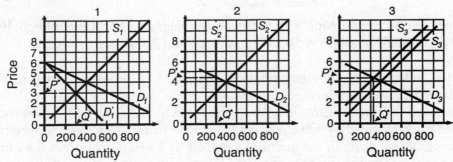

   (b) It would not choose the tariff policy. Price would rise by almost the **full amount of the** tariff, and there would be little change in equilibrium quantity.

2. (a) Canadian production is 120, Canadian consumption is 240, and imports are 120.

(b) The foreign supply curve shifts upward by 20 cents. Domestic production rises by 20, domestic consumption falls by 20, and imports fall by 40. Imports fall by more than domestic production rises due to the decline in total quantity demanded.

(c) At a price of $1.40, domestic production rises to 160, and domestic consumption falls to 200. The government can allow imports of 40 if this is to be an equilibrium position.

3. (a) $2, 15 million units, and $30 million, respectively.
    (b) $3.50 and 10 million units, respectively.

Figure 35-7

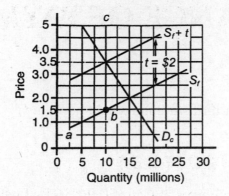

(c) Canadian consumers pay $3.50 per unit, of which $2 goes to the government. Therefore, government tariff revenue is $20 million and that of foreign firms is $15 million.

(d) The new effective supply curve is labelled *abc* in the graph.

(e) The price per unit is $3.50, revenue of foreign firms equals $35 million, and, since there is no tariff, government revenue is zero.

4. (a) and (c) **Figure 35-8**

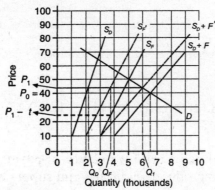

(b) The world price is $40 and denoted P_0 in the above diagram. Approximately 6,500 widgets are consumed, of which 4,500 are imported and 2,000 are produced domestically.

(c) The new price and quantity are approximately $44 and 3.75 thousand units, respectively. They are labelled P_1 and Q_1 above.

(d) The price received by foreign firms is now approximately $24 (i.e., $44 minus the $20 tariff). So the price received by foreign firms is reduced from $40 to $24 (approximately).

(e) The tariff forces a reduction in the quantity supplied by foreign producers (i.e., imports) to Q_F and an increase in the quantity supplied by domestic producers to Q_D.

Practice Multiple Choice Test

1.(c) 2.(c) 3.(b) 4.(b) 5.(b) 6.(a) 7.(c) 8.(d) 9.(d) 10.(c) 11.(a) 12.(a) 13.(a) 14.(c) 15.(d) 16.(a) 17.(a)

CHAPTER 36

EXCHANGE RATES AND THE BALANCE OF PAYMENTS

LO *LEARNING OBJECTIVES*

1 Explain the various components of Canada's balance of payments.

2 Understand why the balance of payments accounts always balance.

3 Understand the determinants of the demand for and the supply of foreign currency.

4 Explain the various factors that cause changes in the exchange rate.

5 Explain why a current account deficit is not necessarily undesirable.

6 Understand the theory of purchasing power parity, as well as its limitations.

7 Explain how flexible exchange rates can dampen the effects of terms-of-trade shocks on output and employment.

CHAPTER OVERVIEW

This chapter discusses the accounting framework for **balance-of-payments accounts** and how these international transactions determine the demand for and supply of foreign exchange. The balance of payments is divided into three major accounts: the **current account** (trade in goods, services, and net capital-service payments); **the capital account** (trade in assets [direct and portfolio]); and the **official financing account** (central bank foreign exchange transactions). A credit entry results from the sale of a good or an asset to a foreigner; it represents extra demand for a county's currency or an extra supply of a foreign currency in the foreign-exchange market. A debit entry results from the purchase of a good or an asset from a foreigner; it represents extra supply of a country's currency or an extra demand for foreign currency in the exchange market.

Transactions that generate receipts for Canada in its balance of payments (Canadian exports, capital inflows into Canada, and firms, banks, and governments that wish to increase their holdings of Canadian dollars by selling other foreign currencies) represent a **supply of foreign currency** and a demand for Canadian dollars. Conversely, payments to foreigners by Canadians (Canadian imports, capital outflows from Canada, and the firms, banks, and governments that wish to decrease their holdings of Canadian dollars in order to buy other foreign currencies) represent a supply of Canadian dollars and a **demand for foreign currency**.

Exchange rates are determined in the foreign-exchange market. Two major types of exchange rate schemes are discussed. Under a **flexible exchange rate** regime, forces of demand and supply determine the equilibrium level of the exchange rate, with no intervention by the central bank. Important determinants of the equilibrium level of the exchange rate are relative inflation rates, relative interest rates, and structural changes in the domestic or foreign economies. At the equilibrium exchange rate, the sum of the current and capital accounts must be zero, with no changes in the official financing account.

Under a **fixed exchange rate** system, the central bank may take steps to set an exchange rate that differs from the equilibrium value. A pegged rate that is set above the equilibrium exchange rate value implies that the sum of the domestic economy's current and capital accounts will be positive (a surplus). To maintain the pegged rate, the central bank increases its holdings of the foreign currency by selling domestic currency in the foreign-exchange market.

The chapter concludes by examining three important policy issues. (1) Is a current account deficit bad for Canada? (2) Is there a "correct" value for the Canadian dollar? (3) Should Canada fix its exchange rate with the U.S. dollar? **Purchasing-power-parity (PPP)** theory and the determination of the PPP exchange rate are important considerations for issue (2). Issue (3) deals with **exchange-rate risk** and the ability of flexible exchange rates to act as "**shock absorbers.**"

CHAPTER REVIEW

The Balance of Payments

Understanding the difference between a *debit* and a *credit* is important for this section. Any transaction leads to two entries (one credit and one debit) in the balance of payments accounts Hence, when all three accounts (current, capital, and official financing) are considered, the sum of all credits must equal the sum of all debits; e.g., the balance of payments must always balance. However, it is possible that any individual account may be in a deficit /surplus position. It follows that the rest of the accounts are in a surplus/deficit position.

A deficit or surplus in the balance-of-payments refers to the combined net position of the current and capital accounts *excluding* the official financing account. Hence, the balance of payments can be in deficit or surplus only if the central bank changes its foreign exchange reserves (this transaction appears in the official financing account).

1. Which of the following international transactions would be recorded as a credit in Canada's balance of payment accounts?
   (a) Canadians buy U.S. bonds.
   (b) Canadians send cash gifts to their relatives in Italy.
   (c) Canadians receive dividend income from Germany.
   (d) Canadian firms pay New York consulting companies for their services.
   (e) The Bank of Canada purchases foreign currency (and sells Canadian dollars).

2. Which international transaction would be recorded in France's current account?
   (a) French banks receive interest payments associated with their holdings of bonds issued by the German government.
   (b) French investors purchase stocks issued by Canadian companies.
   (c) A French investment group buys a mining company located in Bolivia.
   (d) The central bank of France adds to its holdings of U.S. dollars.
   (e) None of the above are correct.

3. Which international transaction would be recorded in Canada's capital account as a credit?
   (a) Canadian sales of agricultural products to China.
   (b) Germans buy farm land in Saskatchewan.
   (c) Canadian investors receive interest payments from their U.S. bond holdings.
   (d) Japanese families book skiing tours to British Columbia.
   (e) The Bank of Canada increases its holdings of gold and/or foreign-currency reserves.

4. If the Bank of Canada decreases its holdings of a foreign currency, then
   (a) this transaction would be recorded as a debit in Canada's capital account.
   (b) this probably represents the Bank's effort to prevent an appreciation of the external value of the Canadian dollar.
   (c) the combined balance of Canada's current and capital accounts must be in a deficit position.
   (d) this transaction would be recorded as a credit in Canada's Official Financing Account.
   (e) Both (c) and (d) are correct.

5. If the Bank of Canada does *not* engage in any foreign-exchange transactions, then
   (a) any deficit in Canada' current account must be matched by an equal and opposite deficit on Canada's capital account.
   (b) any surplus on Canada's capital account must be matched by an equal and opposite surplus on Canada's current account.
   (c) any deficit in Canada's current account must be matched by Canadians buying more foreign assets.
   (d) any deficit in Canada's capital account must be matched by an equal and opposite surplus on Canada's current account.
   (e) the combined balance of Canada's current and capital accounts could be either in a deficit or surplus position.

6. If the Bank of Canada increases its holdings of foreign reserves, then
   (a) this transaction is analogous to a capital inflow to Canada.
   (b) the combined balance of Canada's current and capital accounts must be in a deficit position.
   (c) it may be trying to prevent a depreciation of the external value of the Canadian dollar.
   (d) a deficit on the current account is being matched by an equal and opposite surplus on the capital account.
   (e) None of the above are correct.

The Foreign-Exchange Market

The supply of foreign exchange arises from Canadian exports to foreign countries, capital inflows to Canada, and accumulation of Canadian dollar reserves by foreigners (they supply foreign currency). The theoretical bases for an upward-sloping supply curve for foreign exchange are discussed. If the exchange rate appreciates (the Canadian dollar depreciates), we would expect Canadian exports and purchases of Canadian assets by foreigners to increase.

If the exchange rate appreciates, we would expect the demand for foreign currency to decrease (imports into Canada and purchases of foreign assets by Canadians). Hence, the demand curve for foreign exchange is downward sloping. *Movements along* either the supply or demand curves for foreign exchange are caused *only* by changes in the value of the exchange rate.

7. The exchange rate is
   (a) the ratio of exports to imports.
   (b) the amount of home currency that must be given up in order to obtain one unit of foreign currency.
   (c) the rate at which one country exchanges gold with another.
   (d) the volume of foreign goods that can be obtained for one unit of domestic currency.
   (e) always equal to the external value of a currency.

8. Suppose that one Swedish krona trades for 0.197 Canadian dollars. It follows that the external value of the Canadian dollar is
   (a) 19.7 krona.   (b) 1.97 krona.
   (c) .197 krona.   (d) 197 krona.
   (e) 5.08 krona.

9. Which of the following transactions between Canada and Japan constitutes a demand for Japanese currency (yen)?
   (a) Japanese companies buy real estate in Calgary.
   (b) Ontario producers sell beef to Japan.
   (c) Japanese mutual fund companies buy Canadian securities.
   (d) Zellers (Canada) buys Japanese-produced cameras.
   (e) Canadians receive interest payments on their holdings of Japanese bonds.

10. In the exchange market between Canadian dollars and Mexican pesos, a demander of dollars is also a
    (a) supplier of dollars.   (b) supplier of pesos.
    (c) demander of pesos.   (d) Canadian exporter.
    (e) Canadian who is buying assets in Mexico.

Questions 11 through 17 refer to Figure 36-1. The two countries are Canada (the home country) and Japan. The currency of Japan is the yen.

Figure 36-1

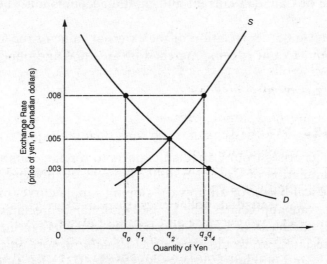

11. A movement down the vertical scale means that
    (a) the Canadian dollar is depreciating.
    (b) the yen is depreciating.
    (c) the external value of the Canadian dollar is fixed.
    (d) the exchange rate is appreciating.
    (e) None of the above.

12. If the current exchange rate is 0.005,
    (a) $200 trades for one yen.
    (b) 0.005 yen trades for one Canadian dollar.
    (c) one yen trades for 0.005 Canadian dollars.
    (d) the quantity demanded of yen is less than the quantity supplied.
    (e) the quantity supplied of yen is less than the quantity demanded.

13. At an exchange rate of 0.008,
    (a) there is an excess demand of yen.
    (b) there is an excess supply of yen.
    (c) there is an excess supply of Canadian dollars.
    (d) 0.008 yen trades for one Canadian dollar.
    (e) the external value of the Canadian dollar is 12.5 yen.

14. At a current exchange rate of 0.003,
    (a) the quantity demanded for yen is q_4 and the quantity supplied is q_1.
    (b) the current external value of the Canadian dollar is 333.33 yen.
    (c) there is an excess demand for Canadian dollars of $q_4 - q_1$.
    (d) the exchange rate has reached an equilibrium level.
    (e) Both (a) and (b).

15. Assuming that the initial exchange rate is 0.008, market forces are likely to cause the
    (a) Canadian dollar price of yen to rise.
    (b) external value of the Canadian dollar to fall.
    (c) yen to depreciate to 0.005.
    (d) external value of the Canadian dollar to rise to 333.33 yen.
    (e) quantity demanded for Canadian dollars to increase and the quantity supplied of dollars to decrease.

16. As the exchange rate changes from 0.008 to 0.005,
    (a) the quantity demanded for yen increases with the decline in the prices of Japanese goods in Canadian dollars.
    (b) Japanese imports from Canada increase.
    (c) the quantity demanded for Canadian dollars increases because Canadian exports rise.
    (d) the prices of Canadian goods imported into Japan decrease.
    (e) external value of the Canadian dollar falls.

17. The supply curve of yen is upward sloping because
    (a) as the dollar price of yen increases, the demand for Canadian exports will rise and Japanese customers will supply more yen.
    (b) as the dollar price of yen decreases, the demand for Canadian exports will fall and Japanese customers will supply less yen.
    (c) as the external value of the Canadian dollar rises (the yen depreciates), the Japanese demand for Canadian assets will decrease and Japanese investors will supply less yen.
    (d) as the external value of the Canadian dollar falls (the yen appreciates), the Japanese demand for Canadian assets will increase and Japanese investors will supply more yen.
    (e) All of the above.

The Determination of Exchange Rates

You should understand how changes in foreign and domestic inflation rates, changes in interest rates and profit expectations, and structural changes in the economy *shift* either the supply

and/or demand curves for foreign exchange thereby causing either an appreciation or a depreciation of a flexible exchange rate. You should also know how changes in the equilibrium value of
the exchange rate have potential policy implications for a fixed exchange rate system.

18. Assuming a flexible exchange rate regime, a lower inflation rate in Canada than in Mexico,
    other things being equal, is predicted to cause
    (a) the Canadian dollar price of pesos to rise.
    (b) the peso price of dollars to fall.
    (c) the demand curve for pesos and the supply curve of pesos to shift to the right, assuming
        that Canadian and Mexican goods are price elastic.
    (d) a depreciation of the Canadian dollar price of pesos.
    (e) an increase in Mexican net exports.

19. A desire by Canadians to invest more in European Union countries than before, other things
    being equal, will cause
    (a) the dollar price of the euro to appreciate under a flexible exchange rate.
    (b) the demand curve for the euro to shift to the right.
    (c) the supply curve of the euro to shift to the right.
    (d) both the demand and supply curves of the euro to shift to the left.
    (e) Both (a) and (b).

20. If short-term interest rates in Canada increase relative to short-term U.S. interest rates, other
    things being equal, then
    (a) capital flows from the United States to Canada are likely to increase and the U.S dollar
        will depreciate under a flexible exchange rate system.
    (b) the supply curve of U.S. dollars will shift to the left.
    (c) the demand curve for U.S. dollars will shift to the right.
    (d) the external value of the Canadian dollar will fall under a flexible exchange rate system.
    (e) capital flows from Canada to the United States will increase thereby causing the exchange
        rate to appreciate under a flexible exchange rate system.

21. Which of the following is not likely to cause an appreciation of the external value of the
    Canadian dollar under a flexible exchange rate?
    (a) An increase in interest rates in Canada relative to rates elsewhere.
    (b) A lower inflation rate in Canada relative to foreign rates, assuming all internationally
        traded goods are price elastic.
    (c) Lower earnings expectations on Canadian assets relative to those elsewhere.
    (d) Economic expansion in the economies of Canada's major trading partners.
    (e) A higher propensity to buy Canadian-produced goods in international markets.

22. An increase in the world demand for a country's products
    (a) leads to an appreciation of that country's currency in flexible exchange rate markets.
    (b) leads to an appreciation of the currency of other countries in flexible exchange rate
        markets.
    (c) leads to a depreciation of that country's currency under a flexible exchange rate system.
    (d) signals that this country has a balance of trade deficit.
    (e) None of the above.

23. If the Bank of Canada sets an exchange rate between euros and the Canadian dollar which is higher than the equilibrium exchange rate, then
    (a) the combined balance of Canada's current and capital accounts will be in a surplus position.
    (b) the Bank will have to buy Canadian dollars by reducing its holdings of foreign exchange.
    (c) the Bank will add to its holdings of euros in its *official financing account*.
    (d) the Bank might try to lower Canadian interest rates in order to increase the demand for Canadian dollars.
    (e) Both (a) and (c) are correct.

Three Policy Issues

Is a current account deficit bad for Canada? The lesson to be learned from Chapter 35 is that the gains from trade depend on the volume of trade (both imports and exports) rather than the balance of trade. A current account deficit is created by changes in private saving, domestic investment, and the government's budget deficit. Hence, knowing the cause of the deficit is crucial to knowing whether the change in the current account is undesirable.

24. A current account deficit
    (a) is viewed to be a "good" situation by Mercantilists.
    (b) can be created by an increase in private saving.
    (c) will increase if governments adopt budget surplus policies.
    (d) can be created by increases in domestic investment.
    (e) necessarily implies a capital account deficit.

Is there a "correct" value for the Canadian dollar? As forces of demand and supply for the Canadian dollar in foreign-exchange markets change, the "correct" value of the Canadian exchange rate is constantly changing. However, some economists argue that, whereas various shocks may cause the exchange rate to rise or fall in the short run, there exists some long-run purchasing-power-parity level to which it will return. According to the PPP theory, the exchange rate between two country's currencies is determined by the relative price levels in the two countries. However, since countries produce different goods and not all goods are traded internationally, we must be extremely careful in selecting the price indices that are used when applying the PPP theory.

25. Consider the purchasing power parity (PPP) hypothesis in its simplest form and how it applies to the price of a McDonald's *Big Mac* in two border cities, Windsor, Ontario and Detroit, Michigan. If the price of a *Big Mac* in Detroit is $2.00 (U.S.), then
    (a) the price of the same burger in Windsor should be $2.00 (Canadian) regardless of the PPP exchange rate.
    (b) the price of a same burger in Windsor should be $2.80 (Canadian) if the PPP exchange rate is 1.40 Canadian dollars per U.S. dollar.
    (c) if the U.S. dollar price of the burger in Windsor is $2.10, then the Canadian dollar is undervalued relative to a PPP level of 1.40.
    (d) if the U.S. dollar price of the burger in Windor is $1.90, then the Canadian dollar is overvalued relative to a PPP level of 1.40
    (e) None of the above.

26. According the purchasing power parity (PPP) hypothesis, if domestic inflation in country *A* exceeds that in country *B* by 10 percent, *B*'s currency (in terms of *A*'s currency) should
   (a) increase by about 10 percent.
   (b) not change, since any trade deficit will be offset by a capital inflow.
   (c) not change, since the theory applies only to fixed or pegged exchange rate systems.
   (d) decrease by about 10 percent.
   (e) not change, since inflation rates are calculated on the basis of domestically produced goods and services.

Should Canada fix its exchange rate with the U.S. dollar? Advocates of a fixed exchange rate argue that exchange-rate fluctuations generate uncertainty for importers and exporters and thus increase the costs associated with trade which in turn decrease the potential gains from trade. On the other hand, advocates of flexible exchange rates stress the importance that changes in exchange rates play in absorbing the effects of international shocks, thereby reducing the impact of these shocks on the domestic economy's output and employment.

27. Suppose that the Liquor Control Board of Ontario agrees to pay 400,000 francs for French wine three months in the future. When the LCBO negotiates this deal the dollar price of francs was $0.20 but when payment is due the dollar price of francs is $0.25. We observe that
   (a) the franc has depreciated.
   (b) French wine producers will receive larger franc payments.
   (c) the costs of the transaction from the LCBO's perspective have increased.
   (d) the LCBO is subject to an exchange rate risk because the contract was in terms of a given number of francs regardless of the level of the exchange rate.
   (e) Both (c) and (d) are correct.

28. If Mexican fruit exporters agree that they will be paid $100,000 (Canadian) in four months by Canadian fruit importers, then
   (a) the Mexican fruit exporters have accepted an exchange-rate risk.
   (b) Canadian importers will lose if the Canadian dollar falls between the period that the deal was negotiated and payment is made.
   (c) Mexican fruit exporters will gain more Mexican pesos if the Canadian dollar price of the peso depreciates between the period that the deal was negotiated and payment is made.
   (d) Canadian fruit importers have accepted an exchange-rate risk.
   (e) Both (c) and (d) are correct.

29. In terms of an *AD-SRAS* framework, a decrease in a country's terms of trade will
   (a) be shown as an upward shift to the left in the *SRAS* curve.
   (b) cause the *AD* curve to shift to the right.
   (c) result in a greater decrease in output and employment if the country has a flexible exchange rate rather than a fixed exchange rate.
   (d) reflect an initial current account surplus.
   (e) generate a smaller short-run output gap if the country's flexible exchange rate system causes its currency to depreciate.

EXERCISES

1. Suppose that the exchange rate between Canadian dollars and German marks is established in a flexible exchange market without any intervention by the Bank of Canada. For each of the following events, indicate whether the exchange rate (in this case the Canadian dollar

price of marks) will tend to appreciate, depreciate, or remain unchanged. Explain your answer briefly and indicate whether the event is likely to affect the demand curve for marks (denoted by D_M), the supply curve of marks (denoted as S_M), or both. Assume that all internationally traded goods are price elastic.

(a) Attendance of German rodeo fans at the Calgary Stampede doubles.

(b) The rate of inflation in Canada increases relative to the German inflation rate.

(c) Short-term interest rates rise in Germany relative to those in Canada.

(d) Prolonged German economic expansion increases Canadian exports to Germany.

(e) Germans buy several farms in southwestern Ontario.

(f) German construction companies expect U.S. lumber prices to increase more than Canadian lumber prices.

(g) The Bank of Canada reduces its holdings of German marks in its Official Financing Account.

2. Figure 36-2 represents the hypothetical market for Canadian imports of Japanese cameras, with prices given in Canadian dollars.

Figure 36-2

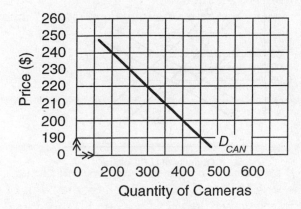

(a) The Canadian demand for imported Japanese cameras is shown in the diagram. The Japanese supply schedule for cameras is given below, with prices shown in yen (the Japanese currency). If Japanese producers quote yen prices to their Canadian buyers, determine what the supply schedule must be in terms of Canadian dollars if the external value of the Canadian dollar is 150 yen per dollar. Put your answers in column (a).

Quantity	Price in yen	Price in dollars (a)	Price in dollars (b)
200	27,000	_____	_____
300	28,500	_____	_____
400	30,000	_____	_____
500	31,500	_____	_____
600	33,000	_____	_____

(b) In the diagram, plot the supply curve you derived in column (a), and determine the equilibrium price and quantity of imported cameras.

(c) If the Canadian dollar depreciates to 129.5 yen (the yen appreciates) enter the values for the new supply curve in column (b) in the table above (round to the nearest dollar). Determine the new equilibrium price and quantity of imported cameras.

(d) By how much has Canadian spending (in Canadian dollars) on imports changed as a result of the dollar's depreciation?

(3.) You are given the demand for and supply of U.S. dollars at alternative prices in terms of Canadian dollars. Assume that the U.S. dollar changes without intervention from any central bank. The curves labelled D_0 and S_0 represent the initial case. The other curves represent changes in economic conditions between the two countries. Use them to answer (b) to (d).

Figure 36-3

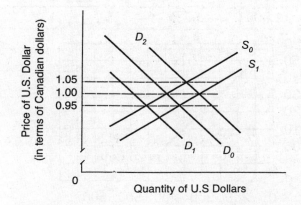

(a) Determine the equilibrium Canadian dollar price of the U.S. dollar, assuming that D_0 and S_0 apply.

(b) Suppose that there is a sizable increase in short-term capital flows from Canada to the United States, other things being equal. Which curves would shift and why? What will happen to the exchange rate (the Canadian dollar price of the U.S. dollar)?

(c) Which curve or curves would shift if Canadians were to import significantly less from the United States? What will happen to the Canadian dollar price of the U.S. dollar?

(d) Suppose that Canadian exports to the United States were to increase significantly, other things being equal. Predict the effect on the price of the U.S. dollar.

4. A "Big Mac" hamburger purchased at a McDonald's restaurant is good example of a standardized product sold around the world. *The Economist*'s website records its **Big Mac Index** for several countries. The most recent edition of the index (at the time of writing the *Study Guide*) appears below for selected countries.

Country	Price in Local Currency	Exchange Rate 7/4/97 Local Currency per U.S. Dollar	U.S. Dollar Price	Implied PPP of the U.S. Dollar	Local Currency Under (−) or Over (+) Valuation
United States	$2.42	—	$2.42	—	—
Canada	C$2.88	1.39	$_____		
Germany	DM 4.90	1.71	$_____		
Mexico	Peso 14.9	7.90	$_____		
Russia	Rouble 11,000	5,739	$_____		
South Africa	Rand 7.80	4.43	$_____		
Sweden	SK 26.0	7.72	$_____		
Thailand	Baht 46.7	26.1	$_____		

(a) Using actual exchange rates (7/4/97) calculate the U.S. dollar price of Big Macs for each of the seven countries and fill in the entries in column 4.

(b) The textbook defines the PPP exchange rate as the value of the exchange rate that equates the local price (in the currency of the country) to the price in the United States (in U.S. dollars). Specifically, $e^{PPP} = P_L$ (local currency price) divided by P_{US} (price in the U.S.) or P_L/P_{US}. Calculate each PPP exchange rate and fill in the values in column 5.

(c) According to the PPP theory, a domestic currency is *undervalued* if the implied PPP exchange rate is less than the current exchange rate. Alternatively, if the Big Mac (valued in U.S. dollars at the current exchange rate) is less than the price at a store in the United States, then the domestic currency is undervalued. Which of the local currencies are undervalued? Fill in the entries in the last column.

(d) Are Big Macs traded goods? If not, does this present a problem for the *The Economist*? Explain.

(5.) *Maintaining a Fixed Exchange Rate*

Figure 36-4 represents the market for pounds sterling. The horizontal axis denotes millions of pounds, and the vertical axis is the Canadian dollar price of pounds.

Figure 36-4

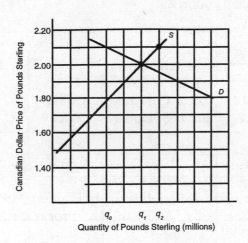

(a) If the exchange rate were flexible, what would be the equilibrium dollar price of sterling?

(b) If the Bank of Canada wants to maintain a fixed value of $2.10, what foreign exchange transactions must it conduct at the current market conditions depicted by the demand and supply curves? What will happen to the Bank of Canada's holdings of international currency reserves?

(c) What would happen in the foreign exchange market if the Bank of England pursued a target of 0.48 pounds per Canadian dollar?

6. *Exchange-Rate Risk*

Exchange-rate risk arises for a person or business who has a liability/receivable in foreign currency sometime in the future and the future value of the foreign currency is uncertain. If the exchange rate changes between the period that a contract is arranged and payment is due, the individual or business may gain or lose in terms of the amount of domestic currency that is actually received or must be paid relative to what receipt/payment was anticipated at the time the deal was made. Hence, "risk" involves both the possibility of a gain or a loss.

In each of the following cases, determine who is taking the exchange-rate risk and calculate the value of the gain or loss in terms of the payment in domestic currency at the time of payment/receipt versus the anticipated cost/earnings in domestic currency at the time at which the contract was negotiated. Assume in each case that the individual or business who is taking the risk anticipates that the exchange rate that prevails when the contract is signed will not change.

(a) A Canadian importer agrees to pay 500,000 yen three months from now. At the time of signing the exchange rate was $0.10 dollars per yen. When payment is made three months thereafter, the exchange rate is $0.15 per yen.

(b) A hotel in Buffalo, New York, agrees to be paid $25,000 Canadian for a June wedding reception booked by a Hamilton, Ontario couple. When the contract was signed in March, one U.S. dollar traded for $1.40 Canadian. Suppose that the exchange rate in June was $1.45 Canadian.

(c) As an investment strategy, Jim buys a Florida condominium in 1997 for $60,000 (U.S.) at a exchange rate of 1.45 Canadian dollars. He intends to sell the condo in 1998 and use the earnings to buy Canadian securities. He sells the condo in 1998 for $63,000 (U.S.) to a couple from North Carolina, but pays $3,000 (U.S.) for real estate and legal services. He then exchanges $60,000 (U.S.) at a rate of 1.51.

EXTENSION EXERCISE

El. A country has a demand curve for foreign currency given by $D = 6 - 2e$ and a supply curve given by $S = 0.5 + 3e$, where e is the price of the foreign currency in terms of the domestic currency and quantities are in millions. The PPP exchange rate value is 1.1

(a) If its policy had allowed the exchange rate to be determined freely on the exchange market, what would the equilibrium levels of e and the quantity of foreign currency have been? Compare the actual exchange rate value with the PPP level.

(b) Now the country's central bank increases domestic interest rates relative to those in other countries with the result that the new demand curve is $D = 5.8 - 2e$ and the new supply curve is $S = 0.8 + 3e$. Explain why both the demand and supply curves for foreign currency changed, and predict the new short-term equilibrium exchange rate value. How does this value compare with the PPP value?

(c) If the country's PPP value is not likely to change in the future, what is likely to happen to the value of e? Explain.

PRACTICE MULTIPLE CHOICE TEST

Questions 1 through 8 refer to the balance-of-payment items for a particular country. Before attempting these questions, you should be familiar with the components of the capital and current accounts discussed in the text. All foreign currency purchases have been converted into millions of the domestic currency (dollars) at a given exchange rate value.

(1)	Long-term capital inflows	785
(2)	Merchandise exports	17,785
(3)	Exports of traded services	1,170
(4)	Short-term capital inflows	932
(5)	Addition to Official Reserves	7
(6)	Merchandise imports	15,556
(7)	Long-term capital outflows	814
(8)	Short-term capital outflows	1,158
(9)	Investment income receipts	545
10)	Investment income payments	1,613
(11)	Net international transfer payments	721
(12)	Imports of traded services	1,348

1. The balance on merchandise trade is
(a) a credit (favourable) balance of $33,341.
(b) a credit balance of $2,229.
(c) a debit (unfavourable) balance of $2,229.
(d) a debit balance of $33,341.
(e) a credit balance of $1,330.

2. Which of the following is not a credit item in the balance of payments accounts?
(a) Item 2.   (b) Item 4.
(c) Item 9.   (d) Item 7.
(e) Item 1.

3. The value of the current account balance is a
   (a) credit balance of $262.
   (b) deficit balance of $262.
   (c) surplus of $983.
   (d) surplus of $2,051.
   (e) None of the above.

4. Which of the following is *not* a capital account item?
   (a) Item 8.   (b) Item 4.
   (c) Item 1.   (d) Item 7.
   (e) Item 9.

5. The value of the capital account balance, excluding changes to official reserves is
   (a) a deficit of $255.
   (b) a surplus of $255.
   (c) a deficit of $262.
   (d) a surplus of $777.
   (e) None of the above.

6. The sum of the current and capital accounts, ignoring the Official Financing Account, indicates that the balance of payments at the current exchange rate is in
   (a) a surplus position of $7.
   (b) a deficit position of $517.
   (c) a deficit position of $7.
   (d) a surplus position of $517.
   (e) an equilibrium position.

7. If there had been no central bank intervention in the foreign exchange market, described by the situation in question 6, then
   (a) the external value of this country's currency would ultimately appreciate.
   (b) the exchange rate would ultimately depreciate.
   (c) at the current exchange rate there is an excess supply of foreign currency or an excess demand for the country's currency.
   (d) the country's balance of payments ultimately would be in equilibrium at a lower exchange rate.
   (e) All of the above.

8. Given your answers to questions 6 and 7, what central bank intervention in the exchange market would be necessary in order to prevent the exchange rate from changing from its current value?
   (a) The central bank would have to buy up the excess supply of the domestic currency of $7 (millions) by reducing its official reserves.
   (b) The central bank would have to supply the excess demand for the domestic currency of $7 (millions) and add to its holdings of foreign currency.
   (c) By increasing the domestic interest rate, the central bank could eliminate the surplus balance of $7 (millions).
   (d) By selling bonds to foreigners, the central bank would finance the deficit in the balance of payments of $7 (millions).
   (e) The central bank would have to buy up the excess supply of the domestic currency of $517 by reducing its official reserves.

Questions 9 through 12 refer to the following exchange rates in Canadian dollars for two years:

Country	1997	1998
German mark	$0.185	$0.187
French franc	$0.243	$0.244
U.S. dollar	$1.445	$1.465
Japanese yen	$0.0107	$0.0105
British pound	$2.368	$2.418

9. Which of the following was *not* true in 1997? The external value of the Canadian dollar was
   (a) 5.405 marks.   (b) 4.115 French francs.
   (c) $1.445 U.S. dollars. (d) 93.458 yen.
   (e) 0.422 pounds.

10. Which of the following was *not* true in 1998? The external value of the Canadian dollar was
    (a) 5.348 marks   (b) 4.098 francs.
    (c) 0.683 U.S. dollars.   (d) 95.238 yen.
    (e) 0.418 pounds.

11. Which of the following statements concerning exchange rate movements between 1997 and 1998 is *not* true?
    (a) The German mark appreciated.
    (b) The British pound depreciated.
    (c) The external value of the Canadian dollar with respect to the Yen appreciated.
    (d) The U.S. dollar appreciated.
    (e) The external value of the Canadian dollar with respect to the franc depreciated.

12. Suppose that a week's skiing vacation (meals, ski tows, accommodations, but excluding travel) costs $1,000 (U.S.) in the United States, 8,000 francs in France and 11,000 marks in Germany during this two-year period. Which of the following statements is *not* correct?
    (a) A Canadian paid $1,445 (Canadian) in 1997 for a skiing vacation in the United States.
    (b) A Canadian supplied 1,952 Canadian dollars and demanded 8,000 francs in 1998 for a skiing vacation in France.
    (c) The Canadian dollar price of a skiing vacation in the United States decreased between 1997 and 1998.
    (d) The Canadian dollar price of a skiing vacation in France increased between 1997 and 1998.
    (e) A Canadian supplied 2,035 Canadian dollars in 1997 to get 11,000 marks for a skiing vacation in Germany.

13. Which of the following events, by itself, will cause the Canadian dollar price of Mexican pesos to appreciate?
    (a) Canadians import less Mexican products.
    (b) Canadians export more raw resources to Mexico.
    (c) Price inflation in Mexico is less than inflation in Canada.
    (d) Canadian interest rates rise while interest rates in Mexico remain constant.
    (e) Canadians receive higher interest payments for their Mexican asset holdings.

14. The short-run expansion of Canadian GDP and employment triggered by an increase in domestic investment will be less if
   (a) Canada operates on a flexible exchange-rate system.
   (b) the *SRAS* curve is relatively flat.
   (c) if the exchange rate is fixed by the Bank of Canada.
   (d) there is no "crowding-out" effect.
   (e) None of the above are correct.

15. If an identical basket of goods in Canada has a price index of 110 and price of index of 200 in Germany, then the PPP exchange rate
   (a) equals 0.55 (dollars).   (b) equals 90 (dollars).
   (c) equals 1.82 (dollars).   (d) indicates that Canadian dollars are undervalued.
   (e) cannot equal the actual exchange rate because the two indices are not equal.

16. What is the value of the current account if $S = 100$, $I = 50$ and $(T - G) = -24$?
   (a) a surplus of 150.   (b) a surplus of 76.
   (c) a surplus of 26.   (d) a deficit of 26.
   (e) a surplus of 126.

17. Which of the following would reduce (a smaller surplus or a greater deficit) the value of the current account balance that you calculated in question 16?
   (a) S increases from 100 to 110.
   (b) I increases from 50 to 56.
   (c) The government's budget deficit changes from −24 to −20.
   (d) S increases from 100 to 110 and investment decreases from 50 to 40.
   (e) All of the above.

SOLUTIONS

Chapter Review

1. (c) 2. (a) 3. (b) 4. (e) 5. (d) 6. (e) 7. (b) 8. (e) 9. (d) 10. (b) 11. (b) 12. (c) 13. (b) 14. (e) 15. (c) 16. (a) 17. (e) 18. (d) 19. (e) 20. (a) 21. (c) 22. (a) 23. (e) 24. (d) 25. (b) 26. (a) 27. (e) 28. (a) 29. (e)

Exercises

1. (a) When more Germans visit Calgary, this is a German import of a Canadian-produced tourist service. Hence, S_M will shift to the right, with the result that the mark should depreciate.
    (b) A greater inflation rate in Canada will cause Canadian exports to Germany to fall and imports from Germany to increase. D_M will shift to the right (Canadian imports increase), and S_M will shift to the left (reduced Canadian exports to Germany). Both are likely to cause the Canadian dollar price of the mark to appreciate (the Canadian dollar depreciates).
    (c) Germany is likely to experience more capital inflows from Canada, and less international capital will flow from Germany to Canada. Hence both the demand and supply curves for marks are affected such that the mark will appreciate.
    (d) S_M will shift to the right, and hence the mark will depreciate.

(e) These transactions constitute capital outflows from Germany. The supply curve for marks will shift to the right, and hence the mark will depreciate.

(f) The mark will depreciate (with respect to the Canadian dollar) as German companies switch away from U.S. suppliers to Canadian suppliers.

(g) S_M will shift to the right, and the mark should depreciate.

2. (a) Column (a) entries are $180, $190, $200, $210, and $220.

(b) The equilibrium price is $200, and 400 cameras are sold.

(c) Column (b) entries are $208, $220, $232, $243, and $255. The new equilibrium price is $220 and 300 cameras are sold.

(d) Spending on imports falls from $80,000 to $66,000.

3. (a) One Canadian dollar trades for one U.S. dollar.

(b) The demand curve for U.S. dollars will shift to the right (such as that labelled D_2). The U.S. dollar will appreciate and will equal 1.05 Canadian dollars.

(c) The demand curve for U.S. dollars will shift to the left (such as that labelled D_1). The U.S. dollar will depreciate to a price of $0.95 Canadian.

(d) The supply curve of U.S. dollars will shift to the right (such as that labelled S_1). The U.S. dollar will depreciate to a price of $0.95 Canadian.

4. (a) U.S. dollar prices: 2.07 (Canada), 2.86 (Germany), 1.89 (Mexico), 1.92 (Russia), 1.76 (South Africa), 3.37 (Sweden), 1.79 (Thailand).

(b) PPP value in local currency: 1.19 (Canada), 2.02 (Germany), 6.16 (Mexico), 4,545 (Russia), 3.22 (South Africa), 10.7 (Sweden), 19.3 (Thailand).

(c) Undervalued local currencies are Canada dollars, Mexican pesos, Russian roubles, South African rand, Thailand's baht. Overvalued local currencies are German marks and Swedish krona.

(d) Big Mac's, although consumed throughout the world, are locally produced and generally are not traded internationally, except perhaps for border towns. Thus, the local price of Big Macs will not adjust to exchange rate changes and we would not expect local prices to be influenced by changes in prices of Big Macs in other countries.

5. (a) $2.00 where $D = S$.

(b) At a fixed price of $2.10, there is an excess supply of pounds (and an excess demand for dollars). Thus, the Bank must sell dollars and buy $q_2 - q_0$ pounds in the exchange market. The Bank's holdings of sterling (which may be held for reserves) will increase.

(c) Probably confusion, increased speculation, and destabilized exchange markets. The Bank of England's target of 0.48 pounds translates into a dollar price of pounds of $2.08, which is different from the Bank of Canada's target of $2.10.

6. (a) The Canadian importer is taking the exchange-rate risk since its liability is in yen. The Japanese seller is guaranteed 500,000 yen. At the time the deal was made, the Canadian importer anticipated paying $50,000 (Canadian) for 500,000 yen. However, at the time of payment, the importer has to pay $75,000 (Canadian). The loss is $25,000.

(b) The New York hotel is taking the exchange-rate risk since its receipt is in Canadian dollars. When the hotel receives its payment in June, it converts $25,000 (Canadian) into $17,241 (U.S.). At the time the deal was signed, the hotel anticipated receiving $17,857 (U.S.) at an exchange rate of 1.40. The loss is $616 (U.S.).

(c) Jim is taking the exchange-rate risk since his asset is valued in U.S. dollars. In 1997 he pays $87,000 Canadian for the Florida condo. However, he receives $90,600 (Canadian) in 1998. Although Jim realized no net capital gain(in U.S. dollars) after deducting transactions costs on his Florida property, the appreciation of the U.S. dollar earned him a gain of $3,600 (Canadian).

Extension Exercise

E1.   (a) Quantity demanded equals quantity supplied at $e = 1.1$; equilibrium quantity is 3.8 million. The current exchange rate equals the PPP rate.

  (b) An increase in the domestic interest rate will cause less capital outflows and more capital inflows. Less capital outflows decrease the demand for foreign currency and more inflows increase the supply of foreign currency. The new equilibrium exchange rate will be 1.0. Relative to the PPP value, foreign currency is undervalued while the domestic currency is overvalued.

  (c) Assuming that no additional interest rate differentials are created, we would expect the price of foreign currency to appreciate (domestic currency depreciates). This might occur through the activity of speculators who gamble that the undervalued foreign currency will rise to its PPP value in the future. Thus, by selling domestic currency and buying foreign currency, speculators may cause the foreign currency to reach its PPP value.

Practice Multiple Choice Test

1. (b) 2. (d) 3. (a) 4. (e) 5. (a) 6. (a) 7. (e) 8. (b) 9. (c) 10. (e) 11. (b) 12. (c) 13. (c) 14. (a) 15. (a) 16. (c) 17. (b)